Labour Law in Bulgaria

Labour Law in Bulgaria

Second Edition

Vassil Mrachkov

This book was originally published as a monograph in the International Encyclopaedia of Laws/Labour Law and Industrial Relations.

Founding Editor: Roger Blanpain
General Editor: Frank Hendrickx
Volume Editor: Frank Hendrickx

Wolters Kluwer

Published by:
Kluwer Law International B.V.
PO Box 316
2400 AH Alphen aan den Rijn
The Netherlands
E-mail: international-sales@wolterskluwer.com
Website: lrus.wolterskluwer.com

Sold and distributed by:
Wolters Kluwer Legal & Regulatory U.S.
7201 McKinney Circle
Frederick, MD 21704
United States of America
Email: customer.service@wolterskluwer.com

ISBN 978-94-035-2720-8

e-Book: ISBN 978-94-035-2721-5
web-PDF: ISBN 978-94-035-2722-2

The Author

Professor Vassil Mrachkov was born in 1934 in Brachlian, Bourgass district, Bulgaria. He studied Law at the Saint Kliment Ohridski University, Sofia, from 1952 to 1957, receiving his Master's in Law in 1957 and a PhD in Law (Sofia) in 1963. Professor Mrachkov received his *agrégé* in Higher Education in 1969. He was a Research Associate and Associate Professor in Labour Law at the Institute of Legal Sciences at the Bulgarian Academy of Sciences from 1962 to 1973 and Director of the Institute from 1982 to 1989, and he has been a Professor since 1980. He became a Doctor of Sciences in 1985. He has been a Professor in Labour Law and Social Security Law at the Saint Kliment Ohridski University, Sofia, from 1981 until 1999. Since 1994 he has taught Labour law and Social Security Law at the Paissii Hilendarski University, Plovdiv. He is Doctor *honoris causa* of Sofia University 'St. Kliment Ohridski'. Since 2014 he is Professor Emeritus.

Professor Mrachkov has also been actively involved in international matters. He was an international civil servant with the International Labour Organization (ILO), Geneva from 1973 to 1979. He is former President of the Bulgarian National Association of Labour Law and Social Security Law and member of the Executive Committee of the International Society of Labour Law and Social Security. In 1993 he was a visiting professor at the Catholic University of Leuven, Belgium. He is Honorary President of the Bulgarian National Society of Labour Law and Social Security Law.

He was a Chairman of the Legislative Council by the 37th Legislature of the National Assembly (1995–1997). From October 2001 until 2005 he was Chairman of the Consultative Legislative Council by the 39th Legislature of the National Assembly.

Professor Mrachkov has written numerous books in Bulgarian, as well as numerous essays and articles in Bulgarian, French, English, Russian, German and Spanish for Bulgarian and international journals. He is also the author of the national monograph on Bulgarian Social Security Law published by Kluwer in the *International Encyclopaedia of Social Security Law* in 1999 (*Social Security Law*, Supplement 26 February 1999), in 2006, Supplement 58 (September 2006), in 2011, in 2014 and in 2017.

His national monograph on Bulgarian labour law was first published by Kluwer in the *International Encyclopaedia of Labour Law and Industrial Relations* in 1979, updated since then in 1995, in 2001, in 2011, in 2014, in 2017 and in the present 2020 publication.

The Author

Table of Contents

List of Abbreviations

BSP	Bulgarian Socialist Party
CEDB	Citizens for European Development of Bulgaria
CITUB	Confederation of Independent Trade Unions in Bulgaria
CL *Podkrepa*	Confederation of Labour *Podkrepa*
D.	Directive – Council Directive of the European Economic Community
Dec. No. of the III C.Ch.	Decision No. of the III Civil Chamber of the Supreme Court of Cassation
EEA	European Economic Area
EU	European Union
ICFTU	International Confederation of Free Trade Unions
ILO	International Labour Organization
LC	Labour Code
LEP	Law on Employment Promotion
MP	Member of Parliament
NCTC	National Council for Tripartite Cooperation
OJ	Official Journal
RCM	Regulation of the Council of Ministers
SIC	Social Insurance Code
UDF	Union of Democratic Forces

List of Abbreviations

General Introduction

Chapter 1. General Background

§1. Geography and Population

1. The Republic of Bulgaria is situated in the south-east of Europe, on the Balkan Peninsula. It has a territory of 111,000 sq km. According to the data of the latest official census, the population of the country as on 31 December 2018 was 7,000,039, having decreased by 153,761 in comparison with 2015.[1] To the east Bulgaria borders the Black Sea, to the north Romania, to the west Serbia and Macedonia, and to the south Greece and Turkey.

§2. History

2. The Bulgarian state was formed in the year 681 and based on the Proto-Bulgarian and Slav tribes that inhabited ancient Moesia. It existed as an independent state until 1018. At that time it came under Byzantine rule from which it freed itself in 1187; thereafter, Bulgaria continued its independent existence up to the end of the fourteenth century. In 1396, the country came under Ottoman domination. It was not liberated until 1878 as a result of the 1878 Russo-Turkish War, and then embarked on the road to free development.

3. On 1 March 1940, during the Second World War, the ruling government of Bulgaria joined the Trilateral Treaty as an ally of Germany. This was a step with far-reaching consequences.

4. After the Second World War, on 9 September 1944, a socialist system with a proletarian dictatorship was established in Bulgaria. The country was placed under the direct political influence of the former Soviet Union. Radical changes were introduced into society. Political pluralism and parliamentary democracy were gradually abolished (1944–1946). Marxism-Leninism was adopted and proclaimed as the official state ideology. The leading force in the state and society was the Bulgarian Communist Party which enjoyed the monopoly of power. Private property was expropriated (1945–1947) and free, private initiative eliminated. A centrally

1. *Statisticheski Godishnik na Republika Bulgaria* [*Statistical Yearbook of the Republic of Bulgaria*] (Sofia: Science and Art Publishing House, 2019), 29.

planned and administered economy on the basis of state ownership was established. This was legally consolidated by the Constitution adopted on 4 December 1947, which was subsequently replaced by a new Constitution on 16 May 1971. The political foundations of both the Constitutions of 1947 and of 1971 were the political ideas and decisions of the Bulgarian Communist Party. This development of the country lasted until the ousting of T. Zhivkov – former General Secretary of the Central Committee of the Bulgarian Communist Party and former President of the State's Council – by reformers in the Communist Party on 10 November 1989.

5. A period of profound political change leading to political pluralism and democratization, began in the country on 10 November 1989. The Union of Democratic Forces (UDF) was created as an anticommunist coalition which rapidly grew to form the political force opposed to the Bulgarian Socialist (former Communist) Party (BSP).

In the meantime, some significant amendments were made to the Constitution of 1971 in December 1989 and in April 1990, such as abolishing the disposition which proclaimed the leading role of the Communist Party, deleting some references to a socialist society, liquidation of the state council, introducing new dispositions recognizing the right to private ownership, the equal treatment of all forms of ownership.[2] In accordance with the agreements reached at the Round Table conference which was held in early 1990, the first elections for the Great National Assembly (a body assembled to draft a new constitution) took place in June 1990. These elections were widely recognized as being free, fair, democratic and pluralistic by the great number of foreign observers who followed them. At the end of these elections, a new Great National Assembly was elected. It was composed of 400 Member of Parliament (MPs): 211 from the Socialist Party, 144 from the UDF, 23 from the Movement for Rights and Freedoms (organization supported by the Turkish population in Bulgaria), 16 from the Agrarian Party, and 6 independents.[3] Its fundamental task was the elaboration of a new Constitution which was adopted on 12 July 1991 (and became effective 13 July 1991).[4] After the adoption of the new Constitution, the Assembly dissolved itself. In accordance with the requirements of the new Constitution, new legislative elections for the ordinary National Assembly took place as follows: in October 1991, December 1994, April 1997, June 2001, June 2005, July 2009, May 2013, October 2014 and March 2017. In the latest parliamentary elections (26 March 2017), the 44th National Assembly with a four-year mandate was elected. It consists of 240 deputies from the following political parties having the following number of deputies: Political Party 'Citizens for European Development of Bulgaria' (CEDB) – 45; BSP 'Left Bulgaria' (a coalition) – 80; 'United Patriots' – 27; Movement for Rights and Freedoms – 26; 'Volya' Party – 12. A coalition government was formed with the participation of two political parties: the CEDB and the 'United Patriots'.

2. *Official Journal*, Nos 6 and 29 of 1990.
3. These data are quoted from: St. Stoichev, *Izbiratelno zakonodatelstvo i izbori* v *perioda na prehoda kam democrazia* [*Electoral Legislation and Elections during the Transitional Period to Democracy*] (Sofia: 'St. Kl. Ohridski' University Printing House, 1993), 254–255.
4. *Official Journal*, No. 56 of 13 July 1991.

In conformity with the new Constitution the first direct presidential elections were held in January 1992. After that direct presidential elections were also held in November 1996, November 2001, October 2006, November 2011 and November 2016 for the posts of President and Vice President of the Republic, respectively, the following candidates were elected for the next five years: Mr Roumen Radev and Ms Iliana Yotova.

All these elections – both legislative and presidential – were also widely recognized as being free, fair, democratic and pluralistic by the international community and the great number of foreign observers who followed them.

As a result of all the developments which started on 10 November 1989, Bulgaria decisively embarked on the road to political democratization and pluralism.

§3. The Political System

6. The political system was established by the new Constitution of 12 July 1991. Bulgaria is a unitary state with local self-government. No autonomous territorial formations are admitted (Article 2 of the Constitution). The functions and the parameters of the state organs are defined on the basis of the principle of separation of powers (Article 8 of the Constitution).

7. Article 1, paragraph 1 of the Constitution establishes a parliamentarian republic as the form of the state. Indeed, the republican form of government was introduced on 15 September 1946, on the basis of a referendum held on 8 September 1946. The results of this plebiscite were impressive: 93% of those who took part voted for the abolition of the monarchy and the establishment of a republic.[5] The new Constitution confirmed the republican form of the state again.

8. By establishing the form of the state as a parliamentarian republic, the Constitution underlines the importance placed on the role of Parliament in the political structure of the state. Parliament is composed of one chamber called the National Assembly (the 44th Legislature). It was constituted after the last legislative elections held on 26 March 2017 (*see* above paragraph 5). Any person who is a Bulgarian citizen and at least 21 years of age, is eligible to become an MP, with the exception of those placed under guardianship or serving a prison sentence (Article 42, paragraph 1 of the Constitution). MPs are elected by universal, equal and direct suffrage and secret ballot by the Bulgarian citizens who have reached the age of 18, with the exception of those placed under guardianship or serving a prison sentence (Article 10, paragraph 1 of the Constitution). The Assembly exercises legislative power and has the function of parliamentarian control over the Executive. It sits permanently and self-determines the periods of time when it is not in session (Articles 62–91 of the Constitution).

---

5. *Istoria na Bulgaria* [*History of Bulgaria*], Vol. 3 (Sofia: Science and Art Publishing House, 1964), 516–517.

9. The Presidency of the republic is a new institution, created for the first time in April 1990. This office was reconfirmed and entirely reregulated by the Constitution of 1991. The President is the Head of State. He/she personifies the nation's unity and represents the state in international affairs (Article 92 of the Constitution). He/she is directly elected for five years. He/she is supported by a Vice President elected *from the same election team.* The main functions of the President are to schedule the elections for the National Assembly and the bodies of local self-government and to set the date for national referenda pursuant to a resolution of the National Assembly, to promulgate laws, to conclude international treaties in the circumstances established by the law, on a motion from the Council of Ministers, to determine the boundaries of the administrative territorial units and their centres, on a motion from the Council of Ministers, to appoint and dismiss the heads of national diplomatic and permanent missions at international organizations, to receive the credentials and the letters of recall of foreign diplomatic representatives to the country, to grant asylum, to exercise the right to pardon, etc. Following consultations with all the parliamentary groups, the President appoints the Prime Minister nominated by the party holding the highest number of seats in the National Assembly to form a government. The President is the Supreme Commander in Chief of the armed forces of the Republic of Bulgaria, presides over the Consultative National Security Council, proclaims general or partial mobilization on a motion from the government, etc. (Articles 92–104 of the Constitution).

10. The next important organ is the Council of Ministers (government or Cabinet). It is the main organ of executive power and is designated by the National Assembly (Article 84, items 6 and 7 of the Constitution). The Council of Ministers heads the implementation of the state's domestic and foreign policy, ensures public order and national security, exercises overall guidance over the state administration and the armed forces. It manages the implementation of the state's budget, organizes the management of the state's assets and concludes, confirms or denounces international treaties when authorized to do so by law. Under the Constitution, the government is accountable to the National Assembly. Pursuant to and in implementation of the laws, the Council of Ministers and the ministers adopt decrees, ordinances, resolutions, rules, regulations, instructions and orders (Articles 105–116 of the Constitution).

11. The judiciary is an independent branch of the state's power. Its main task is to safeguard the rights and legitimate interests of citizens, legal persons and the state. The judges, court assessors, public prosecutors and investigating magistrates are answerable only to the laws of the land. The judicial system consists of the Supreme Court of Cassation, the Supreme Administrative Court, courts of appeal, district, military, administrative and regional courts. The regional courts are established by region and the district courts within the framework of a district. The courts of appeal are located territorially so as to serve as the first authority to hear appeals from some district and regional courts. There are 112 regional courts, 28 district courts and 5 courts of appeal. The Supreme Court of Cassation exercises supreme judicial control over the activities of all courts and secures their exact and identical application of the law. The Supreme Administrative Court is a new court as provided for in the new Constitution. It has not been in existence since 1948 when it was abolished after having been created in 1912. Indeed, this Court, as well as the 28 administrative courts, was re-established by the Law on Judicial Power (2007). Their main functions are to exercise supreme judicial oversight as to the exact and identical application of administrative laws and to rule on all challenges as to the legality of acts of the Council of Ministers and of individual ministers as well as of other acts as established by law. In total, there are: municipal court judges – 1020, district judges – 795, administrative court judges – 330, courts of appeal judges – 136, military court judges – 38, Supreme Court of Cassation judges – 104 and Supreme Administrative Court judges – 96.

The second branch of the judiciary (besides the courts) is the Public Prosecutor's Office. Its structure corresponds to that of the courts. The Public Prosecutor's Office oversees legality by bringing charges against criminal suspects and supporting the charges in common criminal trials, by overseeing the enforcement of penalties and other measures of law enforcement, by acting for the rescindment of all unlawful acts, by taking part in civil and administrative suits whenever required to do so by law. The total number of public prosecutors is about 2,350. The third basic element of the judiciary is the investigating bodies which fall within the system of the judicial branch. They perform preliminary investigations in criminal cases. The total number of investigating magistrates in the National Investigating Office is about 98.[6]

According to the amendment made to the Constitution in February 2007 (prom. OJ, No. 12 of 2007), within the framework of the judicial power (the judiciary) a new body was created at the Supreme Judicial Council, namely the Inspectorate (new Article 132a of the Constitution). It consists of a Chief Inspector and ten inspectors. They have been elected by the National Assembly by a qualified majority of two-thirds of the MPs for a period of five years (the Chief Inspector) and four years (the ten inspectors), respectively. This Inspectorate has to check the activity of the judicial authorities without affecting the independence of the judges, the court assessors, the prosecutors and the investigators in performing their functions, and has to obey the law only. The Chief Inspector and the inspectors are to be independent in performing their functions and to act ex officio on the initiative of citizens, legal entities and state authorities, including judges, prosecutors and investigators. It has to address signals, proposals and reports to other state authorities. The Inspectorate is obliged to present an annual report on its activity to the Supreme Judicial Council as well as to make this report public. The amendments to the Constitution of December 2015 extended the functions of the Inspectorate. The latter has been assigned new functions: to carry out checks on the integrity and conflict of interests of judges, public prosecutors and investigating magistrates; to check the annual declarations on the property status and incomes of the magistrates for the respective calendar year; to check their conduct for violations injuring the reputation of the judicial power, and for breaches of their independence and attempts at interference with their work and the like. On the basis of the results of the checks it conducts,

---

6. The data on the composition of the judiciary (courts, Public Prosecutor's Office and investigating magistrates) are quoted from the Supreme Judicial Council.

the Inspectorate gives information, makes proposals and submits reports to other state authorities, including the judicial power bodies (Article 132a, paragraphs 6 and 9 of the Constitution).

12. Judges, public prosecutors and investigating magistrates are elected, promoted, reassigned and dismissed by the Supreme Judicial Council which is composed of twenty-five members. Three of them, namely the Chairman of the Supreme Court of Cassation, the Chairman of the Supreme Administrative Court and the Chief Public Prosecutor sit ex officio. The other twenty-two are elected members. Practising lawyers of high professional and moral integrity with at least fifteen years of professional experience are eligible for election. Eleven of them are elected by the National Assembly and the other eleven by the bodies of judicial power – judges, public prosecutors and investigating magistrates (Articles 129 and 130 of the Constitution). These amendments to the Constitution of December 2015 introduced significant changes in the structure of the Supreme Judicial Council and the distribution of its functions. Two colleges were set up within the Supreme Judicial Council: the College of Judges and the College of Public Prosecutors. The College of Judges, which consists of fourteen members, comprises the Chairman of the Supreme Court of Cassation, the Chairman of the Supreme Administrative Court and six of its judges elected by all the country's judges, and six members of the Supreme Judicial Council elected by the National Assembly. The College of Public Prosecutors, which consists of eleven members, comprises the Chief Public Prosecutor, four members elected by the country's public prosecutors, one member elected by the country's investigating magistrates and five members of the Supreme Judicial Council elected by the National Assembly. Each of these colleges appoints, promotes, transfers, demotes and imposes disciplinary punishments as follows: the College of Judges does so on the judges, and discusses and resolves specific matters of the courts and judicial activity; and the College of Public Prosecutors does so on the public prosecutors and the investigating magistrates, and discusses and resolves specific matters related to the activities of the Public Prosecution and the Investigation (Article 132a of the Constitution). However, the Constitution preserves the Plenum of the Supreme Judicial Council, which comprises all the members of the two colleges of the Supreme Judicial Council and determines the functions of the latter. These functions concern the general matters of judicial power (court, public prosecution and investigation bodies), for instance: approving the draft budget of judicial power, adopting resolutions for termination of the mandate of an elective member of the Supreme Judicial Council, organizing the qualification of magistrates, managing the real estates of the judicial power (Article 130a, paragraph 2 of the Constitution).

13. Judges, public prosecutors and investigating magistrates cannot be removed from office after having completed five years in their respective position. They may be dismissed only after attaining 65 years of age or upon retirement, resignation, enforcement of a prison sentence for a deliberate crime, or upon an actual inability to perform their functions which has lasted for more than one year, as well as in the case of a grave offence or systematic non-fulfilment of official duties and undermining the prestige of the judicial power (Articles 129 and 131 of the Constitution).

14. For the first time the Constitutional Court was provided for in the new Constitution (Articles 147–152 of the Constitution). The Constitutional Court was first set up in August–September 1991 and has been functioning since 3 October 1991. It consists of twelve judges, one-third of them elected by the National Assembly, one-third appointed by the President, and one-third elected by a joint meeting of the judges of the Supreme Court of Cassation and the Supreme Administrative Court; they are elected or appointed for a period of nine years and are not eligible for re-election or reappointment.

15. The functions of the Constitutional Court are established by the Constitution: to provide binding interpretations of the Constitution, to rule on challenges as to the constitutionality of the laws and other acts passed by the National Assembly and the acts of the President, to rule on 'competence' suits between the National Assembly, the President and the Council of Ministers, and between the bodies of local self-government and the central executive branch of government, to rule on the compatibility between the Constitution and the international instruments concluded by the Republic of Bulgaria prior to their ratification, to rule on the compatibility of domestic laws with the universally recognized norms of international law and the international instruments to which Bulgaria is a party, to rule on challenges as to the constitutionality of political parties and associations, to rule on challenges as to the legality of the election of the President, Vice President and a Member of the National Assembly, and finally to rule on impeachments by the National Assembly against the President and Vice President.

16. The Constitutional Court acts on the initiative of at least one-fifth of all members of the National Assembly, the President, the Council of Ministers, the Supreme Court of Cassation, the Supreme Administrative Court or the Chief Public Prosecutor. Pursuant to paragraph 3 of Article 150 of the Constitution introduced through its amendment of March 2006 (prom. OJ, No. 27 of 2006), the Ombudsman may also approach the Constitutional Court by way of a claim for the establishment of an unconstitutional law which violates the rights and freedoms of the citizens. Through the amendment made to Article 150, paragraph 4 of the Constitution in December 2015, the same function was assigned to the Supreme Bar Council as well (OJ, No. 100 of 2015). A challenge as to competence between the National Assembly, the President and the Council of Ministers, and between the bodies of local self-government and the central executive branch of government may also be filed by a municipal council. Any act found to be unconstitutional ceases to apply as of the date on which the ruling comes into force. However, the areas or sections of a law which are ruled not to be unconstitutional remain in force.

17. The Constitutional Court is quite active. From the beginning of its functioning (3 October 1991) until the end of 2016, 780 constitutional files were formed. The Constitutional Court has pronounced 561 decisions and 150 resolutions.[7] By the end of 2016, six files were pending before the Constitutional Court.

---

7. In performance of Art. 14, para. 3 of the Law on Constitutional Court the decisions and rulings of the Constitutional Court are published in the Official Journal within fifteen days of their being

The practice of the Constitutional Court contains a number of decisions that concern employment relations: Decision No. 12 of 20 July 1995 (OJ, No. 69 of 1995), Decision No. 14 of 30 April 1998 (OJ, No. 52 of 1998) on court disputes concerning wrongful dismissal of responsible executives (Article 360, paragraph 2, items 1 and 2 of the Labour Code (LC)), Decision No. 14 of 24 September 1996 (OJ, No. 84 of 1996) on the right to strike under Article 50 of the Constitution and under Article 16, items 4 and 6 of the Law on the Settlement of Collective Labour Disputes that revoke the right of strikes in certain branches (power supply, communications, health care, etc.), Decision No. 2 of 4 April 2006 (OJ, No. 32 of 2006) on the right to a special protection on the part of the state, consisting in prenatal and postnatal leave, free obstetric care, alleviated working conditions and other social assistance, Decision No. 12 of 11 November 2010 (OJ, No. 91 of 2010) on the right to a paid annual leave (Articles 176, 176a and 224 of the LC), Decision No. 7 of 19 June 2012 (OJ, No. 49 of 2012) concerning the requirements to be met by the trade union and employers' associations for recognition of national representation (Articles 34 and 35 of the LC). These decisions are of major importance for protecting the social rights of citizens and for establishing the Republic of Bulgaria as a law-governed state.[8]

18. The local self-government and local administration are basically regulated by Articles 135–146 of the Constitution. The organization and the procedures of the bodies of local self-government and local administration are further established by the Law on Local Self-government and Local Administration (OJ, No. 77 of 1991, as amended).

19. The territory of Bulgaria is divided into municipalities and regions. There are 265 municipalities and 28 regions. A municipality is the basic administrative territorial unit. Citizens participate in the government of the municipality both through their elected bodies and directly, through a referendum or a general meeting of the population. The organ of local self-government within a municipality is the municipal council elected directly by the population for a term of four years on the basis of universal, equal and direct suffrage by secret ballot. The number of municipal councillors in the different municipalities depends upon the population of the

---

adopted and they take effect within three days of their being published in the Official Journal. In accordance with Art. 14, para. 7 of the Law on Constitutional Court all decisions and rulings of the Constitutional Court rendered during the respective calendar year are published in a separate Annual Collection. Nine volumes of decisions and rulings of the Constitutional Court have been published since the beginning of its activities on 3 Oct. 1991 until the end of the year 2013. The dissenting opinions of the Constitutional judges on the decisions approved are also published therein.

8. N. Nenovski, 'Konstituzionniat sad na Republika Balgaria i zakrilata na osnovnite prava' ['Constitutional Court of the Republic of Bulgaria and the Protection of Fundamental Rights'], *Juridicheski sviat* [*Juridical World*] 2, (2000): 185–191; W. Mratschkov, 'Die Einwirkung der Verfassung vom 12.07.1991 auf die Entwicklung des Arbeitsrechts in Bulgarien', *Recht und soziale Arbeitswelt, Festschrift für Wolfgang Däubler zum 60. Geburtstag*, 2 (1999): 40–49; E. Drumeva, *Konstituzionno pravo* [*Constitutional Law*], 5th edn. (Sofia: Ciela Publishing House, 2018), 518–585; V. Mrachkov, 'Constitutional Protection of Paid Annual Leave', *Juridicheski sviat* [*Juridical World*] 2 (2011): 11–44; P. Penev, *The Attorney, the Constitution and the Governing Law* (Sofia: Faber Publishing House, 2018), 9–18, 25–294.

respective municipality and varies from 11 to 61 councillors. For the capital municipality (Sofia) it is 61. The last local elections for municipal councillors took place on 27 October and 3 November 2019. During these elections 5,135 municipal councillors were elected from the different political parties and movements.[9]

20. The body of executive power within a municipality is the mayor. He/she is elected by the population on the basis of universal, equal and direct suffrage by secret ballot for a term of four years. During the last local elections of 27 October and 3 November 2019, 265 mayors were elected in municipalities and 1,966 mayors in other agglomerations (towns and villages).[10]

21. A region is an administrative territorial unit entrusted with the conduct of a regional policy and the implementation of the state's policy on a local level as well as ensuring the harmony of national and local interests. Each region is governed by a regional governor aided by a regional administration. The regional governor is appointed by the Council of Ministers. He/she ensures the implementation of the state's policy, the safeguarding of the national interest, law and public order and exercises administrative control.

22. The next basic element of the Bulgarian political system is the *political parties*. One of the most salient features of the country's democratic development since November 1989 is the constitutional recognition of the principle of political pluralism as a basic characteristic of the political life of the new Bulgarian society (Article 11 of the Constitution). The political parties contribute to shaping and freely expressing the political will of the citizens. The foundation and cessation of their activities are settled by the Law on Political Parties (OJ, No. 30 of 2001). The main political forces are: CEDB, the BSP, the Movement for Rights and Freedoms and 'Ataka' ('Assault'). Other political parties are: the movement 'Bulgaria for Citizens', UDF, Democrats for Strong Bulgaria, Bulgarian Agrarian Union, etc.

Domestic political life continues to be characterized by fragmentation of political parties. About 250 political parties have been registered.

Politics is characterized by political polarization and the sharp opposition between the BSP, on the one hand, and the CEDB. Their activities and conduct shape political life in contemporary Bulgarian society.

From a constitutional point of view two supplementary remarks should be noted. First, it is forbidden for any political party to declare or to assert itself as a state party (Article 11, paragraph 2 of the Constitution). This principle proclaims the complete separation of the political parties from the state and assures the equal treatment of all political parties which comply with the legal requirements as to their

9. The data on the results of the local elections for municipal councillors are quoted from the Central Commission for Local Elections, 'Bulletin of the Commission for Local Elections' (Sofia: CCLE, 2019), 67–74.
10. These data are quoted from the Central Commission for Local Elections, 'General Results', Vol. I (Sofia: CCLE, 2019), 33–38.

existence. Second, it is forbidden to form a political party on an ethnic, racial or religious basis or a party which has as its objective to obtain possession of state power by violence (Article 11, paragraph 4 of the Constitution).

§4. Economy

23. The economic system of contemporary Bulgarian society is defined in Articles 17–22 of the Constitution. In this area, there have been great changes as part of the profound transformations which have taken place in the country since the end of 1989. As a whole, they characterize the transition from a centrally planned economy, based on state ownership, to a market economy, based on the plurality of ownership forms and by the presence, above all, of private property. These changes are manifested in the following features. First, the economy is based on a free economic initiative (Article 19, paragraph 1 of the Constitution). This means that everybody is free to develop a profit-making activity, to create economic organizations, to make investments and to hire working people in every sector of the national economy. This is a great change in comparison with the situation which existed when the monopoly of state ownership of the means of production did not permit individuals to develop proper economic activities. Second, the new Constitution recognizes the right to private property and proclaims its inviolability (Article 17, paragraphs 1 and 3 of the Constitution). This is a very important progression after the suppression of private property during the socialist era of development. Third, the state enjoys exclusive ownership rights over the subterranean country, the coastal beaches, national thoroughfares, as well as over the waters, forests and parks of national importance and natural and archaeological reserves, established by a law (Article 18, paragraph 1 of the Constitution). Fourth, given the plurality of ownership forms (private, public and so on), the state is obliged to establish and guarantee equal legal conditions for economic activity to all citizens and corporate entities by preventing any abuse of a monopoly status and unfair competition (Article 19, paragraph 2 of the Constitution). The state fosters fair competition and forbids and punishes unfair competition. For these purposes a new Law on the Protection of Competition was adopted (OJ, No. 102 of 2008). This provides for the establishment of a special body for the implementation of the above-mentioned law, namely the Commission for the Protection of Competition. This Commission was formed in May 1991 and has been functioning since that time. Fifth, for the development of economic activity a special protection is provided for on the investments and economic activity of foreign persons. It is established by the Law on Encouragement of Investments (OJ, No. 97 of 1997, as amended). Economic activity and investments made by foreign persons or by national companies enjoy equal rights. The size of foreign participation in newly founded or existing companies is not limited. Foreign persons may acquire ownership of buildings, limited real rights in immovable property, etc. As of 31 December 2000 the foreign investments in the country amounted to approximately USD 4 billion, and for the period 2009–2012 they amounted to USD 28 billion.[11] Sixth, one of the key problems within the framework of the transition to a market-oriented economy is the privatization of state-owned enterprises. To resolve this problem, a special law, the Law on Transformation and Privatization of State-Owned and Municipal Enterprises, was adopted in 1992 (OJ, No. 38 of 1992, as amended). By virtue of this law, the privatization of state-owned and municipal enterprises amounts to the sale of the shares and stocks or entire enterprises or separate parts thereof and property of liquidated enterprises to physical and legal persons.

A decisive step in this aspect was made by the government in the period 2010–2018. As a result of the policy conducted by the governments, a large proportion (about 86%) of state-owned and municipal enterprises were privatized. At the end of 2018 the private sector gave employment to 2,438,948 people, this being about 75% of all the 3,124,247, the total number of all the employees in the country.[12] However, the intensive privatization carried out in the last four years showed serious shortcomings as well. The privatization was carried out hastily. In a number of cases this prevented the conclusion of privatization contracts that were economically advantageous for the state and municipalities, whose property the privatized enterprises and objects were. The needed transparency in performing the privatization was lacking, and in a lot of cases this gave rise to social distrust both in privatization and in those vested with power. No effective post-privatization control was exercised. As a result of that, the clauses of privatization transactions were not always observed by the new acquirers. And thus the expected effective management and efficient use of the enormous mass of assets that turned from public into private property was not provided. These consequences of the mass 'shock' privatization, performed within a short time, create serious difficulties for the new administration of the country. The overcoming of these difficulties is one of the most topical and acute problems in the economic policy of the new government formed after the parliamentary elections of 5 July 2009.[13]

The process of privatization is not yet finally accomplished. The privatization of several large state-owned companies is forthcoming, the latter holding key positions in national economy, such as Bulgartabac, National Electrical Company.

24. Prior to the Second World War, Bulgaria was known as one of the most backward agricultural countries in Europe with a poorly developed industry. The ratio of industrial to agricultural output in 1939 was 25:75. After 9 September 1944, Bulgaria embarked resolutely on the course of industrializing its economy and by the end of 1983, 36.1% of the labour force worked in industry, 21.9% in agriculture and 17.2% in services. The share of the population employed soared from 27.5% in

11. *Statisticheski spravochnik* [*Statistical Reference Book*] (Sofia: National Statistical Institute, 2019), 132.
12. *Ibid.*, 32.
13. I. Angelov, 'Ikonomikata na Balgaria do 2009 g.' ['The Economy of Bulgaria until the Year 2009'], in the collection: *Economics of Bulgaria and the European Union* (Sofia: Science and Art Publishing House, 2010), 13–20.

1950s to 66.4% in 1988.[14] During this period and until the mid to late 1980s the economy grew rapidly: between 1981 and 1985 net material production rose at an annual rate of 3.7% and during 1986 and 1987 rates of more than 5% were recorded. This implied strong growth in output per worker for most of the period – for instance 5.2% in 1986 and 5.3% in 1987. Unemployment was officially non-existent and the official inflation rate was also very low, ranging from 0.1% to 1.8% a year during the period 1981–1989.

25. Towards the end of the 1980s, the economic problems had become more widespread and severe. In 1989, national output declined by 1.9%. For 1990 the drop was about 10%, while since then the slump has apparently intensified: in 1991, the output fell by 20%, in 1992 it fell by 24% and in 1993 by 26%. Some particular but very important branches of the national economy experienced more serious disruption. For instance, the output of industry was 54.3% in 1992 and 49% in 2001 in comparison with the level in 1989; the output in construction in comparison with the level in 1989, was 55.8% in 1992, 48% in 2001,[15] 84% in 2008 and 80% in 2009, in 2010 – 70%, in 2011 – 65%, in 2012 – 62%, in 2015 – 58%.[16]

§5. Employment

26. The cardinal tenet of employment policy after the Second World War was a commitment to full employment. This was achieved: if the absolute number of employed persons in 1946 was 629,204 in 1985 it was 4,588,530, i.e., about seven times more than forty years before.[17] But this full employment had some peculiarities: it was neither sufficiently free (because of the existing limitations in the free movement of working people from one enterprise to another) nor productive because of the general low level of labour productivity. However, all the people were able to work, had jobs, remuneration and a guaranteed standard of living even if it was modest in comparison with the European standards. In this sense the existing full employment was more social than effective.

27. Since 1990 a significant deterioration in employment and a sharp spurt of unemployment has taken place because of the massive fall in economic output. The number of unemployed persons in 1991 was 419,123 (12%), in 1992 – 576,893

14. *Statisticheski Godishinik na Republika Bulgaria* [*Statistical Yearbook of the Republic of Bulgaria*] (Sofia: Science and Art Publishing House, 2013), 14; D. Jones, 'The Bulgarian Labour Market in Transition', *International Labour Review* 130, no. 2 (1991): 212–213.
15. These data are quoted from I. Angelov, 'Ikonomikata na Balgaria do 2002 g.', 20–24.
16. I. Angelov, 'Ikonomikata na Balgaria 2008–2009' ['The Economy of Bulgaria 2008–2009'], *Troud* [*Labour*] *Newspaper*, 22 Dec. 2009; *Statisticheski Godishinik na Republika Bulgaria* [*Statistical Yearbook of the Republic of Bulgaria*] (Sofia: Science and Art Publishing House, 2016), 11–13.
17. *Statisticheski Godishinik na Republika Bulgaria* [*Statistical Yearbook of the Republic of Bulgaria*] (Sofia: Science and Art Publishing House, 1989), 72.

(14%), in April 2001 – 750,000 (18%).[18] This picture of rapidly emerging unemployment is based on the official data but it is an understatement. The official data count as unemployed persons only those who are laid off from jobs and who are eligible for unemployment benefits and who continue to actively search for work. The data, therefore, omit:

(1) first-time job seekers (mainly secondary and higher-school graduates);
(2) involuntarily unemployed workers who do not qualify for the benefits because they have not worked for the firm long enough – minimum nine months during the last fifteen months;
(3) those working part-time who would prefer to work full time (especially the increasing numbers of employees who reportedly are being 'encouraged' or simply obliged to take extended unpaid leave as a way of preserving their jobs;
(4) all those who, for one reason or another, do not register with the local employment exchange office as unemployed.

28. The reasons for the sharp rise in the country's unemployment in the 1991–2001 decade originate in the collapse of the national economy and, first and foremost, of its two main branches of the primary and secondary sectors – agriculture and industry. These were built on public property and were subject to the centralized planned regulation, the latter being incidental to totalitarian rule. And, although they were not distinguished for the high productivity of labour that obtains in advanced, industrially developed countries, they were functioning and producing. However, this economy turned out to be naturally incompatible with the profound changes in the country that took place after the end of 1989. And, instead of transforming this economic sector and ensuring the smooth transition to market economy, it was destroyed. In this regard all governments that took turns in ruling the country during the period 1989–2001 failed to provide for a smooth transition to a market economy and for an active policy to stimulate the economy.

29. In the period 2002–2009 there was considerable economic progress within the country, which brought about an increase in employment and a decrease in unemployment. The total number of unemployed persons in March 2001 was 750,000 (about 18%) (*see* paragraph 27 above); in 2004 it fell to 399,800 (12%), and continued to decrease progressively as follows: in 2005 – 334,200 (10.1%); in 2006 – 305,700 (9.0%); in 2007 – 240,000 (6.9%), in 2008–2009 it was 199,700 (5.6%), in 2013 it was 415,000 (11.5%) and in October 2019 – 164,000 (4.8%).[19] During this period the governments pursued an active policy of encouraging economic development, foreign and national investment and employment. Since 2001 the Council of Ministers has been adopting annual National Plans concerning

18. *Statisticheski spravochnik* [*Statistical Reference Book*] (Sofia: National Statistical Institute, 2001), 57–59.
19. These data are quoted from *Statisticheski spravochnik* [*Statistical Reference Book*] (Sofia: National Statistical Institute, 2016), 46–48; *Troud* [*Labour*] *Newspaper*, 5 Nov. 2019.

employment. They provide for using state budget means for subsidized employment in community service activities, performed in parks, streets, public works and the like, for approximately 100–110,000 unemployed persons. The implementation of these plans was supported by the encouragement set out in Articles 3–55 of the Law on Employment Promotion (LEP) which concern the creation of new jobs and the appointment of disadvantaged unemployed people: young persons under 29 years of age, mothers of children aged 3–5, disabled persons, people of advanced age (women over the age of 50 and men over the age of 55), persons in long-term unemployment, etc. In carrying these plans through, courses were organized and financed for vocational training and retraining of unemployed persons and part-time workers; models were designed of public–private partnership and professional orientation of dismissed persons, including those who belong to the Roma population of the country, as well as for encouraging the mobility of the workforce, etc.[20]

30. Unfortunately, the progressive economic development and the gradual decrease in unemployment within the country were interrupted by the world financial and economic crisis of late 2008, which hit Bulgaria in 2009. At the end of 2009 and in the first quarter of 2010, the crisis greatly affected the private and public sectors and brought about a decrease in gross domestic product of 25%–30%. From mid-2013 the country started to come out of the economic crisis. Economic growth for 2016 is expected to be 3.5%.[21]

§6. Fundamental Political, Social and Cultural Values

31. The basic value in society is the human being. The care of his/her rights, freedoms, dignity and security constitutes the main content and goal of the policy of the state and the first guiding principle of its activities. A juridical expression of the position of man as the main focus of political, social and cultural development is given in the Constitution which stipulates a person's right to dignity and security 'as a supreme principle in the society' (preamble) and that the Republic of Bulgaria guarantees the life, the dignity and the rights of human beings and creates conditions for the free development of man and the civil society (Article 4, paragraph 2). Furthermore, the Constitution recognizes the fundamental rights of citizens, some of which directly relate to labour law (*see* below).

32. Adherence to universally recognized values such as liberty, peace, humanism, equality, equity and tolerance is laid down in a guideline for the overall development of society (*see* preamble of the Constitution). Respect for these values penetrates and dominates the functioning of all the state's institutions and serves as a permanent target to be attained and pursued.

---

20. St. Simeonova, 'Nacionalen plan za deistvie po zaetostta' ['National Action Plan for Employment'], *Employment Relationships Yearbook* (Sofia: Labour and Law Publishing House, 2019), 643–648.
21. Editorial, *Troud [Labour] Newspaper,* 5 Nov. 2019.

33. Democracy is the next fundamental value. It is conceived as a regime in which freedom is considered a fundamental and primordial good. In this context the government by the people is understood as a government for the free development of the nation as a whole and for the free development of each individual. Democracy is a principle of politics not only at the national level but also at the level of local self-government (preamble, Article 2, paragraph 1, Articles 135–146 of the Constitution) as well as being a principle of economic life (*see* below).

34. A lawful state (preamble, Article 4, paragraph 2 of the Constitution) means the submission of the state, the national government, its organs and their functioning to the law, including the Constitution and the laws of the country. The establishment of the Constitutional Court (Articles 147–152 of the Constitution) considerably favours the assertion and the strengthening of a lawful state.

35. Another important value in society is work. This remains the primary means of existence for every able-bodied citizen. He/she performs work in accordance with his/her individual physical and mental capacities. In return he/she receives payment which supports him/her and his/her family. That is why the state protects and guarantees labour (Article 16 of the Constitution). The Constitution proclaims the right of citizens to work in employment which means the right to have a freely chosen job in accordance with their qualifications. The free choice of labour also stems from the expressly declared prohibition of forced labour (Article 48, paragraph 3 of the Constitution). The right to employment includes working under hygienic and safe working conditions, just remuneration for work done, norms set for working times, the securing of sufficient time for daily, weekly and annual rest, etc. (Article 48 of the Constitution). Unfortunately, the profound economic slump which has plagued the country since 2009 and rising unemployment (*see* below under §5) does not always favour the right to work. Nevertheless, labour remains a fundamental value in society, even during these difficult times, and is one of the basic concerns of the state. Great efforts are made to create the necessary economic and social prerequisites for facilitating labour. The current labour legislation develops these constitutional stipulations still further by regulating the conditions for the establishment and termination of employment relations, for giving a central place to the question of the labour contract, and for paid educational leave, etc.

36. Property and especially private ownership of property as well as free economic initiative are recognized as fundamental values in society (Articles 17–19 of the Constitution). The private ownership of property is inviolable. The law creates and guarantees to all physical and legal persons equal conditions for their economic activities and fosters fair competition. During the difficult transition period rapid and intensive development of the private sector, including massive privatization, play an important role in repairing the national economy (*see* below under §4).

37. A fundamental value in society is also the constitutional freedom of citizens to form organizations (political, religious, athletic and the like). This also includes the right of wage earners to form trade unions' organizations and of employers to form their own employers' organizations (Articles 12, 44 and 49 of the Constitution). Trade unions' and employers' organizations are formed to defend and protect the interests of wage-earners and the employers respectively. They are free, autonomous and based on the principle of the pluralistic organization. Under the prevailing socioeconomic conditions in the country both trade unions' and employers' organizations play a very important factor as social partners in labour law (*see* below Part II).

Chapter 2. Definitions and Concepts

§1. Labour Law as a Branch of the Legal System

38. As a separate branch of the Bulgarian legal system, (the specific subject of) labour law is the regulation of labour relations. These relations arise from the hiring (placing at disposal and utilization) of manpower from one physical person (wage-earner) to another physical or legal person (the employer). The peculiar feature of the employment relationship is that it subjects the wage-earner, the bearer of labour power, not only to economic but also to personal and juridical subordination to the employer. The worker is obliged to be at the employer's disposal, to follow and complete his/her orders concerning the manner in which the work should be done; the employer may supervise and control the execution of the entrusted job. The rights and obligations which arise in the establishment, continuation and termination of the employment relation between the wage-earner and the employer form labour relations. These include the concluding of the employment relation, working time, leave, rest, remuneration, labour discipline, safety at work, grounds for termination of the labour relations, collective labour contracts and the like.

Apart from the labour relations, labour law regulates some social relations which are closely connected because they precede, accompany and assist their normal course or are an immediate consequence of them. Relations connected with the freedom of association for professional purposes (trade unions' and employers' organizations, the hearing of labour disputes, supervision of compliance with labour laws, social dialogue and tripartite cooperation, etc.) are derived from employment relations.

Although labour law in general encompasses labour relations and derivative relationships, this does not imply that a hierarchical relationship exists wherein labour relations are primary and derivative relationships are of secondary importance. They are equally important fundamental relationships, which lend themselves to lasting settlement and stable regulation by law (Article 3, paragraph 1 of the Law on Normative Acts). Without the regulation of other relations directly linked with labour relations, the regulation of labour relations cannot be full and complete. In fact, the difference between the two groups of relations does not stem from the degree of importance, but from their link with hired labour. This concept of labour law is now embodied in Article 1, paragraph 3 of the LC.

39. The method of legal regulation in labour law is peculiar; it is a specific combination of legal regulation and regulation by means of collective and individual labour contracts. The amendments to the LC in November 1992, March 2001, June 2004, December 2005, June 2006, December 2008, January 2012, December 2013, January 2014 and until the end of 2019 introduced profound changes in this respect, most of which are immediately linked to the transition to a market economy, as well as to the social problems provoked by the economic crisis. The number of imperative legal provisions which rigidly fixed the volume and content of the rights and obligations of the parties to the individual labour relation as an expression of the centralized planned economy was considerably reduced. The changes transformed many essential legal provisions into norms with a compulsory minimum and indefinite maximum. This now means that a 'lower threshold' has been established below which the parties may not descend, but above which they are free to agree on more favourable provisions in collective and individual labour contracts. For the first time, the amended LC legalized and established by law information and consultation of workers, tripartite cooperation and social dialogue. All this has produced an entirely new appearance to the method of legal regulation of labour relations during the transition to a market economy (*see* below, Sources of Labour Law).

40. Labour relations, which is the basic subject regulated by labour law, needs some further explanation and additional classifications concerning the circle of persons whose labour relations it covers, namely workers, employees and state employees.

41. The notion of 'worker' or 'employee' has no legal definition. The changes in the LC in November 1992 resulted in dropping its legal definition which was given by paragraph 1, item 2 of the Supplementary Provisions of the 1986 LC. But the law still contains sufficient characteristics from which it is possible to reconstruct a definition. A worker or employee is primarily a physical person who has reached the minimum age decreed by the law: in principle the age of 16 (Articles 301 and 302 of the LC). This is a person who submits (places at the disposal) his/her labour force for temporary use in the labour process, meaning that he/she hires out his/her ability of mental and/or physical labour by concluding a labour nexus arising from a labour contract, selection or contest, to another person who is the employer, against payment, and submits to the employer's orders. As a party to the legal labour relationship, the worker primarily hires out physical labour, whereas the employee primarily sells mental labour.[22] The law uses these as alternative concepts in order to underscore the predominant use of physical or mental labour but not in order to contrast them; on the contrary, it places them on a par. Indeed, labour relations deriving from the two forms of labour have the same, not different, legal consequences. This comes from the character of the labour as a conscious and well-conditioned human activity and unity of mental and psychophysical energy, since no physical job can be accomplished without a minimal expenditure of mental effort, and vice versa. Thus the terms 'worker' or 'employee' are employed as equivalents. Also, no distinction is made between 'white-collar workers' and 'blue-collar workers'.[23]

42. It was pursuant to Article 116, paragraph 2 of the Constitution that the Civil Servant Law was adopted in 1999 (OJ, No. 67 of 1999, as amended) and it has been effective since 27 August 1999. Prior to the adoption of this law the legal status of civil servants was regulated under the LC and this status was the same as that of

22. L. Radoilski, *Troudovo pravo na Narodna Republika Bulgaria* [*Labour Law of the People's Republic of Bulgaria*], (Sofia: Science and Art Publishing House, 1957), 191–192.
23. In the subsequent text, for the sake of brevity, instead of 'worker and employee' or 'wage-and salary-earner', the term 'worker' will be used. Whenever it is a question of a worker or employee (wage- or salary-earner) in the precise meaning of these concepts, this will be expressly indicated.

workers and employees. Through this law civil servants were 'taken out' of the field of application of labour law and were placed in a separate branch of effective law – the Civil Servant Law. Their legal status as civil servants in the bodies of central and local executive power is grounded on public law relations called 'civil service legal relations', which are established and exist between the state and the civil servant for the execution of the state power (Article 1 of the Civil Servant Law). The Civil Servant Law regulates the establishment and termination of the civil service legal relation (Articles 2–17, 103–109), the status of the civil servants (Articles 18–87), disciplinary responsibility of civil servants (Articles 89–102), etc. It is on the grounds of the Civil Servant Law that specific acts of subordinate legislation for its application were issued, such as the Single Classifier of the Civil Services in the Administration, and the Regulation on its Application (OJ, No. 23 of 2000), Regulation on the Official Status of Civil Servants (OJ, No. 23 of 2000). Thus a new autonomous branch of public law was established as a part of administrative law – civil service law. Such a part of administrative law, its legal infrastructure and legal science being developed at a European level, existed in Bulgaria from the beginning of the twentieth century until the end of the Second World War, and it was known as 'civil servants' law'.[24] Through the new legal infrastructure, created in 1999, after a fifty years' discontinuance, the traditions of Bulgarian civil service law were restored.

§2. Delimitation of Labour Law from Other Branches of Law

43. Historically having arisen from civil law (from the contract of hiring manpower) and administrative law (labour protection, factory inspection), labour law is now fully independent and separate from them. This does not exclude the possible application of civil and administrative law in some cases. For instance, the LC expressly refers to civil law regulations concerning the financial liability of the worker and employer for damages caused during the existence of the labour relations (Article 212 of the LC – *see* below) or to administrative law in the case of administrative responsibility of the employer for the non-observance of labour laws (Article 416 of the LC – *see* below). Apart from these expressly mentioned cases, civil or administrative law is duly applied to cases without specific regulations and in which the matter can be solved by their application.

44. The relation between labour law and social security law is of further interest. In the same way that a few decades ago labour law was separated from civil and administrative law, social security law is now being completely separated from labour law. This separation is effected on the basis of established differences within the sphere of related social relations. While labour law regulates those relations which arise from and are implemented in the labour process, social security has as its object relations in the specific field of distribution, namely the support placed at

24. P. Stainov, *Chinovnichesko pravo* [*Civil Servant Law*], Vol. I (Sofia: Science and Art Publishing House, 1932), 506; P. Stainov, *Chinovnichesko pravo* [*Civil Servant Law*], Vol. II (Sofia: Science and Art Publishing House, 1934), 266.

the disposal of citizens when they are incapable of working temporarily or permanently. The development of the relations is between insured citizens, the insurers (enterprises or cooperatives) and the insurance body – the state social security administration. Part of this support is given only to persons who are or have been in employment relations: indemnities for temporary incapacity for work, certain kinds of pensions – for retirement and old age, for disablement, for employment accidents and occupational diseases, etc. But again, the distinction from labour law stands out: covered are not only workers but also members of labour cooperatives, persons practising a liberal profession or an independent craft, servicemen, etc., i.e., all persons doing socially useful work regardless of the legal character of the relation in which the performance of this work is organized. Another element of support is placed at the disposal of interested persons regardless of whether or not they are working: pensions for civic disablement, social pensions, etc. Finally, there is a third form of support: the group of persons to whom this is made available is extremely wide: access to and free medical aid for all people (Article 52, paragraph 1 of the Constitution), assistance at childbirth for all Bulgarian citizens regardless of whether they are working, cash benefits for pregnancy and childbirth for working women and school and university students, etc. (Articles 48–54 of the Social Insurance Code (SIC) (1999) and Articles 4 and 7 of the Law on Family Allowances for Children, 2002). As can be seen, social security covers a considerably wider circle of persons, going far beyond the category of workers under labour law, embracing all persons who are working and, in a number of cases, all citizens.[25]

45. Finally, labour law and social security law differ also in their method of regulation. While labour law makes use of the combined application of legal regulation and regulation by means of collective and individual labour contracts, social security continues to be regulated by a central imperative legal determination of the relations between its objects, insured persons, insurers, and state insuring bodies. There are also peculiarities in the positive regulation of labour law and social security law. While Labour Law is regulated by the LC of 1986, as amended and the acts issued for its application (*see* below), the legal regulation of social security is to be found in many different legal sources, such as the SIC, the Law on Health Insurance, the Health Law.

25. V. Mrachkov, *Social Security Law – Bulgaria*, 4th edn. (The Hague: Kluwer Law International, 2014), 58.

Chapter 3. The Historical Background: 1878–2001

§1. Legal Regulation of Labour Law During the Period 1878–1944

I. 1878–1918

46. The 1877–1878 Russo-Turkish War was significant for Bulgaria in two ways: on the one hand, in 1878, the country with the help of Russia, was liberated from five centuries of Ottoman domination and on the other hand, the foundations of Ottoman feudalism were destroyed, which opened up the way for the country's capitalist development. In this respect, the war played the role of a bourgeois democratic revolution in Bulgaria. A comparatively rapid development of industry, banking, the construction of railway lines, etc., began. With the laws of 1894 and 1905 for the encouragement of local industry, the new power gave a number of privileges to private industrialists and traders and gave legislative expression to its liberal policy. Parallel with this, the number of hired workers increased: in 1905, 277,000 of the total population of 3,310,000 and by 1911, the number had increased to 400,000.[26] The workers worked under exceedingly bad working conditions: the average length of a working day was eleven to twelve hours, working premises were unhygienic and workers were subjected to arbitrary dismissal. The situation of women and children was particularly hard. Strike actions were stepped up: as many as thirty-two strikes broke out in 1903, while there were sixty-seven strikes in 1904. In 1891, the Bulgarian Social Democratic Party was founded and the General Workers Syndical Union was set up in 1904. Under the pressure of the struggles of the working class, and guided by the Bulgarian Social Democratic Party and the trade unions, the first laws protecting the workers were passed at the beginning of the century which thus marked[27] the beginning of labour legislation.

47. In 1905, the first labour law was passed: the Law on the Protection of Women's and Children's Labour in Industrial Enterprises. It set the age of 12 as the minimum age for employment, and the age of 10 under certain conditions. The length of the working day was also determined: for children aged 10 to 12 – six hours, 12 to 15 – eight hours, and for women over 15 years of age – ten hours. At that time this law represented an indisputable step forward in the protection of the employment of women and children. But because it was applied only in industry it had a limited effect. Trade, agriculture and the household industries, where the employment of women and children had a wide application, remained beyond the scope of this law. And even within its limited framework, the law failed to be effectively applied in practice. Many years after its adoption, the inspectors who were supposed to secure its application had not yet been appointed. The sanctions for neglecting application of the law also proved ineffective. The employers preferred to violate it, and if punished, to pay the minimal fines laid down rather than to observe it. In 1917, the Law

26. Z. Nathan, *Stopanska istoria na Bulgaria* [*Economic History of Bulgaria*] (Sofia: Science and Art Publishing House, 1957), 335–357.
27. L. Radoilski, *Troudovo pravo, Istorichesko razvitie* [*Labour Law, Historical Development*] (Sofia: Science and Art Publishing House, 1957), 185–200.

on Labour Hygiene and Safety was passed which revoked the Law on Women's and Children's Labour of 1905. The new law established an eight-hour working day for workers up to the age of 16, and an eleven-hour working day for all other persons employed in industry. At the same time, it also provided for certain general rules on labour hygiene and safety in all branches of production.[28]

II. 1918–1944

48. The years 1918–1944 were one of the most tumultuous periods in the recent political history of the country. It began with the Vladaya Insurrection of demobilized soldiers in November 1918, after the end of the First World War, in which Bulgaria took part as an ally of Germany. It was an expression of the profound dissatisfaction of the people with the foreign and domestic policy of King Ferdinand and his government which had brought the country to national catastrophe. This period was also characterized by the bringing down of the legal government by a *coup d'état* on 9 June 1923 and the crushing of the uprising in September 1923. It was, moreover, characterized by the further development of the working class.[29] In 1926, there were 505,000 hired labourers in Bulgaria constituting 16% of the population capable of work; in 1934, their number was 474,000 or 13.8% of the able-bodied population.[30]

49. With the Decree of 1919, Article 18 of the Law on Labour Hygiene and Safety of 1917 was amended and an eight-hour working day was introduced. After signing the Neuilly-sur-Seine Peace Treaty in 1919, as a part of the Treaties of Versailles, Bulgaria entered the International Labour Organization (ILO) in 1920 and has remained a member ever since.

50. In September 1934 the Law on Trade Unions was adopted. This abolished the right to free trade union association and introduced compulsory trade union membership. The new Law on Trade Union Organization of 1941 still more openly established the fascist corporatist principle in the organization of the trade unions. State control over the activities of the trade unions was tightened by means of the State Trade Union Board which was set up especially for this purpose and was given the right to interfere in the internal life of trade unions, in the appointment of their management, the determination of their membership fees, and other aspects.

51. In 1936, two basic laws were passed in the field of labour – a Decree-Law on Labour Contracts and a Decree-Law on Collective Labour contracts – which marked the highest point in the development of Bulgarian labour legislation before

28. I. Zlatinchev, *Borbata za troudovoto zakonodatelstvo v Bulgaria (1878–1944)* [*The Struggle for Labour Legislation in Bulgaria (1878–1944)*] (Sofia: Profizdat Publishing House, 1961), 39–184; K. Sredkova, 'Balgarskoto trudovo zakonodatelstvo – 100 godini i sled tova' ['Bulgarian Labour Law – 100 Years and Beyond'] in *Actual Problems of Bulgarian Labour and Social Security Law*, Vol. 2 (Sofia: University 'Saint Kliment Ohridski' Publishing House, 2007), 19–58.
29. *Istoria na Bulgaria*, 5–433.
30. *Ibid.*, 252.

the Second World War. The Law on Labour Contracts abandoned the civil regulation of the contract of hire according to the Law on Obligations and Contracts of 1892, which until then applied to the relations between worker and employer and gave a comparatively complete regulation on the conclusion, effect and termination of the individual labour contract. In Article 2 it provided that in the labour contract the parties determine the amount of remuneration, the character of the work to be performed by the worker and the place of work. It also established the conditions under which the labour contract could be discontinued on the initiative of the worker, the employer, or by mutual consent (Articles 57, 60 and 66). The grounds on which a worker could be dismissed without warning, were enumerated by way of example. According to Article 1 of the Law on Collective Labour Contracts, collective labour contracts could be concluded only by the legally established corporate organizations of the workers, the individual employers or their legally established organizations. They determined the amount of the remuneration of the individual workers. The amount thus determined was obligatory as far as the employer was concerned: the parties to the individual labour contract were free to agree on a higher amount, but they could not go below it (Article 7). The law introduced compulsory labour arbitration for those cases in which no agreement in concluding a collective labour contract between the parties could be reached. By these means, the state secured its intervention in the terms of the collective labour contract. On the other hand, proceeding from the introduction of collective labour contracts and compulsory labour arbitration, the law prohibited all strikes and lockouts. Workers' responsibility was introduced for instigators of strikes – imprisonment of up to three years. These provisions reduced the positive effect of the entire law.

52. The linkage of Bulgaria to Germany and the waging of the war were elements also reflected in the field of labour legislation. With the Law on Civil Mobilization of 1940, workers were firmly attached to their employers. Failure to appear for work and failure to fulfil the worker's obligations under the labour contract were proclaimed a crime and were severely punished with imprisonment of up to one year, or in time of war, with death. In 1941, the Law on Collective Labour Contracts of 1936 was amended. The new formulation of its Article 6 provided for the possibility to prematurely terminate a collective labour contract if the circumstances under which it was concluded had changed. The principle in civil law of the *clausula rebus sic stantibus*, which was introduced in this way, was in practice used only by the employers. Guided by their economic interests, they renounced their obligations assumed under the labour contracts and, unilaterally, suspended them, with all the unfavourable consequences for the workers. With the amendments to the Law on Civil Mobilization in 1943, a policy of 'freezing prices and remuneration' was introduced and applied. In fact, prices soared and only the remuneration of workers remained 'frozen'. Although the government determined only the minimum amount of individual remunerations, this was the amount which was widely applied in practice. Bearing in mind the growing cost of living, especially during the war years, this action was in fact legalizing workers' misery.

53. From this cursory review of labour legislation during the period 1878–1944, three basic conclusions may be drawn:

(1) With the development of capitalism and the appearance of the working class, the foundation of labour legislation was laid by the adoption of the first laws on the protection of labour of hired workers. Subsequently labour legislation developed gradually. The regulation of labour was contained in individual laws regulating the situation of workers only in part.
(2) The adoption of these laws was the result of the pressure exercised by the workers' struggles against the employers and the state.
(3) As of 1934 the fascist principles of trade union association were adopted; these trampled upon the freedom of trade union association and placed the trade unions under the state's control.

§2. Legal Regulation of Labour During the Period 1944–1989

54. The radical changes in social relations, which began on 9 September 1944, had a profound impact on labour legislation. The period 1944–1989 was characterized by the predominance of ownership of the means of production by the state and central planning of the economy. Labour relations were also regulated in a central and rigid manner, manifested in an administrative-command system approach to labour matters which used imperative legal provisions to regulate in detail the rights and obligations of the parties to the labour relations. The parties were not allowed to deviate from the norms, which paralysed their initiative, limited their free will, and left them no legal space for any manifestation of their own. The parties simply looked up their legally established rights and obligations, strictly observed them and could negotiate only within narrow limits. This legal approach, adopted under the influence of and copied from the Soviet model of labour law regulation, was slowly but surely introduced and completely adhered to during this period.

55. The new government undertook to establish its own labour legislation. A new law was adopted – the Law on the Setting Up of Conciliation Boards for the Interpreting and Application of Collective Labour Contracts, 1945. On the basis of this law, local conciliation boards and the Central Conciliation Board were set up. The local boards consisted of the Chief of the Labour Inspectorate, one representative of the workers and one of the employers. These were competent to interpret collective labour contracts, to settle disputes between workers and employers connected with the implementation of collective labour contracts, to take decisions on questions connected with the increase or decrease in the number of people employed by an enterprise, and other similar matters. Their decisions were subject to appeal before the Central Conciliation Board which also had a tripartite composition: president – the Chief of the Labour Inspectorate under the Ministry of Social Policy – and members – a representative of the General Trade Union of Workers and one of the Union of Employers. Later, in 1946, a special Law on Increasing the Sanctions in the Labour Protection Laws was passed. It expressed the endeavour to guarantee the exact application of the labour laws, providing serious punishments for acts of violation, in this way striving to secure actual application of the laws and thus enable the working people to make effective use of their rights. The Law on

Labour Norms adopted in 1946 helped to restore the economy, which had been destroyed, and to increase labour productivity.

56. Substantial changes were introduced in the field of remuneration. As a result of remuneration having been frozen prior to 9 September 1994, wages had considerably lagged behind rapidly rising prices during the war. That is why in 1945 the remuneration of all wage and salary earners was increased. The freedom to determine remuneration through collective labour agreements was also restored; as a result of this about thirty collective labour contracts were concluded, as early as 1945 affecting a large proportion of industrial workers. New and higher remuneration was thus established. An important step in the remuneration of state employees was also made with the adoption, in 1947, of the Law on the State Employees' Payroll. This law provided that the different posts could be occupied by persons who had the necessary qualifications as regards education and length of service (Article 5, paragraph 1). The law established the basic salary for the different posts of all state employees.

57. The first republican Constitution was adopted on 4 December 1947. It proclaimed the basic place assigned to labour in the new organization of society and entrusted the state with the task 'obligatorily to devote special care to it'. The Constitution also regulated the basic labour rights of citizens such as the right to employment (Article 73, paragraph 1), the principle of payment of labour according to its quantity and quality (Article 73, paragraph 2), the 'right to rest' (Article 74, paragraph 2). It also established the duty to work (Article 73, paragraph 2).

58. On 23 December 1947, nationalization of all private industrial and mining enterprises was carried out by law. This was a national act, broad in scope affecting about 6,000 enterprises in 37 industrial branches.[31] The nationalization secured a commanding position of the new state power in the nation's economy, and determined new trends in the development of labour legislation. Changes also occurred in the sphere of remuneration. With Decree No. 4 of the Council of Ministers of 3 January 1948, a central wages system was established. The level of remuneration in 210 industries and kinds of work in industry and trade was determined. Changes were also made in the regulation of leave; in 1948, the principle of graded paid annual leave was adopted. Paid annual leave of 14 to 30 days was established depending upon the age of the worker, the nature of the work performed, the conditions in which the work was carried out, the length of service, etc.

59. Substantial changes were also introduced in the regulation of collective labour contracts. By virtue of Articles 16–18 of the quoted Fourth Decree of 1948, these contracts could no longer determine remuneration, the amounts of which were established in the wages system. According to the Decree on Collective Labour

31. Prior to this, insurance companies, tobacco firms, and enterprises producing alcoholic beverages had already been nationalized, and after the Law of 23 Dec. 1947, private banks, large urban real estates, private pharmacies and industries were also nationalized.

Contracts of 1948, collective labour contracts continued to be concluded. They preserved their normative character – through them all future conditions of the labour contract could be regulated (with the exception of remuneration). They were concluded in two stages. The first stage covered the conclusion of general agreements between the central committees of the respective branch trade unions and the ministries under whose authority the economic enterprises fell. The second stage covered the conclusion of local collective labour contracts between the workers' representatives and the enterprises within the framework established by the general agreement. This system was in existence until 1950, when, in accordance with a new Decree which repealed the Decree of 1948, the collective labour contract was thoroughly regulated as a contract transaction and its normative character was eliminated.

60. The first LC was adopted on 9 November 1951 and came into effect on 17 November 1951. The Code underwent several amendments and remained in force until 31 December 1986, when it was replaced by the new LC of 1986 (*see* below). It codified the existing labour regulations and introduced new solutions which reflected the 'socialist character of labour relation'. The Code consisted of four parts:

- Part I. Trade union organizations (Articles 2–8).
- Part II. Employment relations (Articles 9–144).
- Part III. State social security, including long-term and short-term social insurance, i.e., pensions (Articles 145–204).
- Part IV. Penalties and general provisions (Articles 205–218). This Code repealed all laws in the sphere of labour and social insurance issued prior to it.

The main characteristic of this LC was its extremely centralized and rigid manner of regulating labour relations. The freedom of the parties to determine the content of the individual labour relations was reduced to specifying the character and the place of work (Article 15). All other questions were exhaustively regulated by the imperative legal provisions; obedience to these provisions was mandatory as far as employers and workers were concerned. Collective labour contracts embraced the reciprocal obligations of the parties (the enterprise and the trade union organizations) to fulfilling and exceeding the production plan, improving the organization of work and the protection of labour and improving the material and cultural facilities for workers (Articles 9–14). On the other hand, the main functions of the trade unions were their cooperation and participation in the implementation of state activities: management of economic and official activities, creation, application and control of the observance of the labour laws, administration of labour law, etc. Trade unions fulfilled some state functions such as the supervision of the observance of labour laws and the administration of social security. Their traditional function of defending the interest of the working people was displaced to second rank within the framework 'of the struggle against bureaucratic distortions of the state apparatus'. As a whole, the LC put the stress on individual labour relations. In this regard, it contained some significant protection of workers (concerning limitation of working time, paid annual leave, protection against arbitrary and wrongful dismissal, etc.). But it almost entirely ignored collective labour relations. This was one of the peculiarities of the totalitarian labour legislation whose legal manifestation was the LC of 1951.

61. The next important step in the development of labour legislation took place on 22 March 1986 with the adoption of the new LC (OJ, No. 26 and 27/1986, as amended) which came into effect on 1 January 1987. With profound changes having been made in November 1992, December 1995, March 2001, June 2004, June 2006, December 2008 and July 2010 (*see* below), it continues to be in force. It was a very extensive act, consisting of about 416 articles, which introduced some new solutions and consolidated by legal means 'the socialist labour society' in the period of transition to the construction of the so-called developed socialist security. Originally, it contained 20 chapters namely:

Chapter I	General provisions (Articles 1–11)
Chapter II	Labour collectives (Articles 12–32, repealed)
Chapter III	Trade unions organizations (Articles 33–49)
Chapter IV	Collective labour contracts (Articles 50–60)
Chapter V	Arising and the modification of employment relation (Articles 61–123)
Chapter VI	Basic rights and obligations of the parties to the employment relation (Articles 124–135)
Chapter VII	Working time and rest (Articles 136–154)
Chapter VIII	Paid annual and other leaves (Articles 155–171)
Chapter IX	Labour discipline (Articles 172–199)
Chapter X	Financial liability and other compensations (Articles 200–228)
Chapter XI	Vocational training (Articles 228a–241)
Chapter XII	Labour remuneration (Articles 242–272)
Chapter XIII	Healthy and safe working conditions (Articles 273–290)
Chapter XIV	Social, communal and cultural services (Articles 291–300)
Chapter XV	Special protection of some categories of workers (Articles 301–324)
Chapter XVI	Termination of employment relation (Articles 325–346)
Chapter XVII	Work book and length of services (Articles 347–356)

Chapter XVIII	Labour disputes (Articles 357–398)
Chapter XIX	Control on the observance of the Labour legislation and penalty for its non-observance (Articles 399–416)
Chapter XX	Administrative collaboration (Articles 417–422)

62. The LC of 1986 was adopted under the conditions of a centrally planned economy built on complete state ownership. It strictly regulated labour relations. The new regulations on self-management of labour collectives and on collective labour contracts (which provided for broader participation of the workforce and trade unions in the management of state-owned enterprises and in the decision-making concerning the regulation of their activities as well as in the collective bargaining) revealed themselves to be incompatible with the true nature of the administrative-command system and the totalitarian regime. The trade unions were overloaded with a variety of supervisory and administrative functions in the planning of socioeconomic activities and in the management of enterprises, and this did not allow them to play their role as representatives and defenders of the working people's interest. Another problem was whether the extensive participation in the planning and management of enterprises was in principle compatible with the trade union's role as defender and representative. On the other hand, and despite all efforts made to improve the proceeding legislation, the 1986 LC provided for the subsequent adoption of some fifty sets of regulations, ordinances and restrictions by the Council of Ministers and by individual ministers (most often jointly with the central leadership of the then existing Bulgarian trade unions). This, in turn, burdened still further the legal regime of labour relations, making it complicated and awkward. Its autocratic character was thereby reinforced.

63. This brief historical review of the developments of labour legislation during the period 1944–1989 makes it possible to draw several conclusions:

(1) Labour legislation during this period became an instrument in the hands of the established state government used consistently for the application of the administrative-command system in labour relations. Generally speaking the legal approach to labour relationships was closely linked to the existing socio-economic and political totalitarian system prevailing in society.
(2) The legal regulation of labour relations during this period concentrated on the individual labour relations. It ensured some important protection and guarantees of the individual workers (working time, paid annual leave, paid educational leave, financial liability, termination of employment relation, etc.), but it did not leave the parties to the individual labour relations sufficient 'legal room' to manifest their free will. The previous legislation neglected collective labour relations – freedom of association, collective bargaining, etc.
(3) Labour legislation was politicized and rendered ideological. It closely followed the tasks set up by the Bulgarian Communist Party and gave juridical

expression to decisions of the Communist Party, made these decisions legally binding and secured the fulfilment of the decisions of the Bulgarian Communist Party by making use of the typical methods and means of legislation. In this sense the labour legislation during the period 1944–1989 was an integral part and an expression of the administrative-command system.

§3. The Legal Regulation of Labour Since the End of 1989 to the Present

64. The radical changes which set in after 10 November 1989 and the transition to a market economy provoked profound changes in the labour legislation. They can be illustrated by three main manifestations: (1) setting up the regulation of unemployment benefits; (2) settlement of collective labour disputes; (3) amendments to the 1986 LC.

65. The emerging unemployment in late 1989 made it necessary for the Council of Ministers to adopt in December 1989 Ordinance No. 57 (OJ, No. 96 of 1989, as amended) which established regulations regarding unemployment benefits, measures to foster the vocational training and retraining of unemployed workers, etc. The Ordinance shapes the legal framework for the activities of the local employment exchange offices to provide job seekers with information regarding job vacancies, to elaborate a programme to assist in the training and retraining of unemployed workers, to administer unemployment benefits to the people entitled to them, etc. The decline in employment and the sharp rise in unemployment due to the massive fall in economic output since 1990 and the gloomy economic prospect for the near future make these regulations extremely important.

66. In early 1990, on 6 March, under pressure from the political upheavals and a rapidly growing massive strike movement, a new Law on the Settlement of Collective Labour Disputes was adopted (OJ, No. 21 of 1990, as amended in OJ, No. 27 of 1991, No. 57 of 2000, No. 25 of 2001 and No. 87 of 2006). For the first time in the history of Bulgarian labour legislation, the right to strike was expressly recognized and both the procedure for peaceful settlement of collective labour disputes and the exercise of the right to strike were established. Despite some deficiencies which plague this act, it marks a significant step forward of the national legislation in recognizing and regulating this fundamental right of workers within the framework of the ongoing process of democratization in the country. Furthermore, it was accepted by Article 50 of the new Constitution.

67. The amendments to the Law on the Settlement of Collective Labour Disputes of March 2001 (OJ, No. 25 of 16 March 2001) introduced changes into the legal infrastructure of the voluntary settlement of collective labour disputes. Article 4 and 4a of this law provide for a new body for voluntary settlement of collective labour disputes through mediation, conciliation and arbitration – the National Institute for Conciliation and Arbitration at the Ministry of Labour and Social Policy. It is built up on the tripartite principle, with representatives of the state and those of the representative employers' and trade unions' organizations. Its main functions are to organize and realize the mediation, conciliation and arbitration regarding the collective labour disputes in order to avoid the workers' resorting to strikes (*see* below).

68. The latest amendment to the Law on the Settlement of Collective Labour Disputes of October 2006 (OJ, No. 87 of 27 October 2006) has repealed §4 of Article 16 of the Law, according to which strikes were forbidden in some economic branches and services, such as the generation, distribution and supply of electricity; communications (post, telegraph and telephone); and health services. In this way, the freedom to strike has been ensured for workers employed in these branches and services as well. By virtue of the same amendment, in order to prevent harm or losses to society as a whole, Article 14 of the Law obliges the workers and employees to ensure – by means of an agreement in writing – the provision, during the strike, of those essential supplies and services the suspension or stoppage of which may create a serious danger to people. These essential supplies and services have to be provided in order to guarantee satisfactory generation, distribution and supply of electricity; communications (post, telegraph and telephone); as well as health services (*see* below).

69. The most important developments in labour legislation are the amendments to the LC adopted in November 1992 (OJ, No. 100 of 1992, effective 1 January 1993). The amendments made to the LC are large in number and essential in substance. They involve the repeal of some 130 articles and a change in almost 240 out of the total of 416 articles of the 1986 edition of the LC. Taking a closer look at these quantitative data is of interest because, no matter how expressive they may appear, no clear idea can be obtained from them concerning the scale of changes which were effectuated.

The rescinded texts comprise provisions which most openly expressed centralized regulation, totalitarian government, and the politicized and ideological orientation of the legal regulation of labour relations. The most 'extensively' repealed of texts are those on the self-management of labour collectives or workforces; also repealed were certain grounds for the establishment of labour relations (such as appointment to a job by order of the head of the local labour and social matters bureau; by a court decision; the appointment of young graduate specialists; membership in a production cooperative). Also dropped were certain trade union prerogatives regarding participation in enterprise management. Provisions which centrally and rigidly fixed wages and salaries also had to go. The system of settling labour disputes was profoundly changed and the new regime provided for labour disputes to be settled and referred to the common courts under civil procedure, which meant an end to the labour dispute commissions, etc.

The amended articles present an interesting picture. According to the degree of change made in them, they can be divided into three groups:

(a) The first comprises some 25 texts of which only the numerical order has been preserved; their content is entirely new. Though technically designated as 'amendments', they actually contain entirely new legal provisions replacing the rescinded former texts, such as the provision on tripartite cooperation (Article 3), the right of employers to associate (Article 5), the entire Chapter IV on collective labour contracts (Articles 50–59), Article 333 concerning preliminary protection in the case of dismissal.

(b) The second group includes some 25 texts in which the amendments made are minor at first sight, but are of major importance. These include the provisions on the right to trade union association and trade union rights (Articles 4, 33, 37, 45). Issues of fundamental concern, such as working hours, paid leave, wages and salaries, and indemnities are the subject of collective and individual negotiation and agreement (Articles 136, 155, 156, 156a, 220, 221, 228, 242, etc.).

(c) The third and largest group of amended texts comprises technical changes relating to replacement of the term 'enterprises' with 'employer', the addition of the word 'employee' to that of 'worker' and the like. Some 150 texts of the LC have undergone a change. As a result of these changes, the LC has been considerably reduced in volume: 271 articles compared to 416 in the old version of 1986. This makes it comparatively easier to study and apply as law.

70. Amendments to the LC were also made in December 1995 (OJ, No. 2 of 1996). They provided legal means for overcoming the practice, which has been extending in recent years, of taking up a job either without concluding labour contracts with workers and employees or without concluding personal contracts, in order to conceal the existence of labour relations and, thereby, to avoid the labour law protection of workers, and for employees to save the expenses on its realization – the payment of security instalments, granting leaves, ease in suspending the legal relations, escaping the regime of protection in unemployment, non-recognition of the time as length of service, etc. (Article 1, paragraph 2, Article 405a LC). The written form of concluding the labour contract as a form *ad solemnitatem* – required for its validity – was abandoned, and the written form *ad probationem* – required for evidencing it – was adopted (Article 62, paragraphs 1–3 LC).

71. Important amendments to the LC were introduced in March 2001 (OJ, No. 25 of 16 March 2001) and they took effect on 31 March 2001. In their scale and scope, they can be compared to the amendments of November 1992 (*see* above paragraph 67) and represent further development thereof. A brief outline of the most considerable changes of the LC is expressed in the following points of major importance:

(a) greater participation of the employers and their organizations, as well as the trade unions, workers and employees in the regulation and self-regulation of labour relations (Articles 2, 3–3f, 51a, 51b, 51c LC, etc.);

(b) consolidation of the independence of the employer and increasing his/her role as a party to the individual labour relation (Article 136a, Article 138, paragraphs 2 and 3, Article 139, paragraph 4, Article 142, Article 173, paragraph 4 LC, etc.);

(c) establishing greater flexibility in the functioning of labour relations in the enterprise and their adaptation to the specific and varying conditions in the activities of the enterprise (Articles 136a, 138, 142 LC, etc.);

(d) intensifying the procedures of coordination and consultation at the national, branch, municipal level as well as within the enterprise in the implementation of the rights and obligations of the parties to the individual labour relations (Article 136a, Articles 138, 139 LC, etc.);
(e) asserting the workers' and employees' right to information from the employer concerning those activities of the enterprise which are essential to the worker's or employee's individual labour relation, or hold interest for all workers and employees in the enterprise (Article 52, paragraph 1, item 2, Article 23, paragraph 4, Article 127, paragraph 1, items 4 and 5, Article 130, 130a LC, etc.);
(f) introducing in the LC some important labour rights contained in the European Social Charter, in the acts of primary and secondary legislation of the European Union (EU) in connection with the country's readiness for its acceptance as a full member of the European Community, in the latest conventions and recommendations of the ILO (Conventions Nos 182 and 183), etc. (Article 8, paragraph 3, Article 123, paragraphs 4–6, Article 130a, §1, item 7 LC, etc.).

72. The changes in the LC dated July 2004 (prom. OJ, No. 52 of 2004) were needed for the adopted course of intensive approximation of the national labour legislation to the directives of the EU in view of preparing the country for its admission as a member of the Community. These amendments concern some additions to the legal regulation of collective dismissals and the requirements for early information and consultation of the representatives of workers and the trade unions in case of contemplated collective dismissals (Article 130a and §1, item 9 of the Supplementary Provisions of the LC), introduction of a new type of parental unpaid leave for raising a young child of 2 to 8 years of age, this leave having the duration of up to six months and being enjoyed by each of the child's parents (Article 167a of the LC), strengthening the protection in case of dismissal of pregnant workers (Article 333, paragraph 5 of the LC), guaranteeing the payment of labour remuneration at the amount of 60%, yet, no less than the minimum salary for country, in case of thorough performance of labour duties on the part of the employees (Article 245 of the LC), etc.

73. The amendments to the LC of 2006 (prom. OJ, No. 48 of 2006) introduced the European requirements regarding information and consultation, on the part of the employer, of both workers and employees, and the representatives of trade union organizations. These amendments provide that the general assembly of workers and employees has to elect representatives for information and consultation, and lay down the employer's obligation to inform and consult these representatives on matters essential to the activity of the enterprise (transfer of the enterprise and other changes in the employer, introduction of extended working time or part-time work, night work and the like), as well as on current issues of the labour organization within the enterprise (Article 7–7d and Article 130–130d of the LC). Thus, the operative labour legislation has adopted 'the two-channel system' of representation of workers and employees – by the trade unions and by the information and consultation representatives.

74. The main accent of the changes in labour legislation in 2008 (prom. OJ, No. 108 of 2008) was on strengthening control over the observance thereof and liability for violating it. The reason for these changes was the general conclusion that in recent years the efficiency of labour legislation has been decreasing, and the number of violations of labour protection laws has been growing. In order for these weaknesses to be overcome, a drastic (tenfold) increase was introduced in the fines in case of non-observance of the rules on healthy and safe working conditions; admission to work of persons without labour contracts being concluded with them; non-observance of the requirement regarding the conclusion of employment contracts in a written form; non-observance of the employers' obligation to send notifications to the National Revenue Agency as regards newly appointed workers and those who quit, so that the centralized electronic information system of the workers working under an employment relationship can be regularly updated; vesting larger powers in the Labour Inspectorate, etc. (Articles 399–416 of the LC).

75. The most recent changes in the LC have been made in February, June, July and October 2010. They are targeted at overcoming the consequences of the economic crisis which hit country at the beginning of 2009. Due to the recorded downturn in economic activity by the beginning of the crisis unemployment had risen substantially: from 5.69% at the end of 2008 to 11.26% in March, 9.13% in September 2010 and 11.5% in January 2014.

In February 2010 (OJ, No. 15 of 23 February 2010) the legal regulation of redundancies was amended by repeal of subparagraph (d) of §1, point 9 of LC in order to bring it into compliance with the requirements of Article 1, paragraph 1, subparagraph (a) of Directive 98/59/EC concerning Collective Redundancies. With the same amendments to the LC a new more flexible regulation of the employment contract for jobs during definite days of the month has been established, this time has been recognized as a time of service.

With the amendments to the LC of June 2010 (OJ, No. 46 of 18 June 2010) a new legal ground for termination of the employment contract has been established in Article 328, paragraph 1, point 10a of the LC. According to the said provision an employer may terminate a contract of employment by giving notice in writing of thirty calendar days to the worker or employee where he/she has become eligible and has exercised his/her right to a retirement pension.

In recent years most workers and employees have refrained from taking their paid annual leave during the calendar year it pertained to, putting it off till the next year, when they still did not take it, etc. This brought about the accumulation of unused paid annual leave of long duration, for which pecuniary compensation was due upon termination of the employment relationship. Under the conditions of continuing recession and increasingly frequent collective dismissals, this creates even more difficulties for employers. The new regulation (Article 173 and Article 176 of the LC, version 2010) provides that, after consulting the representatives of the workers and the trade union organizations, the employer should approve the schedule of the workers' and employees' mandatory taking of their paid annual leave within the calendar year it pertains to. By way of exception, there is a possibility of transferring up to ten working days from the previous year's unused leave for mandatory use during the next calendar year (prom. OJ, No. 58 of 30 July 2010).

The changes in the LC of October 2010 (No. 77 of 1 October 2010) authorize the Executive Agency of the General Labour Inspectorate, which exercises overall control over observance of labour legislation in all sectors and activities in which workers and employees have also been employed to realize its control competence in the civil service and the compliance of the rights and duties of civil servants in their official legal relationships (Article 399, paragraph 2, Article 402, paragraphs 1–4; Articles 403, 404, paragraphs 1–2 of the LC).

In the period 2011–February 2014 a number of amendments and supplements were made to the LC – 14 in total. The most important ones among them were the three newly created sections – VIIIa, VIIIb and VIIIc in Chapter Five 'Occurrence of the Employment Relationship'. Three new types of employment contracts were regulated therein, respectively, those concerning: outwork (Article 107b–107g, prom. OJ, No. 18 of 1 March 2011), remote work (Article 107h–107p, prom. OJ, No. 82 of 21 October 2011) and the performance of work through an enterprise providing a temporary job (Article 107q–107x, prom. OJ, No. 7 of 24 January 2012). They will be dealt with in their systematic place hereinafter (*see* below, Part I, Chapter 1, §2). And yet, here it is worth mentioning the positive thing they have in common: they enlarge and enrich the opportunities for work under an employment relationship ensuing from an employment contract in contemporary conditions. On the one hand, they establish a comparatively complete regulation of a form of employment which has long been known and practised, as outwork, and, on the other hand, they introduce for the first time in Bulgarian legislation two new employment forms in which electronic technology is used – remote work and, under the conditions of globalization, the provision of employment through an enterprise providing a temporary job. This determines their prospective and permanent place in labour legislation.

76. In the meantime, six labour laws were adopted, namely the Law on Healthy and Safe Working Conditions (OJ, No. 124 of 1997, as amended), which gives further development to Chapter XIII of the LC regarding the matters of healthy and safe working conditions; the Employment Promotion Law (OJ, No. 112 of 2002, as amended), which regulates the fostering and support to the unemployed in job placement, their vocational training and retraining; the Law on the Guaranteed Payments of Outstanding Claims to Employees in the Event of the Bankruptcy of Their Employer (OJ, No. 37 of 2004, as amended); the Law on Informing and Consulting the Employees in Multinational Undertakings, Groups of undertakings and European Companies (OJ, No. 57 of 2006) and the Labour Inspecting Law (OJ, No. 102 of 2008, as amended), which establish the legal infrastructure of different aspects of employment relationships; the Law on Establishing by Judicial Procedure of the Length of Service and the Insurance Length of Service (OJ, No. 26 of 2011); the Law on Amendments and Supplements to the LC (prom. OJ, No. 27 of 2014), which creates a new type of employment contract – a traineeship (Article 233a–233c) and introduces changes in the employment contract regulation, stipulating in-house training (prom. OJ, No. 27 of 2014, No. 61 of 2014, No. 54 of 2015); the Law on Amendments and Supplements to the LC of June 2015 (prom. OJ, No. 54 of 17 July 2015), which supplements the regulation of Article 3 on tripartite cooperation and lays down the regulation of a new type of employment contract – the one for short-term seasonal agricultural work (Article 114a), the regulation of the creation of an employment record of the worker or employee (Article 128b) and the regulation of the working hours performed in flexible working time.

In fulfilment of Bulgaria's obligations as a member of the EU and in order to align the national legislation with the European standards, in 2016 the Law on Labour Migration and Labour Mobility was adopted (prom. OJ, No. 33 of 2016). This regulates the access to the labour market on the part of those workers who are citizens of a third country, and also includes the regulation of freelance practice, the exercise of the right to free movement in the Republic of Bulgaria of workers who are citizens of another Member State of the EU or of a signatory party to the Agreement on the European Economic Area (EEA) or of Switzerland, the Bulgarian citizens' employment relating to the free movement within the EU and the EEA, and the bilateral regulation of employment with third countries as well as the employment of Bulgarian citizens within their territory and the employment of their citizens in the Republic of Bulgaria. This law introduces into Bulgarian legislation the requirements of ten Directives of the EU, among which: D. 2003/109/EC concerning the status of third-country nationals who are long-term residents, D. 2004/38/EC on the right of citizens of the Union and their family members to move and reside freely within the territory of the EU and EEA Member States, D. 2014/54/EU on measures facilitating the exercise of rights conferred on workers in the context of freedom of movement for workers, D. 2014/66/EU on the conditions of entry and residence of third-country nationals in the framework of an intra-corporate transfer, etc.

77. The last amendments to the LC, as well as the new labour laws recently adopted, substantially changed the overall aspect of the entire Bulgarian labour legislation and introduced new concepts. The purpose of these changes is to make the labour legislation capable of meeting the new challenges posed by the profound transformations going on in the country from administrative-command to a democratic social system and market economy. As a whole these changes are an important step forward in the development of Bulgarian labour legislation and will facilitate the difficult transition. They approximated the Bulgarian labour legislation to the European standards and prepared for the country's joining the EU on 1 January 2007.

78. Apart from these changes in labour legislation, the adoption of the new Constitution on 12 July 1991 (effective 13 July 1991) should be especially mentioned for two reasons:

(1) its nature as fundamental law which determines the development of all the branches of the national legal system;
(2) the provisions directly oriented to labour law matters. In this regard, reference is made to the special protection and guarantees labour law enjoys (Article 16), to the right to work, to the right to healthy and safe working conditions,

to the formal prohibition of forced labour (Article 48), to the freedom of association both of the workers and the employers (Article 49), to the right to strike (Article 50), etc.

Generally speaking the new Constitution fosters and demands the progressive development of the labour legislation.

79. To conclude this very brief review of the most recent developments of labour legislation from the end of 1989 to the present, some short remarks can be made:

(1) The content of labour legislation is in the process of radical and dynamic change. This process flows very rapidly because the changes in society from which it stems are developing very fast.
(2) These changes cover not only individual but also collective labour relations. Furthermore, since the end of 1989, regulation of collective labour relations has been more dynamic and is trying to make up for lost time in order to prevent it from getting behind.
(3) In recent years Bulgarian domestic labour legislation has adopted European and world standards in regulating labour relations more and more intensively. This finds expression, on the one hand, in the ratification of contemporary international treaties on labour protection (conventions of the ILO, the European Convention on Human Rights, the European Social Charter, etc.), and on the other hand, in the introduction *expressis verbis* of their norms into the domestic legislation, such as the latest among them: ILO Convention No. 181: Private Employment Agencies, 1997, ratified and effective for Bulgaria since 24 March 2006, Directive 2008/104/EC of the European Parliament and the Council of 19 November 2008 on temporary agency work, effective since 5 December 2011. This important point in the latest development of labour legislation is an expression of the efforts of our country for its integration into the international social community and for being accepted as a full member of the EU.
(4) The common determining factor of all changes in the legal regulation of both individual and collective labour relations is to introduce more democracy, freedom, autonomy of the will, creativity, imagination and motivation by the parties to the labour relations and by the social partners.

Chapter 4. Role of the Government and the Social Partners in the Shaping and Administration of Labour Law and Industrial Relations

§1. State Labour Legislation

80. The effective labour law consists of legal norms contained in normative acts issued by state bodies: Laws (Acts) adopted by the National Assembly (the legislative body), Decrees adopted by the former State Council (which existed until 4 April 1990), Regulations and Ordinances by the Council of Ministers, Instructions by ministers and the like. This state labour legislation, according to the principles embodied in the amendments to the LC, must set minimum standards (minimum flow) so that the parties to individual and collective labour contracts can deviate from them by providing a higher but not lower level of labour protection. This basic principle of labour regulation is established in Articles 50, 66 and 74 of the LC. The profound reason for the embodiment of this principle can be explained by the necessity of minimum legal protection and more flexibility in labour regulation of the labour market economy. To this end, contemporary labour legislation has abandoned the principle of central regulation of labour relations from which the parties could not deviate by providing either a higher or lower level of protection.

81. Nevertheless, even after the last amendments (2016) to the LC, there are some imperative legal norms, for example, regulations concerning the termination of employment relations, disciplinary responsibility of the workers, financial liability of the employer and the worker within the framework of the labour relationship. These cannot be subject to any negotiation and contracting of the parties to collective or individual labour contracts. Therefore, in any individual case of interpretation and application of legal norms, careful attention must be paid to determine the legal nature of such norms, i.e., whether they are imperative or supplementary. Normally this is not difficult, though sometimes it may be rather perplexing to qualify the genuine legal nature of some legal dispositions (provisions). Only on the basis of the response to this question is it possible to determine if the contracting parties have the freedom to deviate from the respective legal norm and, if so, in which direction – to establish only higher or also lower levels of protection.

§2. Labour Policy

82. Policy in the field of labour is part of the domestic social policy of the state, the regulation of which is organized by the government (Article 105 of the Constitution). The Council of Ministers performs this function through the order which it introduces, the tasks and goals which it sets, the rights and obligations which it establishes in normative and other administrative acts in the sphere of labour. Acts connected with the application of the LC occupy an important place in labour legislation, namely among provisions concerning healthy and safe working conditions, working hours, leave, rest and so forth. The government also implements state policy in the sphere of employment and remuneration. For this purpose it makes combined use of three main measures concerning:

(1) employment security and unemployment;
(2) minimum wages;
(3) indexation of labour remuneration.

83. The process of transition to a market economy which began after the profound political changes at the end of 1989 was accompanied by industrial restructuring and a massive fall in economic output. This provoked an abrupt decline in employment and a spurt in unemployment. This was and still is a new phenomenon unknown to the population during the period of a centralized economy when unemployment was officially non-existent. It brought about not only general social insecurity and a sharp drop in people's standard of living, but also great psychological stress.

The deterioration in the level of employment from 1990 until the end of 2018 is a cause of great concern. About 40,000 are unemployed for more than one year. About 50% of unemployed persons have only basic education or are illiterate.[32]

The role of the state in solving the crucial problems in this area is limited to establishing legislation protecting employment security, and helping dismissed workers.

84. Legislation regarding employment security consists of regulating:

(1) the unilateral termination of the employment contract by the employer;
(2) the obligation of the employer not to unilaterally change the terms of the individual labour relation, except in important and limited cases;
(3) the preservation of employment in case of structural changes in the enterprise;
(4) the establishment of suspension instead of termination of the individual labour relation in various cases provided for in the legislation.

In other words, the legislation makes an effort to preserve individual labour relations and to avoid their termination whenever possible, making it endurable for the employer and favourable to the worker.

85. The legislation protects employment security above all through the legal regulation which establishes the terms for the unilateral termination of the employment contract by the employer. The employer can unilaterally terminate the employment contract only in some limited cases enumerated by the law and for objective reasons (*see* below, Part I). As a consequence of this development the employer is obliged to justify a dismissal. This principle was confirmed despite some distortions, flexibility and relaxation which were introduced by the last amendments to the LC (November 1992, effective 1 January 1993, March 2001, effective 31 March 2001, January 2014, December 2018). The employer is also obliged to reinstate the worker in the case of wrongful dismissal (*see* below, Part I). All these solutions in

32. *See* Editorial, *Troud* [*Labour*] *Newspaper*, 12 Nov. 2019.

labour law are interpreted as manifestations of the fundamental principle of the LC (Article 1, paragraph 3) concerning the protective role and functions of labour legislation, as well as an important legal means and guarantee for providing employment security.

86. The work entrusted to the worker and the conditions under which he/she agreed to perform his/her work cannot be arbitrarily changed by the employer without the consent of the wage-earner. Only by way of exception, in the presence of precisely defined and exhaustively enumerated instances in the LC, can the employer unilaterally, and in principle only temporarily, change the nature and place of the worker's employment. These instances are as follows: when the production requirements in the enterprise impose such changes, during periods of temporary stoppage of work in the enterprise, by Act of God (force majeure), and in the case of business trips and assignments (Articles 120 and 121 of the LC) (*see* below, Part I, Chapter 2).

87. The employment relation is not terminated when enterprises or businesses merge or amalgamate, when part of one enterprise is transferred to another enterprise, or when the activities of one enterprise are distributed among several enterprises. The employment relation of the worker does not terminate either in the case of change-over of the proprietor of the enterprise or in the case of an enterprise being leased, sold, let out for rent or under concession (Article 123 and 123a of the LC) (*see* below, Part I, Chapter 2).

88. The legislation also contains a provision in which employment relations are maintained although the worker does not actually place his/her labour at the employer's disposal in fulfilment of the functions entrusted to the worker. Such situations include the following: idle time, natural disasters, temporary incapacity to work, different kinds of leave, temporary removal from work, strike participation, etc.

89. Unemployment management is established by the Employment Promotion Law of 2001 (OJ, No. 112 of 2001, as amended). Under this law, the local authority competent in managing unemployment is the employment exchange office. This office is obliged to provide job seekers with information regarding job vacancies in the district and the required professional qualities for such vacancies. This information is submitted by the employers in the district. They are obliged to communicate to the local employment exchange office all newly created vacancies or positions which have become vacant due to the termination of employment, as well as the requirements for these positions.

When a job seeker is interested in a particular vacancy the local employment exchange office directs him/her to the relevant employer to get more details and eventually to discuss with him/her the conditions for employment. Neither the job seeker nor the employer is obliged to conclude a labour contract. This depends upon the free consent of the parties. The role of the state organ is only to serve as 'mediator' and a kind of 'broker' in the labour market, to facilitate direct contact between the two parties in order to negotiate between themselves if they wish to do so.

Programmes to assist in the training of unemployed persons and job seekers were introduced in 1990. Originally, they were designed to retrain workers who had been made redundant but the great majority of those currently participating in retraining programmes are unemployed. Enrolment in these different training and retraining programmes is entirely free. The costs of these training courses are financed out of a special fund to promote vocational training and retraining.

Provisions for unemployment compensation were introduced for the first time in late 1989. They are financed out of a special fund. From 1 July 2010 the amount of compensation for the period of unemployment is 60% of the labour remuneration which the unemployed person used to receive prior to becoming unemployed (Article 54c of the SIC). Only employees who are dismissed and who have worked for a certain period (nine months during the last fifteen months) are entitled to unemployment benefits. The maximum length for which they are paid is fixed at twelve months.

90. In the meantime, while the country is surviving an economic and social crisis, one plan of action in resolving the serious problems of the increasing number of low-paid workers is the policy in the field of national minimum wages as a part of the general state policy. After discussions the minimum wage is fixed by the Council of Ministers (Article 244, item 1 of the Labour Law within the framework of the National Council for Tripartite Cooperation (NCTC). Following a three-year period of stagnation (2010–2012), during which – in accordance with RCM No. 326 of 30 December 2009 (prom. OJ, No. 2 of 2009) – the minimum monthly wage was 'frozen' at BGN 240 (about EUR 120) and the minimum hourly wage was BGN 1.20 (about EUR 0.60), in 2019 the national minimum monthly wage was increased twice. On 1 January 2019 the amount of the national minimum monthly wage was increased to BGN 560 (about EUR 280), the minimum hourly wage being BGN 3.37 (about EUR 1.69) (RCM No. 320 of 2019, prom. OJ, No. 1 of 2019). Of course, this is a low and insufficient amount. However, it shows the state's increased attention and social sensitivity to social issues, although the consequences of the crisis have not been completely overcome yet.

91. The government implements the policy of the state in the sphere of labour and standard of living through ministries and departments. A fundamental place is occupied by the Ministry of Labour and Social Policy. This is a specialized government body in labour questions. Its competency embraces the organization, standardization and payment of labour, the direction, distribution and utilization of manpower, the problems of employment and unemployment, vocational training, the elaboration of drafts of legal acts in the sphere of labour, the exercise of control on the observance of labour legislation, etc. (Articles 2–9 of the Regulation on the Functions and Tasks of the Ministry of Labour and Social Policy, 2010, as amended). The Ministry of Labour and Social Policy has a functional competency: it implements state policy in the sphere of labour on a national scale irrespective of the branch or sphere of activity in which labour is applied. It also has its own local bodies: 122 regional services and bureaux on manpower (employment exchange offices) and 28 regional labour inspectorates. Within the territory of the region they manage the problems of employment and unemployment and supervise the application of the labour laws.

§3. The Role of the Trade Unions and Employers' Organizations in Establishing Labour Policy

92. Trade unions and employers' organizations play an active role in the process of establishing labour policy through tripartite cooperation (tripartism) and social dialogue. This is a completely new mechanism, introduced in early 1990, within the framework of the burgeoning democratization process, which has been applied since its introduction though with some interruptions during 1992–2010. This mechanism was expressly although briefly regulated for the first time by the last amendments to the LC in March 2001 (Article 3–3f of the LC). The tripartism is characterized by:

(1) its subject;
(2) the organs and organizations which take part in it;
(3) the contents and form in which it is carried out.

93. The subject of the tripartite cooperation is defined very broadly. It covers labour and social security relations as well as questions of standard of living. Labour relations arise from or are connected with the hiring and the direct application of manpower of the worker, the rights and obligations of the workers on the one hand and the employers on the other. They include questions about the arising of labour relations, labour remuneration, working hours, healthy and safe working conditions, termination of employment, etc. Social security relations concern the insurance of pensions and temporary incapacity for work, the amount and adjustment of the social security benefits, the payment of social security contributions, etc. Standard of living questions involve relationships between prices, incomes and purchasing power, periodical adjustment of the wages, social security benefits and social welfare payments because of the increasing inflation rate, determining the cost of the social and living minimum, the cost of medical care and the related problems which acquire a vital importance by the constantly increasing impoverishment of the great mass of the population. All these problems are part of and deeply connected with labour policy.

94. Tripartite cooperation is realized between the following actors: state, employers and trade unions. Participants on behalf of the state at a national level include Vice Prime Ministers and members of the Council of Ministers – Minister of Labour and Social Policy, Minister of Finance and other members of the Cabinet according to the questions under discussion – and at a local level include representatives of the local authorities (municipal, mayors, etc.). On behalf of the trade unions and employers, only representatives of the organizations recognized as representative trade unions and employers' organizations participate (Article 3, paragraph 1 of the LC). The criterion and procedure to be followed for recognizing trade unions and employers' organizations as representative are provided for in Articles 34–36a of the LC and they will be discussed further (*see* below Part II, Chapter 2). The idea is that the relevant trade union and employers' organization have relatively great significance at a national level to represent the interest of all workers and employers respectively in discussing the problems of labour relations, social security and standard of living. Every organization which is a member of a trade union or employers' organization recognized as representative on a national level acquires this quality because of its belonging to such an organization (Article 3, paragraph 6 of the LC).

An important step towards the organization and institutionalization of tripartite cooperation was made in 2001 through the adoption by the National Council of Tripartite Cooperation of the Working Rules on the National System of Tripartite Cooperation (OJ, No. 57 of 2001). According to these rules, the national system for tripartite cooperation is built up on national, branch and municipal level (*see* below). The Council of Ministers established a National Council of Tripartite Cooperation. On the National Council, the government is represented by the Deputy Prime Minister as Chairman and by one minister depending on the issues being discussed. The trade unions and the employers' organizations are represented by two authorized representatives. The meetings of the National Council may be attended by no more than two experts of each participant on separate issues. The National Council may reach agreement on issues discussed in the case of consensus between all participants in the respective session.

95. Since the entry in force of the regulation of tripartism (1 January 1993), the Council of Ministers has recognized employers' organizations as representatives. For the period 2016–2020 these are five employers' organizations, namely: the Bulgarian Chamber of Commerce and Industry, the Bulgarian Industrial Chamber, the Confederation of Employers and Industrialists in Bulgaria, the Association of Industrial Capital in Bulgaria and the Union for Private Economic Enterprise – and two trade unions – the Confederation of Independent Trade Unions in Bulgaria (CITUB) and the Confederation of Labour *Podkrepa* (CL *Podkrepa*) (meaning 'support').

At the same time, the National Council of Tripartite Cooperation from the beginning of 1993 has developed intensive activities regarding the determination of the national minimum wage, the new level of adjustment of salaries, pensions and social welfare payments according to the inflation rate, the discussions on the drafts of new ordinances and regulations in the application of the revised LC, etc. Even though its decisions are not binding on the Council of Ministers, the Cabinet, in principle, follows the proposals adopted by the National Council of Tripartite Cooperation. Its role is constructive in finding a solution to the difficult and painful social problems with which the country is confronted and contributes positively to the preservation of social peace.

96. Tripartism has also developed at branch, industry, regional and municipality level. By December 2019, tripartite commissions had been established in 15 ministries and in over 120 out of the 265 municipalities. At industry level, the main issues discussed were measures to reduce the effects of unemployment, the prospect of redundancies and the adjustment of salaries. At municipal and regional levels, the main problems discussed were measures to reduce the effects of unemployment and to create new or alternative jobs, vocational retraining, etc.[33]

§4. Control and Administrative Penal Responsibility

97. An essential element in the management of labour is the control over the observance of labour legislation. It is exercised by the General Labour Inspection under the Ministry of Labour and Social Policy. This is an important state activity which is very wide in scope and diverse in content. Its aim is to observe the application of the labour laws and to control the fulfilment of the obligations which legislation establishes. The functions of the Labour Inspection are regulated by Articles 399–407 of the LC.

98. The Labour Inspection is vested with the overall control over the implementation of labour legislation in all branches, i.e., control which is comprehensive in scope. Its control does not exclude the activity of the organs of ‘specialized’ control (state sanitary control of the Ministry of Health, the control of the fire safety service of the Ministry of Interior, etc.) but it is applied parallel with it.

The Labour Inspection is formed by a central service under the Ministry of Labour and its local organs – 28 regional services of labour inspection which altogether form a system of labour inspection. It is composed of paid employees on the state’s payroll who enjoy the status of civil servants. The total number of labour inspectors in the country engaged in the Labour Inspection in 2016 is 432.

For the effective implementation of control over the observance of labour legislation, labour inspectors are vested with relevant rights, duties and powers as provided for in the LC.

99. The rights of the labour inspectors are established in Article 402 of the LC. They include the right:

(1) to visit at any time of day and night any enterprise or other similar premises used by workers. This right is accorded to enable the labour inspectors to become personally acquainted with the check ‘on the spot’ whether and to what extent the existing labour protection corresponds to that prescribed;
(2) to require from the head of an enterprise ‘the necessary explanation’ concerning working conditions, organization of the labour process and the like;
(3) to request the presentation of all papers, documents, information and materials necessary for the fulfilment of the tasks entrusted to the employer, such as registers, payrolls and the like;

---

33. For more details *see* J.E.M. Thirkel & E.A. Tseneva, ‘Bulgarian Labour Relations in Transition: Tripartism and Collective Bargaining’, *International Labour Review* 131, no. 3 (1992): 355–361; V. Mrachkov in V. Mrachkov, K. Sredkova & A. Vassilev, *Komentar na Kodeksa na trouda* [*Commentary on the Labour Code*] 12th edn. (Sofia: SiBi Publishing House, 2016), 33–59; *Tripartism in Bulgaria* (Sofia: CITUB, 1993), 4–6.

(4) to take or remove for purposes of analysis samples of materials used or handled;
(5) to investigate the causes and circumstances of accidents at work by interrogating eyewitnesses and victims, 'on the spot' visiting of the accident at work, etc. These issues are extremely important for the establishment of the real situation in which the accident occurred and, eventually, for the realization of the responsibility of the guilty persons who have caused it, if any. The employers as well as the managerial staff in the enterprise are obliged to assist the labour inspectors in exercising their rights. This means that they are obliged not only to give them the necessary information but also to facilitate them in making complete, exact and thoughtful inquiries concerning the effective observance over the labour legislation and respect of the rights of the workers.

100. The duties of the labour inspectors (Article 403 of the LC) are the following:

(1) they should not reveal any manufacturing or commercial secrets or working processes which may come to their knowledge in the course of their duties;
(2) they should not utilize these secrets in their own economic activity, if any;
(3) they should treat as absolutely confidential the source of any complaint or information about violation of the labour legislation;
(4) they should not hold any interest in the undertakings under examination.

The justification of these duties is to ensure and guarantee the labour inspectors, objectivity and perseverance in exercising the control.

101. In accordance with Article 404 of the LC, the labour inspectors are vested with certain powers. The powers at their disposal are wide and varied and can be divided into two groups, according to their nature. The first group embraces the power of intervention of a labour inspector with a view to remedying defects observed in plant, layout or working methods. This includes the following:

(1) The power to issue orders with binding effect on the employer and workers for the purpose of eliminating irregularities and other deficiencies in labour safety (Article 404, paragraph 1, item 1 of the LC). This is the 'classical' power of labour inspectors. Its field of action includes the entire sphere of the legal provisions relating to conditions of work and the protection of workers while engaged in work. These orders with binding effect represent orders to perform certain actions, which the person to whom they are addressed to must carry out, so as to eliminate the established violations or deficiencies of labour safety. According to the character of the violation, orders may be accompanied by a time or – in the event of imminent danger to the health or safety of workers – by a no-time limit, i.e., such orders require that immediate measures for the removal of the violations are taken.
(2) The power to suspend actions and activities violating the rules of hygiene and labour safety by which people's life and health are endangered, as well as

those constituting violations in concluding labour contracts (Article 404, paragraph 1, items 2, 3, 7 and 8 of the LC). This measure is applied in cases of the approval of designs of buildings, machines, and equipment, the construction and reconstruction of premises, projects, industries – i.e., executions of projects already approved – the initial exploitation of enterprises – buildings, machines, equipment – i.e., their entering into service – and the immediate performance of production work; repeated hiring of workers and employees without concluding labour contracts with them, as required under Article 62, paragraph 1 of the LC. In fact, this measure embraces the whole cycle from inception and implementation of production activity under concrete working conditions. The labour inspector is authorized to intervene at any stage to check whether measures are being implemented in accordance with the rules of labour hygiene and safety. When such rules have been violated, the inspector is also authorized to stop their further progress and thus to eliminate the materialization of any concealed dangers. The effect of the exercise of this power is strong. The respective actions and activities have to be discontinued: designs are not approved, buildings and machines are not put into operation, construction or reconstruction is stopped, the activities of the enterprise cease. This 'cutting' effect continues until the violations are removed, the faults are set right, i.e., hygienic and safe conditions at work are secured.

(3) The power to suspend illegal decisions of the economic organs and officials connected with labour safety and the everyday life of the labour force (Article 404, paragraph 1, item 4 of the LC). 'The unlawful character' of these decisions is assessed in each specific case and consists in the establishment of contradictions with a legal stipulation, for instance, an illegal order for the performance of extra work (overtime) or undue expenditure from the fund for social, communal and cultural undertakings. 'Suspending' means putting an end to the effectiveness of the decision in question without annulling the decision itself. The law expressly sets a time limit of one month within which the administration or the respective economic body must make its decision conform with the law. This may mean that it might be repealed or changed. This power to suspend is intrinsically important and indicative of the resolve of the legislator to defend the interest of working people against illegal encroachments by the administration or other economic bodies.

(4) The power to remove from work workers who are not acquainted with the regulations on healthy and safe working conditions or do not possess the necessary technical training and qualifications required for the relevant job (Article 404, paragraph 1, item 5 of the LC). The removal in such a case continues while the cause for which the worker was removed exists.

(5) Obligatory instructions for implementation of special regimes for work safety. This power applies when there occurs a serious and imminent danger to the life and health of the workers and employees, or a possibility arises for such a danger to occur. This power is new: it was introduced in the legislation through the amendments to the LC made in March 2001 (Article 404, paragraph 1, item 6 LC). The essence of this measure is that the Labour Inspection should order the employer to take additional safety measures for those workplaces where the danger has occurred and to introduce a new work regime in

compliance with the specific situation, such as reduction of the length of working time, transition to smaller working groups of workers and employees, better personal safety means. And where the danger to the life and health of the workers is a sure and imminent one, the instruction provides that the employer is to suspend work, evacuate the workers from their workplaces where the danger will appear and the like.

(6) Obligatory prescriptions for employers or the persons authorized by them for sending a notification of an employment contract entered into whenever it is established that the deadline laid down in Article 62, paragraph 3 of the LC for sending such a notification has not been met; and for sending a notification for the obliteration of a notification given under Article 62, paragraph 3 of the LC whenever it is established that there is no evidence of the existence of a labour relation (Article 404, paragraph 1, subparagraphs 10, 11 and 12 of the LC).

102. The above-enumerated measures, when taken by the labour inspectors, may be subject to appeal to the administrative courts in accordance with the Administrative Procedure Code. Appeal against any measure does not suspend its execution.

103. The amendments to the LC made in December 1995 established a new power of the labour inspectors under Article 405a of the LC: to proclaim the existence of a labour relationship when discovering that the submission of the workforce was not performed under a labour relationship and no personal labour contract has been concluded between the parties – a contract of manufacture, in most cases. These situations have had a comparatively wide distribution recently and they are typical in maintaining the black market of labour. They are created either by the employer or under his/her pressure, and they are accepted by the workers because of the existing unemployment and lack of other opportunities for work. These contracts provide for lower worker's remuneration, stipulate a longer working day, do not provide social security or payment by the employers of the security instalments due. These workers and employees are not provided with paid annual leave, the time is not recognized as length of service and, as a whole, these workers and employees do not benefit from the protection of labour legislation.

104. In this situation the labour inspectors have the power to proclaim the existence of a labour relationship between the worker and the employer for whom the former is working. This is made by way of a specific written act-ordinance of the labour inspector, which is handed to both parties. Through this decree the labour inspector obliges the employer to offer the worker to conclude a labour contract for the future. This means that the existing state between the parties is to be transformed into a legally adequate state of work under a legal employment relationship between the worker and the employer. Should the employer deem the labour inspector's ordinance a groundless one, he/she is entitled to appeal against it to the administrative court by his/her legal or residential address within seven days of receiving it. The appeal does not suspend the performance of the ordinance. If the court finds that the ordinance has been issued lawfully, the court confirms it and the employer is obliged to sign a written labour contract with the worker concerning the work he/she has performed so far. However, if the court finds that the ordinance has been issued unlawfully, and that the case does not concern performance of work under a legal relationship, the employer is entitled to suspend the labour contract whose occurrence the labour inspector has laid down. The application of this measure by the Labour Inspection has brought about a certain reduction of the black market of labour; however, the latter has not been completely abolished.

105. The trade unions are also involved in the control over the observance of the labour legislation. In contrast with the recent past when they exercised overall state control, they now play a less important, but nevertheless significant, role in the application of labour legislation. From the juridical point of view, this role is characterized by some basic legal rules. They are contained in Article 406 LC and provide for some specific rights of the trade unions. Depending on the content thereof, they can be divided into two groups.

106. The first group comprises their rights of cooperation with the state control bodies. The law assigns a privileged position to them in their relations with the state control bodies. It is expressed in two specific functions that they are provided with. One of them is the signal function of the trade unions. They are entitled to notify the state control bodies of specific violations and violators of labour legislation, specifying the type of violation, the place and the persons who have committed them, describing the features of these violations, etc. The purpose of this right is to draw attention and provoke the interference of the competent control bodies in order to make an examination on the spot, to check the signal and, if they establish that the alleged violation has really been committed, to take the required measures, such as applying coercive administrative measures, administrative criminal responsibility of the guilty persons. Their other function is to seek administrative punishment for the persons who have violated labour legislation. This function has the nature of a proposal made to the administrative punishment bodies to impose administrative punishments (fines) on the guilty persons. On the grounds of this proposal the state control bodies carry out an examination 'on site' and if they establish that there has been a violation of labour legislation by the respective officers, they take measures to punish the persons who are guilty of committing it. The state control bodies that the signals or proposals from the trade unions are given to are obliged to carry out examinations thereupon, and to notify the trade unions, within one month, of their findings regarding the signals and proposals given thereto, and also regarding the measures taken in those cases where violations of labour legislation have been established.

107. The second group is expressed in conferring powers to the trade unions. These powers are set forth in Article 406, paragraphs 2 and 3 LC in their new redraft adopted through the amendments to the LC of March 2001, and their content is the same as one of the control rights of state control bodies under Article 402 of the LC (*see* above). These control rights are expressed in the right of the trade unions and their representatives: (a) to visit at any time the enterprises and other places where the work is done, as well as other premises used by the workers and employees – bathrooms, lavatories, sports facilities, etc.; (b) to demand that the employer give explanations and submit the data and documents the trade unions need; (c) to receive direct information from workers and employees on all matters concerning the observance of labour legislation.

108. However, the trade unions and their representatives do not have the powers to impose coercive administrative measures or administrative punishments for violations of labour legislation they have established. Due to their public character and peremptory nature, these powers are conferred only and solely to the state control bodies for labour legislation observance.

The trade unions are vested with the same duties as the state labour inspectors when supervising the application of labour legislation (*see* above) (Article 406, paragraph 3 of the LC).

109. Another essential element in the management of labour is responsibility for infringement of the labour legislation. Though connected to the control, it nevertheless differs in character and nature from a legal responsibility. It is regulated by Articles 412a–416 of the LC.

110. The LC establishes two basic administrative infringements of labour legislation:

(1) violation of healthy and safe working conditions by the employer, his/her managerial staff and workers (Article 413 of the LC);
(2) violation of other legal protective rules by the employer or his/her managerial staff (Article 414 of the LC).

Only when a person has been found guilty of infringing the rules, can he/she be punished. Establishment of the violation is done by the labour inspectors by drawing up a special statement on the basis of which orders are issued by the competent bodies for fining the guilty persons. Fines range from BGN 100 to BGN 30,000 (USD 77 to USD 23,000)[34] according to the gravity of the administrative violation. Appeal against the act by which the fine is ordered is to the ordinary courts whose decisions on this subject are final.

111. There are special penalties for obstructing labour inspectors in the exercise of fulfilling their duties (Article 415 of the LC). This kind of violation is also established by the labour inspectors on the basis of which orders to fine the guilty employers or their managerial staff may be issued by the competent bodies. The penalty consists of a fine ranging from BGN 2,500 to BGN 20,000 (USD 1,667 to USD 13,333). This responsibility aims at increasing the authority of the labour inspectors and giving more respect to their function and activities.

34. Exchange rate in January 2019: USD 1 is equal to about BGN 1.75. The national minimum wage is BGN 560, i.e., USD 320.

Chapter 5. Sources of Labour Law

§1. International Treaties

112. According to Article 5, paragraph 4 of the new Bulgarian Constitution of 12 July 1991 (effective since 13 July 1991), international treaties ratified in accordance with the constitutionally established procedure, published in the Official Journal and having come into force with respect to the Republic of Bulgaria, become part of the domestic law of the country. Provisions of such treaties have priority over contradicting rules of the domestic legislation. It is a fundamental change in the constitutional approach to international law which adopts and underlines the supremacy of international law over domestic law. Such supremacy has a paramount significance for labour relations because Bulgaria has ratified a great number of international treaties in the labour field. Also expressly mentioned here should be:

(1) 101 ratified ones, among them 63 international Conventions of the ILO in force (out of all 189 Conventions adopted by the International Labour Conference by the end of 2001) including the important Conventions on Forced Labour (No. 29), 1930, Abolition of Forced Labour Convention (No. 105), 1957, the Freedom of Association and the Protection of the Right to Organize (No. 87), 1948, the Right to Organize and to Bargain Collectively (No. 98), 1949, Equal Remuneration (No. 100), 1956, Discrimination (Employment and Occupation) (No. 111), 1958, Tripartite Consultation (International Labour Standards) Convention (No. 144), 1976, Worst Forms of Child Labour Convention (No. 182), 1999, Maternity Protection Convention (No. 183), 2000, Social Security (Minimum Standards) Convention (No. 102), 1952, Employment Policy Convention (No. 122), 1964, Maritime Labour Convention, 2006, Convention C131 (1970) – Minimum Wage Fixing Convention, etc.;
(2) UN International Covenants on Economic, Social and Cultural Rights and on Civil and Political Rights, 1966, other UN Conventions (against Racial Discrimination, against Discrimination Women, concerning the Protection of the Child and so on);
(3) the European Convention for the Protection of Human Rights and Fundamental Freedoms;
(4) the European Social Charter, etc.

According to the above-mentioned constitutional provisions on ratification, official publishing and entering into force with respect to Bulgaria, these international acts not only automatically become part of the national legislation, as their self-executing norms apply without a subsequent domestic legal act to be necessary, but also they have priority over existing domestic legislative rules which contradict them and provide less favourable conditions.

§2. Internal Sources

I. The Constitution

113. The significance of the Constitution of the Republic of Bulgaria (1991) as a source of labour law is revealed along three lines. First, in establishing the basic principles guiding the civil society and social state (Preamble and Chapter I), it also establishes the political and economic climate in which labour is to be performed and working people are to live and work. Within this framework Article 16 expressly defines the place which it assigns to labour as a fundamental value which enjoys legal protection and guarantees. Second, Chapter II which deals with the basic rights and freedoms of citizens, proclaims those connected with labour:

- the right to work, the right to freely choose one's profession, as well as the ways in which the right to work is guaranteed (Article 48, paragraphs 1 and 3);
- the right to a minimum wage and to remuneration in accordance with the work done (Article 48, paragraph 5);
- the right of working people to safety at work and healthy working conditions (Article 48, paragraph 5);
- the right to holidays by the establishment of annual paid leave (Article 48, paragraph 5);
- the prohibition of forced labour (Article 48, paragraph 4);
- freedom of association of workers and employers (Article 49);
- the right to strike (Article 50, Article 116, paragraph 2); etc.

These constitutional provisions form the profound basis of the principle upon which rests the actual regulation of the basic institutions of labour law which are now in force. Third, the Constitution expressly provides that labour protection is regulated by 'law' (Article 16). In this way the Fundamental Law not only obliges the state to subject labour to subsequent legal regulation but also establishes the high rank of the normative act by which this is to be achieved.

II. Laws

114. Laws are the main source of effective labour law in Bulgaria. The most important legal acts in the sphere of labour law are the LC of 1986, as amended, and the Law on the Settlement of Collective Labour Disputes of 1990, as amended, the Law on Healthy and Safe Working Conditions of 1997, as amended, etc. The LC regulates all the basic institutions of labour law: collective labour contracts, individual labour contracts (conclusion, content and termination), hours of work, rest periods, leave, labour remuneration, compensation, financial liability of workers, occupational hygiene and safety, legal labour disputes and their examination, control over the observance of labour legislation and penalties for its violation. From a technical viewpoint the Code manifests certain peculiarities:

(1) After the amendments to the LC of November 1992, March 2001, June 2004, June 2006, December 2008, January 2012 and July 2018, it is no longer imperative law based on the principle of centralized and fixed regulations as it was in the recent past, but now contains flexible regulations which establish minimum standards for the protection of labour. More favourable conditions can be agreed upon in collective and individual labour contracts (*see* above).
(2) Most of the provisions of the LC contain concrete rules of conduct. Consequently, it is not a 'legal framework' but a system of legal norms to be directly applied. The law on the settlement of Collective Labour Disputes is a completely new act in labour legislation which has only been possible within the framework of the fundamental upheavals and democratization which started at the end of 1989 (*see* below). It establishes the procedure for the peaceful settlement of collective labour disputes, and it recognizes the right to strike and regulates the exercise of it (*see* below, Part II, Chapter 6).

III. The Normative *Ukases* (Decrees)

115. The normative *ukases* (decrees) are a legislative inheritance of the past. They were issued by the former Council of State (1971–1990) as by its 'predecessor', the Presidium of the National Assembly (1947–1971), according to the old Constitutions of 1971 and 1947 respectively in periods between National Assembly sessions and approved by the next session of Parliament. These kinds of legal sources were manifestations of the disparaged role of Parliament during the totalitarian regime. The prerogative of the Council of State to edict such normative *ukases* was no longer exercised after 1989, and on 3 April 1990 the Council of State itself was abolished within the framework of the amendments to the Constitution of 1971. However, some normative *ukases* in the social and labour area still remain in force, for instance, Decree No. 1074 of 1974 on the Prohibition of Persons sentenced to the Deprivation of Liberty for Certain Crimes against Property and the Economy to be appointed to and to hold jobs connected with accountancy and financial responsibility.

IV. Acts of the Council of Ministers

116. Acts of the Council of Ministers occupy an especially important place among the sources of labour law. They have become necessary because of the dynamic character of social relations connected with the performance of labour. Also, they have come about out of the necessity for regulation of certain details in the settlement of a number of questions. These acts are government decrees which contain legal norms on questions unregulated by the laws or acts with which ordinances, regulations, or instructions are approved in connection with the application of the LC (Articles 6 and 7 of the Law on Legal Acts, 1973). Regardless of the basis on which they are issued, they affect a number of important fields in the performance of labour: the establishment of employment relations, working time, leave, rest, remuneration, etc. As already noted, these acts are adopted after considering the opinion of the NCTC. Ordinances, for instance, were issued in 1993–1998 for tripartism, for bargaining of wages, for reducing of working hours, for rest and leave, for workbooks and period of service and other sub-normative acts in connection with and for application of the amendments to the LC in November 1992. In recent years such acts of the Council of Ministers have been the following: Order No. 7 of 23 September 1999 on the Minimum Requirements for Healthy and Safe Working Conditions at Workplaces and Utilization of Operating Equipment, Decree No. 85 of the Council of Ministers of 4 April 2001, Decree No. 267 of the Council of Ministers dated 12 December 2005 as regards the enactment of the Ordinance specifying the types of work for which reduced working time is introduced and the Ordinance specifying the types of work for which additional paid annual leave is introduced; Decree No. 4 of the Council of Ministers dated 17 January 2007 as regards the enactment of the Ordinance on the Structure and Organization of Salary, Ordinance on the Working Time, Rest and Leave, prom. OJ, No. 72 of 1986, latest amendment OJ, No. 58 of 2018, etc.

V. Regulations, Directives, Instructions and Orders of Ministers

117. Regulations establish, within the different sectors, rules regulating working hours, safety at work and hygiene, as well as the rules regulating other specific questions affecting labour, or questions falling within the competence of one of the ministries. Within the framework of their competency and after consulting the NCTC, the Ministry of Labour, the Ministry of Finance, the Ministry of Health, and others, may issue acts affecting labour binding on all branches and spheres of activity.

VI. Other Sources

A. *Local Acts*

118. Acts of the local organs of state power and government are issued in accordance with Article 21, item 5 and Article 22 of the Law on Local Self-government and Local Administration, 1991, by municipal councils in connection with the rules in the enterprises under their direction or in connection with the social service of the population in their area.

B. *Internal Rules*

119. Internal rules in individual enterprises are drafted and adopted by the employer (Article 181 of the LC). These rules specify the rights and obligations of the employer and individual workers as well as establishing the organization of work according to the particularities of the enterprise's activity. The internal acts of the employer also comprise the following: the internal rules on salary (Article 23 of the Ordinance on Negotiating the Salary) (OJ, No. 55 of 1991, as amended), Rules on Providing Healthy and Safe Working Conditions (Article 277 of the LC), etc.

C. Collective Labour Contracts

120. Collective labour contracts are also an extremely important source of labour law. Collective bargaining plays a very significant role in the shaping of the rules of labour law even though there is extensive statutory legislation. Collective labour contracts are discussed in the next part devoted to the Collective Labour Disputes (*see* below, Part II, Chapter 5).

§3. Secondary Sources

I. Judicial Practice

121. According to Article 117 of the Constitution and Articles 2 and 5 of the Law on the Judiciary (2007), the judiciary defends the rights and legal interest of citizens, legal persons and the state. The task of the courts is to apply the law and not to create new legal norms. Their decisions reveal the content of effective legal provisions, and in concrete labour disputes the 'law is pronounced' (*jurisdictio*). This also holds good for the interpretative decisions of the General Meetings of the civil and penal departments of the Supreme Court of Cassation (Articles 124 and 125 of the mentioned Law) as well as for the interpretative resolutions of the General Meeting of the Supreme Administrative Court (Articles 124 and 125 of the Law). These decisions of the supreme judicial bodies reveal the content of the respective legal norms, enjoy great authority and possess a definite, though different, binding force. The interpretative decisions of the General Meeting of the departments of the Supreme Court of Cassation as well as those of the Supreme Administrative Court serve as guidance to the courts and special jurisdictions (Article 130 of the Law on the Judiciary), have to be followed by the courts, and the administrative organs. However, the binding force cannot make these resolutions acts of a legal character, because in spite of their binding force they are and remain interpretative (revealing the content of the legal norms) and not law-making acts.

II. Decisions of Tripartite Bodies

122. The decisions taken by the NCTC under the Council of Ministers as well as those taken by the other tripartite bodies, by industry branches or by those created at local (municipality or district) level are not regarded as sources of labour law. These decisions have the character only of commonly agreed proposals to the competent public organs such as the government, relevant minister, municipal council, mayor, prefect. They are not of any legally binding character. Legally speaking, it depends upon the final decision of the competent public organ to accept or not to accept the solutions discussed, drafted and addressed to it. This basic idea is in principle embodied in Article 3, paragraph 1 of the LC in providing that the state carries on the regulation of labour relations and social security as well as questions concerning the standard of living after consultations with the representative trade unions and employers' organizations. The stress is put on the prerogative of the state (and of its competent organs) to regulate labour relations, with the sole duty to do it with the collaboration and after having consulted the social partners. This is also the latest trend in the development of the Bulgarian labour legislation. The redraft of Article 3, paragraph 2 of the LC of March 2001 provided that when adopting normative acts in the field of labour relations and those directly connected therewith, the security relations and the matters regarding the standard of living should be necessarily subject to consultations with the representative trade unions and the employers' organizations prior to their final approval by the competent state bodies (*see* above under Chapter 4, §3). But the final decision to adopt the relevant regulation belongs to the state. It does not mean, however, that the proposals made by the tripartite bodies do not have any value or authority. They do. Such value or authority consists in how well founded these proposals are, and in the moral engagement of the relevant state's organs which have participated in their development and adoption by the competent public authority. The latest amendments to the legal regulation of tripartite cooperation were made in July 2015 through the new paragraphs 3 and 4 in Article 3 of the LC, which lay down a new form of realization of this cooperation (prom. OJ, No. 54 of 17 July 2015). According to these amendments, instead of discussing the issues within the scope of tripartite cooperation at a meeting attended by all the three parties, issues regarding which the state has proposed that a bilateral agreement be signed on the adoption of normative acts are discussed by the social partners (representatives of the representative employers' and trade union organizations) only. This new form of enlarging the scope of tripartite cooperation is only noted here, and will be given detailed consideration in Part II 'Collective Labour Relations', Chapter 4 'Tripartite Cooperation'.

On the other hand, labour relations are becoming essentially power relations, whereby the decision-making authority is challenged by the collective power the trade unions may display. Therefore, the problem is within the framework of tripartite cooperation by means of discussions, mutual concessions and compromises to adopt realistic proposals, taking into account the real economic and social situation actually prevailing in the country, which are likely to be accepted by the relevant decision-making competent authority. Finally, the adoption of the proposals so made is due to the goodwill and fairness innate in the tripartite cooperation. That is why, normally, these proposals are accepted and ratified by the competent authorities. Despite this, the elaborated proposals by tripartite bodies are not legally binding (*see* above under Chapter 4, §3).

Part I. The Individual Employment Relationship (Individual Labour Law)

Chapter 1. Definitions and Concepts

§1. General Prerequisites for the Establishment of an Employment Relationship

I. Capacity

123. The individual employment relationship is established between a natural person, on the one hand, and the employer on the other hand. To enter into an employment relationship the parties must possess contractual capacity.

A. Capacity of Individuals

124. A citizen can be a party to an employment relationship when he/she has the capacity to act under Labour Law, i.e., when the law recognizes the ability actually to be employed and to perform personally the obligations arising from the employment relationship and to enjoy the rights derived from it. All citizens who have reached the age of 16 are deemed to have capacity (Article 301, paragraph 1 of the LC). Only in exceptional circumstances, where the work is light and not dangerous or harmful to health or detrimental to the physical, intellectual and moral development of a young person, and with the consent of the Labour Inspectorate, may a young person between the age of 15 and 16 be lawfully employed (Article 301, paragraph 2 of the LC). In this case, employment capacity arises from the issuance of the permission of the respective District Labour Inspectorate.

The list of jobs which are considered harmful, heavy and dangerous for persons aged between 15 and 16 is attached to Ordinance No. 6 of 2006 for jobs forbidden for persons aged between 15 and 18 (OJ, No. 64 of 2006). It contains 115 jobs in different branches of industry such as mining, iron and steel industry, metallurgical industry.

Parallel with employment capacity runs a person's full civil material and judicial capacity on matters connected with the use made of his/her labour:[35] the person

35. General civil capacity ensues with the completion of 18 years of age (Art. 2 of the Law on Persons and the Family, 1949).

himself/herself enters into the employment relationship, personally receives his/her remuneration and lodges claims and answers them as defendant without the participation of his/her parents or tutors (Article 4, paragraph 2 of the Law on Persons and the Family, and Article 16, paragraph 3 of the Code of Civil Procedure, 1952).

125. The acquisition of general employment capacity presupposes the presence of normal mental health. If a person is affected by weak-mindedness or by mental illness, and cannot look after his/her own affairs, he/she must be placed under guardianship (Articles 336–340 of the Civil Procedure Code of 2007). Where the mental condition of a person is seriously disturbed, he/she is considered fully incapable of acting for himself/herself and is placed under supervision, and is unable to enter into an employment relationship. If the condition is not serious, he/she is placed under limited guardianship. In this case employment capacity is unaffected and thc pcrson is capable of entering into an employment relationship.

B. Limitations

126. The law does not allow any limitation of employment capacity based on differences in nationality, origin, creed, sex, race, education, social, personal and material status, or membership of trade unions and other social organizations (Article 6, paragraph 2 of the Constitution and Article 8, paragraph 3 of the LC).

127. The amendments to the LC of March 2001 and June 2006 introduced important changes in Article 8, paragraph 3 of the LC concerning discrimination in employment relationships. They can be divided into two groups.

The first one encompasses the introduction of new discrimination criteria under which employment rights and obligations are prohibited from being performed. These new criteria are colour of the skin, age, family status, disability, etc. The inclusion thereof enlarges the catalogue of discrimination symptoms and extends the prohibition of practising discrimination, privileges or restrictions in the performance of employment rights and obligations. Most of these newly introduced criteria (colour of the skin, age, family status, presence of physical and mental injuries, as well as differences in contracts and the duration of working time) have been present for a long time in the international legal infrastructure, and their explicit adoption in the domestic legislation is an important step in affiliating with world standards.

Another direction of the new solutions of Article 4, paragraph 3 of the Law on Protection from Discrimination (OJ, No. 86 of 2003, as amended) is the explicit prohibition of indirect discrimination, along with and equally with direct discrimination. This question has acquired practical significance in connection with the still more frequent cases of indirect discrimination and the need for approximation of the national legislation to EU law. And important sources of primary and secondary legislation of the latter explicitly prohibit discrimination: Article 119 of the EU Treaty, Article 2 paragraph 1 of D. 76/207/EEC, Article 5 paragraphs 1 and 6 of D. 86/378/EEC, D. 2000/43/EU, etc.

128. Article 4, paragraph 3 of the Law on Protection from Discrimination gives the legal definition of indirect discrimination. It reads as follows:

> Indirect discrimination is the one in which the permissions used in the realization of employment rights and obligations are seemingly admissible by law, however, they are applied in view of the criteria under Article 8, para. 3 [of the LC] in a way that either actually or virtually puts some workers and employees in a less favourable or privileged position regarding the others.

'Seemingly admissible' requirements are those that formally stem from the nature of work, from the need for its effective performance, and are grounded on the freedom of agreement, but in practice lead to discrimination. There are such examples in practice. For instance, it is announced that only women shall be admitted as school teachers; only men shall be appointed salespersons in commercial shops for foodstuffs; only people younger than 35 shall be employed as bank clerks, etc. This reduces the scope of persons that are eligible and unjustifiably increases the chances of a limited scope of persons in applying for a job. This puts all the others in an unfavourable position. In the examples shown above, these are men, as they cannot apply to be teachers; women as they cannot apply to be salespersons in commercial shops for foodstuffs; persons aged over 35 who are not eligible for bank clerk vacancies, etc. These persons are deprived, from the very beginning, of their chance to apply for the vacancies in the above cases without having their professional qualities assessed. It is against this discriminatory result and virtual inequality that the prohibition of indirect discrimination is targeted.

129. Discrimination against women with regard to employment capacity is not permitted either. This is, from a juridical viewpoint, categorically excluded by the principle of equality of men and women, proclaimed in Article 6 of the Constitution. Consequently, women may, without exception, without additional permission and without the consent of their husbands, enter into an employment relationship. And, in fact, the mass participation of women in social labour, noted above, reaffirms this.

130. As to foreign citizens entering into a labour relationship in Bulgaria, they can be divided into two categories.

The first comprises foreigners who have been allowed a short-term or long-term stay in the country. A short-term stay lasts for up to ninety days, while a long-term stay lasts for up to one year. These categories of foreigners, temporarily residing in the country, are entitled to be employed only after receiving permission from the Ministry of Labour and Social Policy. The permission concerns the employment with a specified employer for a specified term (Articles 23 and 33, paragraphs 2 and 3 of the Law on Foreigners in the Republic of Bulgaria). The second group comprises foreigners who are permanently residing in the country for an unlimited time. They can be employed without any exception in accordance with the procedure set for Bulgarian citizens (Articles 23 and 33, paragraph 1 of the law cited).

131. There are jobs and activities that may be performed under an employment relationship by Bulgarian citizens only. They are explicitly set forth in different laws. For example, entering a job in civil aviation – members of the flight personnel of civil aviation (Article 34, paragraph 1 of the Law on Civil Aviation, OJ, No. 94 of 1972, as amended), members of the ships' staff in commercial navigation (Article 88 of the Code of Commercial Navigation, OJ, Nos 55 and 56 of 1970, as amended), etc. Apart from the job under an employment relationship, only Bulgarian citizens are entitled to be civil servants (Article 7, paragraph 1, item 1 of the Civil Servant Law) (OJ, No. 67 of 1999, as amended). Foreign citizens employed in the above-mentioned two cases enjoy the same rights and have the same duties relating to their conditions of work and labour protection as native workers subject only to any exceptions provided for in the respective international agreements concluded by Bulgaria (Article 22). Therefore, the labour status of the foreign worker is determined by Bulgarian labour law in its capacity of *lex loci laboris*.[36]

132. Bulgarian law allows a certain, in principle, temporary, limitation of the employment capacity of citizens in certain precisely determined cases. These may be divided into four groups. First, deprivation by judicial sentence of the right to occupy a certain state of public post or to practise a certain profession or activity (Article 37, paragraph 1, items 6 and 7 of the Penal Code). This punishment is imposed when occupation of the post or practice of the profession is incompatible with the character of the crime perpetrated (Article 50, paragraph 1 of the Penal Code). When such deprivation of the right to occupy or practise is pronounced independently, the sentence can be imposed for a period of three years, and when it accompanies the punishment of deprivation of liberty, the sentences will run concurrently, not exceeding three years (Article 49, paragraphs 1 and 2 of the Penal Code). Second, according to Article 1 of *Ukase* No. 1074 of 1974, persons sentenced to the deprivation of liberty for certain crimes (against property and the economy, or of falsification or use of false documents) cannot be appointed to and hold jobs connected with accountancy and financial responsibility (Articles 2–4 of the *Ukase*). Third, limitation of employment capacity can also be applied where administrative sentences are imposed for certain violations of the law. This is the case where a driving licence is temporarily withdrawn from a professional chauffeur (Articles 174–176 of the Law on Road Traffic, OJ, No. 20 of 1999, as amended). Fourth, professional drivers, engine drivers and pilots having caused an accident intentionally or while in a state of intoxication resulting in the death of one or more persons will be deprived of the right to practise their professions. This is an instance in which limitation of employment capacity applies indefinitely (Article 342, paragraph 3 and Article 343(b) of the Penal Code).

36. Vl. Koutikov, *Mejdounarodno Tchastno Pravo na Narodna Republika Bulgaria* [*Private International Law of the People's Republic of Bulgaria*] 3rd ed. (Sofia: Science and Art Publishing House, 1976), 528–529; T. Todirov, *Mejdounarodno Tchastno Pravo* [*Private International Law*] 3rd edn. (Sofia: Publishing House Sibi, 2010), 359–362.

C. Capacity of the Employer

133. Paragraph 1, item 1 of the Supplementary Provisions of the LC contains a legal definition of employer which emphasizes his/her employment capacity. This definition is broad and contains two basic characteristics:

(1) The employer is a natural or legal person. When he/she is a natural person, he/she must have civil legal capacity. He/she could also be a legal person (body corporate) which has acquired this status in the legally established procedure (by law, by an act of permission, or with the founders' approval).[37] When the employer is a corporate body, 'employer' not only comprises the corporate body as a whole, but also its subsidiary as well as any other formation (enterprise, office, organization or cooperative) regardless of whether or not that formation itself possesses the status of legal person. Nevertheless, in the last case it must be economically and organization ally independent. This means that it must have its distinct subject of activity or distinct part of it, its separate organization and separate finances (its own balance sheet and bank account).
(2) The next basic characteristic of 'employer' is that he/she hires someone else's labour under a labour nexus, to be his/her worker and employee in the performance of the employer's activity. This means that he/she may independently hire and dismiss persons employed as workers and employees. The number of hired workers or employees makes no difference, nor does the kind of premises on which the employer's activity is performed. It may be public (state or municipal owned), private or of a mixed nature.

In practice these cases are frequent ones – for instance, a branch of a commercial company, bank or enterprise, which performs its activities out of the population centre in which its headquarters are located. This flexible legislative solution allows the employer, as a party to the employment relationship, to be 'closer' to the place where the other party to the same employment relationship – workers or employees – perform their employment rights and obligations, and in general to be closer to the place where the individual employment relationship is realized and functions. The acknowledgement of the employment capacity of the branch or subdivision is of importance regarding both substantive and procedural law. It determines the branch-employer as the bearer of the rights and obligations under the substantive legal employment relationship concerning the respective worker or employee. It also determines the procedural legitimation of the branch-employer as a party claimant or defendant in a labour dispute with a worker of the branch or subdivision, in accordance with Article 357 of the LC in relation to Article 15 of the Civil Procedure Code (*see* below). This attitude is adopted in court practice. It is also consistently carried out by the Supreme Court of Cassation (*see* Dec. 22-98-III C.Ch., Dec. 366-98-III C.Ch., Dec. 447-2000-III C.Ch., Dec. 660-2000-III C.Ch., Dec. 815-07-II C.Ch., Dec. 455-07-II C.Ch., Dec. 549-08-IV C.Ch., Dec. 626-08-IV

37. V. Tadjer, *Grajdansko pravo* [*Civil Law*] (Sofia: Science and Art Publishing House, 1973), 82–84.

C.Ch., Dec. 833-10-IV C.Ch., Dec. 325-11-IV C.Ch., Dec. 467-12-IV C.Ch., Dec. 557-12-IV C.Ch., Dec. 12-16-III C.Ch., Dec. 185-16-III C.Ch., Dec. 163-17-IV C.Ch., Dec. 2609-17-IV C.Ch., etc.).[38]

§2. Grounds Giving Rise to an Employment Relationship

134. An employment relationship arises as a result of exactly determined juridical facts, which are the grounds giving rise to an employment relationship. Under the laws now in force, an individual employment relationship arises from the following three grounds:

(1) a labour contract;
(2) election;
(3) competitive examination.

I. Labour Contract

A. *Conclusion and Content*

135. A labour contract is an agreement concluded between a worker, on the one hand, and an employer, on the other hand (Article 61, paragraph 1 of the LC). The candidate for a job submits a written application for employment. In the formation of a contract, this constitutes an offer. The candidate attaches the following documents to his/her application as enumerated in Article 1 of the Ordinance concerning the necessary documents for the conclusion of a labour contract of 1993 (OJ, No. 44 of 1993): passport, education certificate, medical certificate, abstract of his/her judicial record if the job requires this, permission from the Labour Inspection if the person is between 15 and 18 years of age and a personal health booklet. The reason for the presentation of these documents is to substantiate the person's application and to persuade the employer to accept the candidate. When the employer accepts the offer made to him/her in this way, he/she concludes the labour contract or issues a written order for the person's appointment to the respective job and arranges delivery to the worker. Upon both parties (the worker and the employer) signing the labour contract or the delivery of the order for the person's appointment concord of

38. V. Mrachkov, *Trudovo pravo* [*Labour Law*] 7th edn. (Sofia: SiBi Publishing House, 2010), 182–192; 'Critical Review of the 2007 Practice of the Supreme Court of Cassation on Labour Disputes', *Juridicheski Sviat* [*Juridical World*] *Journal* 2 (2008): 179–218; 'Critical Review of the 2008 Practice of the Supreme Court of Cassation on Labour Cases', *Juridicheski Sviat* [*Juridical World*] *Journal* 2 (2009): 138–197; 'Critical Review of the 2010 Practice of the Supreme Court of Cassation on Labour Cases', *Juridicheski Sviat* [*Juridical World*] *Journal* 2 (2011): 143–144; 'Critical Review of the 2011 Practice of the Supreme Court of Cassation on Labour Cases', *Juridicheski Sviat* [*Juridical World*] *Journal* 2 (2012): 138; 'Critical Review of the 2012 Practice of the Supreme Court of Cassation on Labour Cases', *Juridicheski Sviat* [*Juridical World*] *Journal* 2 (2013): 116–117.

the two wills is effected and the contract is concluded. The moment of its conclusion is receipt by the worker of a copy of the labour contract signed by both parties or of the employer's order for the appointment of the worker (Articles 13 and 14 of the Law on Obligations and Contracts).

136. The labour contract has to be in writing. This requirement is expressly provided for in Article 62, paragraph 1 of the LC. The amendments to the LC of December 2002 (prom. OJ, No. 120 of 2002) repealed paragraph 2 of Article 61 of the LC. This paragraph was created in December 1995 (prom. OJ, No. 2 of 1996) and permitted the conclusion of the employment contract in a verbal form as well. This permission, introduced in 1995, contradicts national legal traditions which, for decades on end, have been providing for and sanctioning the written form of the employment contract as being the form for its validity (*ad solemnitatem*). This regulation did not turn out to be successful. It resulted in the large-scale conclusion of verbal employment contracts which, later on, were arbitrarily terminated by the employer, once again verbally. Because of that, in December 2002, the written form of concluding an employment contract was restored to its importance as the form required for its validity from 1 January 2003 onwards.

137. The requirement regarding the written form of concluding an employment contract is a requirement for the ordinary written form, without any complications, such as notarized authentication of the signatures. This form consists in expressing in writing the content of the concluded employment contract and the signing of it by the two parties.

The time of conclusion of the employment contract is the time it is signed by both parties.

The requirement of the written form establishes clarity in the relations between the parties regarding the labour contract, the time of conclusion, and the content of the labour contract. It is a prerequisite for strict financial and staff discipline in the enterprise: the employer only has to remunerate labour when there is a written contract.

138. The content of the labour contract is an aggregate of the rights and obligations of the parties. In accordance with the source from which these arise, rights and obligations can be divided into two groups: legal and contractual. The legal content is that prescribed by imperative legal stipulations. It includes the rights and obligations of the parties regarding safety at work and hygiene, labour discipline, financial liability, termination of the labour contract, and so forth. Such rights and obligations are directly and precisely established by the legislation and the parties cannot deviate from them. They need not be expressly included in the labour contract, because they constitute part of its content directly by virtue of the law. If, nevertheless, the labour contract contains stipulations of other rights and obligations in contradiction to the legally established rights and obligations, these stipulations will be null and void (Article 74 of the LC); and in the relations between rights and regulations those established by law will apply. Naturally, this does not mean that the labour contract as a legal transaction bears no relation to rights and regulations. Although no agreement can be reached on this point between the parties, their will to conclude the contract in fact signifies their voluntary and conscious acquiescence in rights and regulations. Therefore, the rights and regulations become active in the relations between the parties, embracing the specific individual employment relation as a result of the labour contract.

139. The second group of terms contain the contractual ones. They are directly and immediately negotiated between the parties and exist only in so far as the parties have given them a certain content. Certain terms are necessary, i.e., consent must be reached on them, if we are to consider a labour contract to be concluded. They obligatorily figure in the labour contract. They are exhaustively enumerated in Article 66, paragraph 1 of the LC. These elements are the following:

(1) the place of work;
(2) the name of the job position and the nature of the work;
(3) the date of conclusion of the employment contract and the beginning of its fulfilment;
(4) the duration of the employment contract;
(5) the length of the basic and extended paid annual leave and the length of the additional paid annual leave;
(6) the equal term of notice for both parties upon termination of the employment contract;
(7) the basic and extra remuneration of permanent nature, as well as the periodicity of their payment;
(8) duration of the working day or the working week.

These constitute the core of the labour contract and are of particularly great significance both in the interest of the worker and the employer because they determine where and what labour is to be furnished. This is why the terms must be precisely determined.

Other elements of the contract are optional: they may figure in the labour contract or not.

Such elements are envisaged in Article 66, paragraph 2 of the LC which provides that the parties may include in the labour contract ‘other provisions in connection with the furnishing of labour and not prescribed by imperative legal provisions as well as conditions which are more favourable for the worker than those provided for in the collective labour contract’. These stipulations enrich and widen the content of the labour contract and are aimed at reflecting and consolidating more fully the interest of the parties to the individual labour relationship. Examples of these are an agreement on providing a dwelling for the workers, different kinds of compensation and gratification, etc. It is worthwhile noting that the opportunities of the parties to enlarge this part of the labour contract have significantly increased since the last amendments to the LC of November 1992 and June 2004 and as such represent one of the most evident manifestations of contractual freedom of the parties to the individual labour relationship during the transition to a labour market economy (*see* above).

B. Types of Labour Contract

140. According to their duration, labour contracts can be divided into two basic categories: contracts of indefinite duration and contracts of fixed duration (Article 67 of the LC).[39] Contracts of indefinite duration are contracts which have no stipulated time limit (Article 67, paragraph 1, item 1 of the LC). Such a contract exists when the parties expressly agree upon the unspecified period of its duration at the time of its conclusion and when they do not expressly stipulate a time limit (Article 67, paragraph 2 of the LC). If the parties fail to stipulate a time limit, although they may have wished to do so, or if subsequently they wish to transform a contract of indefinite duration into a fixed-term contract, they may do so by mutual agreement by means of an additional stipulation in writing. In practice, a contract of indefinite duration is the most common one. In most cases, it corresponds to the desires of the parties: for the enterprise it places at its disposal manpower for a long period of time, and for the worker it gives a permanent and stable job.

141. Fixed-term contracts correspond to certain social needs. In certain branches and activities, employment is of a temporary or seasonal nature (construction, agriculture work). Sometimes the performance of a specific task becomes necessary or substitution of a temporarily absent worker is required. In other cases, an individual may wish to work only for a certain time because this is what his/her personal interest and subjective capabilities dictate. Fixed-term contracts are a suitable means of meeting such needs of the enterprise and the worker. Through them, the enterprise secures the necessary labour for a specified period only and averts the risk of a worker leaving precisely at a time when the enterprise needs him/her. The worker, on the other hand, is certain of work during a time when he/she wants it. Fixed-term contracts offer both parties clarity with respect to the duration of the employment relationship and an easy way of terminating it, contained in the very nature of the contract.

142. Recently, there has been a tendency towards a more extensive application of fixed-term contracts as a result of a deterioration in the employment situation in the country. Resort to fixed-term employment contracts and especially to fixed-term contracts with a fixed date (*see* below) of a relatively short duration (one to two months) – periodically or in many cases frequently renewed – is predicated by the insecurity of the economic activities. In these situations, the employer prefers to conclude fixed-term labour contracts, termination of which is simply by expiration

39. Under Bulgarian labour legislation a labour contract cannot be concluded for life. The prohibition of lifetime employment is not expressly proclaimed in the labour legislation but it can be deduced by way of interpretation. Article 67 of the LC permits the conclusion of a labour contract only for a definite or an indefinite duration. A lifetime contract cannot be placed in the group of labour contracts for an indefinite duration nor in the group of labour contracts for a definite duration. On the other hand, the conclusion of a lifetime labour contract will be tantamount to a form of 'forced labour' which is expressly prohibited by Art. 48, para. 4 of the new Bulgarian Constitution (12 Jul. 1991) as well as by Art. 2 of the ILO Convention No. 29 (1930), which has been ratified by Bulgaria. That is why such a clause would be null and void (Art. 74, para. 1 of the LC).

and without the need for notice and, if necessary, to renew them without any limitations instead of concluding contracts of indefinite duration. As the alternative is not having any job at all, workers are economically obliged to accept the proposed temporary work on the basis of a contract of fixed duration and reluctantly assent to concluding such labour contracts of fixed duration. Thus, the practice of the so-called 'chain' fixed-term labour contracts was established. The practice of concluding such contracts has sharply increased since 1997 and has resulted in large-scale transformation of the existing labour contracts of indefinite duration into fixed-term labour contracts, and also to the predominant conclusion of such fixed-term labour contracts of definite duration with the newly appointed workers and employees. 'Chain' fixed-term labour contracts used to create social tension and insecurity in employment relationships and caused an acute reaction from the trade unions and, eventually, necessitated the intervention of the legislator in amending the LC in March 2001 (*see* below paragraph 146).

143. Article 68 of the LC establishes five kinds of fixed-term employment contracts, namely those:

(1) terminating on a fixed date insofar as a law or an act of the Council of Ministers do not provide otherwise (*dies certus*);
(2) for the completion of a given task (*dies incertus quando*);
(3) for the employment of substitutes;
(4) for the completion of a job which will be occupied by the competitive examination;
(5) for a fixed mandate, where such a mandate has been established for the respective body.

144. For a fixed date contract (Article 68, paragraph 1, item 1 of the LC), the parties may use different technical legal methods for determining the date: determining its final day, determining its duration in days, weeks, months, years, reckoned from the day of its conclusion or from another expressly fixed date, and so forth. The duration of such a contract lasts from one day to three years. The maximum period of three years is meant to put a limit on the time for which the parties are bound. Since they have expressed a preference for a labour contract of a certain specified period rather than a labour contract of indefinite duration, their reciprocal commitment should not be too long.

145. Article 68, paragraph 1, item 1 allows that, in those cases which are explicitly specified, the term may be longer or shorter than three years.

According to Article 229 of the LC, in the case of a contract for acquiring professional qualification concluded between an employer and a person who is taking a job or has enrolled in an educational institution for acquiring a qualification, this contract obliging the employer to provide the means of support to the person, the latter undertakes the obligation to work with the said employer, in accordance with the qualification acquired, for a term agreed between the parties which may not exceed six years.

A term shorter than three years is specified under fixed-term employment contracts of definite duration concluded for work under so-called subsidized employment under Articles 52–55 of the Law on Fostering Employment. According to these provisions, employers are allowed to conclude fixed-term employment contracts of duration up to twelve months with people who are in a disadvantaged position on the labour market (the disabled single parents of children under three years of age, unemployed mothers of children aged 3–5, unemployed people who have served a penalty of imprisonment and the like). These employers are granted a subsidy under the 'Human Resources' national operative programme, which covers basic and additional labour remuneration, and the social security and health insurance contributions of the persons employed under these contracts.

146. It is to the legal infrastructure of these fixed-term labour contracts, which are actually those most frequently concluded, that considerable legal changes were made in March 2001. Their main objective is to limit the large-scale and arbitrary application of fixed-term labour contracts of definite duration and to reduce the resort thereto only to those cases where it is necessary and justifiable. The adopted legislative measures consist of three main points.

A new paragraph 3 was established in Article 67 of the LC, this paragraph providing that, in principle, it is inadmissible to transform labour contracts concluded as ones of indefinite duration into fixed labour contracts of fixed duration. The purpose of this prohibition is to prohibit the employer, through pressure exercised on the worker or employee, from forcing him/her to sign a written agreement under Article 119 of the LC to transform a labour contract of indefinite duration into a fixed-term one. The law allows one exception from this principle: the transformation of a labour contract of indefinite duration into a fixed-term one of definite duration is possible only where the worker or employee wishes this and has expressed his/her will thereof in writing. The purpose of this legislative provision is that the transformation of the labour contract of indefinite duration into a fixed-term one is to be rarely admitted – only where it has been asked for by the worker or employee expressing his/her free will. And this expression should be made in a reliable way: the will of the worker or employee is to be expressed in writing.

Under the new legal infrastructure the conclusion of a fixed-term labour contract of a definite duration on taking a job is admissible in two main groups of cases, regulated in detail under Article 68, paragraphs 3–5 of the LC. The first group comprises cases where the conclusion of fixed-term labour contracts is admissible without any exception or limitations (Article 68, paragraph 3 of the LC). What is common to these cases is that the conclusion of fixed-term labour contracts ensues from the nature of work and activities that are to be performed. These are the cases of temporary, seasonal or short-term work and activities, and also the cases of newly employed workers and employees in enterprises that have been declared bankrupt. 'Declared bankrupt' here means that bankruptcy proceedings under Part IV of the Commercial Law (Articles 607–760) are over and that the bankruptcy court has rendered a decision declaring the debtor-employer bankrupt and has suspended the activities of the enterprise thereof (Article 711, paragraph 1, item 1 of the Commercial Law).

The second group of cases admits the conclusion of fixed-term contracts 'by way of exception' (Article 68, paragraphs 4–5 LC). The 'exception' is available where specific objective reasons in the production activities of the enterprise have taken place, these reasons necessitating the conclusion of fixed-term labour contracts of definite duration. These reasons might be technological, economic, market-related and the like (§1, item 8 of the Supplementary Provisions of the LC). What matters is that they should not necessitate workers and employees being employed under fixed-term contracts of definite duration. These are cases of receiving large orders for performance within a specified term, an unexpectedly occurring market situation of demand for a product's calling for a production increase, and this, in its turn, necessitating the employment of new workers and employees for a certain period of time, etc. In this situation of production reasons that have occurred unexpectedly, the law admits the conclusion of two consecutive fixed-term labour contracts of definite duration with one and the same worker or employee, one of them having the duration of at least one year, while the other may have the duration of less than one year. Should the employer conclude a fixed-term contract of definite duration in breach of these legal requirements, the concluded labour contract shall be deemed concluded for indefinite time (Article 68, paragraph 5 LC).

147. In the last 18 years, after the legal regulation of the limitation on the conclusion of fixed-term employment contracts of definite duration under Article 68, paragraphs 4–5 and §1, item 8 of the Supplementary Provisions of the LC took effect, the Supreme Court of Cassation has gained wide experience which helps stabilize this regulation and its lawful application. A number of this Court's decisions declare invalid certain clauses of fixed-term employment contracts which are concluded without mentioning the existence of 'the exception under §1, item 8 of the Supplementary Provisions of the LC' (Dec. No. 180-07 of the III C.Ch., Dec. No. 717-07 of the II C.Ch., Dec. No. 53-08 of the III C.Ch., Dec. No. 235-08 of the III C.Ch., Dec. No. 53-140 of the IV C.Ch., Dec. No. 302-17 of the IV C.Ch., Dec. No. 94-18 of the IV C.Ch., etc.).

There is another group of cases in which the Supreme Court of Cassation declares invalid certain clauses of fixed-term employment contracts of indefinite duration through which more than two consecutive fixed-term employment contracts for the same work are concluded between the same parties in violation of Article 68, paragraph 5 of the LC (Dec. No. 629-07 of the III C.Ch., Dec. No. 895-08 of the V C.Ch., Dec. No. 146-08 of the IV C.Ch., Dec. No. 120-08 of the III C.Ch., Dec. No. 104-10 of the III C.Ch. Dec. No. 284-11 of the III C.Ch. Dec. No. 52-12 of the III C.Ch., Dec. No. 259-14 of the IV C.Ch., etc.).

In these cases the fixed-term employment contracts of definite duration concluded in violation of the limitations provided for in Article 68, paragraphs 4–5 and §1, item 8 of the Supplementary Provisions of the LC are preserved and are deemed to be concluded as employment contracts of indefinite duration, with all the favourable consequences resulting from this for workers and employees.

The operation of the 2001 legal regulation of fixed-term employment contracts of definite duration and the court practice in support thereof has brought about a considerable decrease in the cases of arbitrary conclusion of fixed-term employment contracts of definite duration under the pressure of the employers and in spite of the dissent of workers and employees and has contributed to their higher security in the employment relationships.[40]

148. Labour contracts for a period to be determined (*dies incertus quando*) include contracts for the completion of a given task (Article 68, paragraph 1, point 2 of the LC). The time limit of such a contract is determined by the length of time it takes to complete the task. All aspects of the task must be exactly agreed upon: kind of task, volume, quality, and, if necessary, the stage of completion to which it must be carried out, etc. This kind of contract for a specified period of time is most frequently applied in the field of construction: construction of buildings, roads, dams, plants, etc. Because of modern conditions of technology, construction has a complex and diverse character and workers with different labour functions and vocational qualifications are hired for its implementation. It is exactly for this reason that the task for which the contract is signed with every worker or group of workers must be precisely determined, because it is the completion of the task that determines the duration of the individual labour contract.

149. Contracts for the employment of substitutes is provided for in Article 68, paragraph 1, item 3 of the LC. The worker who normally and permanently holds a certain job must be absent. This means that his/her job is temporarily vacant. The idea of the law is that the labour function normally performed by the absent person has temporarily ceased to be performed and that the work for which the post was set up remains undone. The reason and type of absence are of no significance. The worker may be absent because of sickness, or in the case of a woman because of maternity leave or pregnancy, or he/she may be on leave to study, on regular annual leave, etc. It is of no consequence whether the absent worker is on paid or unpaid leave. There should be a need for the holder of the job to be replaced and the employer does not overcome this condition by redistributing the work of the absent worker among his/her colleagues. The length of the temporary absence may also be a reason for the 'need'. In the case of a comparatively long absence of the holder of the job, it will be more difficult for his/her job to be carried out by his/her colleagues by redistributing his/her functions among them. In any case, the concrete necessity and opportunity of concluding a contract for replacement are evaluated by

40. V. Mrachkov, 'Critical Review of the 2007 Practice of the Supreme Court of Cassation on Labour Disputes', *Juridicheski Sviat* [*Juridical World*] *Journal* 2 (2008): 181–183; 'Critical Review of the 2008 Practice of the Supreme Court of Cassation on Labour Disputes', *Juridicheski Sviat* [*Juridical World*] *Journal* 2 (2009): 141–143; 'Critical Review of the 2010 Practice of the Supreme Court of Cassation on Labour Disputes', *Juridicheski Sviat* [*Juridical World*] *Journal* 2 (2011): 135–137; 'Critical Review of the 2012 Practice of the Supreme Court of Cassation on Labour Disputes', *Juridicheski Sviat* [*Juridical World*] *Journal* 2 (2013): 113–114; *Trudovo pravo* [*Labour Law*] 10th edn. (Sofia: SiBi Publishing House, 2018), 226–249; 'Critical Review of the 2014 Practice of the Supreme Court of Cassation on Labour Disputes', *Juridicheski Sviat* [*Juridical World*] *Journal* 2 (2015): 97–98; 'Critical Review of the 2016 Practice of the Supreme Court of Cassation on Labour Disputes', *Juridicheski Sviat* [*Juridical World*] *Journal* 2 (2017): 125–126; 'Critical Review of the 2017 Practice of the Supreme Court of Cassation on Labour Disputes', *Juridicheski Sviat* [*Juridical World*] *Journal* 2 (2018): 89–91.

the employees taking into account all circumstances connected with the way in which the absence of the permanent worker is reflected in the whole work of the respective unit or service.

In the contract for employment of substitutes the name of the replaced worker must be expressly mentioned. This is absolutely necessary because the duration of the contract for employment of substitutes as well as its termination is determined by the length of the absence of the holder of the job.

150. The next kind of fixed-term employment contract is that concluded for a post the occupation of which is determined by competitive examination (Article 68, paragraph 1, item 4 of the LC). The length of this contract is determined by the duration of the procedure for organizing and developing the competitive examination. It ends upon the successful termination of the competitive examination's procedure when the relevant job is being occupied by the candidate who won the competition (*see* below).

151. The fixed-term contract 'for a fixed mandate' was provided for the first time through the amendments to the LC of March 2001 (Article 68, paragraph 1, item 5 LC). This contract is concluded with persons who attend to and assist in the performance of the official functions of a state body or a public one, the latter having been elected or appointed for a specified period of time ('mandate'). Depending on the nature of the body, its mandate may be specified in the Constitution, in a particular law, in the statutes of a political party or another non-profit making organization. The term for which the body is elected may be different: three to four or four to five years, etc. Such bodies are the Chairperson of the Parliament, the Prime Minister, the Minister, the Deputy, the President of a political party, the President of a trade union, etc. The employees with which this contract is concluded belong to the 'team' of the mandatory body: counsellors, assistants, secretaries, drivers and the like. The relations established between them and the mandatory body (the natural person who performs the functions of the mandatory body) in their joint work in the course of the mandate are those of particular confidence, both personal and professional. On termination of the mandate of the respective body the legal relationship thereof ends, and, together with it, the employment relationships under Article 68, paragraph 1, item 5 of the official team, attendant thereto, also end.

152. A specific type of the fixed-term employment contract was created through the amendments to the LC of January 2012 – the new paragraph 6 of Article 68 of the LC, which provides for the conclusion of a fixed-term employment contract 'for a long-term business trip for holding a position in an overseas representation body of the Bulgarian state', i.e., in a foreign country. With his/her consent, an employee of the diplomatic office of the Ministry of Foreign Affairs or of another department is sent (posted) under an employment contract to hold this position. Where an employee of another department is posted, the consent of the said department is also required (Article 36 of the Law on Diplomatic Service). The Law does not specify the type of this fixed-term employment contract. Most commonly, that would be a fixed-term employment contract of definite duration under Article 68, paragraph 1, item 1 of the LC (*see* above paragraphs 140–146). However, there is no obstacle for the fixed-term employment contract under Article 68, paragraph 6 of the LC to be a contract for the substitution of an overseas representation body's employee during a long-term absence of the latter (maternity leave, long-term sick leave and the like), i.e., a fixed-term employment contract for substitution under Article 68, paragraph 1, item 3 of the LC. Depending thereon, the rules applied to this contract shall be those valid for the respective type of a fixed-term employment contract under Article 68, paragraph 1, item 1 or 3, etc. (*see* above paragraphs 140–146, 149). The provision of Article 68, paragraph 6 of the LC concerns only those employees of the Ministry of Foreign Affairs who work under an employment relationship, and not the other two categories of employees-diplomatic servants in this Ministry – civil servants of diplomatic rank and civil servants of no such rank, to whom the Civil Servant Law applies. The regulation of the employment relationships of the Ministry of Foreign Affairs employees that is laid down in the Law on Diplomatic Service is special with respect to the general regulation of employment relationships under the LC. Therefore it derogates the general regulation and is applied instead of it, in compliance with the general rule of *Lex specialis derogat legi generali* (Dec. 52-12-III C.Ch.).

153. The amendments to the LC of July 2015 created a new type of fixed-term employment contract – the one for short-term seasonal agricultural work (Article 114a of the LC). This employment contract is concluded between a worker and an employer who is a farmer entered into the register of the Ministry of Agriculture. The contract contains: (a) definition of the subject matter of the contract – short-term seasonal agricultural work for the performance of which workforce is acutely needed. As for the type of short-term seasonal agricultural work, it can only be within the sector of plant-growing, and cannot be any other type of agricultural work, such as stock-breeding or the like. However, even in the sector of plant-growing, such contracts cannot be concluded for all types of activities. Such contracts can be concluded for certain activities only, which are explicitly and exhaustively listed, namely: cultivation of plantations and gathering the crop of fruit, vegetables, rose blossom and lavender. These are the only activities listed because they have a definite seasonal nature and gathering the crop takes a fixed period of time during which the respective type of agricultural work must be finished. The agricultural activities included in the short-term agricultural work are: cultivation of the plantations, their maintenance and gathering the crop from the plantations. The performance of these activities does not require any special professional qualification – education, speciality, professional experience or length of service, etc.; (b) duration of the employment contract. The employment contract under Article 114a of the LC is concluded for the duration of one working day. This determines its nature of a fixed-term employment contract, the term thereof being one working day. It is concluded every day. Within a certain calendar year the worker may not conclude such employment contracts for more than ninety working days, i.e., he/she may not conclude more than ninety employment contracts for performing seasonal agricultural work throughout the seasons of spring, summer and autumn; (c) these employment contracts also specify the place of work, i.e., the name of the settlement, the region or the locality in which the work is performed; the exact designation of the work performed – fruit pickers (apples, pears, cherries, strawberries, etc.), vegetable pickers (pepper, tomatoes, cabbage, etc.), pickers of rose blossom, lavender, etc; length of the working day – eight hours or the start and the end of the working day, for instance from 8 a.m. until 3 p.m., etc.; the amount of the labour remuneration. The minimum amount is BGN 20 (EUR 10). The remuneration is paid every day – at the end of the working day – to the worker or employee in person, against a receipt showing the amount. The employment contract under Article 114a of the LC is concluded each working day – at the beginning thereof, prior to the commencement of performance of the job assigned.

The experience in the application of this employment contract in 2015 and 2016 is encouraging. During the second half of 2015 there were concluded 84,000 employment contracts for short-term seasonal agricultural work, and in 2016 there were 140,000.

1. Transformation of a Labour Contract of Fixed Duration into a Contract of Indefinite Duration

154. In accordance with Article 69 of the LC, a fixed date labour contract is considered as one of indefinite duration when upon the expiry of the stipulated time and without any objection on the part of the employer the worker remains at work for five or more days and the job is vacant.[41] The conditions under which a contract for a specified period of time becomes a contract of indefinite duration according to Article 69 of the LC are the following:

(1) The stipulated time has expired. When the stipulated time limit expires depends on each individual case upon the content of the specific labour contract.[42]
(2) The worker must have remained at work for five or more days (working days, not calendar days). It is necessary for him/her to have continued during that time to fulfil his/her functions under the labour contract, and not, for instance, to have been on leave on some legal ground.[43] The idea of the law is to establish that the worker, in a conclusive and categorical manner, has expressed the will and desire for a prolongation of the labour contract.
(3) It is necessary that the employer has not objected to the fact that the worker has remained at work. Lack of objection on his/her part means that he/she has

41. 'Sbornik Postanovlenia i Talkouvatelni Reshenia na Varhovnia Sad po grajdanski dela, 1953– 1991' ['Collection of Decrees and Interpretative Decisions of the Supreme Court on Civil Cases, 1953–1991'] in *Civil Law Cases* (Sofia: Union of Lawyers, 1992–1999), 108.

42. *Sbornik Sadebna Practika na Varhovnia Sad na Narodna Republika Bulgaria* [*Court Practice Collection of the Supreme Court of the People's Republic of Bulgaria, Civil College*] (Sofia: Science and Art Publishing House, 1969). This collection will be quoted further as *Sbornik Sadebna Practika* with an indication of the year to which it refers and the number under which the decision was published.

43. *Sbornik Sadebna Practika*, 1973, No. 197. In the same sense *see* Dec. 180-99-IIIC.Ch., in V. Mrachkov, 'Critical Review of the 1999 Practice of the Supreme Court of Cassation on Labour Disputes', *Juridicheski Sviat* [*Juridical World*] *Journal* 2 (2000): 195; 'Critical Review of the 2007 Practice of the Supreme Court of Cassation on Labour Disputes', *Juridicheski Sviat* [*Juridical World*] *Journal* 2 (2008): 132–133.

not declared to the worker that the time for completion of the work for which the labour contract was signed has ended and that he/she does not desire continuation of the employment relationship. By not objecting to the worker's continuation, and at the same time setting tasks to be fulfilled by him/her and taking notice of their performance even after the time limit has expired, the employer tacitly accepts the continuation of the employment relationship. Under some specific conditions, these rules are also applied to a labour contract for substitution: when the labour contract with the holder of the job is terminated during the substitution (for instance, by dismissal by the employer with due warning, because of death, or similar circumstances) and the job has remained vacant.

155. When the above-mentioned conditions are fulfilled, the labour contract for termination on a fixed date or that for substitution becomes a contract of indefinite duration with all the consequences stemming from it affecting the content of the employment relationship and its termination. This transformation takes place under the legal presumption established by Article 69 of the LC. It occurs by action on the part of the worker – the fact of remaining at work for five or more days – and the silence of the employer – the lack of objection against the worker having remained at work. From these facts, the legislator draws the conclusion that the will exists for the labour contract to be prolonged and to be transformed into a labour contract of indefinite duration.

2. Labour Contract for a Probationary Period

156. The purpose of a probationary contract is to enable the employer to obtain an impression of the professional qualifications and ability of the worker to perform a certain job before concluding a definite labour contract. A probationary clause may be included in a contract for work requiring special qualifications and knowledge as well as in a contract for work which does not require any special training. In the first case, the employer puts to the test the professional training of the worker and in the second case his/her strength, endurance, working methods, etc. But in both cases attention is paid to those qualities which are necessary for the performance of the specific job. The probationary clause, under the laws now in force, may be included in the contract both on the part of the employer – wishing to check the professional qualities of the worker – and on the part of the worker – when he/ she wishes to obtain an immediate impression of the labour conditions under which he/she will be working, the kind of work, and so forth.

Where the labour contract for a probationary period does not explicitly specify in whose favour the probation stipulation is, the latter is regarded as being in favour of both parties. This is an irrefutable presumption (*praesumptiones juris et de jure*) established by law. In this case each of the parties is entitled to cancel the probationary contract on the expiration of the probation period agreed thereunder. And it is to this effect that the latest practice of the Supreme Court of Cassation is directed

(Dec. 238-99-III C.Ch., Dec. 650-99-III C.Ch., Dec. 1054-07-IV C.Ch., Dec. 596-08-V C.Ch., Dec. 429-16-IV C.Ch., etc.).[44]

The probationary clause can precede the conclusion of a labour contract for either a specified or indefinite period of time (Dec. 10-11-IV C.Ch., Dec. 215-12-III C.Ch., Dec. 33-14-IV C.Ch.). When the probationary period has been satisfactorily concluded, a contract for a specified or unspecified period of time respectively will be concluded depending upon which type the parties intended to conclude.

Under the conditions of market economy and growing competition, and the employer's ever greater requirements to the professional qualities of the workforce employed, in recent years the application of the employment contract for probation under Articles 70–71 of the LC has considerably widened. Upon its conclusion, the probation stipulation is usually in favour of the employer and is made at his/her urging. This is explainable by the employer's dominant position in the employment relationship and the existing unemployment in the labour market.

157. What is new to the application of a probationary employment contract in recent years is that it can be concluded even in the case of a change in the labour function of the employment relationship which exists between the parties. In these cases the probationary employment contract is concluded for the new job position to which the worker or employer is transferred or reappointed and which differs from the job position or the labour function performed with the employer until that time: for instance, from the position of 'client inspector' into 'banking operations specialist' (Dec. No. 170-08 of the III C.Ch.), or from the position of 'bank accountant' into 'senior bank accountant' (Dec. No. 475-08 of the IV C.Ch., Dec. 366-10-IV C.Ch., Dec. 344-11-III C.Ch., Dec. 376-11-IV C.Ch.) and others similar (Dec. No. 824-08 of the II C.Ch.). What matters here is the change in the nature of the job position in which the work is done and not the change in the workplace where it is done. The latter might remain unchanged – it might be the same as physical space (e.g., the same room) – while the worker or employee performs another labour function, operates another machine, etc. (Dec. No. 55-08 of the IV C.Ch.).

However, the conclusion of a probationary employment contract is inadmissible where only the name of the job position is changed, e.g., from 'packer' into 'operator', or where the job positions are identical or similar ones (Dec. No. 212-08 of the

44. V. Mrachkov, 'Critical Review of the 1999 Practice of the Supreme Court of Cassation on Labour Disputes', *Juridicheski Sviat [Juridical World] Journal* 2 (2000): 157–158; 'Critical Review of the 2007 Practice of the Supreme Court of Cassation on Labour Disputes', *Juridicheski Sviat [Juridical World] Journal* 2 (2008): 183–184; 'Critical Review of the 2008 Practice of the Supreme Court of Cassation on Labour Disputes', *Juridicheski Sviat [Juridical World] Journal* 2 (2009): 143–145; 'Critical Review of the 2013 Practice of the Supreme Court of Cassation on Labour Disputes', *Juridicheski Sviat [Juridical World] Journal* 2 (2014): 129; 'Critical Review of the 2014 Practice of the Supreme Court of Cassation on Labour Disputes', *Juridicheski Sviat [Juridical World] Journal* 2 (2015): 98–101; 'Critical Review of the 2015 Practice of the Supreme Court of Cassation on Labour Disputes', *Juridicheski Sviat [Juridical World] Journal* 2 (2016): 140–142; 'Critical Review of the 2016 Practice of the Supreme Court of Cassation on Labour Disputes', *Juridicheski Sviat [Juridical World] Journal* 2 (2017): 127–128; 'Critical Review of the 2017 Practice of the Supreme Court of Cassation on Labour Disputes', *Juridicheski Sviat [Juridical World] Journal* 2 (2018): 91–92.

III C.Ch., Dec. No. 495-08 of the III C.Ch., etc.)[45] or in cases of reassignment to another suitable job of a worker or employee who has suffered an industrial accident (Dec. 716-10-III C.Ch.), or in an employment relationship ensuing from a competition (Dec. 342-02-III C.Ch., Dec. 716-10-III C.Ch.) or the like.

158. The length of the period of probation is established by law as up to six months. This length (of six months) is the maximum time period. Therefore, in each specific case, the parties may also stipulate a shorter period according to the qualities of the worker or the requirements of the relevant job to be tested.

159. Final conclusion of the contract is decided on the basis of an assessment of the results of the probationary period given by the party who stipulated the probationary clause. The respective party can make this assessment at any time within the stipulated time limit. It is not necessary to wait for the expiry of the time limit (Article 71 of the LC). If the assessment of the probation is positive, a definite labour contract is concluded. If it is negative, the probationary labour contract is terminated by the unilateral expression of the will of the respective party. The permanent practice of the courts and the Supreme Court of Cassation maintain that a negative assessment of the results of the probation is discretionary and not subject to any control.[46]

160. Article 70, paragraph 5 of the amendments to the LC of March 2001 explicitly provides that the employer is entitled to conclude only one probationary contract with a particular worker for particular work in a particular enterprise. It does not matter in whose favour the probation has been stipulated. The purport of this legislative solution is to disallow the conclusion of 'chain' labour contracts for probation regarding the same work between the same parties, especially where the probation stipulation is in favour of the employer, which is the widespread practice in concluding labour contracts for a probationary period. This creates insecurity and tension for the worker or the employee. This legislative solution is aimed at averting these very consequences, which are harmful for the worker or the employee. It is a just one. The same comprehension has been arrived at by the Supreme Court of Cassation by way of interpretation (Dec. 238-99-III C.Ch., Dec. 297-99-III C.Ch., Dec. 1134-07-II C.Ch., Dec. 1076-07-II C.Ch., Dec. 366-10-IV C.Ch., Dec. 66-16-III C.Ch., Dec. 200-17-IV C.Ch., Dec. 168-17-IV C.Ch., etc.).[47] The advantage of the new legal infrastructure is that it has fixed it into a legal norm and made its application obligatory and irreversible.

---

45. V. Mrachkov, 'Critical Review of the 2008 Practice of the Supreme Court of Cassation on Labour Disputes', *Juridicheski Sviat* [*Juridical World*] *Journal* 2 (2009): 143–144.
46. 'Sbornik Postanovlenia i Talkouvatelni Reshenia na Varhovnia Sad', No. 108. This stand is contested in the literature by Prof. L. Radoilski, *Troudovo pravo*, 283.
47. V. Mrachkov, 'Critical Review of the 1999 Practice of the Supreme Court of Cassation on Labour Disputes', *Juridicheski Sviat* [*Juridical World*] *Journal* 2 (2000): 196; 'Critical Review of the 2007 Practice of the Supreme Court of Cassation on Labour Disputes', *Juridicheski Sviat* [*Juridical World*] *Journal* 2 (2008): 184; 'Critical Review of the 2013 Practice of the Supreme Court of Cassation on Labour Disputes', *Juridicheski Sviat* [*Juridical World*] *Journal* 2 (2014): 129; 'Critical Review of the 2014 Practice of the Supreme Court of Cassation on Labour Disputes', *Juridicheski*

161. The probationary contract in its legal character is a genuine labour contract. During its duration, the relationship of the parties is a genuine employment relationship. The parties have all the rights and obligations which exist under a labour contract: remuneration is paid, the time served is recognized as qualifying service time, there is obligatory insurance, etc. (Article 70, paragraph 2 of the LC). The only peculiarity of the contract is the probationary clause which determines its future status and not its content and legal nature while it is in existence and being fulfilled.[48]

162. However, the labour contract for probation is an independent type of labour contract, which is distinct from the fixed-term labour contract, and particularly from the fixed-term labour contract of definite duration under Article 68, paragraph 1, item 1 of the LC (*see* above paragraphs 143–146), though the contract for probation also contains a clause laying down the term of probation (*see* above paragraph 157). It is the difference between these two types of labour contracts that Dec. 95-12-IV C.Ch. solicits for. What is of key importance in the labour contract for probation is the stipulation of probation. And the term in this contract is a derivative of the stipulation of probation and it only specifies the period of time for which the probation continues, because the time during which the employment relationship exists is immanent to its implementation as a successive (on-going) legal relationship. That is why the labour contract for probation is not terminated upon the expiry of the probation term. Where the labour contract for probation contains the stipulation of probation in favour of the employer – as the mass practice is (*see* above paragraph 157) – its termination depends on the result of probation and on the employer's assessment thereof. The employer's negative assessment, due to which the labour contract is terminated by virtue of Article 71, paragraph 1 of the LC, constitutes his/her sovereign judgment and is not subject to judicial control (Dec. 11-12-IV C.Ch.). And it is to this effect that the practice of the Supreme Court of Cassation is directed (Dec. 1364-05-III C.Ch., Dec. 155-16-III C.Ch., Dec. 147-17-IV C.Ch., Dec. 96-18-III C.Ch., etc.).

3. Labour Contracts in Which the Workplace Is Outside the Employer's Premises

163. The development of labour law in recent years (2011–2012) has made it possible to differentiate a new group of labour contracts in view of the workplace in which the work assigned under the employment relationship is performed.

164. 'Workplace' as a labour law term has its legal definition in §1, item 4 of the Supplementary Provisions of the LC. It is 'a premise, a workshop, a room, a location of a machine, equipment or another similar territorially defined place

---

Sviat [*Juridical World*] *Journal* 2 (2015): 98–101; 'Critical Review of the 2015 Practice of the Supreme Court of Cassation on Labour Disputes', *Juridicheski Sviat* [*Juridical World*] *Journal* 2 (2016): 140–142.

48. *Sbornik Sadebna Practika*, 1970, No. 200.

within the enterprise where the worker or employee – under the instruction of the employer – does his/her work in performance of the obligations under the employment relationship'. Primarily, the said place is within the employer's premises (regardless of whether they are his/her own or rented ones). That is the traditional location of the workplace. It considerably differs from 'the place of employment', which, as a rule, is the place where the seat of the headquarters of the employer – with whom the labour contract is concluded – is situated (Article 66, paragraph 3 of the LC). By the way, though close in their wording, the 'workplace' and the 'place of employment' are substantially different legal terms. The 'place of employment' is – both legally and spatially – the broader term. It is stipulated between the parties and forms an essential part of the required contractual content of the labour contract (Article 66, paragraph 1 of the LC). Unlike the place of employment, the workplace is – legally and spatially – narrower, and it is a part of the place of employment. It is determined and is unilaterally changed by the employer.

This traditional perception of the workplace was considerably changed through several labour contracts, which came into existence in April 2011–January 2012 (*see* below paragraphs 164–187). This new regulation raised the 'workplace' into an essential contractual element of the content of these labour contracts. They differ in their content, but what is common to them is that the workplace is defined by the worker or the employee or by mutual agreement of the parties. These are the contracts for outwork, remote work and temporary work. They are the subject of the exposition coming next.

4. Labour Contract for Outwork (Article 107b–107g and Article 312 of the LC)

165. The LC contains two legal regulations of outwork. Actually, these are two types of labour contracts for outwork: (a) general regulation or a general labour contract for outwork (Article 107b–107g of the LC); (b) special or particular legal regulation, or a particular type of outwork labour contract of a young child's mother (Article 312 of the LC). These contracts will be considered in brief in the next lines (*see* below paragraphs 165–169).

166. The general labour contract for outwork is concluded for activities connected with the manufacture of products (by knitting, weaving, making souvenirs) and the provision of services (typing texts, editing a certain number of pages, organizing trips and the like). This limitation is related to the need for quantitative measurement of the work performed, which – as it is done outside the premises of the employer – is beyond his/her direct 'sensory' control and can be impartially assessed only through its quantitative result, which is objectified in the production output or the number of services performed.

167. The content of this labour contract determines the location of the workplace (the settlement, the address) – it is the worker's or employee's home or some other place he/she has chosen, and, in any case, it is outside the premises of the employer; the procedure of assigning and reporting the work done – the frequency of reporting, the way in which it is carried out; the supply of raw materials, additional materials, consumables, etc.

168. The parties' obligations under this labour contract are specific, too:

(1) The employer is obliged to provide the worker or the employee with conditions for the performance of the work: healthy and safe working conditions, social and health insurance, internal social services as well as cultural ones, conditions for free trade union association in the enterprise and membership in the trade union organizations of the enterprise, participation in the general assembly of the workers and employees, application of the collective labour contracts and, on the whole, the same conditions as those he/she provides to the workers and employees working within his/her premises.
(2) Along with the general obligations under the labour contract laid down in Article 126 of the LC, an outworker also has certain specific obligations which are conditioned by his/her working outside the employer's premises. Such obligations provided for in Article 107e of the LC are:
    (a) to provide the employer's and the control bodies' access to the premises where his/her workplace is;
    (b) not to perform any actions that bother the other owners and inhabitants neighbouring his/her workplace.

169. The outworkers distribute their working time within the working day on their own, in compliance with its duration laid down in law – in the morning and in the afternoon. They also determine the breaks during the working day and the daily rest between two consecutive working days, complying with its minimum duration of twelve hours and with the five-day working week. The paid annual leave is taken in accordance with the general procedures valid for all workers and employees of the enterprise.

An outworker is obliged to notify the employer of the distribution of the working time and rests.

170. The outwork labour contract of the second type can be concluded with the mother of a child under 6 years of age (Article 312 of the LC). The contract for the performance of work at her home can be concluded either with the same employer or with another one. Of course, this contract can be concluded if the nature of the work allows its performance at her home. Where the work does not allow its being performed at home (e.g., the work of a teacher, a doctor in a stationary medical care institution), no labour contract under Article 312 of the LC can be concluded. The employer with whom the female worker or employee used to work before that is obliged to take her back to work when she so wishes or when the child turns 6 years of age.

171. The interrelation between the two types of outwork labour contracts is an interrelation of general and special regulation. This means that those outwork matters which are not regulated by the brief regulation of Article 312 of the LC shall be governed by the general regulation of the general labour contract for outwork under Article 107b–107g of the LC.

5. Labour Contract for Remote Work (Article 107h–107p of the LC)

172. Remote work has two main specific features.

(1) It is performed in a workplace which is outside the premises of the employer. Here again, the 'workplace' is the worker's or employee's home or some other place determined by mutual agreement of the parties to the labour contract (§ 1, item 4, sentence 2 of the Supplementary Provisions of the LC). The workplace is a substantial element of the required contractual content of the labour contract (*see* above paragraph 163).
(2) Information technology is used in the course of performance of remote work. This determines the higher intellectual content of the labour function assigned to the worker or employee. It consists in the use of computers and software support, access to the largest database (the Internet) and maintenance, hardware and software for storing, processing and delivering data or primary information, etc. All this sets higher requirements for the education, professional qualification and skills of the employee in the performance of his/her labour duties, and makes him/her 'more free' and 'more independent', but also 'more lonely' and 'more dependent' on his/her personal self-discipline and self-organization.[49]

173. The labour contract for remote work discloses important particularities in its content, too. Along with specifying a workplace outside the employer's premises (*see* above paragraph 168), the content also concerns:

(1) Workplace equipment (Article 107i of the LC). This denotes the technical facilities it is furnished within view of the work performed – a computer, a printer, Internet connection, consumables, prophylaxis and the like. Because of the decisive importance of the workplace and its equipment, they are the subject matter of detailed legal regulation and arrangement between the parties to the labour contract.
(2) The employer has more obligations. They comprise:
   (a) provision of a monitoring system introduced with the worker's or employee's consent, which acknowledges and respects his/her right to personal

49. R. Blanpain, *Work in the 21st Century,* in *Law in Motion* (Kluwer Law International, 1997), 887–892.

space and personal life. Therefore, the monitoring system cannot extend over the personal life or personal space of the worker or employee, or over his/her behaviour out of workhours;

(b) provision of preliminary written information on the protection of ancillary data connected with the performance of the assigned work at a distance;

(c) notifying the outworkers of the existing requirements as regards the healthy and safe working conditions in the enterprise.

a. Working Time, Rest and Leave (Article 107 'l' of the LC)

174. The working time of the worker or employee who performs remote work is stipulated in the labour contract in accordance with the provisions of Article 136 of the LC and in observance of the requirements of the LC, while the breaks and the daily and weekly rests are stipulated in accordance with the requirements of Articles 151–153 of the LC.

The time worked out remotely by the workers and employees is recorded each month in a document of a standard form approved by the employer. These workers and employees take their leave in accordance with the LC and the labour contract stipulations, observing the paid annual leave schedule under Articles 172 and 173 of the LC.

b. Labour Remuneration (Article 107m of LC)

175. The amount of the labour remuneration, including the additional labour remunerations (for acquired length of service and professional experience, for extra work and night work, etc.) are determined according to the LC, the Ordinance on the Structure and Organization of Labour Remuneration and the individual and collective labour contracts.

The workers and employees performing remote work are entitled on general grounds to benefit from the social programme of the enterprise and from the internal social and cultural services provided to workers and employees under Articles 292–300 of the LC on the same terms and to the same extent as those workers and employees who work in the premises of the employers.

c. Collective Labour Rights of Workers and Employees (Article 107n of the LC)

176. They can be members of trade union organizations of the enterprise and can participate in the activity of the said organizations. Being part of the staff of the enterprise, the workers and employees performing remote work are members of its general assembly and attend it when decisions are taken as regards the collective labour contract of the enterprise under Article 51b of the LC, the election of the workers' and employees' representatives under Article 7, paragraph 2 of the LC, the determination of the way of spending the money granted by the employer for social, domestic and cultural services to workers and employees under Article 293 of the LC, etc.

If the total number of these workers and employees is more than twenty, they are entitled to form an independent group and to choose their own representative under Article 7a of the LC who expresses and represents their specific interests and takes part in the informing and consulting under Article 130c of the LC.

For the purpose of overcoming the social isolation of the workers and employees performing remote work from those working in the premises of the employer, the latter is obliged to have separate working meetings with them which are held in the premises of the enterprise, as well as to set company's virtual meetings for them. These forms of communication and integration of workers and employees performing remote work are specified in the collective labour contract.

d. Training (Article 107 LC)

177. The workers and employees who perform remote work have the same access to training as those who work within the premises of the employer. However, their training should be appropriate, i.e., it should correspond to and be useful and necessary for improving their professional qualification in performing remote work with the technical equipment and the labour organization that are specific thereto. And that is ever more imperative in view of the boundless opportunities and novelties provided by the information technology in modern times and the fast rate at which they are realized. Therefore, training must be compliant with the work done and the information technology used.

178. Those officials who manage the workers and employees performing remote work also have the right to be given training. In order for these officials to be able to exercise competent management of the workers and employees who perform remote work, they should know this work themselves and should be familiar with the particularities of information technology, etc. In labour process management that is known as 'training of trainees', which requires professional knowledge of the information technology used by the workers and employees performing remote work whom the said officials manage.

6. Labour Contract for the Provision of Temporary Work (Article 107q–107x of the LC)

179. Temporary work is a new phenomenon in labour law.[50] In Bulgarian labour law it has made its way under the influence of the ILO Convention No. 181 of 1997 on private employment agencies, ratified in 2005, and effective in Bulgaria since 24 March 2006 (prom. OJ, No. 30 of 11 April 2006) and D. 2008/104/EC, which took effect on 5 December 2011. The domestic law regulation of temporary work is contained in Article 107q–107x of the LC and Article 74f–74p of the LEP. By the way, there exists a thematically differentiated and compact legal regulation of temporary work.

---

50. J. Arrowsmith, *Agency Work* (Brussels: Official Publications of the European Communities, 2006), 1–8.

180. The term 'temporary work' is of key importance in normative regulation. The latter does not explicitly define this term. However, it defines terms that are close thereto: an enterprise providing temporary work (employer), a user enterprise, and basic conditions of labour and employment (§1, items 17, 18 and 20 of the Supplementary Provisions of the LC), from which the basic legal features of temporary work can be derived:

(a) First of all, it is work, i.e., performance of labour on the part of a person who works under an employment relationship and carries out useful activity.
(b) Unlike the customary (conventional) employment relationship between the worker or employee and the employer, which occurs and is realized between the parties, temporary work involves three – and not two – legal subjects: the worker or employee, the employer who has employed the latter, and a third person – the enterprise to which the utilization of the worker or the employee is granted. There are three legal relationships occurring among these three legal subjects: between the worker or the employee and the provider enterprise that provides the temporary work; between the said worker or employee and the user enterprise in which the temporary work is performed; and, lastly, the legal relationship between the two enterprises – the provider enterprise that provides temporary work and grants it to the user enterprise, which uses it. The first two of these three legal relationships – which involve the worker or the employee – intermediate the occurrence, functioning and termination of the temporary work legal relationship, while the third one determines the commercial contractual relationships of the service – the provision of workforce – between the provider enterprise and the user enterprise. The presence of these three legal relationships, each of them having its parties and content, give grounds for the aggregate thereof to be defined in the doctrine as 'triangular relationships'.[51] The specifics here are that there are two legal subjects acting on the part of the employer: the employer who concludes a labour contract with the worker or employee, and an enterprise which makes use of the workforce.
(c) The temporary nature of the work performed is an important specific element. 'Temporary' nature means that the performance of the work will continue for a certain foreseeable period of time – 'until the completion of the specified work' and 'for substitution of a worker or employee who is absent from work' (Article 107q, paragraph 4 of the LC). As for these provisions, it is not difficult to establish that the idea of the term has been borrowed from the fixed-term labour contracts under Article 68, paragraph 1, items 2 and 3 of the LC, which limits the duration of the legal relationship under Article 107q of the LC.
(d) The structure of the temporary work employment relationship under Article 107r of the LC, which was outlined thus far, allows for dividing the said relationship into two 'parts': the one that sets up the employment relationship with the enterprise providing temporary work, and the other – involving the user enterprise – that continues this relationship (*see* above item (b)). One and the

51. J. Arrowsmith, *supra.*, 45; J. Pélissier, Al. Supiot, A. Jeammaud, *Droit du travail* (Paris: Dalloz, 2006), 389–410; V. Mrachkov, *The Contract in Labour Law* (Sofia: Sibi Publishing House, 2010), 203.

same worker or employee is a party to both these relationships. However, the other party to the said two parts of the employment relationship is different – under the first relationship it is the enterprise providing temporary work, while under the second one it is the user enterprise. The content of the two relationships is also different, i.e., the rights and obligations of the parties to these relationships are different. In the course of time, the two parts of the employment relationship occur one after the other: the employment relationship with the enterprise which provides temporary work occurs first, and the employment relationship with the user enterprise occurs thereafter.

a. Labour Contract with an Enterprise for Temporary Work (Article 107q–107r LC)

(1) The labour contract is concluded in accordance with the general procedure laid down in Articles 61–63 of the LC. Its subject does not consist of direct performance of the respective production or service activity by the employed workers with the respective employer, but rather in the provision of temporary work with another employer – in another enterprise, in his/her favour, in his/her interest and under his/her guidance and control (Article 107q, paragraph 1 of the LC). 'Provision' of the activity means that conditions are created, possibilities are sought and are found with other employers. The activity has the nature of a service for the realization of the employment relationship objective: to provide the worker or employee with work he/she will perform. This activity of the employer (the provider enterprise) also comprises the lawful conclusion of the labour contract, sending the notification under Article 62, paragraphs 3 and 4 of the LC to the territorial department of the National Revenue Agency and the like. The second particularity is that the said employer is subject to obligatory registration with the Employment Agency for a term of five years, this registration being renewable (Article 74f–74p of the LEP).

(2) The employer providing temporary work may not send to the same user enterprise more than 30% of the whole staff of workers and employees of the latter (Article 107q, paragraph 2 of the LC). The purpose of this limitation is also addressed to the user enterprise and aims at obliging the latter to perform its activities primarily with its own workers and employees, and to rely only partially on temporary workers and employees.

(3) There are certain enterprises and activities to which the enterprise providing temporary work is not entitled to send temporary workers or employees at all. These enterprises and activities are exhaustively enumerated and comprise activities performed under the conditions of the 1st and the 2nd category of work, the enterprises connected with the national security and the defence of the country, these enterprises being specified by the Council of Ministers, as well as the enterprises in which a strike is held (Article 107q, paragraphs 5 and 6, and Article 107r of the LC). There are various considerations thereof. As for the first two groups of cases under Article 107q, paragraph 3 of the LC, this solution is adopted because of the specific nature of the activity performed, the latter requiring particular qualification and special preparation and selection, permissions for access to classified information, etc., which are best

known to and best performed by the employer carrying out the respective activity. While in the third case (Article 107q, paragraph 3, item 3 of the LC) the said solution is adopted because the purpose might consist in averting the strike or avoiding the satisfaction of the strikers' demands, which is explicitly forbidden by law (Article 21 of the Law on Settlement of Collective Labour Disputes) because of prejudicing the workers' and employees' constitutional right to strike under Article 50 of the Constitution.

(4) The enterprise which provides temporary work (the provider enterprise) has its specific obligations to the workers and employees. They comprise:
   (a) The issue of an explicit written act to the worker or the employee who is sent to temporary work. This act shows: the user enterprise, its address, the place of work, the position, the official he/she must appear to, the initial training he/she will undergo, etc. This is the 'direction' to the work with the user enterprise and the immediate legal ground for the occurrence of the legal relationship of performance of temporary work with the latter. The said written act is handed to the worker or employee against signature, not later than one working day prior to the date specified for his/her entering the job, the date of handing in being marked in the said act as well (Article 107r, paragraph 3 of the LC).
   (b) The enterprise which provides temporary work (the provider enterprise) must also fulfil the usual general obligations of an employer, such as: to allot in the pay-roll records the remuneration due; to pay the labour remuneration due to the worker or employee; if so requested by the worker or employee, to submit to him/her an excerpt of the documents evidencing the paid and unpaid labour remunerations and compensations; to make contributions for his/her social security and health insurance.

(5) The worker or employee under the labour contract of Article 197q of the LC is not obliged to perform any labour function for the employer with whom the labour contract is concluded and who has assigned the work. However, he/she has to perform all the other obligations to this employer under Article 126, paragraph 1 of the LC except for the obligations relating to the performance of his/her temporary work in the user enterprise. Such obligations are: loyal attitude to the employer, no abuse of the employer's trust, maintenance of the employer's good reputation, no divulgence of confidential information about the latter and the like. These are obligations connected with the performance of the work assigned.

b. Contract Between the Provider Enterprise and the User Enterprise

181. It is the first time this contract has been explicitly regulated – Article 107t of the LC. As for its legal nature, this contract is a freelance one, and more precisely, it is a commercial contract between two traders within the meaning of Article 1 of the Commercial Law. It is concluded in a written form, which is its form of validity.

182. The following is included in the content of the contract:

(a) appellations of the positions and nature of the tasks for the performance of which the provider enterprise sends its workers and employees to the user enterprise;
(b) the period of time for which workers and employees will be sent to temporary work at the user enterprise;
(c) the procedure of taking paid annual leave on the part of the workers and employees who have been sent to temporary work at the user enterprise;
(d) the amount of the labour remuneration – basic and additional – of those workers and employees who have been sent to temporary work;
(e) the initial training that will be necessary for the performance of the temporary work.

183. The provider enterprise and the user enterprise are jointly liable for those obligations to the workers and employees which have arisen during or on the occasion of or in connection with the temporary work performance at the user enterprise (Article 107t, paragraph 3 of the LC). Such obligations arise under Article 200 of the LC in case of damages inflicted on the worker or employee as a result of an accident at work or an occupational disease, unlawful non-admission of a worker or employee to his/her workplace (Article 213 of the LC) and the like.

c. Rights and Obligations of the User Enterprise to the Worker or the Employee Performing Temporary Work

184. These are regulated in Article 107s of the LC and consist of three groups:

(1) Determining the workplace of the worker or employee, handing in to him/her the temporary work description, which the employer-user is not entitled to change in the course of temporary work performance, giving instructions to the worker or employee as regards the healthy and safe performance of the work, insuring the worker or employee under Article 52 of the Law on Healthy and Safe Working Conditions, etc.
(2) Provision of equal conditions for the performance of temporary work and equal treatment of the worker or employee sent to temporary work – the same as those the employer provides for its permanent workers and employees who have the same or similar work or position (Article 107s, paragraph 2 of the LC). During the time they perform temporary work at the user enterprise, they are workers and employees of the user enterprise, just like those workers and employees with whom the employer has concluded contracts under Articles 61 et seq. of the LC.
(3) The user enterprise is obliged to give immediate notification to the provider enterprise of any disciplinary breach under Articles 187 and 190 of the LC committed by the worker or employee who performs temporary work with the said employer. 'Notification' includes communication of the fact of commitment of a breach and a description of its nature, the time it was committed and the circumstances relating thereto, hearing out the worker or employee who is at fault or demanding his/her explanations in writing. The user enterprise is

entitled to make a motivated proposal to the employer for imposing a disciplinary punishment on the said worker or employee, as well as a proposal for 'returning' the worker or employee and sending another one instead. However, the employer providing the temporary work has the right to judge the severity of the breach and to make the decision regarding the disciplinary punishment, choosing it from among those under Article 188 of the LC.

185. The legal relationship between the worker or employee and the user enterprise is terminated on specific grounds. These are:

(a) Completion of the temporary work for the performance of which the worker or employee was sent. That confirms the significance of a precise description of the temporary work, as it determines not only the content of the work, but also the importance the completion has as giving grounds for the termination of the legal relationship with the user enterprise.
(b) The return to work of a worker or employee who has been substituted for (Article 107w, paragraph 2, item 2 of the LC). What is meant here is his/her actual return to the work he/she has performed.
(c) Termination of the labour contract between the worker or employee and the enterprise providing temporary work. This contract is terminated in accordance with the procedure and on the grounds provided for in the LC (Articles 325–336 of the LC). As the temporary work relationship is grounded on the existence of a labour contract with an enterprise providing temporary work, the termination of this contract brings about the termination of the temporary work relationship with the user enterprise.
(d) Suspension of the registration of the enterprise which provides temporary work. This means suspension of the activity of that enterprise, and this conditions the termination of the legal relationship of temporary work performance.

186. The legal relationship between the user enterprise and the worker or employee is an employment relationship. This conclusion is based on a number of legal provisions that were analysed in the preceding exposition (*see* above paragraphs 180–185) and will be just summarized here: the worker or employee works under the guidance and control of the user; the worker or employee is obliged to fulfil all those obligations to the enterprise which stem from the performance of the work assigned; while working at the user enterprise, the worker or employee is entitled to labour remuneration, leave, trade union association, healthy and safe working conditions, and, on the whole, he/she is entitled to the entire catalogue of labour rights. The labour disputes arising between the worker or employee and the user enterprise are labour disputes under Article 357, paragraph 3 of the LC. The observance of the provisions on temporary work is subject to the same supervision as the one exercised by the supervision bodies and by the employer in customary employment relationships (Article 404, paragraph 1 of the LC). The violations of labour legislation concerning temporary work are punished by imposing the same administrative penalties as those imposed for violations of labour legislation in customary employment relationships (Article 415e of the LC), and a number of others.

187. Of course, in temporary work, the employment relationship has its specific features, which distinguish it from the customary employment relationship. They consist, on the one hand, in the absence of performance of work assigned to the worker or employee by the employer with whom the labour contract is made, and, on the other hand, in the absence of subordination of the worker or employee to the said employer, the latter not exercising any supervision on the worker or employee.

The regulation contained in Article 107q–107w concerns the specific matters of temporary work. However, a number of important issues connected with temporary work realization and termination are not explicitly regulated. It is the employment relationship regulation of Chapter Five of the LC 'Occurrence and Changes in Employment Relationship' that apply to these matters.

II. Election

188. Elections provide in a democratic manner, on the basis of a plebiscite or vote (in principle by secret ballot) by a certain constituency, the most appropriate persons for the performance of certain state or public and political functions. At its basis lies the electorate's vote of confidence, not only in the professional but also in the moral qualities of the respective person.

The LC (Articles 83–88) contains only the general regulation of the election as grounds for establishing an employment relationship. This regulation is applied subsidiarily in so far as in the respective normative acts or status there are no special provisions in a different sense. At present election as grounds for the establishment of an employment relationship is expressly established in the Constitution for the post of President, Vice-President of the Republic, deputies, President and vice-presidents of the National Assembly, members of Parliament, Prime Minister, ministers, mayors (Articles 63, 64, 76, 84 item 6, Articles 93, 94, etc.) in the different laws, for instance in the Law on the Local Self-government and Local Administration for the post of president of the municipal's council, deputy mayor (Articles 26, 39), the Law on Cooperatives, 1999, for the president and deputy presidents of cooperatives (Article 26), etc.; in the statutes of a number of public organizations for the functioning of their executive bodies (*see*, for instance, Article 21 of the Statute of the Confederation of the Independent Trade Unions in Bulgaria, Article 33 of the CL *Podkrepa*, etc.).

189. The consent of the elected person is needed for the occupation of an elective post (Article 84, paragraph 3 of the LC). This requirement derives from the voluntary character of work, which, without exception, is also applied to the elective employment relationship. The positive vote of the electorate is also necessary. As a rule, the electorate does not coincide with the enterprise with which the person has an employment relationship and is different from it. The composition of the electorate is determined in the different acts regulating the election. They also determine the procedure to be followed for expressing the electorate's will. But, taking into consideration their modalities in every concrete instance, it should be pointed out in this connection that with regard to the expressed positive vote, the decision of the electing body must unambiguously entrust the elected person with the performance of the respective functions or work (Article 85 of the LC).

190. The election must be held in accordance with the established order and the requirements in the respective laws or statutes of public organizations. The requirements for holding state elective posts are, first of all, contained in the Constitution and in the special laws, and the requirements for public organizations in their statutes. Violation, depending on the extent of the violation and the nature of the requirements violated, may lead to cancellation of the election or to it being proclaimed null and void. The competent authority to resolve disputes on the lawfulness of the election is the ordinary court. A plaint may be lodged by any candidate participating in the election as well as by the employer within two weeks of receiving the results of the election. In the case the court establishes that the election was lawful, it confirms this and the employment relationship is deemed to arise from the election. If the court establishes that the election was unlawful, it annuls it and new elections have to be organized (Article 87 of the LC).

The employment relationship arises from the election with the declaration of the candidate as being elected. The office or job to which the person is elected must be on the staff payroll, i.e., it must figure on the staff list of the respective enterprise and certain remuneration must have been provided for its performance. The election of a person to the executive body of a public organization or as councillor, etc., does not give rise to an employment relationship because these posts are not paid for by the respective organization or state body. Finally, the elective employment relation is always for a specified period of time. The election is held for a fixed period mandate, the length of which is determined by the respective laws or statutes of the public organizations. For paid posts such as MPs, mayors, this mandate is four years.

III. Competitive Examination

191. Competitive examination, regulated for the first time by the LC of 1986 (Articles 89–97), is a new condition giving rise to an employment relationship. Its aim is to allow a better selection of the most suitable candidate to occupy the relevant job.

192. Every job which may be occupied by concluding a labour contract could also be occupied by competitive examination. Only jobs filled by means of an election (Article 89 of the LC) are excluded. This means that concluding a labour contract or organizing a competitive examination are alternative conditions giving rise to an employment relationship. The jobs to be taken up by means of a competition are determined by law, decision of the Council of Ministers, competent minister or by the employer. The rule of thumb is that the decision on this issue is to be taken by the employer who knows the specific circumstances in his/her own enterprise best.

193. The law provides for the procedure of organizing a competitive examination: obligatory public announcement of the vacant job and the particular professional requirements giving more people the opportunity to take part in the competition, defining what form the competition will take (documents, exams, interview, test, etc.), salary for the job, the time limit within which candidates must apply and file the necessary documents, etc. The examination itself is held by an examination board jury composed by the employer. Upon completion of the competition, the jury objectively classifies the applicants according to their capabilities and professional qualifications as demonstrated by them during the competition. The decision of the examination board on this issue is of crucial importance, because at this point an employment relationship arises between the employer and the candidate who has been classified as the most successful applicant. The employer is obliged to accept the candidate selected in this manner. Precisely in this consists the role of the competitive examination as a condition giving rise to an employment relationship with the selected applicant (Articles 90–96 of the LC). The labour relationship arises upon receipt of the selection communication (Article 96, paragraph 1 of the LC).

IV. Relationship Between Conditions Giving Rise to an Employment Relationship

194. Among the conditions indicated above which give rise to an employment relationship, the labour contract occupies a central place. It is the typical, most frequent, means of enlisting citizens to do work. Its widespread application is due to the possibilities it offers for combining the parties' interest, expressing their will, initiative and desires. Compared with this, the other conditions have a considerably more limited practical application.

195. The legal significance of the conditions giving rise to employment relationships is that they serve as a legal form for enlisting the participation of citizens in the labour process. Regardless of the condition from which it has arisen, the employment relationship once established has a uniform legal content, i.e., the rights and obligations of the parties are in principle the same for all workers. This is why such rights and obligations are regulated without exception by the LC, dealing of course with the employment relationship, in so far as special rules have not been established in the respective texts. The manner in which the employment relationship has arisen, however, is also reflected in the manner of its termination (*see* below).

Chapter 2. Rights and Duties of the Parties

§1. General Remarks

196. The employment relationship is a complex one because each party has more than one right and more than one duty. It is synallagmatic because the duties of one party correspond to the rights of the other, and vice versa. This is why we shall also be referring to the rights of the employer when we subsequently refer to the duties of the worker (§2). Likewise, when discussing the duties of the employer (§5) there will be a corresponding right of the worker enabling him/her, when necessary, to compel the employer to fulfil his/her duty. Moreover, the duties of the worker and the employer under the employment relationship are complex. They consist of many component elements. The fulfilment of each duty presupposes the fulfilment of all its component elements in all their diversity, and the more generalized the manner in which a duty is formulated, the more diverse and numerous are its concrete manifestations.

197. The LC contains a special chapter regulating the 'general and basic obligations' of workers and employers (Chapter VI, Articles 124–129). They are 'general' because they are entrusted to all workers and employers regardless of the industry branch in which they are employed or act, regardless of the condition from which the employment relationship has arisen (labour contract, election, competitive examination, etc.) and regardless of the kind of property and sector – private or public – to which the employment relationship applies. The obligations are 'basic' because they include the most fundamental duties of the parties to the labour relationship. Obligations regarding working time, leave, working conditions, labour discipline, salary and so on have been developed and realized further on, in different chapters of the LC.

§2. Duties of the Worker

198. The duty to perform the work entrusted to him/her (Article 126, items 4 and 5 of the LC) occupies a central place among the worker's duties and constitutes the basic nucleus. It involves the honest performance, in good faith, of the worker's labour function while observing the established technical and technological rules for the accomplishment of the tasks with which he/she has been entrusted. It has both a quantitative and qualitative aspect. The quantitative aspect embraces the volume of work, the number of tasks, the output the worker must achieve when working under labour quotas, and so on. The qualitative aspect refers to the level at which these tasks must be performed, which reflects the worker's qualifications, his/her knowledge and training. In other words, the duty to perform the entrusted work is the duty to achieve both the quantitative and qualitative indicators it embraces.

199. There is the duty to appear at work in a state permitting the worker to accomplish the entrusted tasks and not to use alcohol and other drug substances during working hours (Article 126, item 2 of the LC). The worker must be rested, in good condition and fit to work. It is strongly forbidden to use alcohol, drugs or other similar substances during working time.

200. The duty to observe working hours (Article 126, items 1 and 3 of the LC) refers to the worker's duty to work during the working hours as agreed upon between the parties. This duty has three components. First, there is observance of its absolute duration. This means that the worker should be at his/her workplace and working every day for such a time, measured in absolute units (hours), as has been established. Second, this absolute duration must fall within certain time limits. This aspect of the labour duty to observe working time reflects the specific way of organizing labour and shifts in the respective enterprise. Third, the worker is bound to make good use of his/her working time. He/she must occupy it with evenly distributed work, i.e., with the expenditure of physical and mental energy used in performing the work entrusted to him/her.

201. There is also the duty to observe the rules of hygiene and safety at work (Article 126, item 6 of the LC). These rules are laid down in regulations, orders and instructions and refer to three different fields: labour hygiene, technical safety and fire protection measures. Life, health, and security, not only of the individual worker but in certain cases also of the whole workforce, depends on the observance of such rules. It is precisely because of the harm and dangers which these rules are called upon to avert, that the strict observance, by every worker, has been raised to the status of a duty (*see* below).

202. The duty to fulfil the lawful orders of the employer (Article 126, item 7 of the LC) reflects the fact that the labour process, by definition, presupposes order and obedience on the part of workers to the rules established in the enterprise, including the orders and instructions of management. Those who can issue obligatory orders to workers include both the managers of the enterprise and their deputies, as well as the local supervisor of the individual component units, workshop, section, shift, etc. To be binding, an order must comply with two conditions:

(1) It must refer to the labour duties of a worker for it is meant to secure their fulfilment in the normal course of the labour process. Orders which exceed these bounds or deviate from them are not binding on the worker.
(2) It must be lawful. It should fall within the official competence of the manager, and the instruction which it contains should follow from the effective legal provisions and should be based on the spirit of the law. An unlawful order is not binding on the worker. This general requirement is expressly formulated in law.

203. Then, there is a duty to protect property (Article 126, item 8 of the LC). This is the duty to guard the objects and implements of labour with which the labourer is in contact, or to which he/she has access in connection with his/her labour activity – buildings, machines, equipment, tools, raw materials and the like. The duty also implies a careful attitude towards such property, i.e., preventing damage, destruction, or waste. It embraces both action and inaction.

204. There is duty to watch over and respect the good reputation of the employer, not to breach the employer's trust and not to disclose the employer's secrets (Article 126, item 9 of the LC). This is a complex duty which embraces four duties, namely:

(1) to be loyal to the employer. This obligation was introduced through the amendments to the LC of March 2001 and it deserves being considered in detail. It poses two main questions: The first one refers to the content of this obligation. 'Loyalty' here means an honest, decent, well-intentioned attitude and respect on the part of the worker or employee towards the employer. It includes both his/her attitude to the interests of the employer (for instance, refraining from participation in companies that are competitors to the employer's, from participation in activities that constitute unfair competition to the employer), and also to the personality of the natural person who performs the functions of an employer on behalf of the employer-natural person and represents him/her in labour relationships. In performance of this obligation the worker or employee has to refrain from any rude and demonstrative disregard of the interests of the employer and from an abusive and scandalous attitude towards him/her. However, this does not mean an attitude of personal devotion and allegiance to the employer, nor does it comprise the obligation of informing the employer about the disposition of the workers and employees and the like. The measure of this obligation and the limits of its extent should not hurt the self-respect of the worker or employee and his/her personal dignity and morality (*see* Article 127, paragraph 2 LC and paragraphs 180–181 above).

The second question concerns the bearing of this obligation on the others that are included therein under Article 126, item 9 of the LC (*see* below items 2, 3 and 4). The 'loyal attitude' of the worker or employee constitutes an obligation of his/her own. It is neither reduced to nor exhausted by the other three obligations under item 9 of Article 127 of the LC. The non-performance of this obligation is also present in those cases where the worker or employee has a dishonest, ill-intentioned and disrespectful attitude towards the employer, although none of the other three specified obligations of the worker or employee is present;

(2) to guard and maintain the good reputation of the employer, as well as the production and services thereof;

(3) to justify the employer's confidence and not to abuse it by one's attitude and behaviour;

(4) to guard details of the employer's production, commercial and other confidential information acquired in the course of duty or otherwise and not to divulge

such information. These duties express the personal character of the employment relationship. Apart from the obligation to complete the relevant job the worker is also entrusted with some personal obligations such as fidelity and loyalty to the employer.

205. The last three obligations specified above (*see* above paragraph 204, items (2)–(4)) have existed since 1992 and there is substantial court practice thereupon. In its practice, the Supreme Court of Cassation is right in differentiating between them as independent and different obligations of the worker or employee. Each of them has attached thereto the meaning of a separate labour obligation of the worker or employee under the labour relationship. The breach of each one of them constitutes a separate breach of labour discipline and engages his/her disciplinary responsibility. And it is to this effect that the practice of the Supreme Court of Cassation is directed (Dec. 492-99-III C.Ch., Dec. 1373-99-III C.Ch., Dec. 1345-07-I C.Ch., Dec. 749-07-I C.Ch., Dec. 7-08-IV C.Ch., Dec. 1013-08-I C.Ch., Dec. 136-16-III C.Ch., Dec. 74-16-III C.Ch., Dec. 239-17-IV C.Ch., etc.).[52]

206. There is a duty on the worker to match his/her work with the work of the other workers, to assist them if necessary and according to the employer's orders (Article 126, item 11 of the LC). This duty stems from the collective character of the contemporary highly organized labour process which involves a great number of workers working together at the same plant, factory, technological line and so on.

207. The duty to observe the internal labour regulations (Article 126, item 12 of the LC) includes all hitherto examined duties of the worker. Consequently, the fulfilment of each one of them implies the observance of the internal labour regulations of an enterprise. In dealing here separately with the observance of the internal labour regulations, a subsidiary employment duty springs to mind, i.e., the duty to observe all its remaining stipulations which do not refer to any of the duties indicated, but reflect specific occurrences in the activity of the respective enterprise or come from the collective or individual labour contract. In Article 187 of the LC, these stipulations are enumerated by way of example: being late for work, leaving work before time, failure to work the full working day, absence from work, nonperformance or grossly negligent performance of any duty, any breach of trust

52. V. Mrachkov, 'Critical Review of the 1999 Practice of the Supreme Court of Cassation on Labour Disputes', *Juridicheski Sviat* [*Juridical World*] *Journal* 2 (2000): 202; 'Critical Review of the 2007 Practice of the Supreme Court of Cassation on Labour Disputes', *Juridicheski Sviat* [*Juridical World*] *Journal* 2 (2008): 208; 'Critical Review of the 2008 Practice of the Supreme Court of Cassation on Labour Disputes', *Juridicheski Sviat* [*Juridical World*] *Journal* 2 (2009): 184–185; 'Critical Review of the 2013 Practice of the Supreme Court of Cassation on Labour Disputes', *Juridicheski Sviat* [*Juridical World*] *Journal* 2 (2014): 155–157; 'Critical Review of the 2014 Practice of the Supreme Court of Cassation on Labour Disputes', *Juridicheski Sviat* [*Juridical World*] *Journal* 2 (2015): 155–157; 'Critical Review of the 2015 Practice of the Supreme Court of Cassation on Labour Disputes', *Juridicheski Sviat* [*Juridical World*] *Journal* 2 (2016): 167–169; 'Critical Review of the 2016 Practice of the Supreme Court of Cassation on Labour Disputes', *Juridicheski Sviat* [*Juridical World*] *Journal* 2 (2017): 151–154; 'Critical Review of the 2017 Practice of the Supreme Court of Cassation on Labour Disputes', *Juridicheski Sviat* [*Juridical World*] *Journal* 2 (2018): 118–122.

accorded by the enterprise, divulgence of confidential information acquired in the course of duty or otherwise, refusal without good reason to carry out work ordered by management. These are the most frequent breaches of discipline, common to all workers. Apart from these, specific breaches of labour discipline may be mentioned in the internal labour regulations of any enterprise (Article 187, item 10 of the LC). It is important to emphasize that a breach of discipline is also every other non-fulfilment of a labour duty even one which is not expressly mentioned in the LC or the internal labour regulations of an individual enterprise.

§3. Labour Discipline

I. Notion

208. The sum total of the labourer's employment duties which have just been elaborated, above constitutes labour discipline. Fulfilment of such duties is their observance. On the contrary, non-fulfilment of a labourer's employment duty constitutes a breach of labour discipline for which a sanction may be applied. Its manifestation in labour law is disciplinary liability. It is legally regulated by Articles 186–198 of the LC.

209. The notion itself of a breach of labour discipline is defined in Article 186 of the LC. It is the negligent or deliberate non-fulfilment of a labourer's employment duty. Consequently, there may be as many breaches of discipline in kind and number as there are labour duties of the worker (*see* above).

II. Disciplinary Penalties

210. Disciplinary penalties are established and enumerated in Article 188 of the LC:

(1) warning;
(2) warning of dismissal;
(3) dismissal.

This enumeration is exhaustive. Besides these, there are no other disciplinary penalties that can be imposed on workers. The practice of the courts has been to constantly uphold this view. The three penalties are applicable to all workers. Disciplinary penalties may be divided into two groups in so far as their unfavourable consequences to the worker is concerned. The first group consists of moral penalties: warning and warning of dismissal. Either of them consists of an official reproach addressed to the worker for the breach of discipline committed. This reproach draws the worker's attention to the breach of discipline and is aimed at arousing an inner psychological reaction of awareness of the violation, and the resolve to overcome it, not allowing it to happen again. Grading of the penalties in an ascending order expresses the strength of the reproach. A relatively light disciplinary penalty, may, in principle, be imposed for a lesser breach of discipline. The second group includes disciplinary dismissal. This is simply, without notice, the abrupt and sudden termination of the labour contract on the initiative of the employer for a serious breach of discipline committed by the worker. The serious breaches are enumerated in Article 190 of the LC. They are, being at least one hour late for work or leaving before time three or more times during the same month, failure to work for two full consecutive days, systematically breaching labour discipline, breaching of employer's trust, divulging confidential information, causing damage to citizens by workers employed in the trade and services by cheating on the weight, price, or quality of an article or service as well as other serious breaches of labour discipline.

211. Disciplinary penalties are imposed according to an established order. They are imposed, in principle, by the employer or by a person designated by him/her (the manager of the enterprise) as an aspect of his/her disciplinary power (Article 192, paragraph 1 of the LC). The employer can also, although only to a certain extent, vest other managers, such as masters of a workshop, section, shift, technical managers of construction projects, supervisors, brigade leaders, with disciplinary authority so that they may fulfil their role as immediate organizers of the labour process. Disciplinary penalties are imposed after hearing the offender's oral or written explanations (Article 193 of the LC). This is an important duty of the employer. Nonfulfilment of this duty by the employer makes a disciplinary penalty unlawful with all the consequences stemming therefrom (Article 193, paragraph 2 of the LC) (*see* below). The purpose of this requirement is to provide the worker with an opportunity to explain the alleged offence. This helps to elucidate the factual situation and enables the manager to make a correct and just decision in determining the penalty. The penalty imposed is intended to be in proportion to the seriousness of the offence, its consequences, including the possible damage to the enterprise, the general circumstances under which it was committed, and its impact on the labour force and especially on the subdivision where the labourer works (Article 189, paragraph 1 of the LC). In determining the penalty, the attitude of the worker towards the offence is also significant: whether he/she is conscious of the misconduct, whether he/she has resolved to avoid repetition in the future, etc. (Dec. 490-07-III C.Ch., Dec. 265-07-IV C.Ch., Dec. 340-08-V C.Ch., Dec. 256-08-IV C.Ch., Dec. 227-12-III C.Ch., Dec. 334-12-III C.Ch., Dec. 82-17-III C.Ch., Dec. 41-18-III C.Ch., etc.).[53] On the other hand, the whole labour record of the worker must be taken into

53. *Sbornik Sadebna Practika*, 1970, No. 10; 1973, No. 159; V. Mrachkov, 'Critical Review of the 2007 Practice of the Supreme Court of Cassation on Labour Disputes', *Juridicheski Sviat* [*Juridical World*] *Journal* 2 (2008): 208–210; 'Critical Review of the 2008 Practice of the Supreme Court of Cassation on Labour Disputes', *Juridicheski Sviat* [*Juridical World*] *Journal* 2 (2009): 185–189; 'Critical Review of the 2012 Practice of the Supreme Court of Cassation on Labour Disputes', *Juridicheski Sviat* [*Juridical World*] *Journal* 2 (2013): 137; 'Critical Review of the 2013 Practice of the Supreme Court of Cassation on Labour Disputes', *Juridicheski Sviat* [*Juridical World*] *Journal* 2 (2014): 159–161; 'Critical Review of the 2014 Practice of the Supreme Court of Cassation on Labour Disputes', *Juridicheski Sviat* [*Juridical World*] *Journal* 2 (2015): 131–132; 'Critical Review of the 2015 Practice of the Supreme Court of Cassation on Labour Disputes', *Juridicheski Sviat*

consideration: whether this offence is incidental or expresses a consistent attitude towards his/her employment duties, etc. For lesser disciplinary breaches lighter penalties are imposed (warning), for more serious disciplinary offences warning for dismissal, and only for the most serious disciplinary offences, dismissal. Disciplinary penalties are imposed by means of a written and reasoned order, no later than two months after the discovery of the offence and up to one year after its commission. The order is delivered to the worker (Article 195, paragraph 2 of the LC). This formal requirement is of great importance: its purpose is not only to record the imposition of the penalty and give it an official character but also to create in the worker the knowledge and certainty that the penalty has been imposed. This is why failure to observe this formality means that the penalty has not been imposed.

212. The commission of disciplinary offences and the disciplinary penalties imposed are not entered in the workbook of the worker (Article 349 of the LC). The purpose of this is not to affect the worker's prestige or to allow the disciplinary penalties imposed to remain permanently on his/her record. If otherwise, this would make it difficult for him/her to get a job at another enterprise.

213. The disciplinary penalties imposed are subject to appeal before the common courts (Articles 357 and 363 of the LC). On appeal, the penalties may be either confirmed or revoked. Under the laws now in force, disciplinary penalties are not 'eternal' and do not accompany the labour record of the worker forever. They are considered expunged after the expiry of a certain period of time. Thereafter, they automatically lose their legal significance and the possible unfavourable legal consequences to which they give rise. The penalties themselves may no longer be taken into consideration when imposing subsequent disciplinary penalties.[54] All disciplinary penalties (except dismissal) are considered expunged once the worker has not been punished with any disciplinary penalty in the course of one year from the date of the imposition of the last disciplinary penalty (Article 197 of the LC). Moreover, if a disciplined worker has not committed a new breach of labour discipline the employer can, with a written order, revoke the disciplinary penalty even before the expiry of this period of time (Article 198 of the LC). This provision, and indeed the whole spirit of the law, which can be deduced from the system of disciplinary responsibility, reveals, above all, its educative role rather than its repressive effect.

§4. Financial Liability

214. The violation of the worker's duty to safeguard property, including machines, equipment, and materials, is sanctioned by a financial liability – the responsibility to reimburse the employer for the damages sustained by him/her. For violation of the duty to safeguard and preserve property (Article 126, item 8 of the

[*Juridical World*] *Journal* 2 (2016): 169–171; 'Critical Review of the 2017 Practice of the Supreme Court of Cassation on Labour Disputes', *Juridicheski Sviat* [*Juridical World*] *Journal* 2 (2018): 121–122.

54. *Sbornik Sadebna Practika*, 1973, No. 159.

LC), disciplinary penalties and financial liability may be imposed, but the employer may choose only to hold the worker financially liable without resorting to disciplinary measures or vice versa. The rule *non bis in idem* cannot be applied here because it is a question of two essentially different legal responsibilities: the disciplinary responsibility of the worker which leads to a disciplinary penalty, and a financial responsibility which leads to the restitution of damages to the employer. In fact, Article 186 of the LC expressly allows the lumping together of disciplinary liability with the financial, administrative or penal liability if the infringement committed contains at the same time all the features of a disciplinary, administrative violation and of a crime. On the other hand, Article 189, paragraph 2 of the LC limits the application of the rule of *non bis in idem* only within the framework of disciplinary liability by providing that for one breach of labour discipline only one disciplinary penalty should be imposed. The financial liability of workers is regulated in Articles 203–212 of the LC. In accordance with the proportion of damages to be covered by the worker's responsibility, this may be classified as limited or full responsibility.

I. Limited Liability

215. Limited liability is the one mainly applied in labour law. It is established in Article 206 of the LC. Its prerequisites, as deduced from Article 206, are:

(1) the existence of damage, i.e., loss of property for the employer. In the calculation of the amount of loss, only actual losses are to be taken into consideration (*damnum emergens*), but not missed opportunities of profit (*lucrum cessans*) (Article 205 of the LC). The damage must have been caused by the worker at the enterprise in which he/she is working in fulfilling the work entrusted to him/her. The damage may consist not only in the damage of objects, equipment, machinery and the like with which the worker is working or which he/ she is producing, but also in the damage of those mentioned objects with which he/she is in contact in connection with the work entrusted;[55]
(2) the act which caused the damage should constitute non-fulfilment of an employment duty by the worker to safeguard property or for the qualitative fulfilment of the work assigned. The worker's act should not be a crime, for in such a case the worker will be responsible for the total amount of damage (Article 203, paragraph 2 of the LC);
(3) between the non-fulfilment of the worker's employment duty and the damage there must be a causal connection, i.e., the damage must be the result of the unlawful conduct of the worker;
(4) the damage must have been caused by negligence. Intentionally caused damage, even when it does not constitute a crime (Article 9, paragraph 2 of the Penal Code) must be fully restored according to the rules of civil liability and does not fall within the category of limited liability. On the other hand, Article

55. *Sbornik Sadebna Practika*, 1972, No. 54.

204 of the LC does not recognize liability for damage connected with the normal production process, constituting the so-called economic risk, which is the result of incorrect or untimely attempts by the management of an enterprise to resolve problems connected with production or with working conditions or which is due to other circumstances beyond the control of the workers.

216. The extent of responsibility depends upon whether it is that of a worker or a manager. The category of workers includes all those working at the enterprise with the exception of the managers (*see* below). The worker is responsible for the amount of damages caused provided this is less than his/her agreed monthly remuneration. If the amount exceeds this remuneration, irrespective of the sum, the worker is still responsible for an amount up to his/her monthly salary. The 'manager', in the sense of Article 206 of the LC, is every executive official in the enterprise, such as the director, the deputies, the head accountant, the technical manager, heads of department, as well as so-called immediate leaders such as masters of a workshop, section, shift, technical managers of construction, project, supervisors, brigade leaders. A manager is responsible for the amount of damage actually caused but not exceeding three times his/her agreed monthly remuneration. The limited character of this form of responsibility is most clearly expressed in the amount of restitution due. On the other hand, defining financial liability in proportion to monthly remuneration reveals the protective nature of this solution – the endeavour of the legislature to secure sufficient labour remuneration to meet the personal needs of the worker and the members of his/her family, even in cases where he/she has, through negligence, caused considerable damage to the enterprise. The differentiation between workers and managers has a dual meaning. On the one hand, it manifests a more favourable protective attitude towards ordinary workers by the fact that it establishes for them a lower maximum amount of compensation. On the other hand, it emphasizes the higher requirements set for managers, upon whom, owing to their position and the experience, more duties and greater responsibilities are imposed as regards the preservation of property. Consequently, when they do not fulfil these duties the law is more severe.

217. A worker who has a labour duty to gather, safeguard, spend and account money or material values is financially responsible to his/her employer for the damages caused within the framework of the so-entrusted labour functions (Article 207 of the LC). The amount of his/her liability depends upon whether or not the causes of the incurred damage can be established. If the causes are established, the worker is responsible for the damages incurred, but not exceeding three times his/her agreed monthly remuneration. If the cause of damage cannot be established, liability is for the so-called financial deficit. The amount of responsibility in this case is both for the full amount of the financial lack and the legal interest estimated from the date on which the damages were caused. If this date is not established responsibility is from the date of discovery of the damages caused (Dec. 290-07-I C.Ch., Dec. 435-07-II C.Ch., Dec. 210-08-III C.Ch., Dec. 767-08-III C.Ch., etc.).[56]

56. M. Kostov, *Imoushtestvena otchetnicheska otgovornost* [*Property Liability*], (Sofia: Publishing House of the Bulgarian Academy of Sciences, 1968), 256–288; V. Mrachkov, 'Critical Review of

218. The profoundly protective character of limited financial responsibility is manifested along two more lines. First, the damage caused by a worker must be established within a time limit of one year after its occurrence. This brief time limit aims at ridding the worker of the unfavourable situation in which he/she would be faced with a claim for damages long after their occurrence. On the other hand, it has a disciplinary effect on the employer and stimulates him/her to follow closely the attitude of workers towards property and to promptly establish any damage caused. Where the damage has been caused by a manager, this time limit is five years. Second, the procedure for the realization of this responsibility is indicative. It is established in Article 210 of the LC and takes into account both the protection of property and the interest of working people. It takes into account the protection of property in that it provides for the payment of damages to be effected in an easy, simplified and speedy manner by means of an order for deductions to be made from the remuneration of the worker. Where damage has been caused by a manager, the order for deductions is issued by his/her immediately superior body (Article 210, paragraph 1 of the LC). Arrangements for these deductions are made not later than one month after the discovery of the loss or damage caused by the worker, and deductions are made in accordance with Article 210, paragraph 4 and Article 272, paragraph 1, item 6 of the LC. But this procedure does not neglect the protection of the worker. It strives to secure this by stipulating that the worker must be notified of the arrangements regarding deductions. This notification is aimed at enabling the worker to take a stand with respect to the arrangement for deductions to be made and possibly to object to its grounds and amount. This is why the employer cannot actually proceed to make the deductions immediately after notification. This can take place only thirty days after notification, provided no objection has been raised against the deductions. If an objection has been raised, deductions are not made and the question is referred by the employer to the court, where the dispute follows the regular procedure for labour disputes. After issuing a resolution that has entered into force, the general rules of the Code of Civil Procedure, 2007 concerning forced execution, are applied in cases of acknowledgement of the claim, and if the claim of the employer is dismissed, liability under Article 206 of the LC is not realized at all, as it has proved to be unfounded.[57]

---

the 2007 Practice of the Supreme Court of Cassation on Labour Disputes', *Juridicheski Sviat* [*Juridical World*] *Journal* 2 (2008): 191; 'Critical Review of the 2008 Practice of the Supreme Court of Cassation on Labour Disputes', *Juridicheski Sviat* [*Juridical World*] *Journal* 2 (2009): 157–158; 'Critical Review of the 2013 Practice of the Supreme Court of Cassation on Labour Disputes', *Juridicheski Sviat* [*Juridical World*] *Journal* 2 (2014): 136–137; 'Critical Review of the 2014 Practice of the Supreme Court of Cassation on Labour Disputes', *Juridicheski Sviat* [*Juridical World*] *Journal* 2 (2015): 111–112; 'Critical Review of the 2015 Practice of the Supreme Court of Cassation on Labour Disputes', *Juridicheski Sviat* [*Juridical World*] *Journal* 2 (2016): 150–152; 'Critical Review of the 2016 Practice of the Supreme Court of Cassation on Labour Disputes', *Juridicheski Sviat* [*Juridical World*] *Journal* 2 (2017): 135–136.

57. For details, *see* L. Radoilski, *Troudovo pravo*, 416–436; M. Kostov, *Imoushtestvena otchetnicheska otgovornost*, 175–248; A. Vassilev, *Ossashtestviavane na imoushtestvenata otgovornost na rabotnika* [*Realization of the Worker's Property Liability*] (Sofia: Publishing House of the Bulgarian Academy of Sciences, 1990), 15–93; V. Mrachkov, *Troudovo pravo* [*Labour Law*], 566–570.

II. Full Liability

219. The worker assumes full liability when he/she is answerable to the employer for the restitution of the whole amount of the damage caused (Article 203 of the LC). This is envisaged in the LC. Although an employment relationship between the worker and the employer exists within the framework of which the damage has been caused, full liability refers to those situations in which a worker cannot avail himself/herself of the protection of diminished responsibility, but is held answerable according to the general provisions of civil law. These cases are as follows.

220. Damages caused by a criminal act (Article 203, paragraph 2 of the LC). This situation presupposes a crime established by a sentence which has entered into force. Since it is a question here of a socially dangerous act proclaimed punishable under the Penal Code (Article 9, paragraph 1 of the Penal Code), the mere fact that it was committed by a worker does not warrant favourable treatment. In fact damage caused in this way must be restituted in full according to the rules of general civil liability.

221. Full responsibility is also provided for in a case of deliberately (wilfully) caused damage (Article 203, paragraph 2 of the LC). The protective regulation of limited financial responsibility regulated by the LC is applicable only to workers who negligently caused damages within the framework of the fulfilment of jobs entrusted to them. It cannot be applied to privilege workers who intentionally cause damage to their employer. In such cases the general rules on civil responsibility must be applied.

222. Full liability also exists for loss or damage caused otherwise than in the execution of labour duties (Article 203, paragraph 2 of the LC). Damages caused by the worker during the course of his/her employment only attracts a limited liability. This main reason in the execution of labour duties for favourable treatment does not exist here and the law returns to general civil liability and full restitution of damages caused. Finally, full liability may be envisaged by specially concluded written agreements between the worker and the enterprise (Article 209 of the LC). Such contracts may be signed by guards, etc. The grounds for their liability in such cases is the special contract. No doubt, this creates greater security for the preservation of the property, but it also calls for a greater care on the part of the worker for its safekeeping.

223. The manner in which full liability is realized is also very different. It takes place on the basis of a civil claim brought in accordance with the Code of Civil Procedure with all procedural guarantees for the lawful resolution of legal disputes which follows the rules of regular civil procedure.[58]

---

58. Zh. Stalev, *Bulgarsko Grajdansko Prozessoualno Pravo* [*Bulgarian Civil Procedure Law*], (Sofia: Ciela, 2012), 190–194; M. Kostov, *Imoushtestvena otchetnicheska otgovornost*, 260–269; A. Vassilev, *Ossachtestviavane na imouchtestvenata otgovornost na rabotnika*, 64–95.

§5. Duties of the Employer

224. The basic and general duties of the employer are provided for in Articles 127–129 of the LC. They embrace only the most important employer's obligations within the framework of the labour relationship. These obligations have been further developed in the LC and other normative acts, as well as new obligations having been established.

I. The Duty to Secure the Necessary Conditions for the Fulfilment of Labour

225. The obligation to provide the worker with everything necessary to carry out the work assigned to him/her is provided for in Article 127, items 1, 2 and 4 of the LC. The employer enters the employment relationship with the worker not simply to retain him/her at his disposal but to make use of his/her labour in production. That is why he/she is first of all obliged to provide work in accordance with the labour function, i.e., that for which the worker has the necessary qualification and training, and to secure the necessary material and technical conditions for its fulfilment – to provide a workplace, instruments, materials, raw materials, and so forth. The employer is also obliged to inform the worker of his/her labour obligations and the manner in which to meet these obligations. The fulfilment of this basic duty of the employer is in accordance with the interest of the worker – through the actual performance of the work assigned he/she secures a stable income, consolidates and enhances his/her professional qualifications, and realizes his/her personal capabilities as an active person.

II. The Obligations Not to Unilaterally Change the Terms of the Labour Contract

226. The work entrusted to the worker and the conditions under which he/she agreed to in person cannot be changed by the employer without the consent of the worker (Article 118, paragraph 1 of the LC). Only by way of exception and in the presence of an instance precisely defined and exhaustively enumerated in the LC, may an employer unilaterally, and in principle only temporarily, change the nature and place of the worker's employment. These instances are as follows:

(1) Where production in an enterprise or needs of an institution require such changes (Article 120, paragraph 1 of the LC). These are instances in which the normal course of activities of the enterprise, or the individual units within it, make it necessary to introduce certain internal changes as a result of which the function of certain workers has to be changed. Such a change cannot last for more than forty-five days in a calendar year. Such a period of change may take place only once or several times provided the total duration does not exceed the maximum duration established by law.

(2) Periods of temporary stoppage, i.e., when the work at an enterprise has been interrupted (Article 120, paragraph 1 of the LC). The nature of the reasons causing the stoppage – organizational, technical, etc. – is irrelevant. It is the result which is significant – the stoppage of work at the enterprise. The change in labour function affects first of all those workers in the sections or units where the work has stopped. Those workers are sent to work in units where activities are continuing as normal or where their efforts may be used to eliminate the causes of the stoppage. The duration of this change depends upon the length of interruption. But since idle time is in principle a temporary and abnormal condition in the activity of an enterprise, the change as a result of it in the nature of the labour function of the individual workers will also be short-lived.

227. The changes in the nature of the labour function in these two types of circumstances have two peculiar features in common. The first refers to the limits within which the change may be effected. According to Article 120, paragraph 2 of the LC, 'In such cases the changes are made in accordance with the qualifications and the state of health of the worker.' The purpose of these circumstances is to make sure that qualified workers and employees are given work akin to that performed by them under normal circumstances, so that their knowledge and qualifications are used most rationally and the type of work with which the worker is entrusted is not in any way harmful to the health of the worker. The second feature is that the change in the nature of the work in these cases may be accompanied by a change in the place of work (Article 120, paragraph 1 of the LC). The worker may be required to perform temporarily his/her new task at another enterprise, if and in so far as this proves necessary in the specific instance. But this other enterprise must be in the same area. The idea of the law is not to permit too great a distance from the place where the worker normally works and in view of which the employment relationship was established.

228. Unavoidable circumstances (Article 120, paragraph 3 of the LC) also constitute an exception. The LC does not define or enumerate them by way of example. In fact, reference is to force majeure whose basic characteristic features are that such events cannot be foreseen, that they are insurmountable and arise from external action.[59] They include natural calamities (earthquakes, floods, etc.), fire and the like. In cases of force majeure, the employer can require the worker to do work of a different nature even though it may not correspond to his/her qualifications. The limitation under Article 120, paragraph 2 of the LC according to which changes in the nature of work should be in accordance with the worker's qualification and his/her state of health is not valid here. The limitation regarding time (of up to forty-five days in a calendar year) is not applicable either. Consequently, the change may

59. Al. Kojouharov, *Obligazionno Pravo, Obshta Chast* [*Contractual Law, General Part*] (Sofia: Science and Art Publishing House, 1958), 271–276, 278–281; A. Kalaidjiev, *Obligazionno Pravo, Obshta Chast* [*Contractual Law, General Part*] 7th edn. (Sofia: Sibi Publishing House, 2017), 326–333.

last for as long as the action lasts, or until the consequences of the force majeure are removed. This is justified by the exceptional nature of the circumstances characterizing force majeure.

229. Business trips and assignments (Article 121 of the LC) constitute an independent case of temporary change of the place of work. In accordance with Article 121, paragraph 1 of the LC, 'when the needs of an enterprise impose it, the employer may assign a wage earner to work outside the place agreed upon by the labour contract'. 'The needs of the enterprise' are circumstances upon which the normal course of its work depends. The existence of such needs is evaluated by the employer. Accordingly, he/she then decides when and for what length of time to assign a mission to a particular worker. Such a mission represents the fulfilment of a task elsewhere, i.e., other than the place agreed upon at the time the employment relationship was established. This 'other place' may be in another enterprise – in the same town or in another. Such a business assignment or mission may not last for more than thirty days, except for certain specific types of work as indicated in the Ordinance on Official Business Assignments, 1987, such as missions for the study of certain objectives, the construction and repair of roads, the shooting of films (Article 6 of that Ordinance). When a worker is sent on an official assignment, he/she is paid travelling expenses and a travelling and accommodation allowance under the conditions established in the Ordinance (Articles 14–28).

III. The Duty to Secure Hygienic and Safe Working Conditions

230. The employer is obliged to secure hygienic and safe working conditions which do not conceal any danger to a worker's life and do not harm the health and safety of workers, and to make known to the worker the specific regulations about them (Article 127, items 3 and 4 of the LC). This duty is subject to further and more detailed regulation in Chapter XIII, Articles 273–290 of the LC (*see* below). It is the duty of the employer to secure the safe operation of machines, so that any possible danger to the life and health of workers is eliminated. This duty falls upon the employer even if the enterprise which produced the machines failed to take the necessary safety measures.[60] The specific content of this obligation varies in every specific case and depends upon the conditions under which the work is being done. But it must always be fulfilled by taking into account the achievement of technology in the field concerned. Hygienic and safe working conditions should prevent employment accidents and occupational diseases among workers, facilitate the fulfilment of their labour obligations and increase labour productivity.

60. K. Sredkova in: V. Mrachkov, K. Sredkova & A. Vassilev, *Komentar na Kodeksa na trouda* [*Commentary on the Labour Code*], 852–886.

IV. The Duty to Pay Remuneration

231. The duty to pay remuneration (Article 128 of the LC) is a contribution by the employer for the labour performed by a worker. It includes basic and additional remuneration. This obligation of the employer stems directly from the law. By providing, in Article 242 of the LC, that 'the labour under labour relation shall be remunerated', it expresses a general principle meaning that for all work under an employment relationship corresponding remuneration is due. Even when the parties have not expressly agreed remuneration in the act establishing the employment relationship, remuneration is still due to the worker. If the parties have expressly stipulated that remuneration shall not be due, such a stipulation shall be null and void (Article 74, paragraph 1 of the LC). This view has been systematically upheld by the court.[61]

232. The changes in Article 128 introduced through the amendments to the LC of June 2004 laid down two new obligations of the employer, connected with his main obligation to pay labour remuneration to the worker or employee. These obligations are: (a) to allot each month the worker's or employee's labour remuneration to the pay-rolls of salaries. This obligation consists in the monthly entering of the amount of the worker's or employee's labour remuneration (basic and additional) in the special books of the enterprise. By entering this amount, the employer recognizes his obligation to the worker or employee and determines the amount thereof; (b) the employer's obligation to issue to the worker or employee – where the latter so requests – an excerpt from the pay-rolls showing the amount of the labour remuneration.

The reasons for introducing these obligations are both internal and external ones. The 'internal reasons' consist in the increasingly frequent delays in recent years (sometimes lasting for months and even a year) of the payment of workers' salaries, which has provoked great dissatisfaction on the part of the workers. The 'external reasons' are the positive impact of the approximation of Bulgarian legislation to the European and international standards: the transposition of Directive 80/987/EC and the ratification of ILO Convention No. 173, which concerns the payment of workers' and employees' labour remuneration in case of the employer's insolvency, and lays down the employer's obligation to pay labour remuneration to workers and employees in a timely and regular manner.

---

61. V. Mrachkov, 'Critical Review of the 2007 Practice of the Supreme Court of Cassation on Labour Disputes', *Juridicheski Sviat* [*Juridical World*] *Journal* 2 (2008): 187; 'Critical Review of the 2008 Practice of the Supreme Court of Cassation on Labour Disputes', *Juridicheski Sviat* [*Juridical World*] *Journal* 2 (2009): 150–151; 'Critical Review of the 2011 Practice of the Supreme Court of Cassation on Labour Disputes', *Juridicheski Sviat* [*Juridical World*] *Journal* 2 (2012): 139–140; 'Critical Review of the 2012 Practice of the Supreme Court of Cassation on Labour Disputes', *Juridicheski Sviat* [*Juridical World*] *Journal* 2 (2013): 117–118; 'Critical Review of the 2016 Practice of the Supreme Court of Cassation on Labour Disputes', *Juridicheski Sviat* [*Juridical World*] *Journal* 2 (2017): 120–121.

V. Obligations to Submit Information and Characteristics of the Worker or Employee

233. These obligations are new ones. They are contained in Article 130 of the LC and are introduced through the amendments to the LC of March 2001 and June 2006. Their inclusion in the LC resulted from the ratification of the European Social Charter and its entry into force for Bulgaria on 1 August 2000, Article 21 thereof raising the workers' 'right to information' as one of their basic social rights. Article 21 of the Charter was adopted as an obligatory one and its introduction in the LC was one of the measures which the state has taken in performance of Article 21 of the European Social Charter, in particular, and in general in introducing the European standards in Bulgarian labour legislation, such as the transposition in the domestic law of D. 80/987/EEC, D. 91/533/EEC, D. 2001/23/EC, D. 2002/14/EC, etc. The new legal infrastructure establishes three new obligations of the employer (*see* below paragraphs 234–236).

234. The first thereof is the obligation of the employer to provide the worker or employee with timely, reliable and comprehensible information regarding the employer's economic and financial state. It is 'timely' when provided at the time the worker or employee needs it in order to use it. The information is reliable when it is truthful and is 'accessible' when it is in compliance with the worker's level of culture and is comprehensible to him/her. However, this information is not general information about the economic and financial state of the employer, and it is only the information that is of importance for the employment rights and obligations of the worker or employee. The latter has the right to this information in cases such as not receiving his/her labour remuneration on time from the employer, who either does not specify the reasons therefor or invokes 'difficulties' in his/her activities in general, etc. The purport of this obligation of the employer is that he/she provides clarification regarding the employment relationship of the worker or employee.

235. The subsequent obligation of the employer is to submit information to the worker or employee when his/her individual employment relationship is changed. Such changes are change of the place and/or the nature of the work or other elements of the content of the employment relationship. The information due in these cases is aimed at explaining and grounding the unilateral change of the content of the employment relationship, this change being undertaken by the employer. This information is necessary for the worker or employee in order for him/her to know the reasons that have brought about a change in his/her labour relationship and to judge whether this change has been a well-founded one and to be convinced of its grounds, or to decide whether to dispute it as incompatible with the law, etc.

236. Lastly, upon the worker's or employee's request, the employer is obliged to give him/her an unbiased and fair assessment of his/her professional qualities as well as the results of his/her work. This will contain the assessment of the employer concerning the professional training and efficiency of the worker's or employee's work. Most often, the worker or employee demands such characteristics upon suspension of his/her labour contract or, if still working with the employer, he/she is seeking and applying for a new, more appropriate job with another employer. He/she hopes that this reference will make it easier for him/her to find and enter a new job. In these cases the employer is obliged to issue the reference and is not entitled to refuse to do so.

237. Significant changes in the domestic legislation on information and consultation of workers and employees were made through the amendments to the LC of June 2006 (Articles 7–7d, 130–130d, etc.). They provided for the institutionalization and differentiation of the information and consultation of workers and employees on the part of the employer. Two types of workers' and employees' representatives were distinguished:

(a) workers' and employees' representatives for those important matters of employment relationships which are explicitly specified in the LC, such as collective dismissals, transfer of enterprises, merger, takeover, distribution of the enterprise's activity and other cases of changes in the employer (the enterprise's being let out for rent, lease or concession), introduction of reduced working time, working day of non-fixed duration, adoption of internal labour regulations on the part of the employer. (Article 7, paragraph 2, Article 130a, 130b, Articles 136a, 138a, 139a, 181, paragraph 2 of the LC, etc.). These representatives are elected at the General Assembly of the workers and employees by a majority of more than two-thirds of the people attending the General Assembly, for a term of three years;
(b) workers' and employees' representatives for information and consultation on the other matters of employment relationships. These representatives are elected at the General Assembly of the workers and employees by a simple majority of the people attending the General Assembly, for a term of three years. It is these representatives of the workers and employees whom the employer informs and consults on matters concerning forthcoming changes in the activity and the economic state of the enterprise; the situation, structure and expected development of employment in the enterprise; the measures in those cases where the level of employment is endangered; considerable forthcoming changes in the organization of labour and the like (Articles 7a–d, 130c and 130d of the LC, etc.).[62]

238. An essential peculiarity of information and consultation of workers and employees under Bulgarian labour law is that, along with the elected representatives of the workers and employees specified above, the employer is also obliged to inform and consult the representatives of the trade union organizations (representative and non-representative ones) in the enterprise. Thus, the so-called two-channel system of representation of the workers and employees – adopted in the country since 2006 – is applied and is really functional at the level of the enterprise.

62. V. Mrachkov, 'Information and Consultation of Workers and Employees in the Enterprise', in: *15 Years' Anniversary of the Faculty of Law, Jubilee Collection* (Plovdiv: University Printing House 'Paissiy Hilendarski', 2007), 18–33; A. Alexandrov, 'Information and Consultation of Workers and Employees in Cases of Changes in the Employer', in: *Juridicheski Sviat* [*Juridical World*] *Journal* 2 (2008): 99–118.

VI. The Employer's Obligation to Maintain an Employment Record of the Worker or Employee (Article 128b of the LC)

239. This obligation of the employer is a new one. It was laid down through the new Article 128b (prom. OJ, No. 54 of 2015) of the LC, which was supplemented in July 2015.

The legal regulation obliges the employer to maintain an employment record of each worker or employee. 'To maintain' means that every worker or employee with whom a labour relation has arisen must have his/her record, which is a collection of all the documents connected with his/her individual labour relation, namely its occurrence, operation, modification and termination: a copy of the concluded employment contract or other documents certifying the occurrence of the labour relation resulting from selection or competition (a protocol of the selection, a decision of the competition commission on the worker's or employee's being ranked first, an agreement under Article 107 of the LC, a document showing his/her taking the job, a job description, agreements on changes in the labour relation, applications and orders on taking paid annual leave and other types of leave, sick notes, business trip orders, orders regarding awards, disciplinary punishments imposed, termination of the labour relation, etc. These documents are kept by the employer – most commonly at the Department of Human Resources – and are periodically updated by adding supplements thereto in the course of continuous operation of the labour relation. This is the worker's or employee's personal employment record. It is started at the time the worker or employee takes the job.

The legal significance of the worker's or employee's employment record consists in its tracing the development of the labour relation of the worker or employee with the employer, documenting it through authentic written expressions of the parties' will and, depending on the circumstances, through documents of other bodies (sick notes, documents of education, etc.), which provides truthfulness and reliability of the content of the record.

Article 128b of the LC lays down the worker's or employee's right to receive – within fourteen days following his/her written request – certified copies of the documents collected in his/her record, which certify the facts relating to the labour relation of the worker or employee. This provides grounds for drawing a general conclusion: the worker or employee at all times has the right of personal access to his/her employment record, so that he/she can get acquainted with its content, and ascertain its completeness and accuracy and, if necessary, request the elimination of any incompleteness or inaccuracy. In spite of being kept by the employer, it is the worker's or employee's *personal* employment record. This increases the mutual trust within the relationship between the parties to the labour relation.

However, the following question is posed: what is the effect of Article 128b of the LC with respect to the 'overtaken' workers and employees? This question should have found its explicit legal regulation; however, there is no such. In this situation the question posed must be answered by interpreting the sense of the regulation in its entirety. The obligation of the employer introduced through Article 128b of the LC is to maintain an employment record of each worker or employee. This obligation, along with its future action, means that from 17 July 2015 onwards the employer must create and maintain such records. As for the 'overtaken' workers and employees, this means collection in a certain place of all the information available about them as well as continuous, regular and timely completion of the records with the new data arising in the course of the labour relation of each worker or employee. As for the newly appointed workers and employees, the employer is obliged to start their records from the day they take the job (Article 128b, paragraph 2 of the LC). The advantage of the proposed solution is the coherence and uniformity of documenting the employment status of each worker or employee and the favourable consequences ensuing therefrom as regards clarity and knowledge, on the part of the worker or employee, of the content of his/her record, as well as reliability, availability and orderliness of truthful information. This will also facilitate the supervisory activity of the labour inspectorates when carrying out the checks on site and will provide a new niche for the on-site control exercised by the labour inspectors.

VII. The Duty Regarding Social Security

240. The employer is obliged to insure the worker against all social security risks which are laid down by social security law (Article 129 of the LC). These risks are provided for in the Mandatory SIC of 1999, as amended. The social security risks are general illness, accident at work, occupational diseases, pregnancy, maternity and child care, unemployment, old age (retirement pensions), death (survivors' pensions), etc. It is worth underlining the fact that the employer has this duty also according to Article 129 of the LC.[63]

§6. Liability of the Employer and His Managerial Staff for Non-fulfilment of Obligations under an Employment Relationship

241. The employer is liable for the non-fulfilment of his obligations. Depending upon the nature of the unfulfilled obligation and the unfavourable consequences for the worker, this liability may be financial – paying the damages caused to the labourer – or may involve the obligation to restore the proper position of the worker under the employment relationship. Financial liability of the employer is applied when damages have been suffered by the worker as a result of the non-fulfilment of the employer's duty to secure conditions necessary for the performance of his/her work or hygienic and safe working conditions, or in the event of non-fulfilment of the obligation to pay remuneration. The extent of this liability depends upon the specific damages sustained by the worker, the remuneration due but not paid, the remuneration which the worker was unable to receive because of the employer's failure to secure normal hygienic and safe working conditions affecting the life and health of the worker. The worker or his/her heirs have the right to be indemnified by the employer under the special civil financial liability for the damages suffered and consisting of the difference between the benefits provided by the social insurance system and the actual loss or damage suffered.

---

63. V. Mrachkov, *Social Security Law – Bulgaria*, 2nd edn. (The Hague: Kluwer Law International, 2006), 58.

242. A special financial employer's liability in the case of death of a worker or damages to his/her health was established by Article 200 of the LC. Until entry into force of this Code as of 1 January 1987, the responsibility of the employer in such cases was regulated by the general rules of common civil liability for unlawful inflicted damage as a consequence of the infringement of the common rule *neminem laedere* (do not damage another) according to Article 45 of the Law on Contracts and Obligations. Since then, Article 200 of the LC has introduced important peculiarities which created a new form of the employer's civil liability for damages caused to a worker. This responsibility consists in the obligation of the employer to indemnify the worker or his/her heirs by means of a lump sum the amount of which represents the difference between the damage caused – moral and material (patrimonial) including not only actual losses (*damnum emergens*) but also missed opportunities to profit (*lucrum cessans*) and compensation and/or pension paid by the social security funds.

243. The financial liability of the employer under Article 200 of the LC has its wide application in practice. The Supreme Court of Cassation renders hundreds of decisions yearly awarding indemnities to workers and employees who have been injured in industrial accidents or suffer from occupational diseases, or, in the event of death, to their relatives (children, parents, spouses).[64] Two new points have been outlined in the court practice since 1998. The first one is a tendency towards an increase in the amount of the indemnities awarded for damages caused by industrial accidents or occupational diseases (Dec. 651-98-III C.Ch., Dec. 747-98-III C.Ch., Dec. 248-07-III C.Ch., Dec. 818-07-IV C.Ch., Dec. 33-08-III C.Ch., Dec. 377-08-II C.Ch., Dec. 125-11-III C.Ch., Dec. 355-12-III C.Ch., Dec. 190-13-III C.Ch., Dec. 235-14-III C.Ch., Dec. 194-15-IV C.Ch., etc.) The second one is the introduction of some social criteria regarding fairness and evaluation of the specific socioeconomic situation in the country, the price outlook, the inflation index and the like, and the accounting thereof in determining the amount of indemnities awarded for financial

64. V. Mrachkov, *Imoushtestvena otgovornost na rabotodatelia* [*Financial Liability of the Employer*], (Sofia: Publishing House Sibi, 2013), 63–215; 'Critical Review of the 1998 Practice of the Supreme Court of Cassation on Labour Disputes', *Juridicheski Sviat* [*Juridical World*] *Journal* 2 (1999): 211–214; 'Critical Review of the 2000 Practice of the Supreme Court of Cassation on Labour Disputes', *Juridicheski Sviat* [*Juridical World*] *Journal* 2 (2001): 161–165; 'Critical Review of the 2007 Practice of the Supreme Court of Cassation on Labour Disputes', *Juridicheski Sviat* [*Juridical World*] *Journal* 2 (2008): 188–189; 'Critical Review of the 2008 Practice of the Supreme Court of Cassation on Labour Disputes', *Juridicheski Sviat* [*Juridical World*] *Journal* 2 (2009): 155–157; 'Critical Review of the 2011 Practice of the Supreme Court of Cassation on Labour Disputes', *Juridicheski Sviat* [*Juridical World*] *Journal* 2 (2012): 140–142; 'Critical Review of the 2012 Practice of the Supreme Court of Cassation on Labour Disputes', *Juridicheski Sviat* [*Juridical World*] *Journal* 2 (2013): 118–121; 'Critical Review of the 2013 Practice of the Supreme Court of Cassation on Labour Disputes', *Juridicheski Sviat* [*Juridical World*] *Journal* 2 (2014): 131–136; 'Critical Review of the 2014 Practice of the Supreme Court of Cassation on Labour Disputes', *Juridicheski Sviat* [*Juridical World*] *Journal* 2 (2015): 107–111; 'Critical Review of the 2015 Practice of the Supreme Court of Cassation on Labour Disputes', *Juridicheski Sviat* [*Juridical World*] *Journal* 2 (2016): 134–139; 'Critical Review of the 2016 Practice of the Supreme Court of Cassation on Labour Disputes', *Juridicheski Sviat* [*Juridical World*] *Journal* 2 (2017): 132–135; 'Critical Review of the 2017 Practice of the Supreme Court of Cassation on Labour Disputes', *Juridicheski Sviat* [*Juridical World*] *Journal* 2 (2018): 95–98.

and moral damages caused by an industrial accident or an occupational disease. These criteria bring about full satisfaction of the claims for damages filed by the injured or relatives thereof.

244. The practice of the Supreme Court of Cassation extends the scope of the employer's property accountability under Articles 200–202 of the LC by way of including cases of so-called excess of a disease and suffering. The 'excess' is a renewal of a preceding disease, renovation and sharpening of the problems of a preceding occupational disease or an accident at work and impairment of the health state, following a period in which the disease slackened and the health state was stable. In this case the employer's property accountability is grounded on the general provision of Article 51, paragraph 3 of the Law on Obligations and Contracts, according to which: 'Where compensation for lost capacity for work has been adjudged, the compensation may be increased or decreased, if the injured person's capacity for work changes.' The 'excess' under Article 200 of the LC concerns the alternative of increasing the compensation in case the injured person's capacity for work changes towards impairment of the health state and lower capacity for work.[65]

245. A compensation for excess is adjudged in cases of injury to health resulting from an occupational disease or an accident at work, these being cases in which, most often, the injured worker or employee used to receive a compensation under Article 200, paragraph 3 of the LC. The compensation covers all damages caused to the worker or employee as a result of the exacerbation of the suffering or disease (expenditures on medicine, rich diet and the like) and the loss of profit, as well as moral damages for pains and sufferings if such damages have occurred (Dec. 253-08-III C.Ch., Dec. 875-08-II C.Ch., etc.). It does not matter when the initial injury to the health – resulting from an occupational disease or an accident at work – has occurred. Nor does it matter what the reason for the renewal of the suffering was – concomitant general diseases, seasonal changes in weather, age-related changes, deterioration of the working conditions, increased concentration of harmful substances in the presence of silicosis disease, etc. What matters is to establish that it is a renewal of a preceding disease, which was caused by an occupational disease or an accident at work (Dec. 742-08-III C.Ch., Dec. 26-08-II C.Ch., etc.).

The excess has to be established and proven just as the preceding impairment to the health from an occupational disease or an accident at work was established. The excess has to be proven in each specific case. Where it is not proven, no compensation for excess under Article 200 of the LC is due (Dec. 320-08-III C.Ch., Dec. 43-08-II C.Ch., Dec. 196-11-IV C.Ch., Dec. 185-12-IV C.Ch., Dec. 226-16-III C.Ch., Dec. 283-17-IV C.Ch., Dec. 168-18-III C.Ch., etc.).

No excess is present where the deterioration of the health state is not caused by an accident at work or an occupational disease, but rather by a general disease (Dec. 541-08-V C.Ch.).[66]

---

65. V. Mrachkov, *Financial Liability of the Employer*, *supra.*, 119–124.
66. V. Mrachkov, 'Critical Review of the 2007 Practice of the Supreme Court of Cassation on Labour Disputes', *Juridicheski Sviat* [*Juridical World*] *Journal* 2 (2008): 189–190; 'Critical Review of the

246. The liability of the employer for damages caused by an industrial accident may be reduced where the injured person has contributed to the occurrence of the industrial accident and the injury through gross negligence (*culpa lata*). According to the practice of the Supreme Court of Cassation gross negligence is present where the worker or employee has violated the most elementary rules on healthy and safe working conditions, which every ordinary and average worker or employee is obliged to have knowledge about, to comply with the requirements of these rules and to abide by them, or where the worker or employee has shown excessive self-confidence and impertinent presumption (*luxuria*) in non-observance thereof. Examples of such gross negligence are a drink-driver who has fallen asleep while driving (Dec. 1507-2000-III C.Ch.); evacuating air from a pump full of sodium base as it has been elementary to presume that the liquid (sodium base) will flow out under the air pressure (Dec. 2014-2000-III C.Ch.); violation of the labour safety rules (Dec. 786-07-V C.Ch.); a worker staying under the boom of the excavator while repairing it (Dec. 289-08-III C.Ch., Dec. 191-13-III C.Ch., Dec. 85-14-IV C.Ch., Dec. 62-15-IV C.Ch.), etc. However, even in these cases of culpable contribution to the injurious result, the financial liability of the employer may be reduced; however, he/she may not be totally released therefrom.

247. The following prerequisites for this responsibility can be deduced from the law:

(1) The occurrence of an accident at work or occupational disease of the worker as defined by law (Articles 55–56 of the SIC). It does not matter whether or not the employer is at fault as regards the occurrence of an accident at work or occupational disease. It is sufficient that the event has occurred. In this sense the envisaged liability is objective and differs from the civil responsibility under Article 45 of the Law on Obligations and Contracts, which always requires the element of guilt bringing about the damage. The basic idea of this prerequisite and the financial liability of the employer as a whole is that the accident at work or occupational disease is a result of the employer's failure to secure normal hygienic and safe working conditions. The employer has this obligation by virtue of the law. The law not only lays down the accomplishment of hygienic and safe working conditions by the employer but also imposes on him/her the risk of failing to secure healthy and safe working conditions. That is why the law in Article 200, paragraph 1 of the LC expressly provides that liability arises irrespective of fault on the part of the employer himself/herself, somebody on his/her managerial staff or any other person in his/her employ as regards the occurrence of an accident at work or occupational disease. The employer is also liable for accident at work due to an Act

---

2008 Practice of the Supreme Court of Cassation on Labour Disputes', *Juridicheski Sviat* [*Juridical World*] *Journal* 2 (2009): 154–155; 'Critical Review of the 2011 Practice of the Supreme Court of Cassation on Labour Disputes', *Juridicheski Sviat* [*Juridical World*] *Journal* 2 (2012): 141–142; 'Critical Review of the 2012 Practice of the Supreme Court of Cassation on Labour Disputes', *Juridicheski Sviat* [*Juridical World*] *Journal* 2 (2013): 119.

of God (force majeure), or occurring as a result of accomplishing or in connection with a task entrusted to the worker, or in connection with any job completed in the interest of the enterprise, even without an order to that effect by the employer. The employer is also liable if an accident at work has occurred during a rest period spent in the enterprise (Article 200, paragraph 2 of the LC). The only case in which the employer does not bear a responsibility for damages caused to a worker during his/her work is when the worker causes the damage to himself/herself with premeditation (Article 201, paragraph 1 of the LC). But in such circumstances there is no accident at work in the legal sense of this term (Article 55, paragraph 2 of the SIC). In the last case the burden of proof (*onus probandi*) rests upon the employer. Also, the responsibility of the employer may be diminished if the worker by his/her serious misconduct has contributed to the accident at work taking place (Article 201, paragraph 2 of the LC).

(2) The accident at work or occupational disease must provoke a temporary incapacity to work, the invalidity or death of a worker. These are the legally recognized types of damages or injuries sustained by the worker. Only these three forms are relevant to any employer's responsibility arising. They are established by the competent medical bodies in the manner prescribed by the law.[67]

248. The employer must also restore the worker's legal position. In a case where the employer unilaterally changes the conditions of the employment while violating his/her duties, his/her respective actions are revoked and he/she is ordered to restore the worker to his/her former job and position. This is the case where the employer changes the place and character of work without there being any production necessity or urgent need for this, without a stoppage being in operation or force majeure. Finally, when the employer unlawfully imposes disciplinary actions correction simply means the performance of actions leading to the restoration of the former employment relationship and of the position of the worker within it. Where damages have been sustained by the worker as a result of such unlawful actions by the employer, the latter is obliged to compensate the worker.

249. In order to avail himself/herself of these employer's responsibilities, the interested worker has the right to file a claim. To realize the financial responsibility of the employer, the worker may bring a claim asking for a condemnatory court decision; to realize the employer's responsibility for an unlawful change of the nature and place of work he/she may lodge a restitutive claim. When the two responsibilities exist simultaneously, he/she may lodge both claims which are objectively united (Article 103 of the Code of Civil Procedure)[68] into one.

---

67. V. Mrachkov, K. Sredkova & A. Vassilev, *Komentar na Kodeksa na trouda*, 659–683; V. Mrachkov et al., *Komentar na Kodeksa za zadaljitelno obshtestveno ossigouriavane* [*Commentary on the SIC*] (Sofia: Labour and Law Publishing House, 2000), 193–219; *Financial Liability of the Employer*, *supra*., 226–259.

68. Zh. Stalev, *Bulgarsko Grajdansko Prozessoualno Pravo*, 417–423.

250. The obligations of the employer, stemming from the employment relationship with the worker, are fulfilled by his administration on his behalf. This includes the manager of the enterprise and his closest assistants: deputies, heads of department of the lower subdivisions of the enterprise (shop, section, shift, construction project, team, etc.). Fulfilling the obligations of the enterprise is part of their duties as employees of that enterprise. It is precisely this dual character – as performers with their personal actions of the obligations of the enterprise towards its workers, and as performers of their own employment duties towards the enterprise – which gives rise to their dual responsibility. When they do not fulfil the employers' obligations towards the state or to the employer's workers in respect of labour hygiene and safety, or their own other duties under the LC, they may have a personal administrative and penal responsibility. This consists of fines imposed as a result of intervention by the control organs (the Labour Inspectorate) for observing labour legislation. The fines thus imposed are payable personally and cannot be charged to the enterprise (Articles 413–415 of the LC).

251. When managers fail to fulfil their employment duties in this way, they are also liable to disciplinary action under Article 188 of the LC. In fact the application of these two responsibilities, although they do not constitute responsibilities of the employer under the employment relationship, but responsibilities of his administration, contribute indirectly and help, in the final analysis, in the fulfilment of the enterprise's duties under its employment relations with the workers.

252. The labour laws now in force do not contain special or express regulations on the responsibility of the enterprise to compensate for damages caused to objects belonging to the worker (clothing, personal belongings, instruments and the like) in the course of his/her work – mutilation, loss or theft. Of course, this does not mean that no responsibility exists in such cases. It does, but it falls under general civil liability for an inadmissible injury as provided for in Article 49 of the Law on Obligations and Contracts. According to this provision 'Whoever has entrusted another person with any job is liable for the damage caused by the latter in the performance or on the occasion of the performance of this job.' However, two conditions are necessary before the provision can be applied:

(1) the object belonging to the worker must have been damaged by a person to whom the enterprise has assigned a job. Normally, this will be a person with whom the enterprise has an employment relationship;
(2) the damage must have been caused to the person performing his/her duties or tasks related to the object. In fact, it is necessary to establish causality between the injurious action and the damage inflicted on the object belonging to the worker. The form of the damage inflicted on the respective objects – theft, destruction, impairment and the like – does not matter. The liability in these cases is borne by the enterprise because the law proceeds from the assumption that the enterprise has not fulfilled the assumed obligation to protect objects belonging to its workers and to prevent any damage being caused to them. It owes the worker full compensation for the damage inflicted on his/her possessions.

Chapter 3. Working Time; Weekly Rest; Holidays; Annual Vacation; Paid Educational Leave

§1. Working Time and Overtime

253. In accordance with the law (the LC) and the acts issued for its application, or, in cases permitted by the law – according to a stipulation between the parties to the employment relationship – working time is the time during which the worker is bound to perform the work entrusted to him/her. The legal regulation on working time has undergone a substantial and progressive development. The main milestones in this development were the 6-day working week with an 8-hour working day and a 48-hour working week with the Decree of 1919, a cutting down of the working week to 46 hours in November 1957 (Article 39, paragraph 1 of the LC, as amended in November 1957), the gradual introduction, between 1973 and 1975, of a 5-day working week of 42.30 hours and finally, the cutting of the 5-day working week to 40 hours as of 1 January 1993 (Article 136, paragraph 1 of the LC).[69]

The amendments to the LC of March 2001 and June 2006 introduced greater flexibility in the legal framework of working time. The adopted legislative measures aim at achieving better adjustment of the length and utilization of the working time to the specific needs of the current manufacturing and official activities of the enterprise and the employer (*see* below paragraphs 256–257).

I. Categories of Working Time

254. Working time can be classified according to various features. In the text that follows, the basic classifications, of legal significance under the current laws, will be discussed.

A. *Standard, Extended and Reduced Working Day and Working Week*

255. The division of the working day and working week into standard, extended and reduced is effected on the basis of their duration. The standard working day is eight hours in the case of day work and seven hours for night work (Article 140, paragraph 1 of the LC). It is called the standard day because it is customary, widespread and most widely applied. It affects the overwhelming majority of working people. This is also the maximum permissible length of the working day and any lengthening is forbidden in principle under Article 136, paragraph 4 of the LC, unless it is explicitly provided for in the LC (*see* below paragraph 256). A standard

69. For more details about working time, *see* K. Sredkova, *Praven regim na rabotnoto vreme* [*Legal Regime of the Working Time*] (Sofia: University 'Saint Kliment Ohridski' Publishing House, 1993), 51–214; K. Sredkova, 'Extended Working Time', *Savremenno pravo* [*Contemporary Law*] *Review* 3 (2001): 7–20.

week corresponds to the standard working day. The same applies to the whole country, its length for the present is forty hours while the number of working days, into which it is divided equally, is five.

256. The new Article 136a of the LC, which was established through the amendments to the LC of March 2001, introduced so-called extended working time. This consists in increasing the length of the established duration of the working day by two hours for the workers and employees working under a normal working day of eight hours, and by one hour for the workers and employees working under a reduced working day of seven or six hours. In these cases, in the presence of 'economic reasons', the working time is extended by way of a written ordinance of the employer. 'Economic reasons' are those connected with the course of activities of the enterprise: greater orders received for performance within a specified term in the conditions of a favourable market situation, need for quick processing of perishable materials and raw stuff, intensive seasonal work, etc. The judgment about the presence of these reasons is made by the employer. However, prior to resorting to the introduction of extended working time, he/she is obliged to make consultations with the representatives of the workers and employees or other representatives or bodies provided for in the collective labour contract – representatives of the trade unions, the General Meeting of the workers and employees, etc. The employer notifies the Labour Inspection of the extension of the working time and keeps a special register, recording therein the extended working time that has been worked out.

The extension of the working time is applied for a term of sixty working days per calendar year; however, it cannot last longer than twenty consecutive working days. Therefore, the employer is entitled to resort to an extension of the working time at least three times during one calendar year (twenty consecutive working days each time) with an interruption between the periods of extended working time. The law does not specify the duration of the interruption. It has to be at least one working day.

257. The extension of the working time is compensated for by its reduction, which is to take place within a term of four months after the extended working day. The reduction has to be a corresponding one, i.e., the number of days and the number of hours per day of the extension of the working time should correspond to the number of days and number of hours of its reduction, so that the extension be 'compensated for'. If the employer fails to organize the compensation for the extended working time within the established four months' term, the worker or employee is entitled to determine himself/herself the time when he/she will work under reduced working time in order to compensate for its extension. In these cases the latter is obliged to give at least two weeks' notification to the employer concerning the days he/she will work under reduced working time. The idea of the law is that the number of days and hours the worker or employee works under reduced working time is to be the same as the number of days and hours he/she has worked under extended working time.

258. If the labour relationship of the worker or employee is suspended when the work under extended working time is over, however, the latter has not yet been compensated for by reduced working time, the employer owes remuneration to the worker or employee for the non-compensated extended working time as overtime work. Extended working time is paid at a higher rate – the one for overtime work, in accordance with the rules of Articles 262 and 264 of the LC.

259. The reduced working day and reduced working week is that working day or week which legally established is shorter than that of the standard working day or week. With the shorter working day, the total length of the working time is correspondingly reduced, although the number of working days remains standard at five. The reduced working day and reduced working week are always established by law. There are two reasons for their introduction: the nature of the work and the conditions under which it is carried out on the one hand, and certain attributes of the worker, on the other. The first reason, in a generalized but nevertheless express form, is given in Article 137, paragraph 1, item 1 of the LC according to which: 'A reduced working day may be adopted for wage or salary earners employed in jobs which are harmful to health or in work of a special character.' In complying with this provision, the government decided to introduce a reduced working day for workers in a number of industries where production takes place under conditions that are harmful to health or dangerous. Only a few general features of the actual regulation are being highlighted here:

(1) The main social function of the reduced working day in these cases is to protect the workers from the noxious or dangerous impact of the working environment by reducing the length of the time during which they are exposed to such an environment.
(2) A reduced working day is introduced whenever, on the basis of medical or technical expert opinion, the harmfulness, difficulty, or dangerous character of the work is positively established. This is why the acts of the Council of Ministers introducing a reduced working day are numerous and issued at different times. Sometimes they coincide with the coming into operation of a certain industry; at other times they follow the establishment of a harm. But they are always aimed at counteracting, as soon as possible, the damage by eliminating or at least diminishing its negative effect.
(3) The reduction of the working day depends upon the intensity of the danger. This is why such a day may vary between four, six and seven hours. Under a five-day working week, the weekly working time for a four-, six- and seven-hour working day is, correspondingly, twenty, thirty and thirty-five hours.
(4) The reduced working day and working week are valid for a number of types of production and activities in the chemical, metallurgical, coal and textile industries, transport, the health services, etc. They embrace a considerable number of workers.
(5) The reduced working day and reduced working week with their fixed length are not established once and for all. They are dynamic in the sense that they can be changed. In production processes and activities, where as a result of an introduction of new technical equipment, the harm, severity or danger of the

work has been overcome, a standard length of the working day or week may be adopted. This is both in the interest of society and the individual worker. For society this means that working conditions have become healthier and the total amount of working time has increased, and as a result of this so has the nation's wealth; for the worker it means improved labour hygiene and safety which is in profound harmony with his/her lasting interest.

260. The second reason why a reduced working day may be introduced is the specific situation in which a male or female worker may find himself or herself. If a worker is physically weak or has little resistance, it is in the interest of his or her health to work shorter hours compared with other, perfectly healthy and able-bodied workers. Under the laws now in force, a reduced working time on these grounds has been established for three categories of persons: minors up to the age of 18, pregnant women, and persons with a reduced capacity for work.

B. Day and Night Work

261. The division of working hours depends upon the part of the day during which work is carried out. Night work is the work between 10.00 pm and 6.00 am (Article 140, paragraph 2 of the LC). Work done during the other hours of the day and night is considered day work. The division of working hours into day and night work is of great juridical significance in three aspects. First, the period of night work is in principle shorter than that of day work. Under the law currently in force the length of day work is a standard eight hours and of the reduced day time work seven, six and four hours, while that of night-time work is seven or six hours. Second, night work is better paid than day work. According to Article 261 of the LC and Article 7 of the Decree of the Council of Ministers, 1993, an additional remuneration of up to 81.5% of the day rate is to be paid for night work. Third, by virtue of Article 140, paragraph 4 of the LC certain categories of people are forbidden to carry out night work: minors up to the age of 18, pregnant women, mothers with a child under the age of three years, mothers with a child between three and six years, mothers with an invalid child irrespective of the child's age, workers with a diminished capacity to work as well as workers who study extramurally. The measures taken in connection with the performance of night work are a result of the fact that such work may be harmful to the human being, because it changes the normal cycle of the physiological functions in the human body.

262. Considering the fact that night work is performed in uncommon time (during the night), which is harmful in principle and may disturb the biological rhythm of human organism and may have a negative effect upon the health state of the night worker or employee, Article 140a of the LC lays down special rules on night work. They are aimed at close observation of the night work's effect on the health state of the worker or employee performing it and, depending on the results of the observation, the law provides measures for prevention or elimination of the harmful consequences this work generates. These measures are:

(a) night workers and employees are admitted to work only after a preliminary medical examination, the expenses on it being borne by the employer;
(b) night workers and employees are subject to regular medical examinations;
(c) where a medical body finds that the health state of the worker or employee has deteriorated as a result of the night work performed, the latter is transferred to another appropriate day job or is reassigned as a person with reduced capacity for work.

C. *Full-Time and Part-Time Work*

263. The classification of full-time and part-time work is based on the criterion of whether the length of the working time in a specific employment relationship is equal to that legally established for the particular type of work and activity, or shorter. If it is equal to the legally established working time, this is full-time work. If it is shorter, this is part-time work, i.e., working time which does not extend to the limits established by law. It is regulated by Article 138 and 138a of the LC. Part-time work can be established by the parties. The length of part-time work may vary to one, two or three and more hours, but in any case working time must be shorter than that legally established for the relevant type of work. The contracting parties are free to stipulate different methods of organizing part-time work: part-time working day, part-time working week or month (with work on certain days of the week or the month), etc. During the last few years, there has been a considerable development and application of part-time work as a result of the rapidly increasing unemployment rate. In these circumstances unemployed persons are prepared to accept part-time work rather than the alternative of no job at all.

264. Part-time work may be introduced in two ways:

(1) by agreement between the parties (Article 138 LC). By mutual consent, the parties are free to negotiate a part-time working day and to specify its duration. By virtue of the amendments to the LC introduced in June 2006, the employees of part-time work, negotiated by mutual consent, may not be put into a less favourable position only because of the part-time duration of their working hours compared to the workers and employees who are a party to a full-time employment contract and perform either the same or similar work at the enterprise. Part-timers enjoy the same rights and have the same obligations as those workers and employees who work full time, unless the law provides for the enjoyment of some rights being dependent on the duration of the working hours performed, the length of service, the qualification acquired, etc.

    Where part-time work is contracted, the parties are obliged to observe it. If a labour contract of part-time work is concluded (e.g., usually for four hours), it is inadmissible for the worker or employee to work full time (eight hours), save where, by way of exception, he/she has to perform extra work in the presence of conditions of its admissibility under Article 144 of the LC (*see* below paragraph 268). The checks of the Central Labour Inspectorate show that the cases of non-observance of the part time stipulated under Article 138 are not rare ones and, by virtue of a secret arrangement between the parties, the worker or employee works full time and is paid in cash for the time worked in excess of the time under the contract. This income is not taxable, no social security or health insurance contributions are made on it; therefore, it is not taken into account when calculating the social security benefits paid to the worker or employee in temporary incapacity for work, the amount of pension, etc. For counteracting this unlawful practice, the new paragraph 4 of Article 138 (prom. OJ, No. 7 of 2012) and Article 404, paragraph 1, item 9 of the LC authorize the supervision bodies to issue an obligatory prescription to the employer 'for changing the employment contract for part-time work into an employment contract for working time of normal duration'. Within the meaning of Article 404, paragraph 1, item 9 of the LC, the normal duration of the working time is '8 hours in the daytime' (Article 136, paragraph 3 of the LC).

(2) unilaterally by the employer (Article 138a LC). The employer has the right to introduce a part-time working day if the amount of work has decreased. 'A decrease in the amount of work' is present in cases of decrease in the production programme or the quantity of products or turnover (in commercial shops) or the services performed, etc. The reasons for it are of no importance: lower demand for the product, shortage of raw stuff and materials, less clientele, lower sales and the like. Where the employer considers that the decrease in the amount of work is temporary, he/she may reduce the working time and keep the staff, in expectation that the unfavourable situation will be a temporary one, that soon it will be over and he/she will be able to continue his/her activities 'in full swing'. The reduced working time is introduced by the employer after discussing the matter with the representatives of the workers and employees. The reduced working time may be set up for the time the amount of work remains lower; however, it may not be set up for more than three months per calendar year. The reduced working time may embrace either all workers and employees of the whole enterprise or only a part thereof – those working in a particular workshop, production department or another unit thereof, where the decrease in the amount of work is actually manifested. On the other hand, at the discretion of the employer, the working time may be reduced by one hour, or two hours or more, depending on the reasons causing it and the extent of their effect, but the reduction may not be more than half of its legally established duration for the period the working time is calculated in (Article 138, paragraph 3 LC). Thus, the duration of the reduced working time for an eight-hour working day cannot be less than four hours, for a seven-hour working day it cannot be less than three hours and a half, etc.

265. According to the amendments to the LC introduced in June 2006, the employer shall be obliged to undertake some specific measures in order to ensure the smooth shifting from full-time to part-time work or vice versa. These measures are the following:

(1) to take into consideration the requests of the employees for shifting from full-time to part-time work, regardless of whether the requests refer to the same working place or to another, if such an opportunity exists in the enterprise;
(2) to take into consideration the requests of the employees for shifting from part-time to full-time work, or for increasing the duration of the part-time work, if such an opportunity emerges;
(3) to provide timely written information for the employees, at a proper place in the enterprise, regarding the vacant full-time and part-time working positions, in order to facilitate shifting from full-time to part-time work or vice versa. This information shall also be provided to the representatives of the trade union organizations and the representatives of workers and employees;
(4) to undertake measures for facilitating the access to part-time work at all levels in the enterprise, including those positions which require certain qualification as well as the managerial positions, and, whcrc possible, to facilitate the access of the part-timers to professional training for the purpose of increasing their opportunities for career advancement and professional mobility.

II. Overtime

266. The regulation of overtime is contained in Articles 143–150 of the LC. According to Article 143 ‘All work done by a wage or salary earner on the orders of or with the knowledge of the employer or of the relevant leader and without his/her objection outside the established standard normal working hours established for him or her shall be overtime work.’ From this legal definition we can derive three constituent elements of the concept of overtime:

(1) Work done by the worker outside the established normal working hours can relate to either the day work time of eight hours or night work time of six hours, the reduced working time of seven, six or five hours, as well as the part-time work agreed by the parties (*see* above). The important thing is that the work done must be outside these limits of the customary or agreed length of working time for the particular worker.
(2) The work done must constitute part of the fulfilment of the function entrusted to the worker. Overtime work is a continuation of the work normally performed, as agreed by the parties. This is why the work done by workers under another labour contract (for instance for part-time work – Article 259 of the LC), on the basis of an additional and express agreement with the employer, is not within the ambit of basic labour duties and, therefore, not overtime work. This is ‘another type of work’ and not a continuation of that agreed upon.
(3) The work must be performed by order or with the knowledge of and without objection from the employer or the relevant leader. Such an ‘order’ is made when the employer directs the worker to work after his/her normal working time has expired. His authority stems from his capacity as employer and organizer of the labour process. This order is compulsory on the worker. ‘Knowledge’ with the employer or the relevant leader exists, even though he/she may

not have expressly ordered the work to be done, when, although he/she knows that the worker is working after working hours and tacitly accepts this situation without objecting. It is assumed that since the employer or the relevant leader, learning that the worker is working beyond normal working hours, is taking no steps to prevent this, he/she must be accepting the situation as necessary and useful for the enterprise. This solution is no doubt a protective measure in favour of the worker as regards the payment of overtime work. *Per argumentum a contrario* drawn from this requirement, it must be concluded that overtime work is not that which the employer or the relevant leader has expressly ordered not to be done, or about which he/she did not know and which on learning about it, he/she ordered to be discontinued.

267. In general, overtime is forbidden. This is expressly proclaimed in Article 143, paragraph 2 of the LC. This means that in principle it is not permissible and its performance is not allowed. This ban on overtime is a protective measure on behalf of the worker. It is aimed at protecting life and health by disallowing the systematic performance of overtime. This is of important legal significance for the employer and his managerial staff because it compels them to organize the work at the enterprise so that tasks are fulfilled by the workers within the established working hours.

268. Nevertheless, the law allows certain exceptions to this principle. But even in those cases, it strives to limit overtime in forbidding it for certain categories of persons, in setting up a special procedure if overtime is required and in determining the maximum length of permissible overtime. The instances in which overtime work can be done are listed exhaustively in Article 144 of the LC. They involve work in connection with the defence of the country, work to avert and overcome a disaster or peril to the community, work of urgent public necessity – for restoring the water supply, electricity, drainage system, transport or communications or providing medical assistance, where it is necessary to continue work which has already been started and which cannot be completed during standard working hours, as well as performance of intensive seasonal work. Instances also involve work in connection with repairs to workrooms, machinery and other equipment of the enterprise where repairs would delay the work of a considerable number of workers and, finally, cases of intensified seasonal work. A common feature of all these instances is their exceptional nature. They all reflect an unusual situation which differs substantially from the normal conditions in which work at the enterprise is organized and performed.

269. Certain categories of persons cannot work overtime. They are listed in Article 147 of the LC: workers below the age of 18, pregnant women workers or mothers with children until the age of 3, mothers with children aged between 3 and 6, as well as mothers who take care of invalid children irrespective of the child's age (except if the mother consents), workers reallocated to lighter jobs because of their state of health (except if they consent and provided it does not unfavourably influence their health as concluded in this respect by a member of the medical profession), workers who continue their education without interrupting the work, i.e., extramural (except if they consent), and workers for whom a reduced working time is introduced because they work in conditions which are harmful to their health or who accomplish work in specific conditions. Nevertheless, overtime for the latter group of workers is allowed in the case of work in connection with the defence of the country, work to avert and overcome a disaster or peril to the community and work as a result of urgent public necessity – restoring the water supply, electricity, drainage system, transport and communications, work involving medical care, as well as for the completion of work which cannot be completed within the regular working hours and for the performance of intensive seasonal work. These cases are exhaustively enumerated in Article 144 of the LC.

270. The laws also determine the maximum permissible amount of overtime. In a calendar year it cannot be more than 150 hours, in a month up to 30 hours for day work and 20 hours for night work, in a week up to six hours for day work and up to four hours for night work, and in two successive days a total of three hours for day work and two hours for night work is allowed (Article 146 of the LC). The legal significance of these regulations is to compel the employer and the management of the enterprise to organize the work in such a way as to have to resort to overtime only by way of exception. But if, for one reason or another, the worker does work more overtime than the permitted maximum he/she must be paid for it (Article 262 of the LC). Executive personnel, however, who order the application of excessive overtime, are financially liable for the damages inflicted by the higher wages bill of state-owned or communal enterprises and are without exception liable to disciplinary administrative and penal action under Article 414 of the LC.

271. Overtime is paid at a higher rate. Moreover, all work performed in overtime whether permitted or not, and whether within the framework determined by the laws or in excess of it, is always paid. The minimal higher rates are established in Article 262 of the LC. They are applied if the parties did not agree upon higher rates than those provided for in Article 262 of the LC. These 'minimal higher rates' are the following: for overtime on working days the rate of time and 50% is paid for every additional hour, for overtime during the weekly rest period the rate of time and 75%. When overtime is done during public holidays it is paid at a rate of time and 100% for every hour (Article 262 of the LC).[70]

§2. Weekly Rest and Holidays

I. Weekly Rest

272. The legal regulation of weekly rest is contained in Article 153 of the LC. In accordance with Article 153, paragraph 1 of the LC the weekly rest period is forty-eight hours. It is uninterrupted, i.e., these forty-eight hours must be given to the worker as an integral block of time on the basis that after a certain number of working days in the week only a relatively longer interruption of one's work secures

70. For more details about overtime, *see* K. Sredkova, A. Vasilev, in: V. Mrachkov, K. Sredkova & A. Vassilev, *Komentar na Kodeksa na trouda*, 500–511, 832–835.

the full restoration of one's physical strength. A few observations have to be made along this line. First, the rule of an uninterrupted weekly rest of forty-eight hours applied to the forty-hour week, according to Article 136, paragraph 1 of the LC. The system has now been changed substantially. In practice, the weekly rest for the five-day working week up to forty working hours per week is longer. If the last working day of the working week falls on a Friday at 18.00, followed by two days' weekly rest, and the new working week begins on Monday at 8.00 the normal weekly rest of a worker working a five-day week will in fact be sixty-two hours. On the other hand, one of the two consecutive days of the weekly rest must in principle be a Sunday according to the national and religious traditions in the country.

273. Second, the law allows two exceptions whereby it is possible to 'fall' below the indicated factual duration of the weekly rest. The first one provides for an uninterrupted weekly rest, the duration of which shall be no less than thirty-six hours. It is applied to the summarized calculation of working hours (Article 153, paragraph 2 LC). The second exception establishes an uninterrupted weekly rest of at least twenty-four hours. This kind of weekly rest is applied to the summarized calculation of working hours in the case of a change in the shifts (Article 153, paragraph 3 LC); in calculation of daily working time when extra work during the two days of the weekly rest was performed (Article 153, paragraph 4 LC); where the Council of Ministers has declared certain days to be either one-time public holidays or days in commemoration of certain professions (Article 154, paragraph 2 of the LC).

II. Holidays

274. Official holidays are days on which workers do not work, but for which they receive remuneration. Workers who, as a result of the nature of their work or for other reasons, work on such days, are entitled to be paid double time (Article 262 of the LC). Official holidays are determined by Article 154 of the LC. There are fifteen such days: 1 January (New Year's Day), 3 March (Day of the Liberation of Bulgaria from Ottoman Domination), 1 May (Labour Day), four days (Good Friday, Holy Saturday, Easter Sunday and Monday), 6 May (Saint George's Day, Day of the Bravery of Bulgarian Army), 24 May (Day of Slavonic Letters and Culture), 6 September (Day of the Union), 22 September (Day of the Independence of Bulgaria), 1 November (Day of People's Awakers), 24, 25 and 26 December (Christmas). Official holidays are secular holidays and are mainly dedicated to national or universal social, political, cultural and religious events of paramount importance.

§3. Paid Leave

275. Workers have a basic right to paid annual leave, reaffirmed by Article 48, paragraph 5 of the Constitution. The enhancement of the legal significance of this right by including it in the basic rights of citizens, recognized by the fundamental law of the state, underlines its importance and place in the country's legal system. On the other hand, as part of the employment relationship it is a subjective right of the worker. This means that the employer is obliged to ensure it. In the event of violations, the worker can seek realization by lodging a claim in the established manner. The actual regulation of paid annual leave is contained in the LC (Articles 155–178) and in the Ordinance on Working Time, Rest and Leave, 1987, as amended.

276. The right to paid annual leave is given to all workers irrespective of the field in which they are employed – industry, agriculture, transport, public services or whatever. According to Article 155 of the LC, the right to paid annual leave arises after a certain period of qualifying service. Two basic elements characterize this requirement. In the first place it refers to its length, which is eight months. In the second place and according to Articles 352 and 354 of the LC, this period of qualifying service includes a number of exhaustively enumerated paid and unpaid periods of leave as well as the time actually served. The former are widely formulated and include all absences from work for reasons beyond the worker's control. This qualifying period of service is necessary only for the initial acquisition of the right to annual leave in a given enterprise. As long as the employment relation exists, having once acquired the right, the worker is entitled to paid annual leave without it being necessary to serve the eight months again.

277. The law regulates the length of annual paid leave. Regular, paid annual leave is established in Article 155 of the LC and is classified as normal (ordinary) or longer. Ordinary paid leave is established in Article 155, paragraph 4 of the LC for all workers except those who are entitled to longer leave (Article 155, paragraph 5 of the LC). Its length is minimum of twenty working days. Article 155, paragraph 5 of the LC provides for longer leave of twenty-six to forty-eight working days for employees whose work requires greater exertion causing greater fatigue. To this group of employees belong teachers, lecturers and educators in educational establishments, actors in theatres, opera, radio and television, flight personnel of the civil airlines, minors under 18 years of age and others (Articles 40–48 of the Ordinance on Leave). Both ordinary and longer leave are regular, as defined by the law, in the sense that, as a rule, they are due to individual workers. Apart from this, certain workers entitled to normal regular leave, i.e., leave under Article 155 of the LC, also have the right to supplementary leave of not less than five working days if they are employed in unhealthy or dangerous occupations (Article 156, item 1 of the LC) or if they work non-fixed working times (Article 156 of the LC). They are enumerated in lists approved by the Council of Ministers or Ministry of Labour (Article 137, paragraph 1, item 1 and Article 139, paragraph 4 of the LC). The actual length of the supplementary leave depends upon the degree of harm, difficulty and the specific nature of the work, and its aim is to introduce greater justice in determining the amount of leave. Those workers who are entitled to longer annual leave under Article 156, item 1 of the LC have in principle no right to supplementary leave because in determining their basic annual leave the harm caused by, or the difficulty and specific nature of the work, have already been taken into account. The most important changes in this area since the amendments to the LC in November 1992 have been that the above-indicated lengths of regular and supplementary annual leave are only minimal, i.e., longer paid annual leaves (regular and supplementary) may be stipulated by the parties in collective and individual labour contracts (Article 156a of the LC). This is one concrete example of restriction of the scope of the imperative central regulation of labour relations and of the extension of the scope of the collective and individual bargaining.

278. The worker receives remuneration for his/her annual leave (Article 177 of the LC). It is calculated on the basis of wages received for the month preceding the month in which the annual leave begins (Article 177 of the LC). The basic idea is to include all payments due for work done which are of a lasting character. Those elements of remuneration in kind which are not used during the period of leave are compensated in cash (Article 17, paragraph 2 of the Ordinance on Leave).

279. Over the past two decades there has been considerable postponement of the actual taking of the paid annual leave on the part of the workers and employees in the calendar year to which the leave pertains. Although the LC used to provide that the leave had to be taken in the respective calendar year, the leave was systematically put off until the next calendar year, and then until the year after the next, and so on. Thus, unused paid annual leave kept accumulating for years, the length thereof reaching 100 working days or even more. And, as the 1992 amendments to the operative legislation abolished the time limitation on unused leave in case of termination of the employment relationship with the worker or employee – as well as in other cases occurring because of the uncertainty of today's conditions and the rise in unemployment – the workers and employees used to receive compensation of comparatively large amounts under Article 224 of the LC. Actually, this 'sparingness' with respect to the paid annual leave was necessitated by the poverty in which a large part of the country's workers and employees live. This 'sparingness' was contrary to the very nature and social purpose of the paid annual leave as a workers' and employees' constitutional right the main purpose of which is to give them time for their annual rest and for overcoming the fatigue accumulated during the year of work, so that they became able to provide full-value performance in the next year as well.

280. The amendments to the LC of July 2010 (prom. OJ, No. 58 of 30 July 2010 and No. 18 of 1 March 2011) provided for legislative measures for the real taking of the accumulated unused paid annual leave for preceding years and ensuring the real full-length use of the leave in the calendar year it pertains to.

281. The main questions considered by the operative regulation can be divided into four groups: (1) ensuring the use of the paid annual leave in the calendar year that it is due for; (2) limiting the legal possibilities of using the paid annual leave in the subsequent calendar year; (3) using the unused paid annual leave accrued in previous years; (4) introducing time limitation on the future use of the paid annual leave acquired prior to 1 January 2010. The legal provisions concerning the first three groups (points (1), (2) and (3)) are of non-retroactive nature, while the fourth group (points (4)) regulates past relationships (*see* below paragraph 285).

282. The basic rule is: the worker or employee uses his/her paid annual leave until the end of the calendar year it is due for (Article 173, paragraph 5 of the LC). The employer is obliged to grant the paid annual leave to the worker or employee until the end of the respective calendar year, except where the use of the leave has been postponed in accordance with the procedure set forth in Article 176 (*see* below paragraph 285). In this case the worker or employee is granted at least one-half of the paid annual leave he/she is entitled to for the respective calendar year.

283. The employer may unilaterally permit the use of the paid annual leave in three cases that are exhaustively enumerated: (a) downtime of 'more than five working days'; (b) simultaneous use of the paid annual leave by all the workers and employees ('vacation leave') as provided for in a normative act (e.g., the leave of school teachers or lecturers at higher educational institutions), a collective labour contract, internal labour rules, etc.; (c) where the worker or employee has failed to request the use of the paid annual leave until its initial date specified in the schedule (Article 173, paragraph 4 of the LC).

284. Postponing the use of the paid annual leave to the calendar year following the year for which the leave is due is admissible, by way of exception, in two cases only:

(1) Because of important production reasons. These are reasons connected with the employer's production activity: large urgent orders, non-performance of activities because of unforeseeable reasons – natural calamities, emergencies and the like. The judgment upon the 'importance' of these reasons is discretionary and is exercised by the employer. It is not subject to judicial control. In this case the employer is entitled to postpone the use of up to ten working days of the paid annual leave to the next year; however, he is obliged to ensure that the other part of the leave be used in the year the leave is due for (Article 176, paragraph 1 of the LC).
(2) Because of reasonable causes on the part of the worker or employee preventing him/her from using the paid annual leave in the calendar year it should be used in. The judgment upon their presence is exercised by the employer and is discretionary. In these cases the use of the paid annual leave is postponed at the request of the worker, yet, at the discretion of the employer. The postponement is made to the subsequent year or years, depending on the duration of the effect of the said reasons. The leave postponed under this procedure is wholly – i.e., entirely – used within the calendar year in which the reason obstructing the use has ceased to exist.

   Where the leave has been postponed or has not been taken until the end of the calendar year it is due for, the employer is obliged to ensure it is being used during the next calendar year, not later than the period of six months commencing from the end of the calendar year it is due for, i.e., not later than 30 June of the calendar year following the one it is due for. However, if the employer has failed to give permission for the use of the postponed leave by the end of the first half of the next calendar year, the worker or employee has the right to determine on his/her own the period of time he/she will take it. In that case the latter is obliged to give a written notification thereof to the employer not later than fourteen days prior to the date from which he/she intends to use his/her postponed paid annual leave (Article 176, paragraphs 2 and 3 of the LC).

285. The amendments to the LC of March 2011 marked one more positive step in ensuring the use of the paid annual leave. This step was taken under the influence of Decision No. 12 of the Constitutional Court dated 11 November 2010. In connection with the July 2010 version of Article 176, paragraph 3 of the LC, which exhaustively enumerates those reasons beyond the will of the worker or employee which prevent him/her from using the paid annual leave in the respective calendar year (temporary incapacity for work, pregnancy, childbirth, adoption and raising a young child), the constitutional jurisdiction points out that 'there are other types of leave (service leave, leave for creative purposes, student leave) as well as other reasons of various nature'. Thus, the Constitutional Court connoted that the exhaustive enumeration under Article 176, paragraph 3 of the LC, July 2010 version, disregards the availability of other types of reasons laid down in law which prevent the worker or employee from using his/her paid annual leave in the respective calendar year. The National Assembly has rightly grasped the message of the Constitutional Court and has made an amendment to Article 176, paragraph 4 of the LC (March 2011 version), adding 'and to the use of another leave laid down in law' to the exhaustive enumeration. This addition is important and deserves being supported. It imparted a model pattern to the list and allowed the inclusion of other types of leave provided for in the LC, apart from those specified in Article 176, paragraph 4 of the LC, such as: service leave and leave for creative purposes (Article 161 of the LC), student leave (Articles 169–171a of the LC), parental leave under Article 167a of the LC, unpaid leave under Article 160 of the LC.

286. A significant novelty in legal regulation is the restoration of time limitation on using the paid annual leave. The limitation was provided for in the amendments to the LC of July 2010; however, its compliance with the Constitution was challenged before the Constitutional Court. Through its Decision No. 12 dated 11 November 2010, the Constitutional Court dismissed this claim – on good grounds, in my opinion – and substantiated its view with the purpose of the time limitation as a general institute of law which creates stability in the exercise of rights within certain time boundaries, and with the traditions of its application to the use of paid annual leave in the period 1952–1992, and infers: 'The stipulation of time limitation is a matter of legal policy of the state, it stimulates the exercise of rights and does not contradict Article 4, Article 16, Article 48, paras. 1 and 5 of the Constitution. The time limitation provided for in Article 176, para. 3 of the Labour Code has ex nunc effect.'[71] According to the March 2011 Law on Amendments and Supplements to the LC, the time limitation on using the leave is two years counted

71. The time limitation on using the paid annual leave was known to our legislation in the past (Art. 83, para. 1 of the LC of 1951, repealed; Art. 176, para. 4 of the LC of 1986, 1986 version, repealed 1992). The time limitation used to be three years counted from the end of the calendar year that the paid annual leave was due for.

from the end of the calendar year that the paid annual leave is due for, and where the leave was postponed under Article 176, paragraph 2 of the LC, the time limitation is two years counted from the end of the calendar year in which the reason preventing its use has ceased to exist (*see supra* paragraph 281). This limitation concerns the use of the paid annual leave for 2010 and thereafter.

The time limitation concerns both the use of the leave and its pecuniary compensation upon suspension. Upon termination of the employment relationship, a compensation for the unused paid annual leave is due by the employer to the worker or employee under Article 224, paragraph 1 of the LC for all the unused paid annual leave the right to which has not been extinguished by the time limitation provided for in Article 176a of the LC, irrespective of the reasons for which the leave was not used within the two years' time limitation laid down in law.

287. The changes in the LC of July 2010 provided for obligatory use – until 31 December 2011 – of the unused paid annual leave accrued in the period of 1 January 1993–31 December 2009 (§3e of the Transitional and Concluding Provisions of the July 2010 Law on Amendments and Supplements to the LC). The unused paid annual leave accrued in the seventeen years (since 1993) preceding the fixed deadline (31 December 2011) was deemed extinguished by limitation, with all the unfavourable consequences ensuing therefrom for the respective workers and employees.

288. This provision was challenged before the Constitutional Court. Through its Decision No. 12 dated 11 November 2010 the latter upheld the claim for declaring this provision unconstitutional, doing so on good grounds. In its motives, the Constitutional Court points out that the said provision 'violates' the general legal 'principle – the prohibition on retroactive effect of Laws' (Decision No. 8 of 1992 on constitutional case No. 4 of 1992), especially where unfavourable consequences shall ensue for the existing cases, and this contravenes the principles of the law-governed and social state and 'restricts a fundamental social right connected with Article 16 and Article 48, paragraph 1 of the Constitution' – the right to work. This means that the unused paid annual leave acquired prior to 31 December 2009 – regardless of the reasons for not using it – has been lawfully acquired and lawfully unused under the law operative as at that date – 31 December 2009, and, because of that, it is preserved for the future.[72] This leave can be used by the worker or employee even after 1 January 2010 at a time of his/her choice and with the permission of the employer. Upon termination of the employment relationship, the paid annual leave unused until 31 December 2009 is compensated for on general grounds in accordance with Article 224, paragraph 1 in relation to Article 177 and Article 178 of the LC.

289. A renunciation of the right to paid annual leave is null and void (Article 8, paragraph 4 of the LC). What is more, the laws now in force create prerequisites for the right to paid annual leave to endure irrespective of whether or not its holder

72. 'Decisions and Rulings of the Constitutional Court – 2010' Collection (Sofia: M. Drinov Publishing House, 2011), 183–184.

claims it. This is why a failure to ask for leave does not deprive a worker or employee of this right. The laws adhere firmly to the principle that the right to paid annual leave should be utilized. This is the inference drawn from Article 178 of the LC, which reads: 'It shall not be permissible to pay cash compensation in lieu of leave, save in the event of termination of employment.' The LC intends to secure the opportunity to make use of annual leave. This is the reason for excluding compensation in cash, because a temporary cash benefit might lure the worker and divert his/her attention from a needed rest. Yet, rest is in the most complete consonance with the worker's enduring personal interests. Of course, the prohibition of monetary compensation and the idea of genuine utilization of annual leave refers to cases where the employment relationship continues to exist. However, the law allows, as a matter of course, cash compensation in cases of termination of the employment relationship in order not to allow the worker to be deprived of any monetary compensation.

§4. Educational Leave

I. Definition

290. Educational leave is given to workers for the purpose of allowing them to continue their education and enhance their vocational training and qualifications. Part of its constituent elements is common to those of paid annual leave: temporary release from the performance of employment obligations, preservation of the existing employment relationship between the parties and payment of remuneration by the enterprise to the worker during the period of leave. The difference between this type of leave and paid annual leave lending it an independent character is its purpose and social role. Educational leave is aimed at enabling the worker to enhance his/her education, to improve his/her vocational training and to acquire knowledge and qualifications during the employment relationship and alongside his/her work. The social role of this type of leave, on the other hand, is to assist the training of qualified workers in all aspects of social life. Legally, this policy is reaffirmed by the Constitution. Article 53, paragraph 1 of the Constitution reads, 'Citizens are entitled to education', and paragraph 2 of the same article says that 'The state promotes education.' From the point of view of these provisions, which are of fundamental significance, paid educational leave constitutes an independent legal instrument in the state's legal repertoire, by means of which the constitutional right to education is realized and the worker's right to employment furthered. The laws establish many instances of paid educational leave; only the basic types will be noted here. For the purpose of this paper, educational leave is divided into two groups according to the nature of the education for which such leave is given.

II. Educational Leave for Study at Educational Establishments

291. Educational leave has long been known to Bulgarian labour legislation. The legal infrastructure thereof has undergone serious restrictive changes through the amendments to the LC of March 2001. Its effective regulation is contained in Articles 169–171a of the LC.

292. Educational leave is granted to workers and employees who are studying in secondary or higher schools or are improving their scientific qualification. The main purpose thereof is to help these workers and employees with combining the two main obligations they have during that time: to continue performing their obligations under the labour relationship and to study in secondary or higher schools, thus either acquiring better education – in secondary or higher schools – or acquiring scientific qualifications through working on and presenting a dissertation to receive the scientific degree of PhD or DSc. Depending on whether labour remuneration is received during educational leave, it is divided into two main types: paid and unpaid educational leave.

293. The right to paid annual leave is granted to workers and employees who study in secondary or higher schools with the consent of the employer. And this is the essential novelty introduced through the amendments to the LC of March 2001 in comparison with the preceding legislation, which allowed workers and employees to study in secondary and higher schools without the consent of the employer. The granting of this consent on the part of the employer is a matter of his/ her sovereign judgment. Most often he/she grants his/her consent when assessing that the education, speciality and qualification that the worker or employee acquires during the studies are connected with his/her work and labour obligations and the acquisition thereof will contribute to his/her efficiency in performing the work under the labour relationship.

294. Depending on the specific purpose thereof, there are several types of paid educational leave:

(1) for entrance examination at an educational establishment. This leave is granted to workers and employees who apply for schools where the admission is based on an entrance examination. This leave is, for applying for a secondary school – six working days; for a higher school or PhD studies, twelve working days;
(2) for studies in secondary and higher schools. These types of leave are:
   (a) for each school year – twenty-five working days. This leave is granted for attendance at obligatory classes, sitting for term and annual examinations and taking them;
   (b) a single time – thirty working days. This leave is granted for sitting for and taking a secondary school graduation examination or a state one, including an examination for working out and presentation of diploma work;

(c) for preparing a dissertation – for receiving the scientific degree of PhD, six months, and for the scientific degree of DSc, twelve months. This right is exercised only with the explicit consent of the employer.

295. Unpaid educational leave complements paid leave. It is granted in those cases where the worker or employee under training asks to use such leave. Such leave is granted in the following cases:

(a) for each school year – up to twenty working days. They are used for sitting for an entrance examination, a secondary-school graduation examination or a state one, including diploma work presentation in secondary schools – up to thirty working days;
(b) a single time, for sitting for and taking an entrance examination, a secondary-school graduation examination or a state one, including diploma work presentation in secondary schools – up to thirty working days;
(c) a single time – for sitting for a state examination or presentation of diploma work in higher schools or presentation of PhD or DSc dissertation – up to four months.

All unpaid educational leave is recognized as time of service.

296. The time of using paid and unpaid educational leave depends on the organization of the training process in the respective educational establishment in which the training is carried out. The worker or employee under training is obliged to notify the employer of using a forthcoming leave and of its duration at least seven days prior to the beginning of the leave, and the employer is obliged to permit him/her to use the leave for the stated time.

Chapter 4. Remuneration

§1. General Remarks

297. The system of remuneration now in effect is established in the LC (Articles 242–272) and Acts of the Council of Ministers issued for its implementation. Its legal regulation was profoundly changed with the amendments to the LC in November 1992 in order to adapt it to the needs and requirements of the transitional period from the command centrally planned to a market economy. It is based on four main ideas:

(1) remuneration of labour as a principle of labour law;
(2) the role of the state and the parties in determining salary and different types of compensation;
(3) guarantee (warranty) of payment of labour remuneration;
(4) manner of establishing the system and amount of labour remuneration.

I. The Remuneration of Labour

298. According to Article 242 of the LC, labour supplied under a labour relationship is always remunerated. This means that the employer is obliged to pay remuneration to the worker for his/her labour supplied within the framework of the labour relationship. This rule is from a public order and parties should not derogate from it. If they do, the clause on this subject will be null and void because of its interference with the law (Article 74, paragraph 1 of the LC). On the other hand, a stipulation concerning labour remuneration is a necessary element of the labour contract. Without it, the labour contract is deemed not to have been concluded (Article 66, paragraph 1 of the LC) (*see* above, Chapter 1).

II. The Role of the State and the Parties

299. In the recent past, during the period of the centrally planned economy, the state, i.e., the government, entirely regulated the system and the rate of remuneration of labour for the whole country and for all branches of the economy. This principle stemmed from the very nature of a planned economy based on state ownership. The situation now is substantially different. According to Article 244 of the LC, the Council of Ministers is empowered to establish:

(1) a national minimum monthly and daily wage;
(2) different kinds of additional labour remuneration and minimum amounts where they have not been determined by the LC;
(3) different kinds of compensation within the framework of the labour relationship and its minimum amounts where they have not been prescribed by the LC.

Therefore, the competency of the Council of Ministers is limited by the legal regulation. The government is competent to establish new kinds of additional labour remuneration and compensation and their minimum amounts. But it is not empowered to establish other components and other amounts of the additional labour remuneration and compensation which have yet to be established by the LC.

300. Apart from the above-sketched competence with which the LC has empowered the Council of Ministers, a lot of room for the participation of the parties in determining the amount of salary (basic and additional payments) and compensation within the framework of the labour relationship is allowed. Here, 'parties' mean the individual employer and his organization and the individual worker and his/her organization (trade union). Indeed they participate very actively in the determination of salary and compensation in individual and collective bargaining, and individual and collective labour contracts respectively. Their role in this area has considerably increased in the last few years because either the LC has left it to them to fix entirely the actual amounts of salary and compensation or it has established only the minimum floor whilst authorizing the parties to negotiate more favourable conditions, i.e., a higher amount than that provided for in the law or in the different Acts of the Council of Ministers (*see* below).

III. Guarantee

301. The general rule in this area is established by Article 245 of the LC. It provides that when the worker completes in good faith his/her labour duties, he/she shall be guaranteed a monthly payment of labour remuneration amounting to 60% of his/her gross labour remuneration, yet no less than the minimum salary for the country. The frequency of the (monthly) payments is expressly provided for because it is the normal and typical frequency of payment of salaries in the country. The difference between the national minimum monthly wage and the actual rate of the individual salary is still due to the worker. It is paid later on, together with the interest fixed by the National Bank for the relevant period. The social meaning of this rule is to secure at least the payment of a minimum wage to a worker necessary for his/her survival in the case of economic difficulties encountered by a number of enterprises. It has often been applied in the last few years.

IV. Determining Wage Systems

302. The wage systems in their entirety represent the main aspect of the entire legal system of regulation of labour remuneration. The system of labour remuneration is the sum total of legal rules establishing the manner in which the ratio between labour and the amount of remuneration due is to be determined. The two main systems of remuneration which are applied in Bulgaria are time work and piece work. In the case of time work, remuneration is determined on the basis of the length of working time. It is applied in cases where work cannot be measured quantitatively and where great accuracy and high-quality performance of the tasks set are needed. The piece work system may be applied where the work, its quantity and quality can be exactly measured and controlled, such as piece work, quota work. Labour quotas are established according to normal intensity of work. They are introduced and modified by the employer after consultation with the workers involved (Article 250 of the LC). The amount of remuneration actually due in these cases is in proportion to the work done and materialized in the output. The amount of remuneration is the amount determined in cash, and in the cases allowed by law, also in kind, and due to the worker for the work carried out. It includes both basic and additional remuneration. The rate of the remuneration for every piece of work produced is determined by the parties to the collective or individual labour contract. The rate determined in an individual labour contract must not be lower than that fixed in the collective agreement, if any (Article 247 of the LC).

§2. Minimum National Wage

303. The policy in the field of national minimum wages is part of the state's general policy aimed at resolving the serious problem of low-paid workers and establishing a minimum level of wages for the whole country. It is becoming of paramount importance in connection with the permanently increasing rate of inflation and the increasing impoverishment of the population. The legal regime now in effect with regard to the minimum national remuneration is characterized by four basic features:

(1) The minimum wage is introduced by the Council of Ministers after tripartite consultation with the social partners (representative trade unions and employers' organizations) within the framework of the National Council for Tripartite Co-operation created by virtue of Article 3 of the LC (*see* above). The trade unions played a very active part in its establishment.
(2) The minimum wage is national – it is obligatory for the whole country, i.e., for all workers irrespective of the branch in which they are employed, the grounds on which the employment relationship arose, its duration and so forth. It is a monthly wage, because a month is the normal period for which remuneration is established by the integrated staff payroll.
(3) The minimum wage is the basic remuneration. As a matter of course, all other remuneration established by law should be added to it: for length of service, for work under harmful conditions, and all others (*see* above). In fact, the amount of minimum monthly remuneration the worker receives is always higher than its established minimum amount.
(4) The minimum wage serves as a basis for determining the amount of unemployment benefits, social assistance payments and so on.

304. The amount of the national minimum wage is determined by taking into consideration the following criteria:

(1) The necessity to meet the basic vital requirements of the worker and his/her family members (food, clothing, rest). Taken into consideration is not only

what is necessary physiologically, but also that which is needed for a modest human existence. In determining this, the prices of all goods and services which make up this vital minimum are taken into consideration. The minimum wage is exempt from income tax (Article 1, paragraph 2 of the 6th Decree of the Council of Ministers). In this way the net amount is kept at the level fixed by the Council of Ministers. This, too, is the expression of a stepped up social protection of the minimum wage.

(2) The amount of the minimum wage is determined with due consideration for the general economic level attained in the country: the increase in the average rate of inflation, prices of foodstuffs, cost of living, etc.

(3) The minimum remuneration is established in accordance with the legally adopted daily and weekly working hours and the number of working days in the month which are established for particular activities and jobs. It is envisaged for the lowest-qualified workers, i.e., those who do not possess any special education or qualifications. In this sense, it is remuneration for simple, unskilled labour which is applied for the performance of lighter and unskilled work. From 1 January 2019, the amount of the national minimum monthly wage is BGN 560 (about USD 320) and the minimum hourly wage is BGN 3.37 (USD 2.18) in the conditions of an eight-hour normal working day and a five-day working week.

305. The legal significance of the minimum wage manifests itself in three ways:

(1) The competent state authorities are under a legal obligation to adhere to such a minimum remuneration in determining the basic salaries on the staff scale and wage rates. This means that the bodies which work them out (the Ministry of Labour and Social Policy) and the Council of Ministers, which approves them, cannot provide for a lower basic remuneration.

(2) The other basic remuneration is determined by taking the minimum wage as a basis so that in determining its rate, the difference in quality, difficulty, and the economic significance of the work is taken into account. An increase in the minimum wage also makes an increase in other rates legally and socially necessary.

(3) The existence of the minimum wage constitutes a juridical obstacle to any lower wage when the non-fulfilment of employment obligations has not been the worker's fault but is due to the lack of the necessary working conditions, to a failure to come to work because of natural calamities and the like (Article 266, paragraph 1 and Article 267, paragraph 1 of the LC). In these cases a reduction in the worker's remuneration cannot lead to it falling below the minimum wage as established on a national scale.

§3. BASIC AND ADDITIONAL REMUNERATION

I. Basic Remuneration

306. Basic remuneration is determined for the fulfilment of a given type of work under existing conditions and for a legally established unit of time within a given period – an hour, a day or a month. It is fixed by bargaining, by mutual consent of the parties in the collective agreement or in the individual labour contract on the basis of the professional qualifications of the worker, his/her knowledge, skills, dexterity, performance, kind of the work, etc. Under no circumstances must it be lower than the national minimum wage. As regard the maximum amount no limitations exist except for civil servants and the employees paid by the national budget resources. Their salaries are fixed at their maximum level by the Council of Ministers.

II. Additional Remuneration

307. Additional remuneration is that which is added to the basic remuneration. Its role is to provide remuneration for certain additional requirements as regards the quantity and quality of the work performed under the employment relationship, over and above the normal rate or to compensate and take into account the specific conditions under which the labour is performed. Different kinds of additional labour remuneration are provided for in the LC and in the Ordinance on Additional Labour Remunerations approved by the Council. There are many. Here only the basic principles of their legal regulation will be pointed out.

A. Form

308. As regards form of payment, this includes remuneration both in cash and in kind. The predominant form is cash payment which is made to the worker in a precisely determined sum (Article 269, paragraph 1 of the LC). A second form consists of payment in kind, which means the placing at the disposal of the worker of some material good for the work performed: free lodgings, heating, lighting (Article 269, paragraph 2 of the LC). When such additional remuneration is not given by the enterprise to the worker under the particular employment relationship, the worker has the right to seek, even by bringing a claim to court, its equal value in cash.[73] Under the laws now in force, additional remuneration in kind is permissible by way of exception and only in so far as is expressly provided in the Ordinance of the Council of Ministers, in a collective labour contract or in an individual contract of employment.

73. *Sbornik Sadebna Practika*, 1971, No. 198.

B. Bases

309. The most important types of additional remuneration are established by the LC. They are as follows:

(1) Additional remuneration in cases of so-called internal replacement (Article 259 of the LC). This embraces the case in which a worker accomplishes apart from his own job also the job of an absent worker. In this case he/she is entitled to additional remuneration, the amount of which is agreed between the parties.
(2) Additional remuneration in the case where a worker holds a plurality of offices which are located in different enterprises (Article 111 of the LC). In such a case he/she receives all basic remuneration from his/her basic employer and additional remuneration from the other employer(s) as agreed (Article 260 of the LC).
(3) For night work, the worker receives an additional remuneration by comparison with day work. According to the regulation now in force, the minimum amount of additional remuneration for night work is determined by the Ordinance concerning the structure and organization of remuneration, approved in 2007 by Decree No. 4 of the Council of Ministers (OJ, No. 9 of 2007, as amended). According to Article 8 of this Ordinance, for every night working hour (from 10 pm until 6 am) or part of it, an additional remuneration of not less than BGN 0.25 per every hourly wage is paid unless the parties have agreed upon a higher rate of additional remuneration (Article 261 of the LC and Article 8 of the Ordinance quoted).
(4) Concerning overtime, a worker is entitled to an additional remuneration according to the length of overtime and the day on which it is carried out – regular working day, day of weekly rest or public holiday (Article 262 of the LC) (*see* above).
(5) For work done during public holidays, irrespective of whether this is overtime or regular work a worker receives an additional remuneration as agreed between the parties. The agreed additional remuneration must not be less than a day's salary (Article 264 of the LC).
(6) Extra remuneration for long service (Article 12 of the Ordinance quoted). The amount of this additional remuneration is at least 0.6% of the basic monthly wage for every year of service after completion of the first three years of service. This type of remuneration aims to reward the greater experience acquired by the worker as a result of the continual performance of the job. That is why the amount increases with the number of years the worker has been employed on the basis of a labour relationship. On the other hand, this additional remuneration stimulates stability in manpower.

C. Payments

310. The determination and payment of additional remuneration is a subjective right of the worker; if the grounds on which the corresponding remuneration is provided are present, then this remuneration is due to the worker. This is why its payment is not within the discretionary power of the enterprise director, but is a legal obligation just like the payment of basic remuneration. And if additional remuneration is not paid, the worker can as a matter of course demand it in a claim brought before the courts. This is, undoubtedly, a legal guarantee for actual payment of all additional remuneration.

§4. The Defence of Payment of Remuneration

311. The defence of payment of remuneration is aimed at guaranteeing actual receipt by the worker. For this purpose the law has made special provisions, in labour law (Articles 269–272 of the LC), in civil law (Article 136 of the Law of Obligations and Contracts), in commercial law (Article 722, paragraph 1, item 4 of the Commercial Law) and in the Law on Civil Procedure (Article 446 of the Code of Civil Procedure), as well as in financial laws and others. From this complex array of legal provisions the aim of the legislature to make effective legal guarantees for the actual payment of remuneration can be discerned. On the other hand, this defence is aimed at the remuneration of all working people, irrespective of the grounds that gave rise to their legal labour relationship. It embraces not only basic pay but also all additional labour remuneration under the employment relationship (Article 242 in conjunction with Articles 269–272 of the LC).

312. Remuneration is paid in cash (Article 269, paragraph 1 of the LC). For workers working in Bulgaria, it is paid in Bulgarian leva, and for those abroad in the national currency of the country in which they work. Remuneration in kind is permissible only as an exception in the presence of exactly specified conditions. Remuneration is paid at the place where the work is performed (Article 270, paragraph 1 of the LC). This area of the law is clear: payment should be effected where the worker is normally employed and not at the headquarters of the enterprise where the employer's finance office is because it may be that these two places do not coincide. If the workplace is at some distance from the headquarters of the enterprise, the latter is obliged to take the necessary measures, for example, by sending a paymaster so that payment of remuneration can take place there. According to a schedule worked out by the branches concerned of the Bulgarian National Bank, payment of remuneration takes place twice a month with an interval of no less than fourteen and no more than sixteen days. Payment is effected to the worker in person, or, on his/her written request, to relatives (Article 270, paragraph 3 of the LC). The law does not determine who the latter must be. As there are no express indications, it should be assumed that relatives are not only family members but also other persons enjoying a worker's personal confidence.

313. The laws now in effect establish a system of material and procedural legal guarantees aimed at securing the actual receipt by the worker of his/her remuneration. They can be divided into three groups. First, any sums received in good faith by a worker from his/her enterprise, institution or organization as remuneration or as additions thereto are not reimbursable (Article 271, paragraph 1 of the LC). This original provision in labour law is of profound protective significance. It is aimed at making it impossible for the employer to seek the reimbursement of sums which he has already paid as remuneration, not only because the legality of the payment is presumed but also because the payment may have been consumed. As remuneration is given to meet the worker's personal current needs, it may prove that it has already been spent, as a result of which reimbursement is sure to put such a worker in a difficult material position. But there is an important condition: the payment must have been received in good faith, i.e., with the worker's subjective assurance that he/she has received his/her due. Moreover, as the Supreme Court has decided, it is of no relevance whether or not, in fact or legally, the sums were really due to the worker. It is sufficient for him to have received them with the conviction that they were due. In such cases they are not subject to reimbursement by a claim duly lodged with a court, or by deductions made from future remuneration by the enterprise.[74]

In practice, the important problem is that, in spite of the categorical provision of Article 128, subparagraph 2 of the LC, according to which the employer is obliged to pay within the term agreed the labour remuneration for the work done by the worker or employee, there are employers who fail to fulfil this basic obligation they have under the labour relation and delay by months the payment of workers' and employees' salaries, invoking economic difficulties in the realization of products. Recently there has been a rise in the number of cases in which workers and employees lodge claims with the court for the payment of their labour remuneration due, yet not paid. The court upholds these claims and sentences the employer to pay the labour remuneration along with delay interest for the period during which the labour remuneration was due but was not paid (Dec. 255-14-III C.Ch., Dec. 239-14-IV C.Ch., etc.).

314. Second, deductions from a worker's remuneration can be made only under strictly determined conditions (Article 272, paragraph 1 of the LC). In this connection, a difference between two situations has to be made. The first situation is that in which the worker consents. Deductions may be made from remuneration against claims and in compliance with the worker's will, since it is quite natural that this agreement is in consonance with his/her interest. The second situation is that in which the consent of the worker is absent. This embraces the following cases: state taxes which can be deducted from wages under special laws, deductions for damage or loss inflicted by the worker on the enterprise under Article 206 of the LC, deductions for distress imposed in the legally established order, deductions for sums

---

74. *Sbornik Postanovlenia i Talkouvatelni Reshenia na Varhovnia Sad*, Nos 117, 118 and 129; *Sbornik Sadebna Practika*, 1970, No. 111; V. Mrachkov, 'Critical Review of the 2007 Practice of the Supreme Court of Cassation on Labour Disputes', *Juridicheski Sviat* [*Juridical World*] *Journal* 2 (2008): 187; 'Critical Review of the 2010 Practice of the Supreme Court of Cassation on Labour Disputes', *Juridicheski Sviat* [*Juridical World*] *Journal* 2 (2011): 147.

owed in connection with property or goods entrusted to the worker and not returned, as well as deductions from remuneration of those sentenced to corrective labour (Article 272, paragraph 1 of the LC and Article 43 of the Penal Code).

Article 272, paragraph 1 of the LC exhaustively enumerates only those cases in which the employer makes deductions from the labour remuneration of the worker or employee without the consent of the latter. The purpose of this regulation is to guarantee the right of the worker or employee to receive the agreed labour remuneration and to rule out the possibility of any deductions being made by an unilateral order of the employer. However, apart from these cases, deductions on other grounds can be made with the consent of the worker or employee, including deductions for damages inflicted on the employer by the worker or employee, these being damages for the recovery of which the latter is liable under the rules of the unlimited property liability under Article 203, paragraph 2 of the LC. The said consent must be expressed in writing (argument under Article 270, paragraph 3 of the LC). The amounts of such deductions can exceed the limits laid down in Article 466 of the Civil Procedure Code (Dec. 364-10-III C.Ch., Dec. 487-10-III C.Ch., etc.).[75]

315. Third, the total amount of deductions from a worker's wages may not exceed the limits established in Article 446 of the Code of Civil Procedure. For workers receiving up to BGN 300 the limit is one-fifth if the worker is without children, and up to one-sixth if the worker has children; for workers receiving from BGN 300 to BGN 600, the limit is one-quarter for a worker without children and one-fifth for a worker with children; for a worker receiving from BGN 600 to BGN 1,200, one-half for a worker without children and one-third for a worker with children; for a worker receiving more than BGN 1,200, one-half for a worker without children and one-third for a worker with children. The main concern of the legislation has been to secure a current monthly income for the worker which does not substantially differ from his/her normal income. The permitted maximum extent of deductions has been established by using two criteria which have a major social significance. The limit is lower for a debtor who is with children, and higher for a debtor who is without children (Article 446, paragraphs 1(a)–(d) of the Code of Civil Procedure). The ruling of Article 446, paragraph 1 of the Code of Civil Procedure is imperative and a debtor's renunciation of the protection given by it is null and void (Article 447 of the Code of Civil Procedure). In this way, the law takes into its own hands the defence of the worker's remuneration and, taking into account the high social interest of its actual receipt by the worker, does not even allow the latter the subjective right to renounce it.[76]

316. The claim of a worker for remuneration is privileged (Article 136, item 5 of the Law on Obligations and Contracts). The first four claims indicated by Article 136 of the Law on Obligations and Contracts enjoy special privileges because they

75. V. Mrachkov, 'Critical Review of the 2010 Practice of the Supreme Court of Cassation on Labour Disputes', *Juridical World* 2 (2011): 147–148; 'Critical Review of the 2013 Practice of the Supreme Court of Cassation on Labour Disputes', *Juridicheski Sviat* [*Juridical World*] *Journal* 2 (2014): 130–131; 'Critical Review of the 2014 Practice of the Supreme Court of Cassation on Labour Disputes', *Juridicheski Sviat* [*Juridical World*] *Journal* 2 (2015): 105–107.
76. Zh. Stalev, *Bulgarsko Grajdansko Prozessoualno Pravo*, 714–717.

are priority debts but they are only paid out of certain property belonging to the debtor. They are claims for expenditure made for guaranteeing the claim and for its compulsory execution, claims of the state for taxes, claims guaranteed by pawn or mortgage, and claims which recognized the right of retention. Remuneration is the first claim payable after these specially privileged four claims and is payable out of all the property of the debtor.[77]

317. Special legal infrastructure and a strong protection of wages due as priority debts is provided in cases of bankruptcy, as well. Pursuant to Article 722, paragraph 1, item 4 of the Commercial Law, where the assets of the debtor-employer, who has been declared bankrupt, are converted into cash and distributed, the fourth place (after those secured by pawn or mortgage, those secured by retention and those for bankruptcy costs) is taken by 'debts stemming from labour legal relationships' that have arisen within a year prior to the decision of commencing bankruptcy proceedings. 'Debts stemming from labour legal relationships' is a broader term than debts due to workers and employees for their wages, these being what we are particularly interested in here. However, the latter are indisputably included in the debts stemming from labour legal relationships within meaning of Article 722, paragraph 1, item 4 of the Commercial Law. The labour remuneration debts include all labour remuneration debts – both basic remuneration and the various types of additional remuneration. Owing to the severe economic situation that the country is still in, more and more bankruptcy cases end up by declaring the debtors bankrupt and suspending the activities of the debtors-employers that have been declared bankrupt, and because of that, the protection of labour remuneration as a priority debt under Article 722, paragraph 1, item 4 of the Commercial Law has acquired great practical importance.

I. Complex Measures Against Delayed Payment of Salaries

318. Since the beginning of 2016 there has been a large-scale increase in the number of cases of delayed payment of salaries. At the end of the year the issue became widely known and acquired nation-wide dimensions because it affected hundreds of thousands of workers and employees. Hundreds of complaints were addressed to the Ombudsman of the Republic, the Minister of Labour and Social Policy, the National Assembly and other state and trade union bodies. At the beginning of 2017 a Temporary Parliamentary Commission was set up for investigating the matters related to the workers' and employees' unpaid salaries. It ended its activities in the middle of the same year. A summary of the results was made. They were alarming: 2,811 employers in the country owed a total of approximately BGN 300 million (USD 175 million) of unpaid salaries to about 261,000 workers and employees. Multiplied by four on average (a spouse and two children), this gives over 1 million Bulgarian citizens affected and brought to a state of severe financial

77. Al. Kojouharov, *Obligatzionno Pravo*, 566–569.

difficulties.[78] On the basis of these data, bills were introduced and adopted on amendments and supplements to certain important laws, providing for complex measures to strengthen the legal protection and to ensure the regular payment of salaries: the LC, the Civil Procedure Code, the Commercial Law and the Law on the Guaranteed Payments of Outstanding Claims to Employees in the Event of the Bankruptcy of Their Employer. The most important among these amendments and supplements are dealt with in the exposition hereinafter.

A. *Changes in the LC*

319. Though not numerous, the changes in the LC are the key points in the newly established complex legal regulation as they give rise to and condition the changes in the other branch laws (*see* below in this paragraph and the next ones – paragraphs 320–324). The newly created paragraph 3 in Article 228 LC lays down that the indemnities due in case of termination of an employment relationship are paid not later than the last day of the month following the month in which the employment relationship was terminated, except where some other term is agreed on in the collective labour contract. Article 228, paragraph 3 of the LC is aimed at obliging the employer to pay the employment relationship indemnities in due time after the termination of employment, instead of postponing, delaying and protracting their payment. The grounds for this limitation consists in its direct connection with the termination of the employment relationship, when the worker or employee finds himself/herself in a situation of insecurity and, therefore, the timely payment of these indemnities in their full amount is labour remuneration on which the latter relies for his/her and his/her family's subsistence. As for their grounds and purpose, these indemnities are closely connected with the labour remuneration and form part of the workers' and employees' labour income ensuring his/her and his/her family's subsistence. That is why the legal protection of their regular payment is justifiably equalled to the protection of labour remuneration. The meaning of the legal provision of Article 228, paragraph 3 of the LC is: just as the employer is obliged to pay the labour remuneration within the established terms under Article 128, item 2 of the LC, so too he is obliged to pay timely and regularly the indemnities under Chapter X, section III of the LC when the employment relationship is terminated and the subjective right to their payment arises under the new provision of Article 228, paragraph 3 of the LC. And yet, because of the dispositive nature of the provision of Article 228, paragraph 3 of the LC, another term can be agreed on in the collective labour contract, either shorter or longer than the term laid down in the said new legal provision. If this term is not observed, the employer owes on general grounds the respective compensation, along with the statutory interest. The non-observance of the term under Article 228, paragraph 3 of the LC also constitutes an administrative violation of labour legislation and, according to Article 414, paragraph 1 of the LC, the employer is punished for it with a financial penalty of BGN 1,500 up to BGN

78. These are data from the Report of the Temporary Commission for investigating unpaid salaries (incoming No. 753-74-I dated 8 Jun. 2018 of the 44th National Assembly).

15,000, and the official at fault – with a fine of BGN 1,000 up to BGN 10,000, if not subject to a more severe punishment.

Two supplements are made to Article 399 of the LC: (a) The first one is: after the words 'and activities' in paragraph 1, the expression 'including those concerning the payment of unpaid labour remuneration and indemnities following the termination of an employment relationship' is added. It is a fundamental principle in law that the parties' rights and obligations are governed by the rules that were in force at the time they arose. Therefore, the worker's or employee's unpaid labour remuneration and indemnities, the right to which arose while the employment relationship was effective or upon its termination, are naturally due even after the employment relationship is terminated, and their payment is subject to the Labour Inspectorate's control on general grounds. Owing thereto, the said supplement has the effect of a legislative reminder that the said principle applies in this case as well. Even without it, the worker or employee whose employment relationship has been terminated is entitled to seek, on general grounds, and to insist on the payment of his/her unpaid labour remuneration for the period during which the employment relationship existed and the subjective right to labour remuneration arose. The latter can also be sought through the courts unless his/her right to claim is extinguished by prescription within the three-year limitation period under Article 358, paragraph 1, item 3 of the LC. The said supplement to Article 399, paragraph 1 of the LC admits no doubt about it. (b) The second supplement is the newly created paragraph 3 of Article 399 of the LC. Its meaning is completely different. It says: 'The General Labour Inspectorate files a written application under Article 625 of the Commercial Law.' Its content is clear: the General Labour Inspectorate is authorized by law to file an application for the opening of proceedings on the trader-employer's bankruptcy. This is a new and important power of the General Labour Inspectorate, which is given the subjective public potestative procedural right to seize the court with the opening of complex, lengthy and specific court proceedings. The law has granted to the General Labour Inspectorate the procedural legitimation of seizing the court in case of opening a trader's bankruptcy proceedings under the Commercial Law. This new power expresses the legislator's trust in the Inspectorate's capacity to cope with its realization.

The new item 2 of Article 412a of the LC adds the partnerships under Articles 357–364 of the Law on Obligations and Contracts to those persons to which administrative punishments are applied. Thus, an unincorporated legal formation (unrecognized as a legal person) comprising two or more persons (partners) is given the opportunity to unite the activity thereof for achieving a common business objective. In case of violation of labour legislation, the administrative sanction of financial penalty is applied to these partnerships as well. This is the punishment which is also applied to legal entities and sole proprietors. The grounds for that is the work activity performed by the partnerships for achieving the common business objective that requires creating and abiding by the respective legal norms of carrying the objective into effect, including appropriate rules on healthy and safe working conditions under the Law of the same name for the persons working at their own expense, either in association or on their own, just as the partners in a partnership do (Article 1, paragraph 1 of the Law on Healthy and Safe Working Conditions). And these partnerships also have persons working under employment relationships that require rules on the working conditions, including the healthy and safe working conditions for work performance. For this reason, the adding of the partnerships created under the Law on Obligations and Contracts to Article 412a, item 2 of the LC, along with the legal entities and sole proprietors, is appropriate and expresses the protection of the rights of these persons through the exercise of state control over the implementation of these rights and the imposition of the administrative sanction of financial penalty on persons who are to blame for violations and omissions in the application of labour legislation, this concerning not only the rules on healthy and safe working conditions but also the provisions on respecting the other rights under the employment relationship, including the provisions on regular payment of labour remunerations and indemnities under the employment contract that are due yet unpaid, etc. As for the partnerships under the Law on Obligations and Contracts, the financial penalty under Article 412a of the LC can be imposed not only for violation of the rules of the Law on Healthy and Safe Working Conditions, but also for other violations of labour legislation. This conclusion ensues from the general provision of Article 412a of the LC, which lays down the types of administrative punishments (a fine and a financial penalty) for legal subjects under items 1 and 2, the partnerships under the Law on Obligations and Contracts forming part thereof henceforth.

B. Changes in the Civil Procedure Code

320. The considerable change here is expressed in the supplement of the so-called order for payment proceedings to Article 417 of the Civil Procedure Code. These proceedings are specially regulated court proceedings applied to those cases in which the civil legal relationship develops unlawfully. The unlawful development consists of a pecuniary receivable remaining outstanding, though it is ascertained through a document provided for in Article 417 of the Civil Procedure Code and is not challenged. The purpose of this supplement is to create judicial grounds for enforcement, ascertaining that the receivable is not challenged. For this purpose, the new item 8 is created in Article 417 of the Civil Procedure Code, according to which the applicant can request an enforcement order where, regardless of its price, the receivable is grounded on '*effective obligatory prescriptions* of bodies of the General Labour Inspectorate Executive Agency' to the employer concerning the payment of pecuniary liabilities under employment relationships delayed by more than two months. This provision is created on the occasion of and as a continuation to the new provision of Article 404, paragraph 1, item 12 of the LC, which introduces the compulsory administrative measure of issue of obligatory prescriptions to the employer and the appointment body by the control bodies of the General Labour Inspectorate in the event of establishing unpaid labour remunerations and indemnities following the termination of employment relationships. The general term 'unpaid labour remunerations and indemnities' under Article 404, paragraph 1, item 12 of the LC should be interpreted here as due, yet unpaid labour remunerations and indemnities under an employment relationship. The purpose of the order for payment proceedings, which systematically comprises the new provision grounded on documents – in this case, the obligatory prescription under Article 404, paragraph 1, item 12 of the LC – is to avoid the conduct of a long adversary conviction-type court procedure and to have an enforcement title of indisputable receivable issued, as well as an enforcement order, which does not replace the writ of execution, but constitutes judicial enforcement grounds for the issue of a writ of execution. Article 417 of the Civil Procedure Code lists the documents which constitute enforcement grounds for the issue of an immediate enforcement order. They reproduce almost literally Article 237 of the 1952 Civil Procedure Code (repealed) concerning the so-called extrajudicial enforcement grounds. The new grounds under Article 417, item 8 of the Civil Procedure Code are now included thereto – the effective obligatory prescriptions of the control body of the General Labour Inspectorate regarding the due, yet unpaid labour remunerations and indemnities under an employment relationship. An obligatory prescription that has taken effect is the document necessary under Article 417 of the Civil Procedure Code as enforcement grounds for the issue of an immediate enforcement order, which spares the conduct of an adversary procedure for establishing the due, yet unpaid labour remuneration or indemnity.

However, the way in which the new item 8 of Article 417 of the Civil Procedure Code is formulated goes beyond the occasion on which it has been created, namely as a continuation of Article 404, paragraph 1, item 12 of the LC. The new provision of item 8 of Article 417 of the Civil Procedure Code raises as grounds for the institution of order for payment proceedings those '*effective obligatory prescriptions* of bodies of the General Labour Inspectorate Executive Agency' to the employer which concern the payment of pecuniary liabilities under employment relationships delayed by more than two months. The scope of the new provision is much broader than that of the grounds for imposing the compulsory administrative measure under Article 404, paragraph 1, item 12 of the LC, providing grounds for order for payment proceedings to be instituted in cases of delayed payments under an employment relationship for the time period in which the employment relationship existed, even without the employer's bankruptcy proceedings being opened, e.g., where the employer's pecuniary liabilities delayed by more than two months ensue from an employment relationship, for example labour remunerations and indemnities, as long as there are effective obligatory prescriptions for the payment thereof issued by the bodies of the General Labour Inspectorate under Article 404, paragraph 1, item 1 of the LC.

What is specific to the order for payment proceedings based on the documents listed in Article 417 of the Civil Procedure Code, including those under Article 417, item 8, is that the creditor of the labour remuneration receivable – a worker or an employee – demands that the court should issue an enforcement order and a writ of execution at the same time regarding the claimed receivable, once an obligatory prescription thereof has been issued by the bodies of the General Labour Inspectorate. The requirement of individualization and enforceability of the receivable justifiably applies to these proceedings as well. The mere statement that a worker or an employee has the right to a receivable is not sufficient – it must be established and evidenced that the said right does exist in the specific case. For the issue of an enforcement order under Article 417 of the Civil Procedure Code, a written application of the standard form according to Annex No. 4 (Article 5 of Ordinance No.

6/year 2008) is filed, which contains a request for the issue of an immediate enforcement order and a writ of execution under Article 417 of the Civil Procedure Code, etc. The application is considered at a closed session of the court, without the parties being summoned.[79]

C. Changes in the Commercial Law

321. Their number is greater compared to the changes in the other laws. These changes concern seven Articles of the Commercial Law and relate to various parts thereof. And yet – in spite of the considerable differences in the subject of regulation they concern – if we try to understand what is common to these changes and what is the general idea they express, it can be summarized that they introduce a spirit of 'sociality', taking into account the interests of the workers and employees. Here 'social' means support, stronger legal protection for that party to the bankruptcy proceedings which is of lower socioeconomic status and is more vulnerable. In this case these are the workers and employees to whom the employer has failed to pay the labour remunerations due. This particularly concerns Part IV 'Insolvency' (Articles 606–760) and Part V 'Trader's Stabilization Proceedings' (Articles 761–797 of the Commercial Law), which comprise four of all the seven Commercial Law articles that have undergone changes. The latter were conditioned by the LC changes aimed at protecting the due yet unpaid labour remunerations and indemnities under employment relationships. The consequences thereof are regulated by the Commercial Law. Here again, what is concerned is the protection of workers against delayed payment of salaries due. Compliance must be sought as well as a combination of labour protection and realization of the constitutional principle of the employer's free business initiative under Article 19, paragraph 1 of the Constitution.

Article 15, paragraph 4 (new) of the Commercial Law introduces an additional requirement regarding the transfer of an enterprise which has its workers and employees: the transfer is only possible after the payment of the due yet unpaid labour remunerations, indemnities and social security contributions, including those of workers and employees whose employment relationships were terminated within three years prior to the transfer of the enterprise. Article 15, paragraph 5 (new) of the Commercial Law allows the parties to negotiate that the transferor's liabilities shall be assumed by the transferee. The rights of the transferor are not withdrawn; however, their exercise is accompanied by preliminary settlement of the obligations he has to the workers and employees under the employment relationships. Here again the Law has made its social choice: free disposition on the part of the transferor, yet only if the relationships are settled and the workers' and employees' security is preserved. This is a fair solution which is aimed at compliance with the constitutional principle of the social state and the protection and provision of employment, and the individual's rights, security and dignity (paragraphs 2, 3 and 5 of the Preamble and Article 16 of the Constitution).

79. V. Popova in: Zh. Stalev et al., *Bulgarsko Grajdansko Prozessoualno Pravo*, 850–913.

According to the changes of Article 129, paragraph 1 of the Commercial Law, a partner in a limited liability company can freely transfer his/her shares to another partner and to third persons as well, if the requirements regarding the admission of a new partner are fulfilled and there are no due yet unpaid labour remunerations, indemnities or obligatory social security contributions of workers and employees, including those among them whose employment relationships were terminated within three years prior to the transfer of the company share. Here again, the requirement regarding free disposition with the shares is preserved; however, new requirements are added – absence of due yet unpaid labour remunerations, indemnities or obligatory social security contributions of workers and employees, including the ones whose employment relationships were terminated within three years prior to the transfer of the company share. The principle to which these legislative solutions adhere is: free disposition with the right to private property (Article 17, paragraph 3 of the Constitution) and use of the free business initiative (Article 19, paragraph 1 of the Constitution), yet not before the settlement of the obligations to the workers and employees, which protects their legal security.

Bankruptcy proceedings have three new points introduced therein:

(a) The new item 4 of Article 608, paragraph 1 of the Commercial Law adds a new case of insolvency to the grounds for opening bankruptcy proceedings – it is the first time that the failure of the indebted trader to pay the labour remunerations due to one-third of the workers and employees as his creditors, i.e., due to a considerable part thereof and not to all of them, has been included among the said grounds. This increases the legal and social significance of the non-fulfilment of the employer's main obligation to the workers and employees under the employment relationship, taking into account the number of workers and employees whose basic employment rights have been affected. This guarantees the workers' and employees' legal security and makes it possible for the General Labour Inspectorate to open bankruptcy proceedings against the trader in case he has failed to pay the labour remunerations due to a considerable part of his workers and employees who are his creditors of their receivable consisting of the unpaid labour remunerations.

(b) The supplement to Article 625 of the Commercial Law explicitly nominates and procedurally legitimizes the General Labour Inspectorate to open bankruptcy proceedings. As it has already been pointed out (*see* above paragraph 318), this is a completely new function of the General Labour Inspectorate in comparison with its current functions of a state body which exercises administrative control over the observance of labour legislation. This new power of the General Labour Inspectorate requires considerable financial, personnel and functional strengthening of the Inspectorate on the part of the state in order for this power to be successfully exercised.

(c) According to the new version of Article 687, paragraph 1 of the Commercial Law, those receivables of the creditors – workers or employees – which ensue from an existing employment relationship or from a relationship terminated within six months prior to the entry of the court decision on the opening of bankruptcy proceedings in the Commercial Register are entered ex officio in the accepted receivables list by the trustee in bankruptcy.

According to the amended version of Article 789, paragraph 1, item 2 of the Commercial Law, the creditors whose receivables represent unpaid labour remunerations and indemnities under existing and terminated employment relationships that have arisen within six months prior to the date of the ruling on the opening of the trader's stabilization proceedings vote as a separate class on the proposed stabilization plan. This enhances the role of this class of creditors and solidifies its specific place in the bankruptcy proceedings. In the performance of the trader's stabilization plan, the participation of these creditors is engaged through their right to submit their proposals for the survival of the enterprise at this stage of the bankruptcy proceedings, from the viewpoint of their specific interests of a 'particular class' of creditors. The change in the Commercial Law provides them with the opportunity to give their contribution to rescuing the enterprise from bankruptcy.

D. *Changes in the Law on the Guaranteed Payments of Outstanding Claims to Employees in the Event of the Bankruptcy of Their Employer*

322. The changes in the Law on the Guaranteed Payments of Outstanding Claims to Employees in the Event of the Bankruptcy of Their Employer (LGPOCEEBTE) concern three provisions (Article 4, paragraph 1, Article 20 and Article 25, paragraph 1) and the repeal of Article 23 of the said Law.

Article 4, paragraph 1 of the LGPOCEEBTE defines the scope of workers and employees who have the right to guaranteed receivables in the event of bankruptcy of the employer. These are all the workers and employees who are or have been in employment relationships with the employer against whom bankruptcy proceedings are open in accordance with the procedure of the Commercial Law, or bank bankruptcy proceedings in accordance with the special Law on Bank Bankruptcy; or in cases of insurer's bankruptcy (Articles 612–622 of the Insurance Code), or bankruptcy of additional social security companies and funds (Articles 317–343 of the Social Security Code). It is of no importance to the workers and employees what the term of the employment relationship is (a fixed-term employment contract or an open-ended one), or what the length and type of their working time is – regular, reduced, part-time, extended, floating or summarized, etc.

'The workers and employees under an employment relationship' who have the right to guaranteed payments under Article 4, paragraph 1 of the LGPOCEEBTE consist of two categories: (a) workers and employees working under an employment relationship as at the time (date) of entry in the Commercial Register of the court decision on the opening of bankruptcy proceedings under Article 6 of the LGPOCEEBTE; and (b) workers and employees who were in an employment relationship with the employer within three years prior to the date of entry in the Commercial Register of the court decision on the opening of bankruptcy proceedings. Here, the three years' period provided for aims at covering all the employment relationship receivables that are outstanding and due, and are not extinguished by prescription (argument under Article 358, paragraph 1, item 3 of the LC).

The workers' and employees' guaranteed payments under Article 4, paragraph 1 of the LGPOCEEBTE amount to the last six accrued yet unpaid monthly labour remunerations and financial compensations in the recent thirty-six months (three years) preceding the month in which the bankruptcy court decision was entered (Article 22 of the LGPOCEEBTE).

The yearly Law on the Budget of the Social Security Tax lays down the maximum monthly amount of the workers' and employees' receivables, which cannot be lower than two and a half minimum monthly salaries established in the country as at the date of entry of the decision in the Commercial Register (Article 22, paragraph 2 of the LGPOCEEBTE). In 2020, when the country's minimum salary is BGN 610 (USD 348), the said amount is BGN 2,600 (USD 1,485) + ½ of BGN 610, i.e., BGN 305, or a total of 2,600 + BGN 305 = BGN 2,905, or about USD 1,660. The amount of the guaranteed receivables is determined as at the date of entry of the bankruptcy court decision under Article 6 of the LGPOCEEBTE.

Article 22, paragraph 3 of the LGPOCEEBTE regulates those receivables of the workers and employees under Article 4, paragraph 1 of the said Law whose relationships were terminated in the recent three years (thirty-six months) prior to the date of entry in the Commercial Register of the decision under Article 6 which concern the accrued yet unpaid financial compensations at the employer's account that continue being due by virtue of a regulation or a collective labour contract. These receivables cannot exceed the four-fold amount of the minimum monthly salary established in the country as at the date of termination of the employment relationship. Thus, for instance, if the compensation is paid in July 2018, and the employment relationship was terminated in June 2016, when the minimum salary was BGN 420, the compensation due will be BGN 1,680 (420 * 4), etc.

Article 23 of the LGPOCEEBTE, which used to regulate the workers' and employees' guaranteed receivables for accrued yet unpaid labour remunerations and compensations in the event of employer's bankruptcy, was repealed as these matters are regulated in the amended version of Article 22 (*see* above paragraph 319). The term in Article 23 of the LGPOCEEBTE is extended from two to three months. This term is the time period during which the worker or employee is entitled to file an application-declaration of a specific form to the territorial department of the National Social Security Institute by the seat of the employer for being granted the guaranteed receivable. The time period starts running on the date of entry in the Commercial Register of the court decision on the opening of bankruptcy proceedings under Article 6, items 1 to 3 of the LGPOCEEBTE. The extension of the term is a favourable legislative solution. It gives a longer period of time during which the workers and employees can file their applications-declarations for being granted the guaranteed receivables under Article 22 of the same Law, which used to provide for granting of guaranteed receivables within two months following the date of entry of the decision under Article 6 of the LGPOCEEBTE in the territorial department of the National Social Security Institute. The two-month term turned out to be too short for checking and processing the applications filed, especially in cases of communication with another state; therefore, it was extended to three months.

323. The entry into force of the complex legislative measures on 1 January 2018, and that of the measures related to the amendments to the LC and the Commercial Law regarding the participation of the bodies of the General Labour Inspectorate in declaring the employer bankrupt in cases of systematic delay in the payment of workers' and employees' salaries on 31 March 2018 (*see* above No. 319 and 321) was accompanied by certain hesitations and disputes in the course of discussing them, as the General Labour Inspectorate's new competence to participate in such proceedings is not typical of its usual administrative functions. On the whole, the results of the almost two years' application of these measures are positive. The General Labour Inspectorate has been successfully coping with the performance of its new procedural function.

324. From 31 March 2018 until 31 December 2018 the General Labour Inspectorate filed forty-four statements of claim for the opening of bankruptcy proceedings against different employers. The total number of affected workers in these enterprises is 1,583. Out of all the instituted proceedings, in 2018 the first instance rendered decisions on twenty-five cases – eighteen companies were declared bankrupt, five proceedings remained pending and only two claims were disallowed as the employers paid in full the labour remunerations due. On the whole, the new regulation of these matters has had its disciplinary effect and seventy employers have chosen to pay in the meantime the salaries to their personnel instead of having the Labour Inspectorate seek an opening of bankruptcy proceedings. It is also important to point out that in 2017 the amount of labour remunerations the payment of which was delayed was BGN 27.3 million, out of which BGN 19.3 million were paid.[80]

The results for 2019 are also encouraging. From 1 January until 30 November 2019 there were nineteen new applications filed with the courts under Article 625, paragraph 1 of the Commercial Law against delinquent employers, who have delayed the payment of labour remunerations due to their workers. The total number of workers and employees affected by the non-payment of labour remunerations is 704. The bankruptcy proceedings against their employers have already been opened. The number of workers in the separate enterprises of delayed payment of labour remuneration is different and varies between 5 and 158. The 19 commercial cases that have been initiated are currently at different procedural stages of consideration before the competent courts: the consideration of six of them is completed, the claims are upheld and the delinquent employers are declared bankrupt; three of the cases have their claims disallowed as ungrounded and the decisions on them are appealed before a higher-instance court, and the other ten cases are in a process of consideration and the court proceedings have not finished yet.[81]

80. These are data from the report on the activity of the General Labour Inspectorate Executive Agency for the year 2018, Ministry of Labour and Social Policy (Sofia, 2018), 17.
81. These are data from the General Labour Inspectorate Executive Agency.

Chapter 5. Safety and Health

§1. Approach to the Problems of Healthy and Safe Working Conditions

325. National legislation on labour hygiene and safety is an important instrument for improving conditions and protecting the working environment. The basis for such legislation is found in the Constitution, of which Article 48, paragraph 5 provides, among other basic rights of citizens, the 'right to healthy and safe working conditions'. In raising the juridical rank of this right to such a high level, the great significance which the state attaches to these questions in its policy is shown. The legal rules now in force on healthy and safe working conditions are contained in the LC (Articles 275–290), the Law on Healthy and Safe Working Conditions of 1997 (OJ, No. 124 of 1997), effective since 1 January 1998, and in a number of other legal acts issued by the government or its organs. These establish requirements regarding labour hygiene, the working environment, and rules for rendering safe the objects and instruments with which a worker comes into contact in performing his/her work. They can be divided into two groups:

(1) general and branch rules on healthy and safe working conditions;
(2) special rules on healthy and safe working conditions for certain categories of workers, especially young people, women and persons with reduced capacity for work.

The first group will be examined in the following paragraph, and the second in the chapter devoted to young people and women (*see* below, Chapter 8).

326. The rules on labour hygiene and safety are applied to all workers, including members of producers' cooperatives. They are applied wherever socially useful work is done, regardless of the kind of employment relationship on the basis of which this has arisen. This wide field of application reveals the endeavour of the legislator to improve the working conditions of all working people. The approach to the problems of healthy and safe working conditions is characterized by its practical goals. The state does not limit itself to the establishment of legal rules alone, however important and necessary they may be, but undertakes measures aimed at improving the production environment in enterprises and organizations. In the present difficult economic situation which the country encounters, the practical measures for improvement of healthy working conditions are laid down by the collective agreements (*see* below, Part II, Chapter 4).

327. It is through the Law on Healthy and Safe Working Conditions, 1997, that new advisory bodies are established for participation in managing the activities related to healthy and safe working conditions. National, branch and municipal councils on working conditions are provided for. They are set up on a tripartite basis. These councils are in charge of the development of projects for the improvement of working conditions, their implementation and the training of the workers and employees in the rules of healthy and safe work. The setting up of working conditions committees and groups in the enterprises is provided for, the latter consisting of two to ten members and based on the principles of parity, i.e., having an equal number of representatives of the employer and the workers and employees elected at their general meeting. They take part in the development of programmes for the improvement of the working conditions in the enterprises and are in charge of their implementation in the workplaces, perform checks concerning their observance, etc. (Articles 27–31, 39–43 of the law cited).

§2. General and Branch Rules for Healthy and Safe Working Conditions

328. The classification of the rules on healthy and safe working conditions into general and branch rules is made on the basis of the field to which they apply. The rules governing those working conditions which are applicable in all branches of the national economy and which regulate the working conditions for all, or at least many types of production, are general rules. They are contained in the LC and in Acts approved by the Council of Ministers or its organs. They aim at rendering the working environment more hygienic and safe and the labour of a worker healthier. The provisions affect all elements of the labour process – material and human – the tools and implements of labour, facilities (heating, lighting, etc.) and the person of the worker. And, they embrace both the preparation and the carrying out of the working process itself.

I. General Rules

A. *Preliminary Requirements for Healthy and Safe Working Conditions and Fire Precautions*

329. While drafting the plans for the building or reconstruction of an enterprise and for changes in the manufacturing and technological processes, it is absolutely necessary to take into consideration the requirements established for healthy and safe working conditions and fire prevention (Article 5 of the Law on Healthy and Safe Working Conditions, 1997). A special chapter in these plans has to be devoted to healthy and safe working conditions. What is more, after the construction or reconstruction of an enterprise, it cannot be opened and put into operation without the permission of the special state commission which, with the participation of the specialized control organs, evaluates the observance of the rules on safe working conditions (Article 6 of the Law on Healthy and Safe Working Conditions). This 'second' preliminary control is aimed at securing that the said requirements, embodied in the construction or reconstruction plans, have actually been taken into account. It is only then that the enterprise or its corresponding subdivision can begin to function. All the machines, tools, implements of labour produced in the country must correspond to the requirements established for healthy and safe working conditions. What is more, these requirements are also obligatory for the tools, implements, technologies and so on produced or applied abroad. They are imported only if they satisfy the national requirements of healthy and safe working conditions (Article 8, paragraph 3 of the Law on Healthy and Safe Working Conditions). This rule corresponds to the international labour standards in this area established by the ILO Convention No. 119, 1963 which has not been ratified by Bulgaria.

B. Labour Safety and Fire Prevention

330. There are special requirements for labour safety regarding fire protection measures during the course of the working process. These are aimed at minimizing the danger of an external traumatic effect of the machines and objects of labour on the physical state of the worker, and at creating conditions for his/her security and safety during contact with them. For this purpose, the machines and equipment which the worker uses must be supplied with protective devices to eliminate all risks (Article 275 of the LC; Ordinance No. 7 dated 23 September 1999 on the minimum requirements for healthy and safe working conditions). The actual precautionary measures for making the machines safe are already determined during the process of their design and production (Articles 8–21 of the Ordinance cited). The fire department establishes specific rules for the prevention of fires, methods and means for combating fires and so forth (Article 276 of the LC).

C. Healthy Conditions

331. The requirements for healthy conditions are aimed at preventing noxious substances affecting the workers and disturbing and hindering their normal functioning. They provide norms to which the environment must correspond with respect to lighting, noise, vibrations, the velocity of air, temperature, moisture, concentration of noxious substances in the air and the like. Corresponding sanitary regulations for this purpose were approved by the Ministry of Public Health in 1997. They also establish certain requirements for securing the worker's personal hygiene: sufficient water for drinking and washing, soap, washrooms, baths, sanitary conveniences, rooms for personal hygiene, and so forth (Articles 276 and 282 of the LC). There are many general rules on labour hygiene and safety in connection with the person of the worker and the basic ones are mentioned below.

1. Preliminary and Periodic Medical Examinations

332. Article 287 of the LC and Ordinance No. 3 (1987) provide for obligatory medical examinations before the entering into employment of all workers who are admitted to work for the first time, of those who have interrupted their work for more than three months and of persons who have reached the age of 18, as well as of workers who are to occupy strenuous or dangerous jobs or jobs damaging to health. The list of these occupations is established in Supplement No. 2 to Ordinance No. 2. Admission to employment is allowed only when the health state of the worker is good and the work and the specific conditions under which such work will be performed are not likely to injure his or her health. Again, for the purpose of following closely the way in which working conditions may reflect on the health of the worker, periodical medical examinations, with the necessary X-ray and laboratory tests, are envisaged, of employees working in dangerous or unhealthy working conditions (Article 12, paragraph 1 of Ordinance No. 3). The frequency of these examinations ranges between three months and one year, according to the type, nature and extent of the danger or strain of the job or the conditions under which work is carried out. Preliminary and periodical medical examinations and the tests connected with them are free, in accordance with the right to free medical care to which all citizens are entitled (Article 287, paragraph 2 of the LC).

2. Special Qualifications

333. In modern industry there are many machines and equipment, electrical and other similar installations which are both complicated to operate and constitute a source of great danger to the life and health of workers. This is why work with such equipment must be entrusted to persons with technical training who know how to operate them, i.e., how to use them safely in a way which will not injure their lives or the lives and health of those around them. Precisely for this reason, Article 281 paragraphs 3 and 4 of the LC expressly provides that complicated machines which are dangerous to human life, such as steam engines, internal combustion engines, electrical installations, apparatus for oxyacetylene or electric welding, large and fast-moving presses, shall be operated by persons having the necessary qualifications, in other words, persons whose special knowledge, training, skill and dexterity are officially attested by a certificate issued by a competent body and in the established order, i.e., by an educational establishment, upon the completion of courses and examinations passed before a special commission, etc. and determined by special laws or regulations approved by the Council of Ministers.

3. Instructions for Workers on Labour Hygiene and Safety and Fire Prevention

334. All newly engaged workers are given detailed instructive induction to become familiar with the rules on labour hygiene and safety and fire precautions at the place where they are to work (Article 281, paragraphs 1 and 4 of the LC). Where the workplace is very dangerous, this induction may last from one to five days depending on the character of the work and the kind and degree of dangers it holds (Article 281, paragraph 3 of the LC; Articles 4–10 of the Ordinance cited). If the nature of the work is such that the dangers it conceals are particularly great, special courses of varying duration may also be held to teach the workers labour hygiene and safety, with or without leave from production (Articles 24–27 of the Ordinance cited). And, finally, when working under specific dangers, workers are given day-to-day instruction before they begin work (Article 23 of the Ordinance cited). Preliminary instruction is also given for every change in working conditions, as well as when the worker is entrusted with incidental work.[82] The organizing and giving of instruction is an obligation on the employer and his managerial staff (Article 127, item 4 of the LC). The purpose of these requirements is to get workers acquainted with labour hygiene and safety rules as well as fire precaution measures, to ensure they learn them well and learn to observe them very strictly. To a great extent the real level of protection of the workers' life, health and capacity for work depends on this.

4. Personal Protective Measures

335. Work consisting of minding or using machinery, apparatus, liquids, gases, molten metals, red-hot objects, etc. is connected with great danger to the life and health of the worker, his/her physical integrity and the normal functioning of his/her anatomical organs. To protect him/her against the danger concealed in these tools and objects, Article 284 of the LC provides that workers shall be supplied with and use special personal protective equipment, protecting their body and securing the safety of their work. Such equipment includes special working clothes, masks, gauntlets, goggles depending on the nature of the work. The enterprise is obliged to place such protective equipment at the disposal of the worker, and the worker is obliged to use them while working for the purposes for which they are intended.

5. Antidotes

336. According to Article 285 of the LC, it is obligatory to provide antidotes for workers employed directly in forms of production which may produce a noxious chemical, have a toxic effect on their health or occupational poisoning. These types of jobs involved are enumerated in a special list attached to the Ordinance cited. The list also indicates the kind and quantities of antidotes which are to be given to workers: fresh milk or yoghurt, sugar, boiled eggs, carbonated water, etc., depending on the type of poisoning. The worker's consumption of such food is compulsory during working hours. The law intends such food to be used in order to neutralize the noxious impact on the environment in which the worker is employed, and in this way to protect his/her health.

6. Refusal of the Worker to Pursue the Accomplishment of the Entrusted Job

337. Refusal to pursue the accomplishment of the entrusted job is a new right and was introduced for the first time by Article 283 of the LC within the framework

82. *Sbornik Sadebna Practika*, 1973, No. 49.

of the legal regulation on healthy and safe working condition. The main element in this right is the possibility which the worker enjoys to refuse or unilaterally suspend work because of safety and the existing unfavourable working conditions until they are improved. By its legal nature it is a subjective reformatory right (*Gestaltungsrecht*). By its social destination, it is a means of reaction of the worker against unsatisfactory working conditions created by the employer and aimed at forcing the employer to improve them and to eliminate the shortcomings in safety and working conditions. The prerequisites for exercising this right as they are established by the law are the following:

(1) the appearance of a serious and immediate danger to the life or the health of the worker. The danger is 'serious' when it may really cause severe and unfavourable consequences on the worker's life and health. It is 'immediate' when it is near and imminent and possesses a high degree of probability;
(2) the appearance of such a danger and the high probability of its occurrence must be connected with shortcomings and breakdowns of existing healthy and safe conditions and not with other factors or causes, such as failure on the part of the worker to use personal protective measures (working clothes, masks, gauntlets and the like depending on the nature of the work);
(3) the danger must seriously and immediately threaten the life and health of the worker as his/her most precious values and not his other goods and rights (e.g., property, other rights arising from the employment relationship – labour remuneration, working time, weekly rest, leave, etc.).

338. The law establishes also the procedure for exercising the envisaged right. The worker refusing to work or suspending his/her work has to inform his/her immediate leader. The law does not prescribe any special form for delivering this information. It could be either orally or in writing. But this information must be given very shortly after refusal or suspension of the work by the worker. The meaning of this information provided by the worker is not to demand permission from the immediate leader or the employer to suspend work, but only to let the employer know the decision to stop accomplishment of his/her job under the existing working conditions on the one hand, and, on the other, to ask the employer to take the necessary measures to improve working conditions and in doing so to eliminate the serious and immediate danger to the life and health of the worker. Suspension of the work by the employee lasts while the immediate and serious danger to his/her life and health exists. He/she takes up his/her work again after the working conditions have been improved and the serious and immediate danger to his or her life and health has been eliminated. In this case, only the employer or the immediate leader may order the worker to resume his/her work. During the period of refusal or suspension the employer has to pay the worker his/her salary. The relevant period is also deemed as a period of employment.

339. Articles 21–22 of the Law on Healthy and Safe Working Conditions, 1997, provide for new measures for protecting the health and life of the workers and employees in those cases where they are not aware of an imminent danger that is threatening them. These articles assign specific obligations to the employer. In these cases the latter is obliged, as soon as possible, to inform the endangered workers and employees about the imminent danger or the probability of its occurrence, and also about the measures that are being taken for their protection. These measures may be: (a) suspension of the workers' and employees' work; (b) their evacuation; (c) prohibition on working until the danger to their life and health is removed; (d) providing an opportunity for the workers and employees to take actions on their own in accordance with their knowledge and the available technical means in order to avert the consequences of the impending danger.

7. Labour Medicine Services

340. The obligation of the employer to establish labour medicine services in the enterprise is also a new one (Article 25 of the Law on Healthy and Safe Working Conditions). These are preventive functions units for consulting and supporting the employers and the working conditions committees and groups in planning and performing the obligations regarding the provision of healthy and safe working conditions for the workers and employees and for promotion of their health and capacity for work.

II. Branch Rules

341. Branch rules are established for workers employed in specific branches of the economy. They are aimed at specific peculiarities and noxiousness of the working process in the given branch and in this they supplement the general rules. They are approved by the head of the department governing the respective branch or activity. Under the laws now in force, such rules have been established, for instance, for shipping and port activities, for building and scaffolding work, for the coal mines, for road transport, for railway transport and in other sectors. Branch rules establish specific requirements governing the hygiene of the working environment, the safety and protection against fire of the tools and objects of labour which the worker uses as well as special protective devices, requirements on qualifications and similar matters.

Chapter 6. Suspension of the Individual Employment Relationship

§1. Definition

342. The parties to an employment relationship usually establish it for the purpose of actually fulfilling their duties and exercising their rights under it. And, in fact, this is its normal course. Alongside this, however, there are also cases in which, although the employment relationship continues to exist, its content becomes poorer because the worker does not actually place his/her labour at the disposal of the enterprise for the fulfilment of the functions entrusted to him/her. These situations constitute exceptions, expressly provided for in law. They are always temporary and, as a rule, short-lived. Upon their elimination, the employment relationship becomes effective again. These situations comprise various cases differing from each other in the reasons that led the worker to non-fulfilment of the work agreed upon. These reasons may be due to the enterprise (idle time as a result of machines being out of order, lack of raw materials, power failure, etc.), to the worker (temporary incapacity to work, leave, strike, etc.), or to causes and circumstances outside the employment relationship (natural calamities). In each case legislation intervenes to regulate its modalities and to provide whether or not, how much, and what kind of payment is due and by whom: labour remuneration by the enterprise, social security compensation and the like. All these instances are grouped here under the common term ‘suspension of the employment relationship’. This term is not used in Bulgarian law. It has been introduced for the purpose of this study as a term in jurisprudence and doctrine under which the different types of cases are grouped, the more important ones of which will be examined below.

§2. Idle Time

343. Idle time is a situation in which the worker is present at the workplace but in fact does not do the work entrusted to him/her. This means that he/she remains idle at the workplace, inactive. The laws now in force distinguish between two kinds of idle time depending upon the position of the worker. The first kind is that caused through the fault of the worker (Article 267, paragraph 2 of the LC). In this case, although conditions are adequate, the worker does not work or, if there are problems with the conditions, the worker does not manifest the normal care and initiative which he/she is expected to manifest to overcome them. For such idle time, no remuneration is paid to the worker (Article 267, paragraph 2 of the LC). In such cases where working time has not been utilized because of a breach of discipline, the worker may, as a matter of course, be charged with the corresponding disciplinary responsibility (*see* above).

The second kind of idle time is that which is not the result of the worker’s fault, but is due to reasons and circumstances beyond his/her control and which he/she could not foresee or avert. It may be the fault of the enterprise (e.g., failure to supply raw materials, machines, or malfunctioning of machines), or it may be due to the actions of third parties with whom the enterprise maintains contractual relations. Finally, idle time may be due to natural calamities, such as storms, floods, blizzards, fires. These are all of an exceptional nature, they are unforeseeable and unpreventable by the normal efforts of a worker. They are, in fact, the so-called insurmountable circumstances (force majeure) in civil law. They prevent the worker from appearing at the place of work. And precisely for this reason, temporarily, i.e., so long as the circumstances exist, the worker does not perform his/her employment duties and the employment relationship is suspended. In these cases, it is sufficient that the above-mentioned circumstances are not due to the guilty conduct of the worker. With this kind of idle time, the worker is paid by the enterprise the whole remuneration (Article 267, paragraph 1 of the LC). In such cases, the employer can transfer the worker to another type of work in the same or another enterprise until the stoppage ends (*see* above). If the idle time continues for more than fifteen working days, the employer can terminate the contract of employment by giving the necessary period of notice according to Article 328, paragraph 1, item 4 of the LC (*see* above).

§3. Temporary Incapacity for Work

344. The most frequent reason for suspension of the individual employment relationship is a worker's temporary incapacity for work. What all these cases have in common is that the health of the worker has deteriorated or changed so that he/she cannot or is prevented from being able to place his/her labour at the disposal of the enterprise. That is why he/she is absent from work and is on lawful leave. His/her condition is established by attending a doctor and by the Consultative Commission of Physicians and is attested by a certified copy of the patient's record. During the whole period, from the first day of his/her temporary incapacity until recovery or certification of permanent incapacity, he/she is entitled to compensation in cash from the social insurance scheme (Articles 40–41 of the SIC, 1999). If disablement is established, the worker is granted a pension (Article 79 of the SIC). Cases of temporary incapacity for work are provided for in the insurance laws (Article 2 of the same Code). There are twelve such cases which, for the purpose of this study, may be divided into three groups.

I. Impairment of Health

345. The first group comprises cases in which the temporary incapacity is due to impairment of the worker's health. This includes general disease, accident at work, occupational disease and sanatorium and resort treatment prescribed by a doctor to restore the worker's health (Articles 40–67 of the Code). During the period of temporary incapacity for work due to general disease or to the worker's sanatorium and resort treatment, compensation in cash is paid to the worker amounting to 80% to 90% of his/her normal remuneration depending upon the length of uninterrupted service. In cases of an accident at work or occupational disease, compensation amounts to 90% of the worker's remuneration regardless of the length of service.

II. Pregnancy and Child Care

346. The second group covers two risks: pregnancy and confinement and the mother's care for her child. A working mother is entitled to various kinds of leave, each of a precisely determined length. For pregnancy and confinement, she is entitled to maternity leave of 410 calendar days. As a rule, 45 days are to be taken before the birth of the child and the remainder after confinement. A female worker or employee who adopts a child is also entitled to such leave, regardless of the type of adoption – a full or a partial one. The length of her leave is equal to the difference between the adopted child's age as at the day it is handed over for adoption, and the length of the childbirth leave due, which currently is until the adopted child attains the age of 1 (Article 163, paragraph 6 of the LC). During this leave, the working mother receives compensation from the social insurance system amounting to 90% of her normal remuneration (Article 163 of the LC and Article 49 of the SIC).

The legal regulation contained in the December 2008 amendments to the LC has provided for 'paternity leave' for the first time (Article 163, paragraph 7 of the LC). A father who is married to the mother (his spouse) or lives in the same household with her has the subjective right to this leave. When a child is born, the father is entitled to a fifteen-day leave counted from the day the child is released from the hospital institution. The purpose of this leave is to allow the father to be of assistance in raising the child and to share with the mother the care for the child in the first days of its life in the new world of family environment.

347. Upon request, a working mother is entitled to two kinds of leave for the care of her infant.

The first is paid and is granted after maternity leave; it lasts up to the age of two years for a first, second and a third child, and six months for a fourth and every successive child (Article 164, paragraph 1 of the LC). During this time, she receives compensation from the social insurance system amounting to the national minimum wage. In December 2013, the amendments to the LC (the new Article 164b) and to the SIC (the new Article 53a), effective since 1 January 2014, and the amendments to the LC of April 2018 (prom. OJ, No. 30 of 2018) created a new type of paid leave for the adoption of a child aged 2–5 (prom. OJ, No. 104 of 2013). According to Article 164b of the LC, a female worker or employee who adopts a child aged 2–5 under the conditions of full adoption has the right to a leave of 365 days following the day of the child's handover for adoption, yet not later than the time the child attains five years of age. After the expiry of six months following the handover of the child for adoption, yet not later than the time the adopted child attains five years of age, and on condition that the adoptive mother has given her consent thereto, the leave may as well be used by the adoptive father. Full adoption, which gives rise to the right to the leave under Article 164b of the LC, can be performed by a single female worker or employee, or a single male worker or employee, or by a female worker or employee and a male worker or employee (a woman and a man) who are spouses, i.e., who have contracted a civil marriage, or by a man and a woman – a female worker or employee and a male worker or employee – who are co-habitants, i.e., who have not contracted a civil marriage. Where such leave is requested by the adoptive mother or the adoptive father, the employer is obliged to permit it. During this leave, the female worker or employee – adoptive mother (the male worker or employee – adoptive father) having twelve months of insurance length of service has the right to a benefit in the amount of 90% of her (his) average daily gross labour remuneration or of her (his) average daily insurance income on the basis of which the social security contributions were made during the eighteen months' period preceding the month of the child's handover to the adoptive mother or father (Article 53a of the SIC).

The second type of leave is the so-called unpaid leave for raising a child under eight years of age provided for in Article 167a of the LC since 2004 (prom. OJ, No. 52 of 2004). It is granted to both parents (adoptive parents). If the parents work under an employment relationship and the child has not been placed in an establishment of full state support, after using the leave under Articles 163 and 164 LC (*see* above) each of the parents has the right to use unpaid leave of up to six months for raising the child until it attains the age of eight years. Where both parents have died before the child attains two years of age, and the parents have not used the leave under Article 167a, paragraph 1, the guardian shall be entitled to such leave amounting to twelve months, and where the parents have used only a part of the leave, the guardian shall have the right to use the remainder thereof, i.e., the unused part of the leave. With the consent of the guardian, this leave may be used by one of the parents of the child's mother or father. During this time, the enterprise keeps open the job of the absent working mother who assumes it upon her return. This leave is recognized as a period of service.

III. Preventive Measures

348. The third group embraces circumstances connected with preventive measures for the worker's health and his/her family. Absence from work in these cases is necessary in order to protect health or to render help to family members who are ill. These cases are treated by law as a type of temporary incapacity for work. They are quarantine, urgent medical examination or tests, removal from work of a worker suffering from a contagious disease, a carrier or one who has been in contact with a person suffering from a contagious disease, looking after a sick or quarantined family member, the urgent accompanying of a sick family member to a medical establishment in another town or for treatment abroad. In all cases, the length of leave depends on the individual case. During such leave, the worker is entitled to compensation as in cases of temporary incapacity for work due to general disease, i.e., 80% of his/her remuneration.

§4. Leave

349. The employment relationship is suspended during the time the worker is on annual paid educational leave, the regulation and payment of which have already been examined above (Chapter 3, §3 and §4).

350. The employment relationship is also suspended during a so-called short leave given to a worker, as established in Articles 157 and 158 of the LC. This is the case where the worker is summoned to court or by another authority to act as a party, a witness, or an expert, where absence is required because of the death of a close relative, where a summons for conscription or military service is issued, or the worker marries, etc. Such cases of leave are paid, with the exception of a summons to court or by another authority to act as a party, a witness or an expert. The absent worker receives remuneration from the enterprise.

351. A special situation in which the employment relationship is suspended is the case of unpaid leave under Article 160, paragraph 1 of the LC. There are two kinds of such leave. First, there is leave not exceeding thirty working days in any calendar year. This may be granted by the enterprise at the request of the worker. The enterprise has discretionary power to allow it or not by taking into consideration the reasons for which the worker requests it and the needs of the unit in which he/she works, the possibility of a replacement and the like. When such leave is granted, it is acknowledged as a period of service. Second, leave of more than thirty days, the maximum of which has not been fixed by law, may be granted. This is provided in accordance with the evaluation of the enterprise after considering the view of the trade union committee, only in exceptional cases where important personal considerations of the worker make it necessary, i.e., family reasons, prolonged absence from the country, etc. This leave is recognized as a period of service.

352. The period during which a worker has been called up for military training in the armed forces is considered as service leave and the employment relationship is suspended. During this period the enterprise pays the worker his remuneration (Article 158 of the LC). Should the training mobilization last for fifteen days or more, the employee shall be entitled to two calendar days of paid leave before departure and two more days following his return, which shall be included in the paid annual leave. The employee's remuneration for the time of training mobilization and the leave shall be at the account of the Ministry of Defence.

353. Article 161, paragraph 1 of the LC provides for leave for 'service and for creative purposes'. During such leave, the employment relationship is also suspended. Such leave is allowed to workers to accomplish important social tasks or tasks with a creative character and purpose, such as participation in some official service manifestation, carrying out of trade union activities, carrying out scientific and research studies. The duration, payment, conditions and procedure for granting such a leave are either set forth in the collective labour contract or agreed upon by the worker or employee and the employer.

354. A special kind of service leave is provided for trade union activists and officials in two cases:

(1) for carrying out trade union tasks by unpaid activists, such as participation in collective bargaining, negotiations for settlement of collective labour disputes (Article 159 of the LC);

(2) for fulfilling trade union functions by a paid trade union official (Article 161, paragraph 2 of the LC).

This type of leave is only mentioned here for the sake of completeness but will be analysed further in the chapter devoted to the trade unions (*see* below, Part II, Chapter 2). During such leave, the employment relationship is also suspended.

§5. Temporary Removal from Work

355. Temporary removal from work is a temporary discontinuance of the performance of the work entrusted to the worker on the basis of an order issued to this effect, without terminating the employment relationship. The law permits it in four instances:

(1) when the worker has committed an offence in connection with his/her work (Article 69 of the Code of Penal Procedure);
(2) for workers suffering from a contagious disease who constitute a danger to those around them (Article 19, paragraph 1, item 5 of the Law on Health);
(3) removal by the employer (Article 199 of the LC);
(4) removal by the Labour Inspector (Article 404, paragraph 1, items 5 and 7 of the LC).

I. Criminal Action by the Worker

356. Temporary removal for an offence is ordered when two precisely determined requirements are present:

(1) Where there is definite evidence of the commission of an offence by a worker, i.e., sufficient data indicating that the worker is the perpetrator of a crime under the Penal Code. This evidence must be of such a nature as to indicate with a high degree of certainty that it was he/she who committed the criminal act.
(2) It is necessary that the crime is connected with the work performed under the employment relationship. It may be a criminal breach of trust, a crime involving violation of official duties, a crime in the commission of which he/she availed himself/herself of the opportunities given by his/her job, etc.

The temporary removal here is aimed at making it impossible for the worker to commit again the crime of which he/she is accused, preventing him/her from concealing traces of the crime, or because it is considered that the crime committed is incompatible with continued employment in the job. Removal may be ordered by the District Court hearing the case (Article 69 of the Code of Penal Procedure). In this case the temporary removal is subject to appeal by the interested worker. The temporary removal continues until the necessity of this measure disappears.

357. The temporary removal may come to an end in four ways:

(1) The court which heard the appeal, revokes the temporary removal as unfounded or inexpedient.
(2) The proceedings which were instituted are being terminated or the worker is acquitted by the court. In these two cases, the worker is paid compensation amounting to his/her normal remuneration for the period of suspension, but for not more than two months.
(3) The worker has been found guilty and sentenced, but the enterprise does not resort to dismissal and the punishment imposed is compatible with the continuous existence of the employment relationship, for instance, when the punishment imposed is corrective labour, or public censure (Article 37, paragraph 1, items 2 and 11 of the Penal Code). But, in this case, because the worker has been sentenced, he/she is not entitled to compensation for the period of suspension of work.
(4) The employment relationship is terminated definitely. This will occur in the case of a condemnatory sentence, where the worker is dismissed as a disciplinary penalty for the crime committed (Article 330, paragraph 1 of the LC), or where the court's sentence is incompatible with the continuous existence of the employment relationship, e.g., deprivation of the right to hold a certain state or public post or to carry out a certain profession or activity (Article 37, paragraph 1, items 6 and 7 of the Penal Code). In these cases no compensation is due for the time a worker was removed from his job because he/she has not worked and the temporary removal has proved to have been ordered with good reason.

II. Health Factors

358. The second case of temporary suspension concerns workers suffering from a contagious disease, carriers of infection, or carriers of vermin. It is necessary to establish that their condition is dangerous for those around them, i.e., that the worker creates a danger of also infecting or infesting other members of the labour force, clients, visitors, etc. Temporary removal in this instance is prompted by the necessity to check the spread of infection or vermin to other persons. It is ordered by doctors of the organs of the state sanitary control. The worker thus removed becomes temporarily incapable of work (due to disease or quarantine), so receives corresponding compensation from the social insurance system (Article 43, item 1 of the SIC). According to the nature of the case, a worker is subjected to compulsory treatment (Article 19, paragraph 2, subparagraphs 5–6 of the Law on Health). In such a case temporary removal continues until the worker is cured or the danger of transmitting the infection or vermin of which he/she is the carrier has definitely ceased to exist.

III. Temporary Removal by the Employer

359. Temporary removal by the employer is regulated by Article 199 of the LC. It consists of the right of the employer to unilaterally suspend the employment relationship removing the worker from his/her job. The grounds on which the employer is authorized to exercise this right are the following:

(1) The worker appears at work in a condition which does not permit him/her to fulfil the entrusted job. This condition may consist in a general indisposition of the worker, his/her illness or his/her mental or physical strain and the like. It is not important whether or not this condition is due to the guilty attitude of the worker. His/her objectively poor condition is important. Furthermore, it is necessary that this poor condition leads to the impossibility of the worker fulfilling his/her labour duties. Actual appreciation of this depends upon the real condition of the worker, the nature of the work with which he/she has been entrusted and the eventual negative consequences which the worker could provoke if he/she continued in his/her job in such a condition.
(2) The worker uses alcohol or drugs during working time. His/her removal in such circumstances is justified by the presumption that the use of such substances (alcohol, drugs) may lead the worker to a condition which does not permit him/ her to carry on his/her duties. Such conduct of a worker represents also a violation of the disciplinary rules which may result in disciplinary action (*see* above). The temporary removal in this situation may be ordered irrespective of the eventual disciplinary sanction of the worker.

The above-mentioned grounds are alternatives. Either of them is sufficient and capable of authorizing the employer to order the temporary removal of the worker.

360. The temporary removal from work consists in prohibiting the worker from pursuing the effective accomplishment of his/her job, despite the fact that the employment relationship continues to exist. This is the essence of the suspension of the employment relationship; it may be ordered either by the employer or by the immediate leader of the worker. The temporary removal of the worker lasts while the conditions which provoked it exist. Their non-existence is established by the employer or the leader who has ordered the temporary removal.

361. During the period of the temporary removal, the worker does not receive remuneration. This legal solution (Article 199, paragraph 3 of the LC) is justified by the nature of labour remuneration. Remuneration is due for the labour supplied as it counts as allocation (payment).

IV. Temporary Removal by the Labour Inspector

362. Temporary removal by the Labour Inspector is established in Article 404, paragraph 1, item 5 of the LC. This is a coercive preventive administrative measure. It is one of the functions of the labour inspector to impose this measure (*see* above) which is pronounced most frequently with regard to blue-collar workers in the presence of the following prerequisites:

(1) The worker in question is not acquainted with the regulations on healthy and safe working conditions established for his/her job and necessary for its accomplishment, or the worker is under 18 years of age and has his/her work permit revoked, this permit having been issued by the Labour Inspectorate under Article 302, paragraph 2 or Article 303, paragraph 3 LC.
(2) The worker in question does not possess the required special technical qualifications to safely carry out his/her job.

This means that carrying out the entrusted job in such circumstances may provoke harmful consequences for the worker himself/herself as well as his/her colleagues. It does not matter if the worker is guilty or innocent concerning the lack of the necessary technical qualifications. If the worker is guilty, this may have consequences on his/her disciplinary liability but not for his/her temporary removal from work. For removal, the objective lack of such qualifications is sufficient justification.

363. The measure of temporary removal is ordered by the competent Labour Inspector, i.e., normally the Inspector who has established the above-mentioned circumstances. By virtue of this measure, the worker is temporarily removed from his/her job and the employment relationship is suspended. This lasts until the worker acquaints himself/herself with the regulations on safely carrying out his/her job or acquires the necessary technical qualifications for the relevant job.

§6. Participation in Strikes

364. Since the recognition of a worker's right to strike by the Law on the Settlement of Collective Labour Disputes (OJ, No. 21, 1990, as amended), a new important case of suspension of the employment relationship was introduced in the national labour legislation. It concerns the participation of workers in strikes organized according to Articles 11–19 of the cited law. The questions which are raised by this law will be further discussed (*see* below, Part II, Chapter 5). Here, only three remarks should be made. First, participation in each form of strike permitted by the law cited, such as an ordinary strike, warning strike or strike of solidarity, is recognized as a ground for suspension of the employment relationship. It embraces the whole period of participation in a strike. Second, suspension of the employment relationship includes participation in a strike which was recognized either as lawful or as unlawful. The participation both in a lawful or unlawful strike provokes a suspension of the employment relationship. Third, during participation in a strike the worker does not receive his/her salary (Article 18 of the law cited). His/her employment is only suspended, not terminated. After the end of the strike the worker resumes his/her job and the employment relationship continues its normal and full existence.

Chapter 7. Employment Security; Termination of the Individual Employment Relationship

§1. Stability of the Employment Relationship

365. Securing employment has been one of the most salient problems of Bulgarian labour legislation for many years. Nevertheless, there has been a fundamental change in the legal approach to this problem since 1990. Before 1990, in the era of full but not always free and productive employment which existed during the centrally administered and planned economy, there was a shortage of manpower. Efforts were directed at combating fluctuations in manpower and at avoiding the free replacement of workers in an enterprise. Efforts were also directed at workers leaving work on their own initiative because of bad working conditions, unsatisfactory salaries and services of workers in individual enterprises. Some unfavourable consequences and legal sanctions were provided for in the legislation to combat the 'instability' in employment relations stemming from the fluctuations in manpower provoked by the above-mentioned circumstances. The result was a substantive limitation of the freedom of employment as part of the employment policy conducted at this time by the state.

The approach to employment security is now completely different. Limitations regarding the free movement of the labour force across the country have been abolished. The freedom of the wage-earner to terminate the labour contract through serving a term of notice has been reinstated in the framework of the new employment policy which is part of the process of democratization in Bulgaria. The crucial problem in securing stability in employment relations is now arising from the continually deteriorating employment conditions and a surge in unemployment since 1990 (*see* above, general Introduction). Securing employment relations is in the domain of the local employment exchange office, which is the competent authority for managing unemployment.

§2. Qualifying Service

I. Definitions

366. Qualifying service is that period during which the worker works in an employment relationship (Article 351 of the LC). The work of the worker in every employment relationship is counted as a period of qualifying service. This is the rule. An exception to it, established in Article 43, paragraph 3 of the Penal Code, is work done in an employment relationship while serving a sentence of corrective labour; in this case it is not recognized as a period of qualifying service. On the other hand, the labour laws expressly treat as a period of service certain absences from employment during which the employment relationship does not exist, or if it exists, is suspended: the period during which a worker is unemployed as a result of unlawful dismissal, cases of paid leave and certain cases of unpaid leave, etc. (Articles 352–354 of the LC). The period of qualifying service is measured in days, months, and years (Article 355 of the LC).

II. Benefits of Length

367. There are a number of important positive legal consequences stemming from the total length of qualifying service. The main advantages are the following:

(1) The rate of additional remuneration is paid for length of service. This rate is minimally 0.6% of the basic monthly remuneration for each year of qualifying service. The right to this additional remuneration arises upon completion of three years of qualifying service (Article 12 of the Ordinance on the Structure and Organization of Labour Remuneration, 2007, as amended).
(2) The worker or employee acquires the right to a basic and extended paid annual leave after at least eight months of qualifying service. This requirement is necessary for the initial acquisition of the right to paid annual leave, i.e., in those cases where the worker or employee takes a job under an employment relationship for the first time (Article 155, paragraph 1 of the LC).
(3) The right to compensation in cash in the cases of temporary incapacity for work due to general disease and in the cases treated as equal thereto – quarantine, sanatorium and resort treatment, looking after a sick member of the family, removal from work on the prescription of the health bodies (Article 40, paragraph 1 of the SIC).
(4) The right to some forms of compensation paid by the employers in the case of a termination of the employment relationship on specified grounds (illness, retirement) depends on the length of qualifying service (Article 222, paragraphs 2 and 3 of the LC).
(5) The right to compensation in cash is acquired by the unemployed who have at least nine months of qualifying service within the preceding fifteen calendar months (Article 54b and 54c of the SIC).
(6) The rate of unemployment benefits depends upon the length of qualifying service: workers whose length of qualifying service is longer are entitled to a higher percentage of unemployment benefits (Article 54c of the SIC).
(7) The right to, and rates of retirement and old-age pensions, of disablement pensions, etc., are determined according to the length of qualifying service (Articles 68, 69, 70, 74 of the SIC). In all these cases, the sum of the total time the worker has worked in an employment relationship is calculated, regardless of whether it was spent at one and the same or at various enterprises, whether it consists of periods of time interrupted by intervals in which the worker has not worked, and so forth.

§3. Termination of the Employment Relationship

368. The system now in force regarding the termination of employment relationships is based on three basic principles. They are dictated by the concern to establish lasting employment relations, to secure legality when they are terminated, and to protect workers. These principles are as follows. The first one is the freedom of a worker to terminate the employment relationship on his/her own initiative with prior notice. This principle is most fully manifested in the labour contract which is the typical basis of employment relations in Bulgaria (*see* above). The employment relationship can also be terminated by the worker without notice in certain exhaustively enumerated cases. The second principle governing termination is the right of the employer to dismiss a worker, i.e., to terminate the employment relationship on his own initiative with or without notice but only in certain individual cases and on certain grounds specified by law. However, the employer is entitled to dismiss a worker by serving a notice or without notice only in the cases laid down by the LC. In both instances (dismissal with prior notice or without such notice), the LC expressly and exhaustively enumerates the grounds on which the employer may dismiss the wage earner (Articles 328 and 330 of the LC). This principle was confirmed during the profound amendments to the LC in November 1992 and in March 2001 (OJ, No. 100, December 1992 and No. 25 of 16 March 2001); it was somewhat relaxed but the legislator has not wavered from it (*see* below, §4). The principle is known as the principle of 'legally established grounds for dismissal' and constitutes an important legal guarantee for wage-earners and a resolute protection against arbitrary and unfounded dismissals, as well as for employment security. Third, once dismissal has become a fact, its legality is subject to subsequent control. As a rule, this control is jurisdictional. It is exercised by the courts, and offers the greatest procedural guarantees and possibilities for checking the lawfulness of the dismissal. If as a result of subsequent control, it is established that the dismissal was unlawful and it is countermanded, then the worker is paid compensation and is restored to his/her former job (*see* below, §7).

369. The termination of the employment relationship is made in writing (Articles 326, 327, 328, 330, 331, 335 of the LC). This means that the employer issues a certain official document in which he proclaims or certifies the dismissal. This document is delivered to the worker. The legal grounds on which the employment relationship is terminated are indicated in it. In current juridical language this document is called 'an order for dismissal'. The term 'order' is not accurate because it does not only concern the unilateral termination of the employment relationship by the employer. By means of such an order, every termination of the employment relationship is formally established, e.g., termination of the employment relationship by mutual consent of the parties, by declaration of the worker, and so forth. But this name has gained universal acceptance. It is also used in law (Article 195, paragraph 3 of the LC), and it will be used in this monograph.

370. On termination of the employment relationship, the workbook is returned to the worker (Article 350, paragraph 1 of the LC). Only the legal grounds for the termination are entered in it (the article, paragraph, item number, etc. of the law) and the date on which it took place (Article 349, paragraph 1, item 8 of the LC). No other description or circumstances, even if they constituted an element of the factual circumstances that gave rise to the termination, are entered in the workbook.

371. The employment relationship does not terminate when enterprises merge or amalgamate, when part of one enterprise is transferred to another enterprise, or when the activities of one enterprise are distributed among several enterprises. In fact, changes that have taken place as a result of structural changes, the reorganization of an enterprise or other similar changes, even when they affect the legal personality of the enterprise, are not reflected in employment relations provided that their economic or other official purpose remains, albeit in a different organizational form. In these cases, according to Article 123 and Article 123a of the LC, the employment relationships of the workers continue to exist in the new or reorganized enterprise set up as a result of structural changes. In transferring part of one enterprise to another, both enterprises are jointly liable for obligations towards the workers, stemming from the employment relations that have arisen prior to the reorganization. During the amendments to the LC in 1992, 2001 and 2006, Article 123 and 123a of the LC provided that the employment relationship of the wage-earner does not terminate if the enterprise or a separate part thereof has its proprietor changed, or has been rented out, or leased out or granted under a concession. In all these instances the LC expressly provides that the new employer is a new proprietor (acquirer) or tenant respectively. The transfer itself does not constitute a reason either for the transferee or for the acquirer (the new proprietor or tenant) to dismiss the wage-earner. Transferred wage-earners can, however, be dismissed later by the new employer if he proceeds with a total or partial closing of the enterprise, or with a restructuring for economic, technical or organizational reasons. This means that the principle of automatic transfer of the employment relationship in the case of a transfer has been substantially relieved of its real content: it may postpone dismissal for some time but cannot avoid dismissal of wage-earners at a later stage.

372. The amendments to the LC of March 2001 supplemented the legal framework regarding the preservation of the labour legal relationships of the workers and employees in cases of changing the proprietor and organizational restructuring (merger, takeover, separation and division of the enterprise) or in cases of changing the ownership of the enterprise or the use thereof (sale, privatization of the enterprise or its renting out or leasing out or granting under concession). A new obligation has been laid on the employer in cases of his/her being changed: to notify the workers and employees or the representatives thereof regarding the forthcoming change, and particularly about the nature of the change and the date of its performance, the reasons necessitating it, the probable consequences of this change concerning the preservation of the workplaces of the workers and employees and the measures provided for in this aspect. The notification has to be given by the employer not later than two months prior to the performance of the change. The idea of the law is to create transparency regarding the changes undertaken in the enterprise, to provide clarity to the workers and employees concerning the future of their labour legal relations, employment, etc. This part of the new legal framework reproduces the requirements of Directive 2001/23/EC of the EU (Council Directive on the approximation of the laws of the Member States relating to the safeguarding of employees' rights in the event of transfers of undertakings, businesses or parts of businesses) and is an expression of the approximation of the national labour legislation to the European Community law.

§4. TERMINATION OF THE LABOUR CONTRACT

373. The system of terminating employment relationships is differentiated in accordance with the grounds giving rise to an employment relation and takes into account their nature (*see* above). This is why in the text that follows the termination of the labour contract, new employment relations arising from competitive examination, election, and sentences of corrective labour shall be examined. Employment relations arising from these are terminated according to the rules established for the termination of the labour contract (Article 336 of the LC).

374. The grounds established for the termination of a labour contract may be divided into three groups:

(1) termination of the labour contract on general grounds;
(2) termination of the labour contract on the initiative of the worker;
(3) termination of the labour contract on the initiative of the employer.

I. Termination of the Labour Contract on General Grounds

375. The general grounds for termination embrace ten types of instances, established in Article 325 of the LC.

A. Mutual Agreement of the Parties

376. Article 325, paragraph 1, item 1, of the LC provides that either party may take the initiative for terminating the labour contract by coming forward with a proposal for the other party to accept. Legally, it is not necessary for the proposal to be reasoned. But normally it is reasoned in order to convince the other party. The party to whom the proposal is directed is obliged to take a position regarding the proposal within seven days of its receipt. During this period the party may or may not accept the proposal and must let the other party know his/her position. If the proposal is accepted, the labour contract terminates because of the mutual agreement obtained. Acceptance of the proposal must always be made expressly. If the proposal is not accepted, the employment relationship continues to exist. The seven-day delay is introduced to provide clarity between the parties concerning the proposal made. In the case where the party to whom the proposal is addressed does not express any position within the seven-day period the proposal is deemed to be unaccepted. Non-acceptance may be either expressed within seven days or tacitly if the party does not take any position within seven days from the date of receipt.

That is why the question of termination of the labour contract by mutual agreement of the parties is also regarded as being over. If, despite that, after the expiry of the seven days' term the employer terminates the labour contract by mutual agreement, the termination is unlawful with all the consequences ensuing therefrom: the worker or employee is entitled to challenge the termination as unlawful dismissal under Article 344 of the LC (*see* below, §7). And it is to this effect that the practice of the Supreme Court of Cassation is directed (Dec. 515-97-III C.Ch., Dec. 884-2000-III C.Ch., Dec. 976-2000-III C.Ch., Dec. 1814-2000-III C.Ch., Dec. 667-07-I C.Ch., Dec. 15-07-III C.Ch., Dec. 940-08-II C.Ch., Dec. 26-08-IV C.Ch., Dec. 714-10-III C.Ch., Dec. 69-12-III C.Ch., Dec. 383-12-III C.Ch., Dec. 244-16-IV C.Ch., Dec. 10-17-III C.Ch., Dec. 49-18-IV C.Ch., etc.).[83] If the proposal for termination of the labour contract by mutual agreement has been made by the worker or employee and the employer has not accepted it, the worker may terminate the labour contract on general grounds with a notification under Article 326 of the LC (*see* below, II.A).

377. Termination of the Employment Contract on the Initiative of the Employer against Agreed Indemnification: according to Article 331 of the LC the employer, on his initiative, may propose to the employee termination of the employment contract against indemnification. If the employee makes no written comment on the proposal within seven days, it shall be considered rejected. Where the employee accepts the proposal within seven days, the employer shall owe him an indemnification of no less than the quadruple amount of the employee's monthly gross remuneration, except where the parties agree upon a larger amount of the indemnification. If the agreed indemnification is not paid within one month following the date of termination of the employment contract, the grounds for termination shall be considered to have dropped off.

B. Death of the Worker

378. When a worker dies, one of the two parties to the labour contract ceases to exist, together with the worker's labour, the contribution of which constitutes the basic element of this type of contract. This is why the contract is terminated (Article 325, paragraph 1, item 11 of the LC).

83. V. Mrachkov, 'Critical Review of the 1997 Practice of the Supreme Court of Cassation on Labour Disputes', *Juridicheski Sviat* [*Juridical World*] *Journal* 1 (1999): 265; 'Critical Review of the 2000 Practice of the Supreme Court of Cassation on Labour Disputes', *Juridicheski Sviat* [*Juridical World*] *Journal* 2 (2001): 167; 'Critical Review of the 2007 Practice of the Supreme Court of Cassation on Labour Disputes', *Juridicheski Sviat* [*Juridical World*] *Journal* 2 (2008): 193–194; 'Critical Review of the 2008 Practice of the Supreme Court of Cassation on Labour Disputes', *Juridicheski Sviat* [*Juridical World*] *Journal* 2 (2009): 159–161; 'Critical Review of the 2010 Practice of the Supreme Court of Cassation on Labour Disputes', *Juridicheski Sviat* [*Juridical World*] *Journal* 2 (2011): 161–162; 'Critical Review of the 2012 Practice of the Supreme Court of Cassation on Labour Disputes', *Juridicheski Sviat* [*Juridical World*] *Journal* 2 (2013): 123–124; 'Critical Review of the 2013 Practice of the Supreme Court of Cassation on Labour Disputes', *Juridicheski Sviat* [*Juridical World*] *Journal* 2 (2014): 142–144; 'Critical Review of the 2014 Practice of the Supreme Court of Cassation on Labour Disputes', *Juridicheski Sviat* [*Juridical World*] *Journal* 2 (2015): 114–116; 'Critical Review of the 2015 Practice of the Supreme Court of Cassation on Labour Disputes', *Juridicheski Sviat* [*Juridical World*] *Journal* 2 (2016): 153–155; 'Critical Review of the 2016 Practice of the Supreme Court of Cassation on Labour Disputes', *Juridicheski Sviat* [*Juridical World*] *Journal* 2 (2017): 137–138; 'Critical Review of the 2017 Practice of the Supreme Court of Cassation on Labour Disputes', *Juridicheski Sviat* [*Juridical World*] *Journal* 2 (2018): 101–102.

C. Death of the Person with Whom the Worker Has Concluded a Labour Contract Relating to That Particular Individual

379. Article 325, paragraph 1, item 10, of the LC concerns the situation where a labour contract is concluded with an employer who is a natural person and with whom the worker has established an employment relationship *intuitu personae*, with a view to his/her personal qualities and needs, such as to act as a private secretary, assistant, chauffeur, household servant. It is precisely because of this, i.e., the natural employer having died, that the labour contract loses not only one of its parties but also the grounds for its existence, as a result of which it terminates.

D. Reinstatement of the Unlawfully Dismissed Worker in His/Her Job

380. Article 325, paragraph 1, item 2 of the LC provides that the employment relationship terminates in some specific situations following reinstatement of an unlawfully dismissed worker. This situation occurs where the worker is dismissed, his/her dismissal is recognized as unlawful and he/she is reinstated in his/her previous job by virtue of the court's or another competent authority's decision (*see* below, §8 of this chapter). In these cases, the reinstated worker has to appear for work and occupy his/her previous job within a period of fifteen days from the delivery of the announcement of his/her reinstatement according to Article 345, paragraph 1 of the LC (*see* below, §8 of this chapter). If he/she fails to appear for the job in which he/she has been reinstated without serious cause his/her 'reinstated labour contract' is terminated by virtue of Article 325, item 2 of the LC.

E. Lighter Jobs Destined for Pregnant Women or Reallocated Workers with Reduced Capacity for Work

381. This general ground is laid down in Article 325, paragraph 1, item 6 of the LC. It applies to the employment relationship of workers who occupy lighter jobs which were originally destined to be occupied by pregnant women or workers with a temporary or permanent (invalid) diminished (reduced) capacity for work. Every employer employing more than fifty workers must provide such lighter jobs – ranging from 3% to 10% of the personnel (Article 315 of the LC). When these jobs are occupied by workers who are neither pregnant women nor workers with a reduced capacity for work, and later on there appears among the workers in the enterprise a candidate belonging to one of these two above-mentioned vulnerable groups and who applies to be reallocated to the relevant lighter job, the employment contract with the worker who does not belong to one of these groups is terminated. This is in order to vacate the relevant lighter job for the entitled worker, i.e., the pregnant woman or the worker with a temporarily or permanently reduced capacity for work. The social meaning of this general ground is to guarantee an appropriate lighter job for the above-mentioned categories of vulnerable workers. In the conflict of interest between, on the one hand, the healthy worker who occupies a lighter job and, on the other hand, the pregnant woman or worker with a reduced capacity for work who occupies a job harmful or inappropriate to them, the lawmaker has given priority to the latter because of their vulnerability due to their health conditions.

F. *Entering into a New Employment Relationship on the Basis of Election or Competitive Examination*

382. This ground for termination is provided for in Article 325, paragraph 1, item 8 of the LC. It concerns two groups of workers, namely those who:

(1) have been elected to occupy an elective paid post;
(2) have won a competitive examination.

In both cases the worker has to occupy the new post. In order to facilitate immediate entry into the new job, the law establishes this as a ground which permits an easy termination of the existing employment relationship.

G. *Illness of the Worker*

383. Article 325, paragraph 1, item 9 of the LC refers to a situation in which the health of a worker has deteriorated to the extent of constituting a lasting incapacity such that he/she is incapable of doing the work for which he/she was engaged without the danger that his/her condition may deteriorate still further. The law also prescribes certain additional requirements which must be observed when the labour contract is terminated on these grounds:

(1) The opinion of the Industrial Medical Board which must certify that the worker's disability has stabilized or that he/she is not capable either of doing the work for which he/she was engaged or of being allocated to other work appropriate to his/her state of health within the enterprise.
(2) No other job exists in the enterprise which is appropriate with regard to his/her capacity of work or health condition. If there is such a job and the worker has agreed to occupy it, the employment relationship must not be terminated and the worker has to be allocated to this job.

The opinion of the Industrial Medical Board must be given before the order for termination of the labour contracts is issued.[84] The aim of these requirements is to protect the worker, to guard against summary and unfounded infringements on the part of the management of the employment relationship, and to establish legal guarantees that the resort to termination of the labour contract will ensue only after a careful and objective examination of every actual case.

---

84. *Sbornik Postanovlenia na Varhovnia Sad*, No. 108.

384. It was through the amendments to the LC of March 2001 that a new item 12 was established to Article 325, paragraph 1 and according thereto the labour contract is terminated 'due to designating the post as one for being occupied by a civil servant'. This provision was introduced through the adoption of the Civil Servant Law in 1999 (OJ, No. 67 of 1999, as amended). The legal situation that item 12 is applied to, is the following: a part of the posts occupied and held by employees prior to the entry into force of the Civil Servant Law, are designated as posts that shall be occupied and held by civil servants. Owing thereto, the labour legal relationship of the persons who have been occupying the said posts has to be terminated and a civil service relationship under the Civil Servant Law, 1999, has to be established in its place.

The grounds for termination of the labour contract is the designation of the post, the latter being occupied until that time under a labour legal relationship, as a post which is to be occupied by a civil servant. This designation as a post occupied by a civil servant is made on the grounds of §2, item 1 of the Concluding Provisions of the Decree of the Council of Ministers No. 35 dated 20 March 2000 by the heads of administration (ministers, presidents of state agencies, presidents of state and state public commissions) who approve the staff list of the ministry concerned or another department. The grounds for the occurrence of the labour legal relationship under which the respective post has been held so far do not matter. Most often these grounds are labour legal relationships stemming from labour contracts of fixed or indefinite duration. However, the post may also be one occupied under a labour legal relationship, stemming from a competition, etc. If the post is vacant (vacancy), this means that no labour legal relationship has been established for the respective post, and owing to that, there is no question of the termination thereof, and therefore, there is no question about the application of item 12, either. However, in the event that the post designated as one to be occupied by a civil servant is being held under a labour legal relationship established for it, the latter is terminated on the grounds of item 12 just because the post has been designated as one to be occupied by a civil servant, i.e., under a civil service legal relationship, which is different from the labour legal relationship by its legal nature. This exhausts the effect of item 12. As to the application of item 12, it does not matter whether the post designated as one to be occupied by a civil servant, shall be occupied or not by the person who has been holding it so far under a labour legal relationship. This is a question under the Civil Servant Law, and not under the LC, and especially under Article 325, paragraph 1, item 12 of the LC.

385. These grounds and all those examined above (*see* paragraphs 334–345) are applicable to the termination of labour contracts of both fixed and indefinite duration. The following three cases refer to labour contracts of fixed duration only.

H. Expiry of the Agreed Time Period

386. Labour contracts under Article 68, paragraph 1, item 1 of the LC (*see supra*) are terminated for reasons of expiry of the agreed time period. Their duration is fixed in the contract and is known in advance to the parties. It ends with the expiry of the period for which the contract was concluded in the manner stipulated in it (Article 325, paragraph 1, item 3 of the LC). If there is disagreement between the parties about the expiry of the agreed period of time, the content of the labour contract concluded between them is taken into consideration, subject to interpretation in accordance with the general rules for the interpretation of contracts, these rules being set forth in Article 20 of the Law on Obligations and Contracts.

1. Completion of a Given Task

387. Article 325, paragraph 1, item 4 of the LC reiterates the normal grounds for termination of a labour contract under Article 68, paragraph 1, item 2 of the LC, including termination on completion of the task for which the contract was concluded. Consequently, here again, thc context of the contract and the way in which performance of the task was agreed are valid and decisive.

2. Return of the Original Holder of a Job

388. Article 325, paragraph 1, item 5 of the LC provides this typical ground for terminating a labour contract for substitution for a specific period of time (*see* above). Since the original holder of the job has returned to resume his/her work, or if the labour contract with him/her has been terminated in the meantime, the ground for existence of a labour contract for substitution ceases to exist. In the first case, the original holder of the job resumes performance of the contract, and in the second, the job remains vacant and a new labour contract to fill the position can be concluded as a matter of course. Of course, there is no obstacle for a labour contract to be concluded between the enterprise and the substitute if such is the wish of the parties. But this will be an entirely new labour contract and not a continuation of the contract for substitution.

389. The January 2012 amendments to the LC (prom. OJ, No. 7 of 2012) created a new ground for the termination of an employment contract. This ground applies to the termination of the employment contract under Article 68, paragraph 6 (*see* above paragraph 152): termination of a long-term business trip under the Law on Diplomatic Service. And, as this employment contract is a fixed-term one, the newly created ground is the termination of the period of a long-term business trip under the Law on Diplomatic Service. The said ground shows a certain closeness to the grounds under Article 325, paragraph 1, items 1–3 of the LC (*see* above). However, closeness does not mean sameness. While the term's expiration, as a ground for termination of the fixed-term labour contract under Article 325, paragraph 1, items 1–3 of the LC, takes place irrespective of the will of the parties – which confirms its nature of a legal event – the ground under Article 325, paragraph 2 of the LC, i.e., the termination of a long-term business trip comprises different hypotheses. It may take place in two ways: (a) upon the expiry of the term of the business trip. In this hypothesis the ground under Article 325, paragraph 2 of the LC is the same as the ground under Article 325, paragraph 1, item 3 of the LC (*see* above).

That is the most common hypothesis; however, it is not the only one; (b) early termination of a long-term business trip. It occurs in certain cases, which are exhaustively enumerated in Article 68, paragraph 2 of the Law on Diplomatic Service, and include: a written request of the employee, a motivated proposal from a permanent secretary of the Ministry of Foreign Affairs or from the leadership body of the respective overseas representation, closure of the overseas representation, and other cases explicitly specified in Article 68, paragraph 2 of the Law on Diplomatic Service. Some of the said cases are borrowed from the Code of Labour and the Law on Diplomatic Service, others are new. However, they all express the specificity in the content of diplomatic service, which encompasses employees under an employment relationship and civil servants, i.e., employees under a service relationship. The main idea of these provisions is to regulate the explicitly enumerated cases in which the termination of a long-term business trip may be carried out even prior to the expiry of its term, which brings about early termination of the fixed-term employment contract under Article 68, paragraph 6 of the LC.

II. Termination of the Labour Contract on the Initiative of the Worker

390. The worker may terminate the labour contract on his/her own initiative in two ways: with due notice or without notice.

A. *Termination With Due Notice*

391. According to Article 326, paragraph 1 of the LC a worker has the right to terminate the labour contract with the employer at will after giving due notice. Under the laws in force, the following peculiar features characterize this way of terminating the labour contract. The notice must expressly and unambiguously reflect the will of the worker to terminate the labour contract.[85] It need not give motives. Notice must be given in writing.

392. In addition, notice has to be of a determined length which is established in Article 326, paragraph 2 of the LC. This is a minimum of thirty days for all workers (skilled or otherwise, white- and blue-collar workers and so forth). The parties may agree upon longer periods of notice in collective as well as in individual labour contracts (Article 326, paragraph 2 of the LC).

393. During the notice period, the labour contract remains in existence with the fulfilment of all rights and obligations of the parties. The worker is also obliged to work during that time. If he/she wishes to leave his/her employ before the expiry of the notice period, he/she is liable to pay compensation to the amount of remuneration for the period of notice during which he/she has not worked (Article 220 of the LC). This period of notice also places the employer under an obligation. If he decides to terminate the labour contract with the worker before the notice period has

85. *Sadebna practika po troudovi dela*, No. 149.

expired because he has found a substitute for him/her, the employer, too, may be bound to pay compensation for the remaining time of the notice period.[86]

394. The labour contract terminates with the expiry of the last day of notice.[87] If the worker does not wish to work out his/her period of notice or if the employer terminates the contract before the notice period has expired, the labour contract terminates the moment the worker voluntarily ceases work or the employer decides.

395. The above-mentioned issues (*see* paragraphs 391–394) concern the termination of a labour contract of indefinite duration. But, according to the laws now effective, the worker may also terminate with due notice an employment contract of definite duration. Nevertheless, there are in this regard some peculiarities established in Article 326, paragraph 2, sentence 2 of the LC which are worth mentioning. These concern only the length of the due notice. This is fixed at three months, but cannot exceed the remaining time of the contract itself. If the remainder is more than three months, the notice is three months and if it is shorter than three months, the length of notice will be equal to the remainder of the labour contract. In the last instance the worker does not need to give notice because, in any way, the employment contract will terminate before the three months are up. If a worker under a labour contract for a fixed period of time decides to terminate it without giving due notice, he/she, likewise, owes the employer the amount of his/her remuneration for three months or for the period which remains to the expiry of the period specified in the labour contract if it is shorter than three months (Article 220 of the LC).

B. Termination Without Notice

1. Impossibility for the Worker to Perform the Assigned Work

396. A worker is entitled to terminate without notice a labour contract for a specified period of time as well as one of indefinite duration on any of the grounds exhaustively enumerated in Article 327 of the LC. The first case is one in which it is impossible for the worker to perform the assigned work as a result of illness and where he/she has not been offered another suitable job (Article 327, paragraph 1, item 1 of the LC). In this situation, the worker must have contracted an illness which does not allow him/her, at the risk of further complications to his/her health, to continue performing the agreed work. If necessary, he/she must prove the illness with a medical certificate. Unlike termination of an employment contract under Article 325, paragraph 1, item 9 (*see* above), the illness need not have led to the worker's disablement. An illness under which the performance of the assigned job is harmful to the worker is sufficient. Furthermore, the worker must have made a request to the employer to be transferred to other work suitable to his/her state of health and the employer must have refused to comply with this request. It is irrelevant whether the employer refused because he had no suitable vacant job or if, although he had such

86. *Sbornik Sadebna practika*, 1970, No. 241.
87. *Sbornik Postanovlenia na Varhovnia Sad*, No. 125.

a job, he did not wish to satisfy the request of the worker. It is sufficient that no other suitable job has been offered to enable the worker to proceed to terminate the labour contract on the grounds examined.[88]

2. Failure of the Employer to Pay Remuneration in Due Time

397. A worker may terminate without notice if the employer fails to pay remuneration in due time (Article 327, paragraph 1, item 2 of the LC), namely when the employer fails to pay in good time a fixed and due claim of the worker for remuneration (Article 270, paragraph 2 of the LC). Since the regular payment of remuneration is one of the basic obligations of the employer and lack of remuneration is of a nature to cause financial difficulties to the worker, failure on the part of the employer entitles the worker to react by terminating the labour contract without notice.

3. Changes in the Essential Terms of the Labour Contract by the Employer

398. The third case in which the worker may terminate without notice is where the employer makes changes in the essential terms of the labour contract (Article 327, paragraph 1, item 3 of the LC). This refers to unilateral changes made by the employer to the character and place of labour as agreed in the labour contract beyond the permissible cases, namely: in view of the production requirements of the enterprise, when there is a stoppage, unavoidable circumstances, assignments (Articles 120 and 121 of the LC) (*see* above). The law considers such a change an impermissible violation of the essential elements of the labour contract stipulated between the parties which the employer cannot change unilaterally without the consent of the worker. An example of this is where an employer, without the consent of the worker, reappoints him/her to another job or transfers him/her to work in another branch or in another area.[89] However, the Supreme Court has ruled that there is no essential violation of the conditions of the labour contract where the employer introduces shift work.[90]

399. According to Article 327, paragraph 1, item 3a of the LC, the employment contract may be terminated by the worker or employee without prior notice where, as a result of a change in the employer under Article 123 and 123a, the working conditions with the new employer are considerably deteriorated. This constitutes a new ground among those laid down through the amendments to the LC of June 2004 (prom. OJ, No. 52 of 2004). It consists of three elements:

---

88. *Sbornik Sadebna practika*, 1972, No. 254.
89. *Ibid.*
90. *Sbornik Sadebna practika*, 1969, No. 212.

(1) a change in the employer under Article 123, paragraph 1 and Article 123a of the LC has to be present. This change consists in merger of enterprises, takeover of an enterprise by another one, distribution of the activity of an enterprise among two or more enterprises, transfer of a separate part of an enterprise to another one, change of the legal organizational form of the enterprise, change of the owner of the enterprise or of a separate part thereof, transfer of an activity from one enterprise to another, as well as the cases of letting out the enterprise or a separate part thereof for rent, lease or concession;
(2) considerable deterioration of the working conditions with the new employer should have occurred. This deterioration might consist in moving the worker or employee to a job in severe and harmful working conditions, decrease in the length of the paid annual leave, transition to shift work and the like;
(3) there has to be a causal relation between the change in the employer and the considerable deterioration of the working conditions. In other words, the deterioration of the working conditions should have occurred after the new employer has joined the employment relationship as a party thereto, after the change under Article 123, paragraph 1 and Article 123a of the LC was effected.

4. Passing to a New Job

400. The next case of termination by the worker without notice is one where the worker goes to a new job on the basis of election, or scientific work (in institutions of research, universities and the like, on the basis of successful scientific competitive examination) (Article 327, paragraph 1, item 4 of the LC). The procedure of the election is regulated by Articles 83–88 of the LC (*see* above). As to the procedure and organization of scientific competitive examinations, these are regulated by the 2010 Law on Development of Academic Staff in the Republic of Bulgaria (OJ, No. 38 of 2010). Therefore, Article 327, paragraph 1, item 4 of the LC is not applicable in the case of a worker going to a new job on the basis of competitive examination organized according to Articles 89–96 of the LC (*see* above), but is applied only to cases of scientific competitive examination. This conclusion stems from the express terms in which this ground for termination without notice is formulated. In this way the law expresses its particular favourable attitude towards elective and scientific posts and strives to facilitate their occupation by the worker.

5. Enrolment at an Educational Institution

401. The next case is enrolment at a higher, secondary or technical educational institution or for a postgraduate study to prepare for a PhD thesis (Article 327, paragraph 1, item 6 of the LC). This arises where the worker enters one of the enumerated educational establishments to study or to pass his/her obligatory probation there.[91] The law considers this condition particularly important from the viewpoint of the worker: this is why it gives him/her the right to terminate his/her employment contract without notice. In all the cases indicated above, the labour contract is terminated at once with the worker filing a written request in which he/she adduces one of the above-enumerated grounds.

6. Termination of a Contract for Substitution

402. Another case is where a worker is engaged under a contract for substitution for a specified period of time according to Article 68, paragraph 1, item 3 of the LC (*see* above), and during the period of substitution he/she finds a permanent job (Article 327, paragraph 1, item 7 of the LC). Whereas normally a contract for substitution ends upon the return of the original job holder, the contract can terminate earlier in this instance. This specific solution has been adopted by the law in order to facilitate the short-time worker to enter into a permanent job without having to wait for the 'natural' termination of his/her contract by way of the return of the original jobholder, which would probably be too late to enter into the new permanent job.

7. Conclusion of a New Employment Contract with Another Employer

403. This ground was provided for in the new item 7a of Article 327, paragraph 1 of the LC, which was introduced through the January 2012 supplements to the LC (prom. OJ, No. 7 of 2012). The right to unilateral termination of the employment contract without prior notification on the part of the worker or employee is granted only to a worker or employee who works under an employment contract with an employer providing him/her with temporary work under Article 107q–107x of the LC (*see* above paragraphs 181–187). The worker or employee is entitled to terminate unilaterally and without prior notification the employment contract with the employer providing him/her with temporary work, in order to take a job with another employer who provides him with work that will be performed with the said employer under a fixed-term employment contract or a contract of unlimited duration. This ground is laid down in order to make it easier for the worker or employee working under the conditions of temporary work to terminate his/her employment contract with the temporary work enterprise when he/she finds appropriate work that will be performed with the employer with whom he/she concludes the employment contract. The new employment contract provides work giving him/her greater legal security and he/she prefers this new work to the temporary work under Article 107q–107x of the LC.

---

91. *Sbornik Sadebna practika*, 1973, No. 184.

8. Reinstatement of the Unlawfully Dismissed Worker

404. Finally, there is the case of reinstatement of the unlawfully dismissed worker in his/her old job (Article 327, paragraph 1, item 8 of the LC). In this situation the worker is entitled to terminate without notice a labour contract concluded after the unlawful dismissal in order to resume the work in which he/she has been reinstated. The meaning of this ground is to permit and facilitate the reinstated unlawfully dismissed worker to occupy his/her old job according to the procedure and within the delay prescribed by Article 345, paragraph 1 of the LC (*see* below, §8 of this chapter).

405. New grounds for the termination of the labour contract without notice were provided for in 1999 under Article 327, paragraph 1, item 9 of the LC through the adoption of the Civil Servant Law (OJ, No. 67 of 1999). It provides for the right of the worker or employee to terminate the labour contract without notice in the event of 'entrance into civil service'. The purpose of these grounds is to facilitate the recruitment of staff for civil service by providing for a prompt and easy way of terminating the labour contract on the part of the worker or employee, so that the latter are able to take up the job of a civil servant.

The essence of these grounds is entrance into the civil service. This implies that civil service legal relations have been established between the civil servant and the state under Articles 6–11 of the Civil Servant Law, including the delivery of the act of appointing the civil servant (Article 11, paragraph 4 of the law cited). Pursuant to Article 14, paragraph 1 of the Civil Servant Law, it is only from that moment on that the appointed civil servant may enter the civil service – within ten days of being delivered the act. He/she is entitled to make the entrance into civil service he/she has been appointed to on any working day of this ten-day period. The 'entrance into civil service' means: signing the act of entrance into civil service, taking an oath and proceeding to the performance of the official obligations of the newly appointed civil servant. It is just at this time that the person who used to be a worker or employee under a labour legal contract until that time, may, i.e., has the right, to terminate, by way of a unilateral written declaration of intention to the employer, the labour contract on the grounds of Article 327, paragraph 1, item 9 of the LC. Usually this is the day preceding the day on which the person appointed to civil service makes his/her entrance in service. As at this moment he/she should have been released himself/herself from the labour legal relationship in order to be able to make the 'entrance into civil service' and to start performing the official duties thereof. The general formulation of the grounds of 'entrance into civil service' implies that these grounds may be applied not only on entrance into office as a civil servant under the Civil Servant Law, but also on entrance into another civil service – for instance, civil service in the Ministry of Foreign Affairs, the Ministry of the Interior as an officer or a sergeant, etc.

406. In accordance with Article 221, paragraph 1 of the LC, when, by virtue of Article 327, paragraph 1, items 2 and 3 of the LC, the worker terminates his/her labour contract without notice, he/she is entitled to compensation equal to his/her remuneration for the period of notice which is applicable if the contract has been terminated on his/her initiative with due notice. On the other hand, according to Article 222, paragraph 1 of the LC, the worker who has terminated the labour contract under Article 327, paragraph 1, item 1 of the LC is entitled to compensation equal to two months' salary. This is universal because of the damage sustained from the sudden termination of the labour contract which the employer imposed on the worker without the approval of the latter. The law proceeds from the view that a worker needs a certain period to find another suitable job. And the time during which he/she is presumed to be able to do so is measured by the length of notice which he/she might have served for the termination of the labour contract. The compensation will secure an income for this period of time. When a worker terminates the labour contract without notice in the other cases provided for in Article 327 of the LC, the question of finding a new job does not arise and, consequently, such compensation is not provided. If, however, by virtue of Article 327, paragraph 1, items 2 and 3 of the LC, the worker terminates a labour contract of fixed duration (or for the performance of a certain task) on the strength of Article 221, paragraph 1 of the LC, the employer will have to compensate 'equal to the loss actually suffered'. The latter is measured by the remuneration which the worker would have received had the contract continued in force.

407. The amendments to the LC dated July 2010 created a new ground for termination of the employment contract by the worker or employee without prior notice. Article 327, paragraph 1, item 10 of the LC provides for the worker's or employee's right to terminate the employment contract without prior notice 'where the employer terminates his activity'. The establishment of this ground was necessitated by the increasingly frequent recent cases in which the employer (most often, private employers, part of them being foreign investors) suspends or actually terminates the activity and leaves the country without announcing the temporary suspension of the activity and its duration, and without appointing a person authorized by the employer to settle the termination of the employment relationships with the workers and employees. This gives rise to uncertainty in the employment status they have. The new ground that has been established is aimed at creating a legal procedure for termination of the employment relationships with those workers and employees who do not actually work in the enterprise as it has been closed down; however, their employment relationships have not been terminated.

In these cases, the new paragraph 2 of Article 327 of the LC provides the workers and employees with the opportunity of filing a request for employment relationship termination to the local labour inspectorate by the seat or head office of the enterprise. On the grounds of this request, a check is undertaken by the inspectorate jointly with representatives of the National Social Security Institute and the National Revenue Agency. If this check shows that the employer has really terminated his activity without leaving an authorized person to settle the termination of the employment relationships with the workers and employees, the labour inspectorate terminates the employment relationships with the workers and employees on the grounds of Article 327, paragraph 1, item 10 of the LC as from the date of registration of the worker's or employee's request and enters the said grounds in their Labour Records.

408. The other new ground for termination of the worker's or employee's employment contract without prior notice – established in July 2010 as well – is provided for in Article 327, paragraph 1, item 11 of the LC. It applies 'where the employer has granted unpaid leave to the worker or employee without the consent of the latter'. The employer is entitled to grant such leave to the worker or employee on the grounds of §3e of the Transitional and Concluding Provisions of the Law on Amendments to the LC of July 2010. According to this provision, in time of economic crisis that the country is going through, a temporary measure is envisaged, consisting in the employer's right – in case of a decrease in the amount of work – to grant unpaid leave of up to sixty working days to the workers and employees until 31 December 2010 without their consent, this leave being recognized as length of service. If the worker or employee is dissatisfied with this unilateral decision of the employer, he/she is entitled to terminate the employment contract without prior notice, on the grounds of Article 327, paragraph 1, item 11 of the LC. Within this context, the ground under Article 327, paragraph 1, item 11 of the LC forms a means of the worker's or employee's counteraction to the unilateral decision of the employer to grant the unpaid leave that the worker has not asked for.

409. The acquisition of the right to an insurance pension for length of service and the old age of the worker or employee constitutes grounds for his/her subjective right to terminate the employment contract with the employer without prior notice. This right of his/hers is provided for in Article 327, paragraph 1, subparagraph 12 of the LC, which was created through the supplements to the LC of July 2015 (prom. OJ, No. 54 of 2015).

The acquisition of the right to an insruance pension for length of service and old age is regulated under Article 68 and Article 68a of the SIC. They regulate the acquisition of different types of pensions for insurance length of service and old age: (a) the acquisition of the right to full pension for insurance length of service and old age under Article 68, paragraphs 1–2 of the SIC; (b) the acquisition of the right to reduced pension for insurance length of service and old age under Article 68, paragraph 3 and Article 68a of the SIC. These provisions have been effective since 1 January 2016. The prerequisites in the presence of which the right to a certain type of pension is acquired are different, and this requires that they be considered separately (*see* below). However, the grounds for termination of the employment contract under Article 327, paragraph 1, subparagraph 12 of the LC are the same in both cases of acquisition of a right to pension – either full or reduced one – for insurance length of service and old age.

In 2016, the right to *full pension* for insurance length of service and old age under Article 68 of the SIC is acquired upon attainment of the age of 60 years and 10 months for women and 63 years and 10 months for men, and insurance length of service of 35 years and 2 months for women and 38 years and 2 months for men. From 31 December 2016 onwards the age keeps increasing from the first day of each calendar year as follows: the age for women increases by 2 months each calendar year until 31 December 2029, and from 1 January 2030 – by 3 months until reaching 65 years of age, while the age for men increases each calendar year by 2 months until 31 December 2017 and by 1 month from 1 January 2018 onwards, until reaching 65 years of age. From 1 January 2020 the right to full pension is acquired upon attainment of the age of 61 years and 6 months for women and 64 years and 3 months for men, and insurance length of service of 35 years and 10 months for women and 39 years for men; and in 2021 – at the age of 61 years and 8 months for women and 64 years and 4 months for men, and insurance length of service of 36 years for women and 39 years for men, etc.

From 1 January 2017 onwards the insurance length of service increased by 2 months from the first day of each calendar year until reaching 37 years for women and 40 years for men.

The right to *reduced pension* for insurance length of service and old age under Article 68, paragraph 3 of the SIC arises when the person attains the age of 65 years and 10 months for both women and men, and has at least 15 years of insurance length of service. From 31 December 2016 onwards the age will increase by 2 months from the first day of each calendar year until reaching 67 years of age for both men and women.

The other type of reduced pension is provided for in Article 68a of the SIC. The right to this pension is acquired by the person if he/she has the required insurance length of service of 37 years for women and 40 years for men, but falls short by no more than one year (12 months) of the age required under Article 68, paragraph 1 of the SIC for acquiring the right to full pension for insurance length of service and old age, in 2016 this age being 60 years and 10 months for women and 63 years and 10 months for men.

Upon acquiring the right to any type of pension from among those under Article 68 and 68a of the LC, the worker or employee also acquires the right to terminate the employment contract under Article 327, paragraph 1, subparagraph 12 of the SIC without prior notice.

The advantage of the new legislative solution under Article 327, paragraph 1, subparagraph 12 of the LC is that the worker or employee is entitled to terminate the employment contract at his/her own will quickly and easily.

III. Termination of the Labour Contract on the Initiative of the Employer

410. Termination of the labour contract on the initiative of the employer, irrespective and in spite of the will of the worker, constitutes dismissal in the precise juridical meaning of this concept. It may be effected in two ways: with prior notice or without such notice. In both instances the LC, in principle, expressly and exhaustively enumerates the grounds on which the employer may dismiss a worker. This legal approach constitutes an important legal guarantee for the worker and a serious protection against unfounded dismissals.

A. Termination With Notice

411. With due notice under Article 326, paragraph 2 of the LC the employer may dismiss a worker in the following cases as enumerated in Article 328 of the LC.

1. Total Closure

412. The first case arises in the event of total closure of an enterprise (Article 328, paragraph 1, item 1 of the LC). Total closing implies the complete termination of the production activity of that enterprise. This decision is taken by the employer (in the private sector) or by the competent organ which set up the enterprise (in the public sector). And since employment relations exist for the development and implementation of the production activity of the enterprise, termination of these relations becomes necessary with the total closing of such activity. The reasons for the total closing, economic considerations for cessation of the enterprise, etc. are not important. As a rule, the total closing is connected with collective dismissal.

Dismissal in these cases takes place with due notice under Article 326, paragraph 2 of the LC, i.e., at least thirty days or a longer period but not exceeding three months.

413. The grounds under Article 328, paragraph 1, item 1 of the LC has recently been most frequently applied in bankruptcy proceedings under Articles 607–760 of the Commercial Law and Articles 79–97 of the Banking Law. The number of these proceedings has sharply increased under the conditions of the grave economic situation that the country is in. It is reflected in the severe financial condition of enterprise employers and the great indebtedness thereof, which brings about the frequent institution of bankruptcy proceedings. These court proceedings are complex and multiphase. In the course thereof the grounds for dismissal, these being grounds under Article 328, paragraph 1, item 1 of the LC, of the workers and employees in the enterprise-debtor that the proceeding has been instituted against come into existence only after, at the end of the court proceeding, the bankruptcy court declares the debtor-employer bankrupt through a decision under Article 711, paragraph 1, item 1 of the Commercial Law, and rules the termination of the debtor-employer's activity. It is from that time on that the trustee in bankruptcy, as an employer, is entitled to proceed to the dismissal of the workers and employees under Article 328, paragraph 1, item 1 of the LC. This view is based on the nature of bankruptcy proceeding under Article 630, paragraph 1 of the Commercial Law and Article 328, paragraph 1 of the LC. The Supreme Court of Cassation has consistently upheld this view since 1998, when the bankruptcy proceedings of commercial companies became more frequent (Dec. No. 473-98-III C.Ch., Dec. No. 1751-98-III C.Ch., Dec. No. 914-07-III C.Ch., Dec. No. 1004-07-IV C.Ch., Dec. No. 100-08-II C.Ch., Dec. No. 668-08-III C.Ch., Dec. No. 526-10-III C.Ch., Dec. No. 210-12-III C.Ch., Dec. No. 58-14-III C.Ch., Dec. No. 27-17-IV C.Ch., etc.).[92]

92. V. Mrachkov, 'Critical Review of the 1998 Practice of the Supreme Court of Cassation on Labour Disputes', *Juridicheski Sviat* [*Juridical World*] *Journal* 2 (1999): 220–221; 'Critical Review of the 2007 Practice of the Supreme Court of Cassation on Labour Disputes', *Juridicheski Sviat* [*Juridical World*] *Journal* 2 (2008): 197; 'Critical Review of the 2008 Practice of the Supreme Court of Cassation on Labour Disputes', *Juridicheski Sviat* [*Juridical World*] *Journal* 2 (2009): 166; 'Critical Review of the 2010 Practice of the Supreme Court of Cassation on Labour Disputes', *Juridicheski Sviat* [*Juridical World*] *Journal* 2 (2011): 164; 'Critical Review of the 2012 Practice of the Supreme Court of Cassation on Labour Disputes', *Juridicheski Sviat* [*Juridical World*] *Journal* 2 (2013): 127;

2. Partial Closure

414. The second case arises in the event of partial closing of an enterprise (Article 328, paragraph 1, item 2 of the LC). Partial closing is the termination of the production activity of a production unit of the enterprise – a shop, section, department, service, etc. That unit and its activity as part of the enterprise or establishment ceases to exist. And that is why the workers employed to carry out of that activity have to be dismissed. The reasons for partial closing – economic considerations, rationalization of work, etc. – are not important. As a rule, partial closing is connected with collective dismissal.

3. Reduction of Staff

415. The third case involves a reduction of staff (Article 328, paragraph 1, item 2 of the LC). It is the cancellation of a given job and of its function from the staff payroll of the enterprise. The reasons for this may be of a widely differing nature – rationalization of work as a result of which the total of tasks are assumed by a smaller number of workers, elimination of certain labour functions, their transformation into other functions and the like. The evaluation of the economic expediency of this is made by the employer.

4. Reduction in Production Output

416. The next ground is a reduction in production output (Article 328, paragraph 1, point 3 of the LC). This is a new ground for dismissal introduced with the amendments to the LC in November 1992. It means a reduction in the volume of the whole production of the enterprise. Reasons, such as the following, are unimportant: decreasing demands of production, loss of markets, disturbance of supply of raw materials and the like. The evaluation of the economic expediency of this measure is made by the employer. As in the case of a total or partial closing, as a rule, this ground is connected with collective dismissals. This ground is frequently applied during periods of economic difficulty and slump, which currently pervade the national economy (Dec. No. 348-15-IV C.Ch.).

'Critical Review of the 2013 Practice of the Supreme Court of Cassation on Labour Disputes', *Juridicheski Sviat* [*Juridical World*] *Journal* 2 (2014): 144–153; 'Critical Review of the 2014 Practice of the Supreme Court of Cassation on Labour Disputes', *Juridicheski Sviat* [*Juridical World*] *Journal* 2 (2015): 116–124; 'Critical Review of the 2015 Practice of the Supreme Court of Cassation on Labour Disputes', *Juridicheski Sviat* [*Juridical World*] *Journal* 2 (2016): 158–159; 'Critical Review of the 2017 Practice of the Supreme Court of Cassation on Labour Disputes', *Juridicheski Sviat* [*Juridical World*] *Journal* 2 (2018): 106.

5. Suspension of Work

417. The fifth ground is a suspension of work for more than fifteen working days (Article 328, paragraph 1, item 4 of the LC) as a result of a discontinuation or termination of the production activity of the enterprise or of one of its independent units or subdivisions – shop, section, etc. The cause of such a discontinuation or termination is of no significance – repair of machines, lack of raw materials, natural calamities and the like. In these cases, according to Article 120 of the LC, the employer can transfer the workers concerned to work of a different nature. But when the activity of an entire enterprise or of a considerable part of it is suspended, this will not always be possible. And because, in such cases, there is a prolonged stoppage of the work (more than fifteen working days) and the enterprise cannot make use of the labour of the workers, creating insecurity in the employment relationship,[93] the law allows its termination.

418. The cases of enterprises that do not work rhythmically and often incidentally discontinue their work for lack of raw stuffs, materials, warehouses, markets, etc., have become more and more frequent under the severe conditions in the country. This brings about the frequent application of the grounds for dismissal under Article 328, paragraph 1, item 4 of the LC. On the other hand, these grounds are applied where the work has been actually and virtually discontinued for more than fifteen working days, and not where it is only expected or presumed that the discontinuance will last for fifteen or more working days. Owing thereto, the dismissals carried out prior to the expiry of more than fifteen working days after the commencement of discontinuance are recognized as unlawful ones. And it is to this effect that the practice of the Supreme Court of Cassation is directed (Dec. No. 582-98-III C.Ch., Dec. No. 765-98-III C.Ch., Dec. No. 364-2000-III C.Ch., Dec. No. 570-2000-III C.Ch., Dec. No. 497-07-IV C.Ch., Dec. No. 953-07-V C.Ch., Dec. No. 442-08-III C.Ch., Dec. No. 44-08-II C.Ch., Dec. No. 270-11-IV C.Ch., Dec. No. 386-11-IV C.Ch., Dec. No. 12-12-IV C.Ch., etc.).[94]

93. *Sadebna practika*, No. 197.

94. V. Mrachkov, 'Critical Review of the 1998 Practice of the Supreme Court of Cassation on Labour Disputes', *Juridicheski Sviat* [*Juridical World*] *Journal* 2 (1999): 223–224; 'Critical Review of the 2000 Practice of the Supreme Court of Cassation on Labour Disputes', *Juridicheski Sviat* [*Juridical World*] *Journal* 2 (2001): 171–172; 'Critical Review of the 2007 Practice of the Supreme Court of Cassation on Labour Disputes', *Juridicheski Sviat* [*Juridical World*] *Journal* 2 (2008): 200; 'Critical Review of the 2008 Practice of the Supreme Court of Cassation on Labour Disputes', *Juridicheski Sviat* [*Juridical World*] *Journal* 2 (2009): 169–170; 'Critical Review of the 2011 Practice of the Supreme Court of Cassation on Labour Disputes', *Juridicheski Sviat* [*Juridical World*] *Journal* 2 (2012): 151–152; 'Critical Review of the 2012 Practice of the Supreme Court of Cassation on Labour Disputes', *Juridicheski Sviat* [*Juridical World*] *Journal* 2 (2013): 129; 'Critical Review of the 2014 Practice of the Supreme Court of Cassation on Labour Disputes', *Juridicheski Sviat* [*Juridical World*] *Journal* 2 (2015): 119–120; 'Critical Review of the 2015 Practice of the Supreme Court of Cassation on Labour Disputes', *Juridicheski Sviat* [*Juridical World*] *Journal* 2 (2016): 160–161; 'Critical Review of the 2016 Practice of the Supreme Court of Cassation on Labour Disputes', *Juridicheski Sviat* [*Juridical World*] *Journal* 2 (2017): 142; 'Critical Review of the 2017 Practice of the Supreme Court of Cassation on Labour Disputes', *Juridicheski Sviat* [*Juridical World*] *Journal* 2 (2018): 107–108.

6. Lack in Qualities of the Worker

419. Further, there is the case of lack in qualities of the worker for the effective accomplishment of the work with which he/she has been entrusted (Article 328, paragraph 1, item 5 of the LC). What the law has in mind here is the worker's practical incompetence or unsuitability for the job. This embraces the situation where the physical powers and capacity of the worker or his/her knowledge, training and professional capacity do not satisfy the requirements of the work assigned. An example of this is where the eyesight of the worker is failing as a result of which he/she cannot work in a laboratory involving the use of a microscope, or when he/she lacks sufficient knowledge to manipulate the introduced new technology,[95] but also when his/her professional qualities and efficiency in the work do not satisfy the requirements of the employer. The basic idea of the new formulation of this ground is to give more possibilities to the employer to free himself from workers who are not suitable for the job assigned. The worker's condition is always assessed with a view to the specific tasks assigned to him/her and its requirements.[96] The Supreme Court steadily maintains the view that incompetence exists when objectively the worker lacks the ability to perform the assigned work although subjectively he/she may be making the necessary efforts and endeavours.[97] This is why disciplinary violations do not include incompetence because, by definition, they involve blame on the part of the worker.[98]

7. Lack in Required Education of the Worker

420. The next ground is connected with the lack in the worker's required education or vocational training for the entrusted job (Article 328, paragraph 1, item 6 of the LC). This ground is applied when the assigned work requires expressly some determined type and degree of general or technical education, for instance secondary general or mechanical education, higher education for a post in accounting, chemical or mining engineer, etc. These requirements are provided for in the law or in the other sublegal acts in force. They are of an obligatory character and change according to alterations in the character of the entrusted job, introduced new technology, and so on. For this ground to apply resulting in dismissal of the worker, it is necessary to establish that, following the alterations that have occurred in the nature and the character of the work, new (normally higher) professional and educational requirements for the relevant work have been introduced which the worker cannot meet.

---

95. *Sbornik Postanovlenia na Varhovnia Sad*, Nos 184, 187, 190 and 191.
96. *Ibid.*, No. 190.
97. *Ibid.*, Nos 183 and 192.
98. *Sbornik Sadebna practika*, 1971, No. 225.

8. Refusal of a Worker to Transfer to Another Enterprise

421. Another type of situation in which the enterprise may terminate the employment contract with due notice involves the refusal of a worker to transfer to another enterprise or area when the enterprise is relocated (Article 328, paragraph 1, item 7 of the LC). There are several component elements:

(1) Change of the locality in which the enterprise or one of its subdivisions performs its production activity. The decision to change is taken by the employer or by the competent body to which the enterprise is subordinated (the respective Ministry, district council, etc.).
(2) An offer by the enterprise addressed to the worker whose work is connected with the activity that is being transferred to relocate or else to be transferred to another enterprise.
(3) Refusal on the part of the worker to accept the proposal thus made. In fact, he/she is not obliged to accept it because it would mean a change of the place of work for which he/she has signed a labour contract. Under these circumstances, the only way out for the enterprise is to discharge the worker.

9. Reinstatement of Unlawfully Dismissed Worker

422. The next type of circumstance arises with the reinstatement of an unlawfully dismissed worker who formerly did the work in question (Article 328, paragraph 1, item 8 of the LC). Every dismissed worker can appeal against the order of dismissal and demand its recognition as unlawful, its countermanding, and reinstatement in the job prior to dismissal (*see* above). When the competent body to which the matter is referred finds that the dismissal is unlawful and reinstates the worker in his/her former job, the worker has a right to return to it. If the employer has, in the meantime, appointed another worker in his/her place, he must transfer such a replacement to another job suitable in respect of his/her qualifications, or if there is no such job, discharge him/her with notice. In fact, faced with conflicting interests of the two workers – the one who is unlawfully discharged and the worker appointed in his/her place – the legislation gives preference to the unlawfully discharged worker. It is the law's intention to secure his/her consistent protection, and not to allow the employer, on the pretext that the job is no longer vacant, to frustrate the actual reinstatement of the unlawfully dismissed worker.

10. Entitlement of Worker to a Retirement Pension

423. Furthermore, there is the issue of entitlement of workers to a retirement pension (Article 328, paragraph 1, item 10 and 10a of the LC). When a worker reaches the necessary age and has completed the necessary length of service entitling him/her to a retirement pension in accordance with Article 68 of the SIC, 1999, he/she can, without exception, terminate the labour contract with the enterprise, by mutual agreement or with notice (*see* above). However, this is not the position with regard to the situation examined here, an entirely different case is when the worker is entitled to a retirement pension but does not wish to abandon his/her job.

And these are the most common cases in practice, because under the existing severe economic and social conditions of large strata of workers and employees in the country and the low pensions, the workers prefer to continue working even after they have acquired the right to retirement and an old-age pension. In such a case the worker or employee may be dismissed by the employer on the grounds examined under Article 328, paragraph 1, item 10 of the LC.

424. The latest amendments to Article 328, paragraph 1, subparagraph 10 of the LC made in July 2015 (prom. OJ, No. 54 of 2015), through which a change in subparagraph 10 was introduced, brought about the restoration of the employer's right to terminate unilaterally – by giving prior notice – the employment contract with a worker or employee who has acquired the right to pension for insurance length of service and old age. This right used to exist until 2012, but was revoked. Its restoration in 2015 was due to the solicitation on the part of employers – after the amendments of 2012 they experienced serious difficulties in discharging workers and employees who have acquired the right to pension for insurance length of service and old age.

425. This ground (Article 328, paragraph 1, item 10 of the LC) is applied only to associate professors, professors and DSc. They acquire the right to a retirement and old-age pension on reaching the age of 65 – both for women and men. After reaching this age they can be dismissed with a notice under Article 328, paragraph 1, item 10 of the LC. The greater age (65 for men and women) for habilitated persons and DSc is adopted here in order to take into account the higher scientific qualification of these persons and to provide the opportunity of employing these people for a longer time in lecturing and research.

426. The amendments to the LC dated July 2010 introduced a new ground for termination of the employment contract with prior notification after the worker's or employee's retirement. This ground is provided for in Article 328, paragraph 1, item 10b of the LC. This ground applies to those workers and employees who have not only acquired but also exercised their right to pension under Article 68 of the SIC. The pension under Article 68 of the SIC is a pension for insurance length of service and age. According to the operative Bulgarian legislation, it is admissible for a person to receive a pension for insurance length of service and age, and to work under an employment relationship, the person receiving the full amount of the pension and the full amount of the labour remuneration for the work performed. Bearing in mind the low amount of these pensions within the country (about 48%–50% of the labour remuneration the person used to receive), a large part of those people receiving a pension for insurance length of service and age who have their capacity for work preserved take this opportunity and continue working even after retiring. This is the group of the so-called working pensioners. The purpose of the new ground under

Article 328, paragraph 1, item 10b of the LC is to make it possible for the employer to terminate the employment contract of pensioners working with him, following the serving of prior notice.

427. The supplement to the LC of July 2015 (prom. OJ, No. 54 of 2015) provided for two new grounds for termination – by way of prior notice given by the employer – of the employment contract with a worker or employee who has acquired the right to pension for insurance length of service and old age.

The first one of these grounds is provided for in Article 328, paragraph 1, subparagraph 10a of the LC. According to this new provision, the employer is entitled to terminate unilaterally, by giving prior notice, the employment contract with a worker or employee who has been granted a pension for insurance length of service and old age under Article 68a of the SIC. The workers' and employees' insurance length of service for granting this pension is increased by two months at the beginning of each calendar year from 31 December 2016 onwards until reaching 37 years for women and 40 years for men. These people are entitled to retire within a year prior to reaching an insurance length of service of 37 years for women and 40 years for men. This pension is granted for life.

The second ground is provided for in Article 328, paragraph 1, subparagraph 10c of the LC. On this ground the employer may terminate the labour relation with a worker or employee who has been granted a pension of a reduced amount under Article 68a of the SIC.

In the cases of termination of the employment contract with a worker or employee under Article 328, paragraph 1, subparagraph 10a, 10b and 10c of the LC, the employer may request and obtain ex officio information from the National Social Security Institute as to whether the respective worker or employee has exercised his/her right to pension for insurance length of service and old age. This information is submitted to the employer free of charge (Article 328, paragraph 3 of the LC).

11. Changes in Requirements for an Assigned Job

428. Changes in the requirements for an assigned post which the worker does not meet is the next ground for termination with notice (Article 328, paragraph 1, item 11 of the LC). This is a new ground created by the last amendments to the LC of November 1992 in order to make the system of dismissal more flexible. The meaning of this ground is to permit the employer to discharge the worker when the professional requirements for the assigned work have changed. These changes may concern any professional requirement for the entrusted job and refer not only to the required education and vocational training as the case is of Article 328, paragraph 1, items 5 and 6 of the LC (*see* above). Such other requirements may involve computer knowledge, knowledge of foreign languages, new and modern technical and technological knowledge in the relevant job, etc. Nevertheless, if the worker has the necessary new required knowledge, skills and dexterity the employer does not have the right to dismiss him/her but has to assign him/her to the relevant job with the new requirements.

12. Objective Impossibility of Accomplishing the Employment Contract

429. The next ground is the objective impossibility of accomplishing the employment contract (Article 328, paragraph 1, item 12 of the LC). This is also a new and generally formulated ground for dismissal the purpose of which is to make the whole regime of dismissal more flexible as compared with that of the past. The objective impossibility of accomplishing the labour contract in the future may come from either the worker (e.g., sentenced to imprisonment which according to Decree 1074/74 is a hindrance to the further occupation of the relevant work) or the employer (e.g., changes in the technology making the relevant post redundant). The reasons for such objective impossibility are not important. However, what is important is the fact that such reasons really exist and that they make further accomplishment of the employment contract impossible. This ground expresses the general rule of the civil law on cancellation of bilateral civil contracts in the case of accomplishment being objectively impossible which has been known for a long time (Article 89 of Law on Obligations and Contracts, 1950).

The difference is, however, that instead of the intricate procedure of judicial cancellation of these contracts as provided for in the civil law, Article 328, paragraph 1, item 12 of the LC establishes a relatively easy and light way of unilateral termination of the employment contract. The consequences, however, are not at all lightweight, especially for the worker who is the subject of the dismissal.

430. Apart from the above-mentioned general grounds which are applicable to the dismissal of any workers, the amendments to the LC of November 1992 have also introduced a special ground for dismissal of specific categories of employees which is effected by serving a term of notice. It is provided for in Article 328, paragraph 2 of the LC.

13. Dismissal of Managerial Staff

431. Article 328, paragraph 2 of the LC establishes a special ground for dismissal of employees on the managerial staff. They may be dismissed when the management of the enterprise is entrusted to a manager on the basis of a civil contract for management concluded with him. The procedure for concluding these contracts is established by the Regulations approved by Decree No. 112 of the Council of Ministers of 2003 (OJ, No. 51, 2003). Upon the conclusion of this contract, the newly appointed manager, who becomes the employer, has the right to dismiss the members of the former managerial staff (i.e., the director, deputy-directors, heads of departments and services and other employees who were entrusted with the management of the labour process such as defined in §1, item 3 of the Supplementary Provisions of the LC) and to appoint in their place other suitable persons. The ground for doing this lies in the fact of concluding the contract for management itself. The employer is not obliged, in these cases, to give any other special reasons or motivation. Nevertheless, termination of the labour contract with the managerial staff is effected by serving a term of notice according to Article 326, paragraph 2 of the LC, i.e., a minimum of thirty days unless a longer period has been stipulated by the parties. The meaning of this ground for dismissal is to permit the newly appointed manager to discharge the former managerial staff and to select a new team of leaders to direct the company's activity in order to accomplish his/her own managerial obligation in accordance with the contract for management.

432. The amendments to the LC of March 2001 supplemented paragraph 2 of Article 328 with a new sentence – the second one. It reads: 'The dismissal (under Article 328, paragraph 2 of the LC) may be carried out after the commencement of the performance of the contract, but not later than 9 months.' This addition has been a necessary and useful one. Prior to its introduction there was no explicit legal framework on this matter, which brought about hesitations and contradictory practice. The supplement to Article 328, paragraph 2 of the LC solves two important questions.

The first of them concerns the length of time during which the new employer, with whom a contract for managing the enterprise has been concluded, is entitled to exercise his/her right to dismiss managerial staff. At present this length is fixed at nine months. This term is the same for all management contracts regardless of their length. The legislator has regarded this time as optimum. It allows the new manager to get to know and evaluate the professional qualities of the managerial staff of the enterprise and to decide who should be discharged and who should be retained in the new manager's team.

The second question concerns the commencement date that the nine months' period of time is to be counted from. Article 328, paragraph 2 of the LC explicitly specifies it 'from the commencement of the management contract'. This means that the management contract should not only be concluded, but its performance should have been started as well. And its performance can be started after the procedure for electing the respective manager of the commercial company is over and the name of the elected manager has been entered in the commercial register in accordance with the requirements of Article 231, paragraph 3 and Article 244, paragraph 4 of the Commercial Law. It is to this important judicial point that the operative legal framework imparts constitutive effect, i.e., it is since that time that the legal relationship between the manager and the commercial company concerned has arisen. However, along with this judicial point, there is one more factual point that is important: the performance of the management contract should have started. This means that the manager concerned should have proceeded to the actual performance of his/her obligations and the execution of his/her rights under the contract. In order to avoid the hesitations and difficulties regarding the determination of that moment, what is actually done in practice is to specify in writing the date of the manager's 'entrance into office'.

433. All grounds for dismissal under Article 328 of the LC are objective ones. Once present, dismissal is necessary because of important changes in the situation of the enterprise (closing, reduction of staff, stoppage, termination of the activity of the enterprise or its transfer to another location, etc.) or in the worker's capacity for work (unsuitability, becoming pensionable) which have occurred during the fulfilment of the labour contract. But in no case have changes resulted from fault on the part of the worker. Taking into consideration the lack of fault on the part of the worker, the law provides that dismissal here shall be effected with due notice, enabling a worker to seek and find another suitable job. The grounds enumerated in Article 328 of the LC are applicable to the dismissal of workers under labour contracts of both definite and indefinite duration. This conclusion stems from the general way in which Article 328 is formulated. Indeed, it establishes the grounds for unilateral termination by the employer of any employment contract without specifying its type – of definite or of indefinite duration.

434. Some of the above-mentioned grounds (Article 328, paragraph 1, item 1–4 of the LC; *see* above, paragraphs 409–410) by their nature and form are of an economic character. For the most part (total and partial closing, reduction of production output, suspension of work for more than fiftten working days), reductions of staff are connected with collective dismissal. These grounds have frequently been applied in the past few years during periods of economic difficulties, slump, massive and abrupt falls in production output, which currently prevail in the national economy.

435. The cases of collective dismissal, which have become more and more frequent in the recent years, have necessitated the adoption of special rules for the protection of workers and employees in cases of collective dismissal. These rules were laid down in Article 131a and §1, item 9 of the Supplementary Provisions of the LC. They are inspired by the Council Directive 98/59/EC on the approximation of the laws of collective redundancies. The introduction of these rules in the domestic legislation is a specific expression of the state policy of approximation to the EU law of the labour legislation of Bulgaria as a Member State of the European Community since 1 January 2007.

436. Collective dismissals are a new phenomenon in Bulgarian labour law. Here are its basic features according to the operative labour law:

(1) This is a dismissal which is performed on strictly specified legal grounds. Pursuant to Article 130a of the LC, these dismissals are made on one of the following grounds: closing the total enterprise or a part thereof, reductions of staff and reduction of production output (Article 328, paragraph 1, items 1–4, 8, 9, 11 of the LC). These grounds are not related to the definite employee.
(2) It is this feature which gives it the character of a collective, large-scale dismissal. §1, item 9 of the Supplementary Provisions of the Labour Code provides that a dismissal is a collective one if the number of the dismissed employees is:
    (a) at least 10 in enterprises employing more than 20 but fewer than 100 workers in the month preceding the collective dismissal;
    (b) at least 10% of the number of employees in enterprises employing more than 100 but fewer than 300 workers in the month preceding the collective dismissal;
    (c) at least 30 in enterprises employing at least 300 workers in the month preceding the collective dismissal.

(3) The dismissal of these workers and employees must be made simultaneously or in a short period of time, within one month.

437. The law establishes a particular procedure that must be followed in the performance of collective dismissals. It consists in assigning specific obligations to the employer concerning notification and consultations. And it is the observance of this procedure that expresses the specific protection for these dismissals.

Where the employer intends to undertake collective dismissal, he/she shall be obliged to start consultations under Article 7, paragraph 2 LC with the representatives of the trade union organizations and those of the employees in due time, not later than forty-five days beforehand, and to make efforts to reach an agreement with them in order to avoid or restrict the collective dismissal and to mitigate the consequences thereof.

Regardless of whether the employer took the decision which led to collective dismissal before the beginning of the consultations, he/she shall be obliged to present written information to the representatives of the trade union organizations and those of the employees under Article 7, paragraph 2 LC regarding the following points:

(1) the reasons for the contemplated dismissal;
(2) the number of the employees to be dismissed and the basic economic activities, groups of professions and positions in the enterprise to which they relate;
(3) the number of the employees working in the basic economic activities, groups of professions and positions in the enterprise;
(4) the particular indicators for application of the criteria under Article 329 LC for choosing the employees to be dismissed;
(5) the period during which the dismissal shall take place;
(6) the indemnities due in relation to the dismissal.

The employer is also obliged, within a term of three working days, to send a copy of the above to the respective unit of the Employment Agency.

438. On the other hand, the laws now effective also provide for some specific rules regarding dismissal for economic reasons. They are applied only in cases of dismissal on the grounds of partial closure, reduction of staff and reduction in production output (*see* above paragraphs 410–416). They concern the right of selection on the part of the employer.

439. The meaning of the right of selection on the part of the employer is that he/she can dismiss a worker who occupies a job similar in character to that which has been abolished. At the same time, the employer can retain in employment the person or persons whose job has been abolished following partial closure, reduction of staff or in production output. The essence consists in the right of the employer to choose who to dismiss among the workers subject to dismissal. This choice is not arbitrary but it is founded on some criteria provided for in Article 329 of the LC.

440. The criteria are provided for in Article 329, paragraph 1 of the LC. According to these, selection is made on the basis of professional qualifications and efficiency of the worker in order to retain those who work better and more efficiently and to dismiss those who do not work so well, have lower qualifications and achieve less efficiency.

441. Assessment of the above-mentioned criteria and their application belongs to the employer. Indeed, the established criteria are objective and form part of the right of the employer to dismiss the worker on the relevant ground. But according to the lasting jurisprudence of the Supreme Court since 1959, this assessment of the employer based on objective criteria is subject to the control of the courts. Moreover, the burden of proof that a selection has been made in accordance with the criteria provided for in Article 329 is on the employer.[99]

442. The right of selection is a subjective right of the employer, which accompanies his/her right of dismissal. The right of selection can be applied only where the dismissal is performed on one of the following three grounds: closure of a part of the enterprise's activity, reduction in staff, or a decrease in the amount of work (*see* above paragraphs 411–413). In the cases of dismissal on any other grounds, no right of selection exists and the employer is entitled to dismiss only those workers or employees for which the respective legal ground for dismissal is present.

443. The exercise of the employer's right of selection under Article 329 of the LC is subject to judicial control. The selection criteria laid down in law (*see* above paragraphs 436–437) have their objective features and the observance thereof forms part of the employer's right of dismissal, which is judged by the court if a dispute on its exercise arises. The court has been adhering to this view for decades now (Dec. 532-91-III C.Ch., Dec. 1046-01-III C.Ch., etc.). In the context of this constant practice of the Supreme Court of Cassation, in 2010 and 2011 there were decisions of the III and IV C.Ch. in which certain panels of judges started soliciting for the discretionary nature of the employer's right of selection and, owing thereto, they refused to exercise judicial control over the employer's judgment in the exercise of

99. *Sbornik postanovlenia na Varhovnia Sad*, 658; V. Mrachkov, 'Critical Review of the 2007 Practice of the Supreme Court of Cassation on Labour Disputes', *Juridicheski Sviat* [*Juridical World*] *Journal* 2 (2008): 205–206; 'Critical Review of the 2008 Practice of the Supreme Court of Cassation on Labour Disputes', *Juridicheski Sviat* [*Juridical World*] *Journal* 2 (2009): 178–181; 'Critical Review of the 2011 Practice of the Supreme Court of Cassation on Labour Disputes', *Juridicheski Sviat* [*Juridical World*] *Journal* 2 (2012): 155–157; 'Critical Review of the 2012 Practice of the Supreme Court of Cassation on Labour Disputes', *Juridicheski Sviat* [*Juridical World*] *Journal* 2 (2013): 133–137; 'Critical Review of the 2013 Practice of the Supreme Court of Cassation on Labour Disputes', *Juridicheski Sviat* [*Juridical World*] *Journal* 2 (2014): 153–155; 'Critical Review of the 2014 Practice of the Supreme Court of Cassation on Labour Disputes', *Juridicheski Sviat* [*Juridical World*] *Journal* 2 (2015): 124–126; 'Critical Review of the 2015 Practice of the Supreme Court of Cassation on Labour Disputes', *Juridicheski Sviat* [*Juridical World*] *Journal* 2 (2016): 165–167; 'Critical Review of the 2016 Practice of the Supreme Court of Cassation on Labour Disputes', *Juridicheski Sviat* [*Juridical World*] *Journal* 2 (2017): 148–150; 'Critical Review of the 2017 Practice of the Supreme Court of Cassation on Labour Disputes', *Juridicheski Sviat* [*Juridical World*] *Journal* 2 (2018): 115–117.

this right (Dec. 310-10-IV C.Ch., Dec. 14-11-III C.Ch., etc.). In 2011 and 2012 the number of such decisions started growing gradually. This court practice, though incidental, did not conform to the letter, the reason and the traditions in the application of judicial control over the employer's right of selection. On the other hand, inconsistency was created in the court practice of applying Article 329 of the LC. This necessitated the adoption of Interpretative Decision No. 3 of the General Assembly of the Civil College of the Supreme Court of Cassation dated 16 January 2012, according to which the employer's judgment under Article 329, paragraph 1 of the LC as to which workers and employees have a higher qualification and work better is subject to judicial control in proceedings over a claim grounded on Article 344, paragraph 1, item 1 of the LC. In the course of exercising the said control, the court examines whether the assessments made by the employer under the criteria laid down in Article 329, paragraph 1 of the LC are based on the qualifications actually held by the workers and employees and the level of performance of the work assigned.

This solution conforms to the sense of Article 329 of the LC and to the decades-long traditions in court practice, and deserves being supported. The latest practice of the panels of the Supreme Court of Cassation is to that effect, too (Dec. 121-12-III C.Ch., Dec. 154-12-IV C.Ch., Dec. 382-12-IV C.Ch., Dec. 52-13-III C.Ch., Dec. 189-13-IV C.Ch., Dec. 347-14-III C.Ch., Dec. 197-15-IV C.Ch., Dec. 320-16-III C.Ch., Dec. 414-16-IV C.Ch., Dec. 317-17-IV C.Ch., Dec. 280-17-IV C.Ch.). A dismissal accomplished in violation of the selection criteria is unlawful on general grounds.

B. Termination Without Notice

444. An employer can dismiss any worker, without notice, whatever the type of employment contract, in the following circumstances as provided for exhaustively in Article 330 of the LC.

1. Detention of the Worker

445. The first case is that of detention of the worker as a result of the court's sentence to imprisonment (deprivation of freedom), currently being implemented (Article 330, paragraph 1 of the LC). Because he/she is detained, the worker is not in a position to go to his/her place of work and to carry out his/her employment duties. It is important to emphasize in this connection that in all the above-indicated cases detention takes place for a crime committed by the worker under the Criminal Code: a crime for which he/she has been sentenced. The nature of the crime is of no significance – it may be a crime either connected with the worker's job or not. Furthermore, the duration of imprisonment to which the worker has been sentenced is not important. It may be one, two or more years. However, Article 39 of the Criminal Code now in force, provides for that the minimum imprisonment imposed by courts is three months.

2. Deprivation of the Right of the Worker to Perform His/Her Job

446. The second case is that of deprivation by means of an imposed sentence by the Court or an administrative order of the right of a worker to perform his/her job in which he/she is appointed (Article 330, paragraph 2, item 1 of the LC). This may be the case:

(1) where the competent court has, by virtue of Article 37, items 6 and 7 of the Criminal Code, imposed on the worker as a supplementary penalty deprivation of the right to perform the relevant job (e.g., to be an accountant, a teacher, a doctor);
(2) where the worker has been deprived by means of an administrative order on expressly provided occasions to perform his/her job to which he/she has been appointed (e.g., withdrawal of the driving licence of the driver after using alcohol, etc.). These cases are provided for in the Law on Administrative Infringements and Penalties, 1970 (Articles 13 and 16) and in the Law on Road Traffic, 1999 (Articles 174–176).

3. Withdrawal of a Scientific Title or Degree

447. The third case is where the scientific title or degree on which the employee relied for his/her appointment in the relevant post is withdrawn (Article 330, paragraph 2, item 2 of the LC). This ground is very rarely applied and normally concerns research workers and university scholars. The ground and procedure for withdrawal of scientific titles and degrees are established by Article 35 of the Law on Development of the Academic Staff in the Republic of Bulgaria (prom. OJ, No. 38 of 2010) and apply where:

(1) it has been established that the works or a considerable part of the works on the basis of which the scientific title or degree was acquired, or the academic position was occupied, have been written or created by another person (the so-called plagiarism);
(2) a person has received a negative assessment in two consecutive performance appraisals.

The withdrawal of the scientific title or degree and the discharge from an academic position is carried out by the Rector of the higher school. This decision can be contested before the Minister of Education, Youth and Science and is considered by the Arbitration Council of the Ministry of Education, Youth and Science.

4. Striking a Doctor or Dentist off the Register

448. This ground for dismissal is a new one. It was established in 1998 through §7 of the Transitional and Concluding Provisions of the Law on Professional Organizations of Doctors and Dentists, 1998 (OJ, No. 83 of 1998). This ground provides for the employer's unilateral suspension of the labour contract with a doctor or dentist where the latter is struck off the registers of doctors or dentists because of infringements of the rules of professional ethics and fair medical practice. The 'striking off' itself is an administrative penalty. It is imposed by way of a penalty warrant issued by the President of the Bulgarian Union of Doctors or by the President of the Union of Dentists in Bulgaria for severe professional infringements for a term of three months to two years. The unilateral suspension of the labour contract in these cases is a consequence of the administrative penalty imposed and constitutes a way of its execution, as the striking off of the doctor or dentist from the register disallows him/her to perform his/her professional duties, and owing to that, he/she cannot occupy his/her post. In these cases, the employer is obliged to make the dismissal in performance of the administrative penalty imposed and is not entitled to judge whether or not to suspend the labour contract with the respective doctor or dentist, who has been struck off the professional register. After the expiry of the term that the 'striking off' penalty has been imposed for, the dismissed doctor or dentist is entitled to enter a job in the general procedure by way of signing a new labour contract (Articles 61–71 of the LC).

5. Refusal of the Worker to Occupy a Suitable Job

449. The next case is where a worker refuses to occupy a suitable job recommended to him/her by the Industrial Medical Board because of his/her reduced capacity for work (Article 330, paragraph 2, item 5 of the LC). This ground contains two basic components:

(1) a decision of the competent Industrial Medical Board for the reallocation of the worker to another suitable job because of his/her reduced capacity for work, taken in accordance with Articles 314 and 317 of the LC;
(2) refusal of the worker to occupy the job to which he/she has been reallocated.

In this case the employment contract no longer exists and the only solution is termination according to Article 330, paragraph 2, item 4 of the LC.

6. Disciplinary Offence

450. The last and the most important instance is that of a disciplinary offence (Article 330, paragraph 2, item 6, in connection with Article 190 of the LC). This punishment is imposed for a serious breach of labour discipline committed by the worker (*see* above). As a rule, disciplinary dismissal, which is the most severe form of punishment and a specific form of drastic termination of the labour contract, is applied when the employer finds it necessary and justified. It depends upon his assessment of whether and when to resort to this kind of dismissal by taking into consideration the offence committed, the damage caused by it (if any), the circumstances under which the offence was committed, as well as the conduct of the guilty worker (Article 198 of the LC).[100] This is an expression of the right of dismissal as an exercise of disciplinary power by the employer.

7. Incompatibility in Cases of a Conflict of Interest

451. It was through Article 330, paragraph 2, items 7, 8 and 9 that the 2003 and 2008 changes into the LC introduced three new grounds for termination of the employment contract without prior notice. What is common to them is that they provide for termination of the employment contract where a conflict of interest is present. However, the grounds for termination in these three cases are different, and that requires their being considered separately.

452. Non-performance of the obligation to give notice of the presence of a conflict of interest (Article 330, paragraph 2, item 7 of the LC). It applies to employees of the state and municipal administration working under an employment relationship. According to Article 107a of the LC, it is inadmissible to conclude such a contract with a person who would thus turn out to be in a hierarchical connection of governance and supervision with his/her spouse, or with a person with whom he/she is in real cohabitation, or with lineal relatives without limitation, or with collateral relatives and relatives by marriage within the fourth degree, or with a person who performs activities or holds positions such as: a deputy or a councillor serving on the municipal council, if the employee works in the same municipal administration. In these cases of incompatibility, the employee is obliged to notify the employer (Article 126, item 12 of the LC). Should the employee fail to perform this obligation, the employer has to terminate the employment contract with him/her under Article 330, paragraph 2, item 7 of the LC.

453. In those cases where such incompatibility arises subsequently, i.e., after the employment contract was concluded (contraction of marriage or real cohabitation with a person who is in a hierarchical connection of governance and supervision), the employer is obliged to terminate the employment contract of one of the two employees, without prior notice, so that the job-related dependence between them be discontinued (Article 328, paragraph 2, item 8 of the LC).

454. Establishment of a conflict of interest under the 2008 Law on Prevention and Detection of a Conflict of Interest (prom. OJ, No. 94 of 2008, as amended). This Law (Article 3) gives a list of the public positions the taking and holding of which requires that the person be guided only and solely by common interests and – in the

100. K. Milovanov, *Disziplinarno ouvolnenie* [*Disciplinary Dismissal*] (Sofia: Science and Art Publishing House, 1967), 70–118.

course of exercising his/her official duties – allow no private (personal) interest of his/hers and no interest of his/her relatives (a spouse, a person with whom he/she is in real cohabitation, children, parents and the like) to exert influence over him/her. Item 3 of the Law contains a list of the persons holding 'public positions' which comprises the employees working under employment relationships in the state or municipal administration. The law classifies the presence of such influence as a conflict of interest, which constitutes grounds for termination of the employment contract with the respective employee without prior notice (Article 30, paragraph 2, item 9 of the LC).

455. The supplement made to the LC in October 2015 (prom. OJ, No. 79 of 2015) provided for a new ground for the termination, on the part of the employer, of an employment contract with a pedagogical specialist. According to Article 330, paragraph 2, subparagraph 10 of the LC, 'The employer may terminate the employment contract without prior notice where: … 10. a pedagogical specialist within the meaning of the Law on Preschool and School Education has been sentenced for a deliberate crime of general nature, regardless of rehabilitation.'

This ground is only applicable to those employees who are pedagogical specialists. This category of employees is specified in Article 217 of the Law on Preschool and School Education and includes: teachers, school and kindergarten headmasters and headmistresses and their deputies, educators, pedagogical employees and the like, exhaustively listed in Article 217 of the law. According to this legal provision, it is inadmissible for a person sentenced for a deliberate crime of general nature to hold the position of pedagogical specialist, regardless of rehabilitation. 'Crimes of general nature' are those crimes under the Penal Code which have pre-trial proceedings (preliminary investigation) conducted on them and have a prosecutor, judges and jurors participating in the court hearing. These crimes are regarded as ones of great social danger. The crimes of general nature are exhaustively listed in Article 194 of the Code of Penal Procedure. The sentencing concerns any deliberate crime of general nature, irrespective of the punishment imposed for the crime committed – from the most severe punishments of 'life imprisonment' or 'imprisonment of up to 30 years' to the lightest ones – 'probation' or 'public censure' under Article 37, paragraph 1 of the Penal Code, regardless of rehabilitation that obliterates the punishment imposed and eliminates the future consequences thereof.[101] According to this legal provision, the sentencing of a person for a deliberate crime of general nature is incompatible with his/her holding the position of a pedagogical specialist, and the labour relation with him/her is terminated without prior notice, on the grounds of Article 330, paragraph 2, subparagraph 10 of the LC.

101. Death penalty in the Republic of Bulgaria is abolished. A decision of the Seventh Great National Assembly dated 20 Jul. 1990 postponed the execution of the effective sentences of death penalty 'until the matters regarding the application of death penalty in Bulgaria are resolved' (prom. OJ, No. 60 dated 20 July 1990). The supplement to Art. 36 of the Penal Code created the new para. 3, according to which: 'There is no death penalty in the Republic of Bulgaria' (prom. OJ, No. 153 of 23 December 1998).

IV. Preliminary Protection Against Dismissal

456. Certain categories of workers enjoy a greater protection against dismissal (Article 333 of the LC). These are workers who find themselves in a more demanding or special condition (health, family status), who are temporarily absent from work (on leave), or who in addition to the employment relationship, also perform other social functions (trade union activists, etc.). In the first two cases, the social role of this protection is to give priority to a higher public interest underlying the special situation in which the worker finds himself/herself, protecting him/her from hasty and unjust dismissal. In the third case, special protection is aimed at prohibiting the employer from exercising his right to terminate the employment relationship with workers in cases provided by the law, to dismiss any of them because of their public functions and possible critical remarks which may be addressed to him in fulfilment of their public or social functions. In this way the law creates security for trade union functionaries in the performance of their work and the free and unhindered development. The essence of this protection consists in the obligation, established by the law, on the employer to obtain preliminary permission from certain state or trade union bodies; he may only then proceed to dismiss the protected persons. A dismissal which has taken place without a request for permission, or when a request has been refused, is unlawful and can be countermanded by the competent bodies with all the consequences stemming therefrom (Article 344, paragraph 3 of the LC). What is more, the Supreme Court holds the view that consent of the respective authorized body, received after the dismissal has been effected, cannot validate the dismissal, which remains unlawful as a matter of course and must be countermanded.[102]

This protection is preliminary because it precedes the dismissal. It consists of prior consent for the dismissal of the worker concerned on the basis of each individual case. Such prior consent is not necessary for every dismissal, but only for dismissals in the case of partial closing, staff reduction, reduction in production output, when the wage-earner does not possess the required qualities for fulfilment of the job, in the case of a change in the job requirements where the wage-earner does

102. *Sadebna practika po troudovi dela*, Nos 247, 249, 250, 251, and 252; *Sbornik Sadebna practika*, 1970, No. 220; 1971, Nos 212 and 223; 1972, No. 237; *Sbornik Postanovlenia na Varhovnia Sad*, No. 108; V. Mrachkov, 'Critical Review of the 2007 Practice of the Supreme Court of Cassation on Labour Disputes', *Juridicheski Sviat* [*Juridical World*] *Journal* 2 (2008): 210–213; 'Critical Review of the 2008 Practice of the Supreme Court of Cassation on Labour Disputes', *Juridicheski Sviat* [*Juridical World*] *Journal* 2 (2009): 189–192; 'Critical Review of the 2011 Practice of the Supreme Court of Cassation on Labour Disputes', *Juridicheski Sviat* [*Juridical World*] *Journal* 2 (2012): 163–164; 'Critical Review of the 2012 Practice of the Supreme Court of Cassation on Labour Disputes', *Juridicheski Sviat* [*Juridical World*] *Journal* 2 (2013): 144–148; 'Critical Review of the 2013 Practice of the Supreme Court of Cassation on Labour Disputes', *Juridicheski Sviat* [*Juridical World*] *Journal* 2 (2014): 161–167; 'Critical Review of the 2014 Practice of the Supreme Court of Cassation on Labour Disputes', *Juridicheski Sviat* [*Juridical World*] *Journal* 2 (2015): 132–134; 'Critical Review of the 2015 Practice of the Supreme Court of Cassation on Labour Disputes', *Juridicheski Sviat* [*Juridical World*] *Journal* 2 (2016): 176–177; 'Critical Review of the 2016 Practice of the Supreme Court of Cassation on Labour Disputes', *Juridicheski Sviat* [*Juridical World*] *Journal* 2 (2017): 155–158; 'Critical Review of the 2017 Practice of the Supreme Court of Cassation on Labour Disputes', *Juridicheski Sviat* [*Juridical World*] *Journal* 2 (2018): 155–158.

not possess the suitable qualifications, if it is objectively impossible to further perform the labour contract and in the case of disciplinary dismissal for serious misconduct of the wage-earner (Article 328, paragraph 1, points 2, 3, 5 and 11 and Article 330, paragraph 6 of the LC).

The authority competent to give the prior permission is the relevant service of the Labour Inspectorate according to the seat of the enterprise.

457. A female worker or employee who is on confinement leave in accordance with Article 330, paragraph 6 of the LC may be dismissed only in the event of closing the enterprise (Article 328, paragraph 1, item 1 of the LC – *see* above paragraph 410). The pregnancy and confinement leave has the length of 410 calendar days and is granted on a medical prescription, usually for 45 days prior to the confinement and the 365 days thereafter (Article 163 of the LC). During this period the female worker or employee enjoys full and direct protection against dismissal by virtue of law and may not be dismissed on any other grounds except those under Article 328, paragraph 1, item 1 of the LC, and no permission of the Labour Inspectorate may derogate the established imperative legal prohibition. This legal provision reproduces the prohibition on dismissal of female workers who are availing themselves of a pregnancy leave as provided for in Article 4 of the Maternity Protection Convention No. 3 of the ILO dated 1919 as well as in Article 8 of the Maternity Protection Convention No. 183 of the ILO dated 2000, which have been ratified by Bulgaria and have taken effect for the country.

458. During the whole period of pregnancy – from the conception and ascertainment of pregnancy until she takes her leave for pregnancy and childbirth (*see* above paragraph 453), the female worker or employee who is either pregnant or in an advanced stage of *in vitro* treatment may be dismissed with prior notice on the grounds of Article 328, paragraph 1, item 1 (closure of the whole enterprise), item 7 (refusal to follow the enterprise or the establishment she works in when the latter moves to another population centre), item 8 (where the position held by the worker or employee has to be vacated for the purpose of reinstatement of an unlawfully dismissed worker or employee who was previously holding the said position), item 12 (in the event of an objective impossibility of executing the employment contract), as well as in the event of a disciplinary dismissal, however, in this case she may be dismissed only after the Labour Inspectorate has given its permission (Article 333, paragraph 5 of the LC).[103]

459. Prior consent is required for the dismissal of the following categories of wage earners:

- working mothers with a child under the age of three;
- handicapped workers;

---

103. As for the preliminary protection in case of dismissal *see* V. Mrachkov in: V. Mrachkov, K. Sredkova & A. Vassilev, *Komentar na Kodeksa na trouda*, 1039–1057 and the court practice quoted therein.

- workers who are suffering from a specific disease such as tuberculosis, cardiac troubles, psychiatric diseases, cancer or occupational diseases;
- wage earners who have commenced their leave. The nature of the leave is irrelevant: regular, annual, educational, sick leave, paid or unpaid and the like. The important thing here is that the leave should have been given in the established manner and the worker should have commenced it;
- workers or employees who have been elected as representatives of the workers and employees under Article 7, paragraph 2 or Article 7a of the LC and workers and employees elected as safety and health at work representatives either by the general assembly of workers and employees or by the assembly of representatives under Article 6 of the LC – for the period of time they are in this capacity;
- workers or employees who are members of a specialized body for negotiations, a European works council or a representative body in a European commercial or cooperative society – for the period of time they carry out their functions.

A dismissal without a request for permission, or a dismissal without a request for permission from the Labour Inspectorate, or where a request has been refused, is unlawful and can be countermanded by the court with all the consequences stemming therefrom (*see* below, Chapter 4).

460. Prior permission for the dismissal of trade union officials is discussed in Article 333, paragraph 3 of the LC.

The circle of trade union officials enjoying this protection is determined by the law. It includes wage-earners who are members of trade union committees at local, branch and national levels as well as presidents and secretaries of the committee in the respective enterprise (*see* Article 1, paragraph 6 of the Supplementary Clauses of the LC). Unfortunately, the vice-presidents (if any) and all other members of the enterprises' trade unions committees are not included in the circle of protected trade union officials. They are in the most direct and permanent contact with the enterprise, often entering into disputes with the administration and the employer and his managerial staff. That is why members, as well as the presidents and the secretaries of these committees, are in a real need of legal protection against unscrupulous dismissal.

The trade union organs competent to give prior permission for the dismissal of different categories of trade union officials are specified by the Central Direction of the trade union concerned.

This protection is enjoyed by all trade union officials, exhaustively enumerated in Article 333, paragraph 3 of the LC, irrespective of whether they are recognized as the most representative in the sense of Article 3, paragraphs 3 and 4 of the LC or not. This protection is applied to the cases of the limited, enumerated grounds in Article 333, paragraph 1 of the LC (*see* above).

This protection against the dismissal of trade union officials is applicable while they hold their respective trade union posts and for six months after their release.

461. A prior protection exercised by the trade unions against dismissal may be provided for in collective agreements (Article 333, paragraph 4 of the LC).

All the wage-earners to which the respective collective agreement applies enjoy this protection. The protection is applicable in so far as it expressly provides for dismissal on only two grounds – reduction of staff and reduction in the volume of the work (*see* above). It is difficult to find a reasonable explanation for this legislative approach which limits the contractual freedom of the parties to negotiate for prior protection against dismissal on other grounds. The former administrative methods have, without thought, been carried over to a purported new employment policy instead of leaving sufficient room for the social partners to negotiate between themselves and to find the most suitable solutions.

Prior permission for the dismissal of wage earners in these cases is given by the trade union committee in the respective enterprise which concluded the collective agreement and was a party to it.

462. A dismissal for which prior permission by the respective trade union organ is required either by law or by the collective agreement (*see* above) and which is made without such permission is unlawful with all the consequences stemming therefrom (*see* above, Chapter 4). This is the most reliable and valuable legal guarantee assuring the observation of the envisaged protection against arbitrary dismissal and job security. It is, at the same time, a guarantee for trade union activists performing their social functions against hasty and unjustified dismissal.

§5. Termination of the Employment Relationship Established by Election

463. Articles 337–340 of the LC contain specific regulations for the termination of the employment relationship established by election. They concentrate on the general questions arising from a termination of the employment relationship established by election. As regards the detailed regulations these are scattered among separate sources – the laws and statutes of public organizations. Here, attention will be focused on certain typical grounds for terminating this type of employment relationship.

464. The usual reason for terminating an employment relationship established by election is the expiry of the period of time for which the person was elected (Article 337 of the LC). The length of this time period differs for different elective officials and is determined in the appropriate laws or other acts – for paid posts in the municipal councils it is four years and so forth. With the expiry of this period the employment relationship is terminated. If the next election is delayed, the employment relationship continues until the elections are held and the newly elected persons have accepted office (Article 337 of the LC). This is to assure the continuous functioning of public and other bodies where the employment relationships are established by election.

465. The next specific reason for terminating this type of employment relationship is that of recall, provided for in Article 338 of the LC. This is a decision of the electorate to terminate the employment relationship, regardless of the will of the elected official, when it has lost confidence in the official. The proposal for recall must be reasoned, i.e., it must include facts and data concerning the work and conduct of the elective official which has acted to the loss of confidence. In fact, recall implies a negative evaluation of the work and conduct of the elected official and, as a rule, has the significance of a sanction. But it may also be provoked by objective reasons, for instance, illness, lasting absence of the elected official.

466. An employment relationship arising from election may also be terminated by the application of the grounds established for termination of the employment contract, except for disciplinary dismissal (Article 339 of the LC). When, in applying the grounds for termination of the employment relationship established by election, a manifestation of willingness by the employer is required, this is replaced by the decision taken by the electorate body for the recall of the elected employee. In the case of disciplinary dismissal, the specific procedure of recall is applied (*see* above).

§6. Legal Defence Against Unlawful Dismissal

467. The law places at the disposal of the worker a solid subsequent legal defence against unlawful dismissal.[104] The main legal provisions here are Articles 344–346 of the LC. The general prerequisites in the presence of which this defence is established are the following:

(1) a dismissal;
(2) the unlawful nature of the dismissal.

I. Dismissal

468. Dismissal in the sense of Article 344 of the LC constitutes a termination of the employment relationship on the initiative of the enterprise against and irrespective of the will of the worker. Dismissal occurs when the employer terminates the labour contract with or without notice. Those cases must be added in which, although the termination of the employment relation assumes an express manifestation of the will of the worker or desire for this (such as mutual agreement, termination on the initiative of the worker with or without notice), termination has in fact been effected against his/her will. In fact, the important thing here is that the worker did not genuinely desire the termination of the employment relationship by the employer.

---

104. For further details, *see* L. Radoilski, *Trudovo pravo*, 577–584; V. Mrachkov, *Pravna zashtita srechtou nepravilno ouvolnenie* [*Legal Protection against Wrongful Dismissal*] (Sofia: Publishing House of the Bulgarian Academy of Sciences, 1971), 52–254; V. Mrachkov, *Troudovo pravo*, 684–701.

II. Unlawful Dismissal

469. An unlawful dismissal is one effected on grounds that do not correspond to those established by law, or although based on it, fails to be supported by the factual circumstances of the specific case. It exists when the necessary prior permission and consent have not been obtained (Article 344, paragraph 3 of the LC). An unlawful dismissal for breach of discipline is a dismissal which has been effected in violation of the rule *Non bis in idem*, or after the expiry of a two-month period from the discovery, or a one-year period after the commission of the offence (Article 189, paragraph 2 and Article 194, paragraph 1 of the LC). Finally, a dismissal is unlawful when the employer fails to fulfil the obligation to audit or to demand written explanations from the worker before his/her disciplinary dismissal (Article 193, paragraph 3 of the LC). The unlawfulness of a dismissal is an objective quality. It makes no difference whether or not the employer is well-acquainted with the law or whether or not he acts in good faith.

These circumstances may be of significance eventually as regards the personal legal liability of the employer or the manager of the enterprise who dismissed the worker, but they are irrelevant for the dismissal's juridical characterization as either unlawful or legal. This follows from Article 344 of the LC in which such prerequisites for unlawful dismissal are not envisaged. It stems also from the social nature of the whole effective legal defence placed at the disposal of the worker in the event of unlawful dismissal. The practice of the courts consistently upholds this view.

470. At the request of the interested worker, an unlawful dismissal must be reaffirmed and proclaimed by the employer or the court. The employer may recognize the dismissal as unlawful when the worker refers the question to him and adduces reasons convincing him that he acted unlawfully (for instance, if a female worker produces a medical certificate attesting her pregnancy, or a worker produces a medical certificate saying that he/she is suffering from a certain disease or has been reallocated to a lighter job), yet the employer failed to ask the competent bodies for consent. The courts may recognize the dismissal as wrongful in examining labour disputes within the framework of legal proceedings and the procedural guarantees which they contain when the matter is referred to them by the worker (*see* below, Chapter 10). The claim can be brought within a period of six months from the date of receipt of the order for dismissal (Article 358, paragraph 1, item 2 of the LC).

471. The burden of proof (*onus probandi*) in a dispute for unlawful dismissal rests on the employer. He must prove its legality. At the basis of the legal dispute lies the exercise of the subjective right of dismissal which the law has placed at the discretion of the employer. When the worker concerned objects that dismissal is lawful, the employer must prove its legality. Naturally, this does not mean that the worker is a 'passive observer' in the process. He/she also takes part in collecting evidence, adducing data and considerations in support of his/her assertion that the dismissal is unlawful. But the employer is the party that must prove its legality.

472. The substance of the legal defence against unlawful dismissal consists, according to Article 344, paragraph 1 of the LC, in the worker's right to request:

(1) recognition of the dismissal as unlawful and if so to cancel it;
(2) reinstatement in his/her job;
(3) condemnation of the employer to pay him/her compensation for the time he/she was without work because of the unlawful dismissal;
(4) correction of the ground for which the worker was dismissed to be entered in the workbooklet and in other documents of or on the worker.

473. Once the court recognizes the dismissal as unlawful it will annul/cancel it. This is a consequence of the recognition of the dismissal being unlawful because the legal order cannot tolerate acts whose unlawfulness has been established by the courts. If the court considers the dismissal lawful, it confirms the dismissal but is not competent to exchange one ground for dismissal for another. The jurisprudence of the courts is consistent in this regard. This is because determination of the ground for dismissal is a right of the employer, as a party to the employment contract, granted to him by the law and the court as the competent organ to administer and apply the law but not to exercise rights with which the law has entrusted the parties to the employment relationship.

474. When, upon the worker's request, dismissal is recognized as unlawful:

(1) the worker is reinstated in his/her job (*see* below); and
(2) the employer is compelled to pay the worker compensation for the time he/she was without work due to the unlawful dismissal (*see infra*).

The worker is reinstated in the same job held prior to the dismissal and from which he/she was unlawfully dismissed. If, in the meantime, another worker has been appointed, the employer must transfer him/her to another job suited to his/her qualifications, and if this proves impossible, dismiss him/her (*see* below). If the job of the worker has been eliminated, he/she is, none the less, reinstated in his/her previous job. But here we have to distinguish between two situations. The first is when the dismissal is caused by a reduction of staff. In this case, the worker is automatically reinstated in his/her job and the employer must proceed to dismiss the other worker. The second situation is when the worker is dismissed for some other reason (breach of discipline, incompetence, etc.) but subsequently, in the course of the dispute over unlawful dismissal, his/her job was cancelled. In this case, after the ruling by the court on reinstatement and after the worker appears to resume his/her job (*see* below) the employer may dismiss him/her because of the elimination of that job. But this constitutes an entirely new dismissal. The worker is interested in such reinstatement, not only because it has been ruled after the establishment of the unlawfulness of his/her dismissal prior to the second dismissal and he/she is the winner in the legal dispute. As a result of this, the time during which he/she was jobless is recognized as a period of service (*see* below). In connection with the second dismissal, the appropriate procedures will have to be followed again, its legality will have to be assessed afresh, and the necessary prior permission and consent will have to be requested again. The practice of the Supreme Court accords with this.

475. After the unlawfully dismissed worker is reinstated in his/her job, if he/she wishes to take it – which most often happens in practice – he/she must 'appear for work' (Article 345, paragraph 1 of the LC). This means that he/she must actually present himself/herself to the employer and declare his/her desire and readiness to resume work. The law insists on the actual appearance for work of the reinstated worker, so that there will be no doubt as to his/her willingness to continue. The appearance for work must take place within a period of fourteen days from the delivery of the announcement of his/her reinstatement. This period of time may be prolonged only if the failure of the worker to appear is due to a 'reason beyond his/her control', such as illness, absence from the country. In these cases it is prolonged for so long as those reasons remain valid. If, however, he/she fails to appear without serious cause after the expiry of the fourteen-day period, he/she can no longer claim to hold the job in question.

476. The employer is obliged to admit the worker to the job in which he/she has been reinstated and to allow him/her to actually perform it. This is the profound sense of reinstatement and its final role – actually to restore the effect of the employment relationship which the enterprise had wrongfully terminated. And, in order to guarantee reinstatement, the law has established a system of legal liability of the employer aimed at compelling him to admit the worker to his/her former job and to create the conditions for its actual normal performance. These include a financial liability of the enterprise and its management to pay the reinstated worker remuneration from the date on which he/she appears to resume work to that of the actual resumption of work, i.e., when he/she in fact starts working. This responsibility is aimed at compensating the worker for damages he/she may have sustained as a result of having been wrongfully prevented to resume work. The compensation due in this case replaces the remuneration which he/she would have received if he/she had been admitted to his/her job and had actually been working. If the compensation is paid by the enterprise, the manager who wrongfully prohibited the re-instated worker from resuming work owes, by way of a regressive claim, restitution to the enterprise for the compensation paid. Second, the employer or manager who wrongfully disallowed the reinstated worker to resume work is administratively liable. This liability is personal and assumes the form of a fine of BGN 250 to BGN 1,000 (USD 190 to 770) imposed on the basis of reports drawn up by the labour inspectors in accordance with Article 414 of the LC. Third, there is criminal liability under Article 172 of the Penal Code. According to this provision, an official who fails to fulfil a decision which has entered into force for the reinstatement of a wrongfully dismissed worker or employee shall be punished with deprivation of freedom for up to three years. In fact, in these cases the actions of which the employer or his competent official, manager, his deputy and the like, has been found guilty are raised to the status of crimes against the labour rights of citizens.

477. In conclusion, it should be pointed out that reinstatement, with the detailed regulation devoted to it by the laws in force and with the legal guarantees of actual implementation which these establish, constitutes a culminating point in the legal defence against unlawful dismissal and is thus an important stipulation in the protection of the right to employment of the citizens of Bulgaria.

478. Compensation is also adjudicated to the dismissed worker for the time during which he/she was jobless (Article 225 of the LC). It is necessary to establish the length of this period as well as the fact that the worker's unemployment was due to unlawful dismissal. This means that it has to be subsequent to the wrongful dismissal and was caused by it. It is not necessary to prove whether the dismissed worker actually looked for work or not, whether he/she made an effort to find work, etc. It is sufficient to prove that he/she did not work at the time for the compensation to be awarded. This compensation is for the whole period during which he/she was jobless, but not exceeding six months. The limit of six months has been set because normally within this period of time the examination of the labour dispute for unlawful dismissal comes to an end with a decision of the respective competent body to the effect that the dismissal is unlawful or its lawfulness is reaffirmed. The basis on which this compensation is calculated is the last month's salary/wages received by the worker prior to dismissal. It includes all payments under the employment relationship owed by the employer to the worker for work done and of a permanent nature. This liability is a financial, contractual liability of the employer for violation of the labour contract which he has committed by the unlawful termination and the damage inflicted on the worker as a result of this expressed in the worker remaining without a job.

479. When a dismissal is found to be unlawful, the whole period of time during which the worker was jobless as a result of this dismissal is recognized as a period of employment (Article 354, item 1 of the LC). The employer must record in the workbook of the worker that the dismissal has been found unlawful and that the order for his/her dismissal has been countermanded. If the employer refuses to do so, the Labour Inspector does it (Article 346, paragraph 2 of the LC). In fact, the intention of this piece of legislation is to remove all possible unfavourable consequences which may arise or have arisen from the employer's unlawful termination of the employment relationship.

480. The worker may also request a change of the ground on which he/she has been dismissed as recorded in his/her booklet and in other documents (Article 344, paragraph 1, item 4 of the LC). For example, there may be different favourable juridical and moral consequences, such as the receipt of certain indemnities which may be due based on specific grounds of termination of the employment relationship (e.g., in the case of retirement pension, illness, reduction of staff, unemployment benefit), if the ground is, for instance, mutual consent rather than disciplinary dismissal. If the court finds the worker's request legally justified, its decision will be to change the ground. The changed ground is recorded in the worker's workbook by the employer on the basis of the court's decision and if the employer refuses to do so, is recorded by the Labour Inspector (Article 346, paragraph 2 of the LC).

481. All the substantive, subjective rights of the worker which form the core of the legal defence against unlawful dismissal are lodged as lawsuits before the competent court. They are heard by the courts within the framework of individual labour disputes (*see* below, Chapter 10).[105]

105. As for the protection in cases of unlawful dismissal, there is abundant and constant court practice. As for the latest court practice regarding these matters, *see* V. Mrachkov, 'Critical Review of the 2007 Practice of the Supreme Court of Cassation on Labour Disputes', *Juridicheski Sviat* [*Juridical World*] *Journal* 2 (2008): 213–214; 'Critical Review of the 2008 Practice of the Supreme Court of Cassation on Labour Disputes', *Juridicheski Sviat* [*Juridical World*] *Journal* 2 (2009): 189–192; 'Critical Review of the 2010 Practice of the Supreme Court of Cassation on Labour Disputes', *Juridicheski Sviat* [*Juridical World*] *Journal* 2 (2011): 180–183; 'Critical Review of the 2012 Practice of the Supreme Court of Cassation on Labour Disputes', *Juridicheski Sviat* [*Juridical World*] *Journal* 2 (2013): 148–151; 'Critical Review of the 2013 Practice of the Supreme Court of Cassation on Labour Disputes', *Juridicheski Sviat* [*Juridical World*] *Journal* 2 (2014): 161–167; 'Critical Review of the 2014 Practice of the Supreme Court of Cassation on Labour Disputes', *Juridicheski Sviat* [*Juridical World*] *Journal* 2 (2015): 132–134; 'Critical Review of the 2015 Practice of the Supreme Court of Cassation on Labour Disputes', *Juridicheski Sviat* [*Juridical World*] *Journal* 2 (2016): 177–181; 'Critical Review of the 2016 Practice of the Supreme Court of Cassation on Labour Disputes', *Juridicheski Sviat* [*Juridical World*] *Journal* 2 (2017): 156–157; 'Critical Review of the 2017 Practice of the Supreme Court of Cassation on Labour Disputes', *Juridicheski Sviat* [*Juridical World*] *Journal* 2 (2018): 122–124.

Chapter 8. Special Protection of Certain Categories of Workers

482. The existing laws provide special protection for certain categories of workers who, because of peculiarities due to such factors as age, health or physiological condition, are in need of special care by society. Such categories are: young people under the age of 18, women, and persons with reduced working capacity. The special protection in these cases consists in the establishment of higher requirements in connection with their appointment to a job and working conditions as compared with other workers. It is regulated by Articles 301–321 of the LC.

§1. Special Protection of Minors

483. The minimum age at which a child may be employed is 16 and is regulated in Article 301, paragraph 1 of the LC. This age limit is applied in general and refers to the employment in all branches of activity: industry, trade, agriculture, non-industrial activities, etc. There are two exceptions to this minimum. The first is contained in Article 301, paragraph 2 of the LC where it is provided that in exceptional circumstances, young persons between the age of 15 and 16 may be employed provided the work is light and not harmful to their health or their normal physiological or intellectual development.

484. Certain types of jobs and functions, about 135, enumerated in the special Ordinance No. 6 of the Ministry of Labour and Ministry of Health Care in 2006, are excluded from being performed by persons between the age of 15 and 16. These are jobs in mining, in the metallurgical, chemical, textile, polygraphic and wood-processing industries, in the transport by hand of loads above 8.2 kg and others. These functions and jobs are assessed as being strenuous and harmful to persons of this age as a result of which access to such jobs is absolutely closed. However, for admission to other kinds of employment a special procedure is to be followed and special requirements have been established. First the young person is subjected to a thorough preliminary medical examination (Article 302, paragraph 1 of the LC). The conclusion of this examination regarding the unfitness of the minor to occupy the specific job must take into account the nature of the work and any strenuous, unhealthy or dangerous features connected with it (Article 302, paragraph 1 of the LC). Second, alongside a medical report for every individual case, the consent of the appropriate district Labour Inspectorate is required for the appointment of the young person to the job to which he/she aspires. The Labour Inspectorate takes into consideration the medical report. If it is negative, the Inspectorate may not give its consent because of the specific nature of the circumstances on which the report is based. At the same time, if the medical findings are positive, it is not bound to grant permission and with a view to the actual working conditions (remoteness from the worker's domicile) the specific organization of the labour force and the specific circumstances, it may refuse to issue it. Without such permission, employment under the conditions of Article 302, paragraph 2 of the LC is not allowed. As has been shown, this exception does not constitute a 'mass exception' but has a strictly individual character and refers to individual cases. It aims at allowing access of minors to light jobs and functions only.

485. The second exception is established in Article 301, paragraph 3 of the LC. It reads:

> Persons under the age of 15 shall not be admitted to employment, except to take part in the artistic sphere in the making of films, in the rehearsal and presentation of theatrical, operatic, ballet, circus or other performances, subject to special conditions as are or may be prescribed by ordinance.

In item 2 of the Ordinance, issued for this purpose in 2006, the conditions indicated above for the persons under the age of 15, are adduced and developed still further, with a view to actual cases. On the one hand, emphasis is placed on the establishment of a good state of health and also on the possibilities of a beneficial, moral and physiological development of this category of persons and, on the other hand, on the nature of the work – it must not be 'dangerous to the life, health, and morals of these persons'. The Ordinance specifies further the text of Article 301, paragraph 3 of the LC, providing for the admission of minors to work in two cases:

(1) that of film-making and taking part in the rehearsal and presentation of theatrical, operatic and other productions, which as a rule is work for a shorter period. For this category of work, neither the law nor the Ordinance restricts the lower age limit;
(2) that of their appointment as students or apprentices in circuses (item 1, paragraph 2 of the Ordinance cited). Here, girls must have reached at least the age of 14 and boys 13.

In these two cases, the same special procedure as established in Article 302 of the LC, is to be followed for the admission to employment of these minors (item 2 of the Ordinance cited).

486. According to Article 303, paragraph 4 of the LC, 'It shall not be lawful to employ any person of the age between 16 and 18 in strenuous, harmful or dangerous jobs.' In fulfilment of this legal stipulation, in a special list issued by the Ministry of Labour and Ministry of Health Care in 2006, eighty types of work and activities in the mining, metallurgical, chemical, leather and fur industries, and others have been exhaustively enumerated. Persons between the age of 16 and 18 may not be employed in these jobs. They may be admitted to other jobs only after a careful and detailed preliminary medical examination and with the permission of the Labour Inspectorate, provided that the medical examination establishes good health and due account has been taken of the nature of the work and of any strenuous, unhealthy or dangerous features connected therewith (Article 303, paragraphs 2 and 3 of the LC).

487. It was through the amendments to the LC of March 2001 that Article 304 established a general prohibition on the performance of certain heavy and dangerous jobs and activities by persons below the age of 18. The jobs and activities enlisted under Article 304, paragraph 1 of the LC are ones whose performance:

(1) is beyond the physical and mental capabilities of these persons;
(2) is connected with exposure to harmful physical, biological or chemical action, and particularly to the action of toxic, carcinogenic and other agents, causing hereditary genetic or intrauterine injury;
(3) is connected with harms that have a constant unfavourable effect on health in any other way;
(4) is carried out under the conditions of radiation;
(5) is carried out in extremely low or high temperature, noise or vibrations;
(6) is connected with a risk of accidents at work, the persons not being able to realize this risk because of their physical or mental immaturity.

488. The explicit prohibition on these types of jobs and activities was introduced in the LC in fulfilment of Article 3, subparagraph (d) and Article 4 of Convention No. 182 of the ILO concerning the worst forms of child labour, 1999. This Convention was ratified by Bulgaria on 21 June 2000 and on 28 July 2001 took effect for the country (OJ, No. 54 of 2000 and No. 68 of 2001). And pursuant to Article 3, subparagraph (d) of the Convention cited, the worst forms of child labour prohibited under the Convention for persons below the age of 18, comprise jobs and activities that, owing to the nature or conditions of performance thereof, might injure their health, safety and morality. Pursuant to Article 4, paragraph 1 of Convention No. 182 these types of jobs and activities must be specified either in the national laws and decrees or by the competent bodies after consultations with the employers' and trade unions' organizations concerned. And the purpose of enlisting the harmful and dangerous types of jobs in Article 304, paragraph 1 of the LC is to designate those which constitute one of the worst forms of child labour within meaning of Convention No. 182 and to prohibit the performance thereof by persons below the age of 18.

489. Observance of minimum age requirements is guaranteed by the consequences for their violation. An employment contract concluded in violation of these provisions is null and void. Invalidity is proclaimed in a quick and simplified way by the Labour Inspectorate (Article 74, paragraph 2 of the LC), which is to be explained by the necessity of reacting at once against the violation. On the other hand, in cases of violation of these rules, administrative criminal liability is applied under the labour laws as provided in Article 414 of the LC. This is addressed to the employer and other persons responsible. The obligation to have preliminary and periodical medical examinations for minors under the age of 18 and the prohibition of night work and overtime of minors have been discussed above in respect of the liability arising from any violation.

490. Finally, minors up to 18 years of age who, by way of exception, are admitted to light jobs in accordance with Articles 301–304 of the LC enjoy a reduced working week (up to thirty-five hours) and day (up to seven hours) in a five-day working week (Article 305, paragraph 2 of the LC, Article 1, paragraph 2 and Article 4 of the Ordinance on Working Time, 1987). They also enjoy a longer paid annual leave of twenty-six days including also such leave for the calendar year in which they reach the age of 16 (Article 305, paragraph 3 of the LC).

§2. The Protection of Women

491. At the beginning of this work the extensive and far-reaching participation of women in social labour has been noted (*see* above, Introduction §I, IV). Naturally, this does not mean that the participation of women in the labour process does not give rise to problems. There are problems: the still continuing traditional preference of women for certain professions, the unsatisfactory vocational qualifications of a section of women workers, unsatisfactory working conditions, etc.

492. Equal remuneration to women and men performing the same work is based on the principle of equality between men and women, proclaimed in Article 36 of the Constitution and in Article 41, paragraph 1 of the Constitution setting up as the main criterion for determining remuneration – quantity and quality of work done. And the wage rates take into account these two criteria. The rate for additional payments is based on the strenuousness of the work, the conditions under which it is performed and its significance for the national economy. But, in both instances, it is a matter of objective criteria. The laws in force and their practical application make no distinction on the basis of gender of the person occupying a particular job in the amount of remuneration. And as a matter of course, all jobs are equally accessible to both men and women provided they fulfil the occupational requirements.

493. Nevertheless, the characteristics of females and the need to protect women from certain dangers or harm that might adversely affect their maternal role, which is of paramount social significance, their function of motherhood, especially when their children are small and in need of constant care, necessitate the establishment of a greater protection of women in the labour process when compared to men.

Women who may benefit from the increased protection provided by the law may be divided into two groups: the first includes all women workers and the second, pregnant women and mothers of small infants.

494. Traditionally, since the end of the Second World War, Bulgarian labour legislation has been providing for special (stronger) protection of women's labour at two levels: (a) protection of the labour of all women; (b) protection of the labour of pregnant women and mothers of young children until attaining three years of age.

495. The protection of labour of all women (*see* above paragraph 489) is based, on the one hand, on the understanding that the bone, muscular and locomotor systems of the female organism are more delicate, this making the woman physically weaker and less resistant to constant physical strain, and, on the other hand, on the need for preservation of the fertile potential of her unique biological natural function of being a mother.

This protection was laid down in Article 307 of the LC (1986 version) according to which it is illegal to employ women workers of any age on jobs strenuous and harmful to their health or function as a mother (Article 307, paragraph 1 of the LC). In fulfilment of this legal stipulation, a special list, approved by the Ministry of Labour and the Ministry of Public Health in 1987 enumerated the types of work in which women were prohibited from being employed because the work was considered to be particularly strenuous and harmful to health. This included thirty-two kinds of work in various branches of material production: all underground jobs, some jobs in the metallurgical, chemical, leather and fur, polygraphic, and canning industries, in construction, the carrying of loads over 15 kg, and others.

496. In the early 1980s, under the influence of the ideas of removal of sex discrimination, the special protection of the labour of all women was classified as discriminating against women and as limiting women's chances of having their full-value participation in labour, on an equal footing with men. These ideas were adopted by the EU as well as by the Bulgarian policy of approximation of Bulgarian legislation to the European standards in the course of preparing the country's accession to the EU. The amendments to the LC of June 2004 almost totally neglected the protection of all women's labour. In return, they introduced stronger and extended special protection for pregnant women and women-mothers in pregnancy, childbirth and raising a young child until the latter attains three years of age, or even eight years of age in certain cases (*see* below). The special employment protection of pregnant women workers and of mothers of children of up to three years of age and in certain cases up to the age of eight is especially far reaching. Protection begins with the establishment of pregnancy of the woman worker and continues through the whole period of pregnancy. The increased protection during this period is in the interest of the life and health both of the mother and the expected child. This protection continues with the same strength after the birth of the child and the return of the mother to work, after having availed herself of pregnancy and confinement leave, until the child reaches the age of two. During this period increased protection is established because of the early age of the child and the constant and special care which the mother must devote to its health and its upbringing.

497. Increased protection of pregnant women workers and mothers of infants mainly manifests itself as follows. Women who perform harmful and laborious work are transferred to other suitable and safe work upon the establishment of their pregnancy (Article 309 of the LC). This transfer should be effected within seven days upon the establishment of the pregnancy and lasts until the birth of the child. The LC makes this transfer the mutual obligation of both the employer and the pregnant woman. The obligatory nature as regards the employer is aimed at compelling his management to determine the strenuous and unhealthy jobs 'at the enterprise, from which pregnant workers and mothers of children up to three years of age must be transferred', the 'suitable jobs' to which they can be transferred, and to actually transfer them. The obligatory nature of this transfer as regards pregnant women workers and mothers is aimed at securing the consistent defence of the interests of women and their future maternity. This apparently personal interest is also the expression of an overriding social interest: the life and health of the mother and the expected child. That is why the legislator does not leave the protection to be assessed by the mother but removes it from her discretion and, with the juridical mechanism of a legal obligation, demands certain conduct. During the period of transfer, a pregnant woman or mother receives the remuneration of the new job. If this is less than the average gross remuneration received during the last twelve months before reassignment to the lighter job, the difference is paid to her by the social security system (Article 309, paragraph 3 of the LC). In addition, protection manifests itself by the establishment of pregnancy and maternity leave, the preservation of the employment relationship and the establishment of certain payments by the social security during such leave as discussed in another context. The prohibition of night work and overtime and special consideration given to women as regards dismissal have already been discussed (*see* above, Chapter 7, §4, IV).

§3. Special Protection of Persons with Reduced Capacity for Work

498. Special rules regulate the reassignment to other work and the conditions under which persons with a reduced capacity for work may be employed. They are contained in Articles 314–320 of the LC and the Ordinance on the Reassignment of Persons with Reduced Capacity for Work, 1987. The purpose of these rules is dual: on the one hand, it is to help the people concerned and place them in labour conditions favourable to the delicate state of their health and, on the other, it is to enable the utilization of their capacity for work, reduced as it may be. The main part of this legal regulation deals with workers whose capacity for work is reduced in the course of employment at an enterprise. The law secures such a worker the opportunity to remain at work in the same enterprise under working conditions favourable to his/her altered state of health and reduced capacity to work. These persons have, more specifically, to satisfy the following conditions:

(1) As a result of their reduced capacity for work, they must not be in a position to perform the work entrusted to them under the existing employment relationship. Their reduced capacity for work, moreover, must be due to illness (general or occupational), or an accident at work, and must last more than fifteen days.
(2) Without doing any harm to their health, they must be in a position to perform another job suitable to their qualifications, or else to be able to perform the same job, but under lighter conditions (Article 1, paragraph 1 of the Ordinance cited).

499. These are precisely the workers who are reassigned to other jobs, either by changing the job or the conditions under which the work is performed. This means:

(1) They should be transferred to other, lighter work, suitable to their state of health. In these cases and in the interest of their health, either the nature of the

work or the place where it is performed is changed, or both. For example, a worker may be transferred to another shop or another type of production where harmful conditions are absent: he/she is allocated another job in accordance with his/her qualifications, etc.

(2) A worker may remain on the same job but under less strenuous conditions. Alleviation of the conditions may consist, for instance, in reducing the number and complexity of the tasks, a reduction of the length of the working day, a reduction of the labour quotas.

These are the two means by which readjustment is effected in the enterprise where the worker was employed before his/her capacity for work was reduced.

500. Lighter and generally more suitable jobs for reassigned workers are specified in each enterprise by a special commission consisting of the employer or his representative, a representative of the trade union committee, the company's physician, a representative of the medical board, and a representative of the Social Welfare Department of the appropriate people's council. This composition facilitates a serious and objective selection of such jobs. They must constitute up to 10% of the total number of jobs in an enterprise, and in certain enterprises, such as for instance those producing consumer goods, or in certain local industries, even up to 50%. Only workers reassigned to lighter work are appointed to these jobs. Naturally, if there are no such workers, these jobs may be occupied by others. However, as soon as a worker needs to be reassigned, a fully capable worker occupying a lighter job is transferred in order to vacate it for the reassigned worker (Article 11 of the Ordinance cited).

501. In each individual case, the necessity of reassignment, the nature of the work to which the person must be reassigned, and the manner in which the reassignment is to be effected is decided by a medical body, the doctor in charge, the medical consultative board or the Industrial Medical Board. Any one of these may order reassignment for a certain maximum period of time: the doctor in charge for up to thirty days and the medical consultative board for up to six months, but it can also prolong this period. The Industrial Medical Board reassigns persons with a permanently reduced capacity for work when it is necessary to determine their disability group. Within this framework, the medical bodies decide in every specific case the duration and form of the reassignment. The employer is obliged to comply with the decision of the medical bodies within seven days by either transferring the worker to a job earmarked for persons with a reduced capacity for work or leaving him/her in the same job but making working conditions lighter in accordance with the medical reports. If the reassignment is to be effected in the form of a transfer to another job which is currently occupied by an able-bodied worker, then the latter must be transferred to another job, or, if that is impossible, dismissed (Article 3 of the Ordinance cited). However, in every case reassignment must be actually effected in full conformity with the ruling of the competent medical organs. It then continues for as long as the worker's working capacity is reduced, or until employment relationship is terminated in the established manner (*see* below). As soon as a worker is able to work normally, the reassignment is terminated and he/she is returned to his/her former job.

502. The employer is obliged to pay special attention to adjusting and maintaining the places of work occupied by disabled persons and to keep these in a condition suitable to their health and reduced working capacity. For this purpose he might have to introduce mechanization, automation or make other (re)adjustments so that working entails less physical or mental effort on the part of the worker (Article 8 of the Ordinance cited).

503. While employed in the new job, the worker receives remuneration for the work done, i.e., for the job to which he/she has been reassigned. If, however, he/she is paid less than the compensation he/she received because of temporary incapacity for work, the social security system pays the difference (Article 320, paragraph 2 of the LC).

504. The employment relationship with reassigned workers is terminated in the normal fashion. But, a dismissal, i.e., a termination of the employment relationship on the initiative of the employer, is effected only upon receipt of the consent of the Labour Inspectorate (Article 330, paragraph 1, item 2 of the LC; *see* above, Chapter 7, §4, IV).

Chapter 9. Covenant of Non-competition; Inventions by Employees

§1. Covenant of Non-competition

505. The operative legislation does not establish an explicit obligation of the workers and employees not to perform actions constituting unfair competition regarding their employer. Such an obligation used to exist under Article 15, paragraphs 2 and 3 of the Law on Protection of Competition, 1991. It was repealed through the law of the same name – the Law on Protection of Competition, 1998 (OJ, No. 52 of 1998). The operative Law on Competition Protection (prom. OJ, No. 102 of 2008, am. and suppl.) does not contain such an explicit provision.

506. However, this does not mean that this obligation is alien to the operative legislation. Such an obligation exists now. It can be deduced from the obligations of workers and employees set forth in Article 126, item 9 of the LC. This obligation becomes even more topical under the conditions of the market economy that is being created in the country. In this aspect it is indicative that the provision of Article 126, item 9 of the LC was supplemented through the amendments of the LC of March 2001.

507. According to the new redraft of Article 126, item 9 of the LC 'The worker or employee is obliged to be loyal to the employer by not abusing his trust, not divulging his confident information and maintaining his good reputation.'

Actually, this provision contains four specific obligations of the worker or employee. These obligations are: (a) to be loyal to the employer; (b) not to abuse his trust; (c) not to divulge the employer's confidential information connected with the activity thereof; (d) to maintain his good reputation. These obligations have a common direction – the worker and employee are supposed not to perform actions that either directly or indirectly affect or would affect unfavourably the competitiveness of the economic activity of his/her employer. They have already been considered here and are mentioned again only for the sake of completeness. As for their content, one should refer to the description thereof made above (*see* above, Chapter 2, §2).

508. On the other hand, the parties are not barred from specifying these obligations by mutual consent and providing for specific manifestations and modalities of these obligations, depending on the nature of the employer's activity and the character of the worker's or employee's job function, the parties being allowed to do so either on concluding the labour contract or by way of a subsequent amendment thereto. Such agreements are fully admissible under Article 66, paragraph 2 and Article 119 of the LC.

§2. Inventions by Employees

509. The protection of inventions is assured by the Law on Patents and Utility Models Registration (OJ, No. 27 of 1993, as amended). The legal protection of inventions as products of ingenious thinking is ensured by the patent irrespective of the character and position of its author. The patent testifies the fact of the invention, its priority, authorship (paternity) and exclusive right of the patentee (inventor) over the invention.

The system established by the Law on Patents applies to all inventions. Special attention is devoted to the service invention (Article 15 of the law cited). According to Article 15, paragraph 1 of the Law cited 'service invention' is an invention created within the framework of the obligations stemming from the labour contract with the inventor unless provided otherwise.

510. Article 15, paragraph 2 of the law cited distinguishes between three types of 'service invention':

(1) inventions created by the employee in the course of fulfilling his/her service (labour) obligations;
(2) inventions created by the worker outside of the framework of the job assigned to the worker according to the labour relationship but within the framework of tasks which are especially assigned to him/her;
(3) inventions created by the worker using material and/or financial resources granted by the employer or using knowledge, experience and the like accumulated as a result of work done within the framework of the relevant individual labour relationship.

The main idea is to protect inventions created by workers during and in connection with the fulfilment of a task entrusted to them.

The inventor who, as a patentee, has created a 'service invention' is entitled to two basic rights:

(1) the right to the paternity (authorship) of his/her invention and to protection of his/her name as the inventor;
(2) the right to fair (equitable) remuneration. The amount of this remuneration may be fixed in two ways: by contract or by some criteria for fixing fair remuneration. These criteria such as laid down in Article 15, paragraph 3 of the law cited are the following:
    (a) profits realized from the exploitation of the invention during the effective period of the patent (twenty years);
    (b) the worth of the invention;
    (c) contribution of the employer (investments, equipment, materials, knowledge, experience, technology, staff, etc.). In principle this remuneration is payable by the employer.

511. Disputes about the conditions under which an invention was made – whether or not it was made during and in connection with the fulfilment of a task entrusted to the worker under the employment relationship – are settled by the District Court of Sofia (Article 61 of the law cited) following the procedure established by the Code of Civil Procedure.

Chapter 10. Resolution of Labour Disputes

§1. Definition

512. Labour disputes are regulated in Articles 357–362 of the LC; the concept of a labour dispute is found in Article 357 of the LC. Its constituent elements derive from the legal definition established by Article 357 of the LC. First, a labour dispute is a dispute over a subjective right. It is an instance of disagreement between contending parties about actual or alleged violations of rights and obligations. Such a dispute presupposes the existence of subjective rights and duties granted or imposed respectively by legislation. The different standpoints of the parties stem from the actual or alleged non-fulfilment of these established duties. The disputes are based on claims. Any party whose subjective right is recognized by the law may defend it against infringements and claim its recognition and respect by turning for help to law-administering bodies or other bodies expressly vested with the power to defend such rights. Disputes like these are rights disputes. They are substantially different from the so-called interests labour disputes for which no legal regulation exists. A dispute between the parties in the latter case is precisely for the establishment of respective legal provision. These kinds of individual labour disputes are provided for in Article 107 of the LC. They are resolved by negotiation between the individual worker and the employer. In fact, here, the dispute is about what the law should be[106] while in labour claims the issue is about the violation or non-fulfilment of an established subjective right or obligation respectively.

513. The immediate object of a dispute is indicated in Article 357 of the LC. A labour dispute is a legal dispute (dispute over rights) which arises from and deals with 'the coming into being, existence, performance and termination of the employment relationship as well as the disputes about the performance of collective labour contracts'. Hence, there are two main groups of labour disputes as regulated by Chapter XVII of the LC. First, there are disputes based on rights and duties stemming from the individual labour relations such as regulated by Articles 61–356 of the LC and in Acts issued for their application. Examples are disputes concerning working time, remuneration, leave, rest, compensation, labour discipline, the entering into and termination of employment relationships, nullity of the labour contract, etc. Within this framework disputes connected with any employment relationship are included, regardless of how they have arisen – by means of a labour contract, by election, competitive examination, etc. This is the first basic group of individual labour disputes covered by Article 357 of the LC. Second, there are disputes about the performance of collective labour contracts. Because collective labour contracts are of a normative character (*see* below, Part II, Chapters 4 and 5) they provide rights and obligations for the workers and employer which become part of the individual labour relationship. Therefore, non-performance of the relevant collective labour contract may give rise to individual labour disputes between the parties involved. This is the second group of individual labour disputes over rights.

---

106. V. Mrachkov, *Troudovo pravo*, 723–737.

514. The legal definition of labour disputes in Article 357 of the LC permits two supplementary remarks. First, besides labour disputes there are disputes under social security law dealing with short-term and long-term social insurance. These disputes are examined by the instruments of social security in accordance with Articles 117–120 of the SIC, 1999. An explanation for this legal resolution is to be sought in the specific nature of the object of such disputes – the calculation and the payment of cash compensation, aid and allowances for children. Although connected with labour relations, the disputes are based on different legal relations – those of insurance – as a result of which Article 357 of the LC does not cover a specific method of settlement. The disputes are of a different legal nature (labour disputes over interests) and their settlement is regulated by the Law on Settlement of Collective Labour Disputes, 1990. They shall be examined in the second part of this monograph (*see* below, Part II, Chapter 5). In conclusion, it must be underlined that this chapter is devoted only to individual labour disputes as regulated by Articles 357–362 of the LC.

515. Parties to labour disputes are the subjects of the employment relationship – the worker and the employer. The rights and obligations giving rise to a disagreement between them, are theirs, and that is why the dispute is conducted between them. Moreover, the question here is one of an individual labour dispute, i.e., a legal dispute based on an individual employment relationship. It is of no significance whether only one worker or more – by a subjective unification of their claims – are in dispute with the employer on one and the same question. The important thing is that the object of the dispute stems from an individual labour relationship, and not the number of workers engaged in it.

516. In accordance with Article 358 of the LC the claims of a labour dispute must be lodged by the interested party within a definite time period. These periods differ according to the nature of the object of the labour dispute as established by law:

(1) within one month in the case of labour disputes about diminished financial liability of the worker and the cancellation of a disciplinary punishment entitled 'reprimand';
(2) within two months in the case of disputes about a cancellation of disciplinary punishment entitled 'warning for dismissal', change in the place and the nature of the assigned work as well as termination of the employment relationship;
(3) within three years in all other cases of labour disputes (leave, compensations, salary, etc.).

It must be clear that the procedural right to bring an action (lodge a claim) is extinguished by the passage of time. In other words, a claim lodged after the expiration of the period laid down is inadmissible.

§2. Hearing of Labour Disputes by the Courts

517. Labour disputes are examined by the ordinary courts (Article 360 of the LC). The competent law-administering body in the cases examined here is the regional court. In hearing labour cases as a Court of First Instance, the regional court is composed of a district judge. Labour disputes are heard in accordance with the Code of Civil Procedure (Article 360, paragraph 1 of the LC). They usually follow the general procedure of civil dispute claims which are heard by courts of first instance, with all the requirements typical of this procedure: filing a claim with the court, the constitution of the parties, the acts of procedure to be performed by the parties and the court, collection of evidence, pronouncing of the decision and its effect (Articles 103–309 of the Code of Civil Procedure). These questions are studied in the Civil Procedural Law.[107] Appeal against a decision of the district court in these disputes may be brought before the district court in the generally established way, within a period of fourteen days from the date on which the party has been informed of the decision, with the accompanying reasons (Articles 258–273 of the Code of Civil Procedure). An appeal to the Supreme Court of Cassation ('cassation appeal to the Supreme Court of Cassation') against this decision follows the normal civil procedure in the third instance (Articles 280–295 of the Code of Civil Procedure).[108] Judgments of the court of second instance are made in last resort from which there is no appeal.

518. One of the most difficult problems in labour disputes, which has given rise to workers' and employees' justified discontent in the recent years, is the length of time it takes for the labour disputes to be considered. Actually, the termination of a legal labour dispute takes from two to four years. Under the on-going inflation in the country, a lawsuit – even one in which the rendered decision is in favour of the worker or employee – loses a great part of its significance for the latter, because the awarded compensation or another receivable has a sharply deteriorated purchasing value. Owing to that, the task is to expedite the court proceedings of labour disputes and achieve a speedy enactment of the court's decisions thereupon that have taken effect, of course, without having the quality of the court proceedings lowered because of their being expeditious. This is a common problem for the whole jurisdiction; however, in the field of labour jurisdiction it is of greater importance, as the labour rights – the subject matter of labour disputes – are of existential significance for the workers and employees. Guided by these considerations, the legislator has provided in the amendments to the LC of March 2001 that the main types of labour disputes shall be processed under the procedure for the so-called summary proceedings (Chapter XXV 'Summary Proceedings', Articles 310–317 of the Civil Procedure Code). These disputes are:

(a) disputes over unlawful dismissal under Article 344, paragraph 1, items 1–3 of the LC (acknowledging the dismissal as an unlawful one, countermanding it,

107. Zh. Stalev et al., *Bulgarsko grajdansko protzesualno pravo*, 179–392.
108. *Ibid.*, 503–583.

reinstating the worker or employee into the job and paying compensation for the time for which he/she has been out of job, but not exceeding six months);

(b) disputes over money due under labour legal relationships: for labour remuneration, compensations and the like.

519. The time limits for performing the various procedural actions in considering the dispute in summary proceedings are shorter: sending a copy of the statement of claim to the defendant as early as the day of its being filed with the court, the obligation of the defendant to submit his/her reply thereto within a seven-day term, the obligation of the court to render its decision within a seven-day term after the session at which the oral pleadings were closed, instead of the thirty-day term in ordinary proceedings, etc.

The conduct of summary proceedings is regulated as a claimant's right, and the usual claimants in labour disputes are the workers and employees.

520. Examination or hearing of labour disputes is free of charge for the worker. This principle, established in Article 359 of the LC, means that the worker is exempted from the payment of any taxes and fees for the conducting of labour cases, such as state taxes, court costs, deposits for witnesses, experts. Exemption from the payment of fees or taxes is applicable to all courts examining labour disputes in all kinds of proceedings and in all instances to which the labour dispute may be referred by way of appeal. This encourages the worker to refer his/her dispute to the competent body for examination and settlement. In addition, legal assistance at the hearing of labour disputes is available to workers who are claimants or defendants in labour cases at low fees of up to BGN 1,000 for defending a case in each instance (Article 1, item 4 of Ordinance of the Ministry of Justice, 1993). This constitutes substantial assistance for workers in seeking and finding qualified aid in the conducting of labour cases.

521. Some peculiarities are established regarding the jurisdiction of labour disputes involving:

(1) foreign employers;
(2) nationals who work abroad;
(3) certain categories of nationals who work in Bulgaria.

These are examined briefly in the subsequent text.

522. Labour disputes between foreign workers and foreign employers, or employers who manage joint-ventures and whose seat (head office) is in Bulgaria, are heard by the Bulgarian courts according to the seat (head office) of the employer. But this rule is applied only when the parties have not agreed upon another competent court (Article 361 of the LC). If they have done so, the competent court is the one agreed upon by the parties. Therefore, priority is given to the contract. The same principle is adopted by Article 31 of the Law on Encouragement of Investments (OJ, No. 97 of 1997, as amended). The main idea is to allow more flexibility and to facilitate the contracting parties settlement of labour disputes arising from the employment relationship.

523. Labour disputes between national workers who work abroad and their Bulgarian employer is heard by the relevant court of the capital Sofia when the worker is the claimant (plaintiff). If the worker is the respondent, the competent court is the court of his/her permanent place of residence in the country (Article 362 of the LC). Therefore, this rule establishes only the local competent court in the country when both parties to the employment contract are nationals. Even if the assigned work is performed abroad the competent court is the national court and national legislation is applicable. The only peculiarity concerns the designation of the regional (local) Bulgarian court as being competent to hear the local dispute.

524. The last particularity regards some specific labour disputes of two categories of employees. Instances of this nature are provided for in Article 360, paragraph 2 of the LC.

The first group includes labour disputes concerning the discharge of elected employees, employed in representative bodies of the state, in social organizations, by political parties or movements, as well as other responsible civil servants, as established by law or by Act of the Council of Ministers, which are expressly excluded from the courts' jurisdiction. The exclusion of disputes involving elected officials (employees) does not seem to give rise to problems. Discharge of such persons depends solely on the supreme power of the relevant electoral body and no other organ is competent to appreciate or control its justification and foundation. This is provided for in Articles 338 and 360, paragraph 2 of the LC. Within the framework of this general principle, special cases may also be provided for, in other special laws. This solution is in accordance with Article 119 of the Constitution.

525. The second group of labour disputes are connected with the discharge of persons under Article 28, paragraph 2 of the Law on Administration, 1998. These are the members of the so-called political cabinets of the Prime Minister, the Deputy Prime Ministers and the ministers. They include: the Head of the Cabinet, the Parliamentary Secretary and the Head of the Public Relations Department, as well as the deputy ministers in the political cabinets of the ministers. The labour legal relationships of these employees are based on political trust and political expedience. And the courts are lawfulness appraisal bodies. Owing to that, the appraisal of political trust and political expedience upon discharging these persons may not be a matter of judicial control. And because of that the LC excludes the consideration of disputes relating to discharge of these employees from the competence of the courts.

526. The amendments to the Law on Settlement of Collective Labour Disputes (March 2001) also gave a new legal framework to the procedure for considering the disputes regarding the establishment of the unlawfulness of a strike (Article 17 of the law cited). Prior to the amendments these disputes used to be considered by the district courts. Their decisions were final and unappealable. The amendments provide that the decisions of the district courts considering these disputes are subject to appeal to the courts of appeal. However, their decisions are final ones and are not subject to cassation appeal to the Supreme Court of Cassation. Actually, by way of these amendments, an important step forward was made in the complex labour legal disputes, which are of great social importance. And the single-instance consideration thereof was changed into normal three-instance one (*see* below, Part II, Chapter 4).

Part II. Collective Labour Relations

Chapter 1. General Remarks

527. Collective labour relations are those existing between workers collectively or their organizations (trade unions) and employers or employers' organizations. They embrace the body of rules which regulate the right of association for workers and employers, the right to set up organizations of their own choice, workers' participation, collective labour contracts, collective labour disputes and their peaceful settlement, as well as the rules concerning economic warfare, namely regarding strikes, lockouts, etc. These issues are of paramount significance in the transition period from a totalitarian to a democratic society.

528. Collective labour relations were systematically neglected during the socialist period of development of labour law. The totalitarian state emphasized and developed above all labour legislation concerning individual labour relations between the individual worker and employer and determined centrally, and almost exhaustively, their content without leaving any room for the free will of the parties. The administrative command system did not allow real participation of workers' and employers' organizations in the determination of rights and duties of the parties through collective bargaining.

529. Since the very beginning of 1990, labour legislation regulating collective labour relations has developed intensely. This rapid development of collective labour law strives to respond to the country's needs and to overcome its proverbial backwardness inherited from the recent past. Progress developed in two ways:

(1) the adoption on 6 March 1990 of the Law on Settlement of Collective Labour Disputes;
(2) the amendments to the LC in November 1992. The amendments provided for completely new regulations of fundamental chapters on collective labour relations such as: trade unions and employers' organizations, tripartism, collective labour contracts, collective labour disputes, and so on. In doing so labour legislation now effectively contains a relatively complete body of rules governing collective labour relations.

Real collective bargaining started in the beginning of 1990. Despite the predominance of the imperative character of the legal regulation on labour relations existing at this time, the newly created or reorganized trade unions successfully tried to 'discover', find and explore all the possibilities to bargain with employers, especially in the field of labour remuneration and working conditions where the problems were sharply felt and where the situation was very strained.

530. The law treats five basic institutions as being characteristic of labour collective relations at a given enterprise or of any working people working under an employment relationship in Bulgaria:

(1) the trade union and employers' organizations;
(2) workers' participation;
(3) tripartite cooperation;
(4) collective labour contracts;
(5) collective labour disputes.

Relatively detailed and far-reaching regulations have been devoted to trade unions and employers' organizations, workers' participation, tripartite cooperation, information and consultation, collective labour contracts and collective labour disputes. The relations arising are different from those of an individual employment relationship. Nevertheless, in the final analysis they are aimed at the individual employment relationship, influence its content and the rights and obligations to which the individual employment relationship gives rise. In the text that follows, these four institutions are examined.

Chapter 2. Trade Unions and Employers' Organizations

§1. Freedom of Association and the Right to Organize

531. According to Article 49 of the Constitution 'Workers and employees shall be free to form trade union organizations and alliances in defence of their interests related to work and social security' (paragraph 1) and further 'Employers shall be free to associate in defence of their economic interests' (paragraph 2). Thus the Constitution recognizes the right of association in the social and economic interest of workers and employers respectively. Developing this fundamental right of workers and employers, the LC devotes to trade unions and employers' organizations a special chapter, namely Chapter III, entitled 'Trade Unions and Employers' Organizations'. From the amendments to the LC in November 1992 and in March 2001 three points are worth noting. First, the volume of legal provisions devoted to the trade unions diminished. The chapter contained seventeen articles in the LC of 1986; now only ten remain (Articles 33, 34–36a, 37, 42, 45, 46 and 49). All disposals providing for several rights of the trade unions not customary to their protective function (such as participation in the drafting and adoption of legislative acts, participation in planning, in technological improvements of the quality of production, organizing rests and holidays of employees, organizing activities of the workers' collectives and the collective bodies of management) and including the trade unions in the totalitarian society were abolished. Only the disposals which are typical for trade unions and their activity were preserved. Second, the legal regulation in Chapter III embraces not only freedom of association and the right to organize in relation to workers and employees, but also for the first time in relation to employers. What is more significant is the fact that the legal regulation recently established deals on an equal footing with freedom of association and the right of workers and employees to organize, on the one hand, and of the employers on the other hand, without any preferences or advantages for one or the other of the two professional groups (workers and employers). Third, the new regulation of the freedom of association and the right to organize is established in conformity with the requirements of international instruments and standards as provided for by Article 8 of the International Covenant on Economic, Social and Cultural Rights and by international conventions Nos 87 and 98 of the ILO which have been ratified by Bulgaria.

§2. Trade Unions

532. Trade union association in the country is free. This principle proclaimed in Article 4, paragraph 1 of the LC means that the legal system not only allows the setting up of trade unions, and does not establish any preliminary conditions, requirements or restrictions in connection with their membership or with the holding of meetings, etc., but also encourages implementation of trade union activities. Finally, the setting up of trade union organizations does not require any preliminary permission from any state or trade union body. Workers are free to join a trade union of their own choice and to leave it. It is the legal basis of pluralistic trade unionism which has really been established in the country since the very beginning of 1990 (*see* below). The only obligation of a worker who is a member of a trade union is to observe its statutes and standing orders and to obey them.

533. As a result of real pluralism in the trade union movement since 1990, there are now some four trade unions in the country. The most important and most influential among them are the CITUB and the CL *Podkrepa*. CITUB was founded on 17 and 18 February 1990 by the Extraordinary Congress of the former Bulgarian Trade Unions. On the initiative of the delegates the Congress became the Constituent Congress, which adopted a new statute, a working platform and a new name for the organization: Confederation of Independent Trade Unions in Bulgaria. CITUB won recognition as the biggest and most influential trade union organization, enjoying prestige and position in the economic, social and political life of the country. Following the last organizational census in December 2012, CITUB unites about 280,000 workers and employees in almost all branches and spheres of activities. Members of the confederation are: 79 federations, unions and trade unions formed on the basis of branch and professional principles.[109] After having left the World Federation of Trade Unions (1990), it is now a member of the East European Trade Unions Forum (1991) and the International Confederation of Free Trade Unions (ICFTU) since 1995. CL *Podkrepa* was created in February 1989 as an informal independent anticommunist organization in opposition. During the congress in March 1990, the organization became legitimate as a Confederation with a new statute of working platform. CL *Podkrepa* has experienced a substantial evolution. After the change in the political system in 1990, it altered the priorities of its activities: now it is oriented towards trade union work, towards defending the rights, interests and living standards of its members.[110] CL *Podkrepa* has been a member of the ICFTU since 1991. Following the last organizational census in December 2012, CL *Podkrepa* unites about 80,000 workers and employees, 22 federations on the basis of branch. The tendency towards a decrease in the membership of trade union organizations, including the two largest ones thereof – CITUB and CL *Podkrepa* – continues after 2007 as well.

It was through the Council of Ministers' decisions No. 667 and No. 666 of 11 August 2016 (prom. OJ, No. 64 of 11 August 2016) that the Confederation of the Independent Trade Unions in Bulgaria and the CL *Podkrepa* were recognized once again as representative trade union organizations at the national level for a four years' period.

534. As a result of pluralism in the trade union movement Articles 34–36a of the LC introduce and regulate the criteria and procedure of recognition of the representative trade unions. The criteria as established by Articles 34 and 35 of the LC, as amended in January 2012 (OJ No. 7 of 2012) and in January 2016 (OJ No. 8 of 2016) are the following:

---

109. *Tripartism in Bulgaria: Legal Framework, Institutions, Social Partners* (Sofia: CITUB, 1993), 25–26; *Otcheten doklad na Koordinazionnia Savet na KNSB 8–10 oktomvri 1993* [*Report of the Coordination Council of the KNSB 8–10 October 1993*] (Sofia: KNSB, 1993), 143.

110. *Tripartism in Bulgaria*, 27–28; G. Nikolova, I. Assiova, 'Democraziata e trouden i machitelen prozess' ['Democracy Is a Difficult and Painful Process'], *Podkrepa Newspaper*, 9 Feb. 1994.

(1) membership of the trade union must be of at least 50,000 workers and employees;
(2) the trade union must have organizations of workers and employees in more than one-quarter of the activities designated by a code of up to two digits in the Economic Activities Classification approved by the National Statistical Institute, with a membership of at least 5% of the people employed in each economic activity or at least fifty organizations of at least five members in each economic activity;
(3) the trade union must already have local bodies in more than one-quarter of the municipalities within the country and a national leadership body;
(4) it must have the capacity of a legal person, acquired under the procedure of Article 49, paragraph 1 of the LC at least three years prior to submitting the request for recognition of representativeness.

535. The provisions of items 1 and 4 (*see* above paragraph 530) were challenged before the Constitutional Court as being unconstitutional and inconsistent with the generally accepted norms of international law and the international treaties that Bulgaria is a party to (Article 149, paragraph 1, items 1 and 4 of the Constitution). In its Decision No. 7 of 19 June 2012 on constitutional case No. 2 of 2012, the Constitutional Court did not uphold this claim, acting reasonably, in my opinion (prom. OJ, No. 49 of 2012). As pointed out by the Constitutional Court in the motives to the said decision, the new regulation has preserved the quality characteristic of the trade union organization, while the changes have only a quantitative nature, as they concern the number of its members and the length of registration of the legal entity prior to submitting the request for recognition of its representativeness. These changes do not affect the internal relations within the trade union organization, as they do not set any restrictive regime of its establishment that would contradict the right of free trade association proclaimed by Article 49, paragraph 1 of the Constitution. Collective bargaining and the exercise of the other functions of the trade unions will not be hindered. On the other hand, the higher norms of national representation are a matter of legislative and administrative expedience, which does not concern the freedom of trade union association, as the trade unions continue existing and carrying out their activity, even where they fail to satisfy the requirements regarding representativeness. The challenged provisions do not contradict those international treaties signed by Bulgaria which, by virtue of Article 5, paragraph 4 of the Constitution, have priority over our national law in case the latter contravenes them. The challenged provisions do not contravene Article 3, paragraph 2 of the ILO Convention No. 87 on trade union freedom, according to which the public authorities must always refrain from any interference that might restrict or obstruct this freedom. The new provisions are not discriminative, as the new requirements set out therein do not introduce different treatment of trade union organizations.[111]

---

111. 'Decisions and Rulings of the Constitutional Court – 2012' (Sofia: M. Drinov Publishing House, 2013), 106–107.

536. Representative trade unions on a national level are acknowledged by the Council of Ministers. Any refusal of acknowledgement could be litigated at the Supreme Administrative Court. Its decisions are final and not subject to appeal. The most important consequence of the acknowledgement of trade unions as representative at national level is that all their organizations and sections are also (*ipso jure*) recognized as representative (Article 36, paragraph 4 of the LC). Representative trade unions enjoy two special rights which no other organizations of workers and employees have. They are the following:

(1) only the representative organizations are entrusted to participate in the tripartite cooperation;
(2) only the representative organizations may conclude collective labour contracts at municipal and branch levels (*see* below).

537. Both these rights, provided for in the LC (Article 3, paragraph 1 and Article 51, paragraph 1), are sufficiently important to justify the interest and aspiration of trade unions to be acknowledged as representative. Up to now only two trade unions have been acknowledged as representative, namely the CITUB and the CL *Podkrepa*.

538. The main function and vocation of the trade unions are to represent and protect the interests of the workers related to labour and social security relations as well as those connected with the living standard (Article 4, paragraph 2 of the LC). The scope of these interests is very broad. The purpose for which trade unions are set up is to formulate these interests, to bring them to cognizance of the established competent organs, and to defend the demands for the improvement of working conditions. This is the *raison d'être* for their existence, which goes on to determine further their organization and activities.

539. Trade unions are autonomous non-profit-making organizations. They are independent of the state, political parties and employers' organizations. The domination of former trade unions by the Bulgarian Communist Party as it existed in the recent past during the totalitarian period, was definitely rejected. Now trade unions enjoy internal organizational autonomy and self-government. They adopt their own statutes, standing orders and other internal regulations, freely elect their organs and representatives, organize their own internal government. They also adopt their own programmes of activities, etc. They determine the manner and approach in the realization of their functions. The only limitations in determining and performing the functions of trade unions are that they are in conformity with their own statutes and national laws. Conformity with their statutes stems from the very nature of their free and voluntary organization. And the requirement for their statutes and activities to conform with the national laws stems from the necessity to observe generally established standards in society. Nevertheless, these generally established standards in the laws do not restrict. On the contrary, they warrant the free exercise of the right to organize. This conclusion is also confirmed by Article 8 of the ILO Convention No. 87.

540. In exercising their protective function, the trade unions take an active part in the drafting of internal rules and regulations at enterprise level and in the discussion of labour and social security issues at a local and branch level. These specific rights of trade unions have some general characteristics. First, all trade unions are entitled to these rights, including both representative and non-representative trade unions. Second, these rights are exercised by their organs and bodies as defined in the statutes of the respective trade unions. This is a normal way of action as all collective formations (and trade unions are also such a formation) normally exercise their functions through their organs and bodies, which are established for this reason, i.e., to act on behalf of the relevant trade union organizations. Third, according to their essence, these rights are of a different character:

(1) According to Article 37 of the LC, the organs and bodies of trade unions have the right to take part in the preparation of the draft of all internal regulations and ordinances concerned with terms of employment. The scope of these internal regulations is quite wide. It embraces all regulations in the enterprise, such as regulations about safety and health, arrangement of working time, internal order in the respective enterprise, salaries and their payment, and so on. The employer is obliged to invite the trade union representatives to participate in the preparation of the internal regulations. Having invited them, the employer has to indicate the agenda, the place and date of the respective meeting and to dispatch to them the preliminary materials about the questions to be discussed, if any. This is a consultative function of the trade unions. Of course, the final decision and approval of the internal regulations is the employer's. Participation of trade union representatives in the drafting of these regulations consists only in expressing the opinions of their members and defending their interests.

(2) According to Article 42 of the LC, trade union representatives may participate in the discussion of labour and social security issues. This prerogative belongs only to central bodies of the trade unions or to the organs and bodies entitled by them. The essence of this right consists in taking part in the discussion of labour relations and social security questions which concern the workers and employees in the relevant ministry, administrative body, enterprise or local administrative unit. In participation in the discussion on labour relations and social security issues, the trade union representatives express and defend the interests of the workers and employees. The final decision in these cases again is made by the employer, the administrative body or organ respectively, minister, and so on.

541. By virtue of Article 45 of the LC: 'The trade union organizations and their subdivisions shall be entitled, at the request of the workers and employees, to represent them before the courts.' This refers to the representation as a matter of procedure in court hearings of labour disputes. It may be effected by the trade union committee of the trade unions, the regional council of the trade unions (if any), by the Central Council of the relevant trade union, and so forth. The formulation of the law 'the trade unions and their subdivisions' is quite wide and establishes no limitations. In this way not only members of the relevant trade union can be represented but any worker or employee. This procedural representation can be effected when the worker authorizes the respective trade union organ to represent him/her. This is the general voluntary representation arising on the basis of a unilateral authorizing action (Article 20 of the Code of Civil Procedure in connection with Article 36 of the Law on Obligations and Contracts). The scope of representation in these cases is normally within the bounds of an ordinary power of attorney. The trade union representative may perform all acts of procedure on behalf of the person he represents without being able to accept claims from the other party, to deny the claims of the worker or employee, to negotiate compromises or to receive money or valuables on behalf of the worker or employee.[112] But if the trade union representative is expressly authorized by the worker he can also perform these acts (Article 45 of the LC). The main significance and purpose of this procedural representation by the trade union organizations and their subdivisions is to assure the competent and free of charge defence of the rights and interests of the workers before the courts. This kind of procedural representation is quite widely used in practice.

542. The laws now in force not only establish the legal framework of freedom of association for trade union purposes but, as a legal obligation, also provide for assistance to the trade unions in the performance of their activities. According to Article 46 of the LC 'The state authorities and employers create conditions conducive to the activities of trade unions and assist them. They shall submit gratuitously for use real and movable property, buildings, rooms and other facilities necessary for the performance of their functions.' This legal provision regulates the attitude which the state authorities and the employers ought to have towards all trade unions, representative and non-representative.

543. Article 46 of the LC establishes an obligation on state bodies, local self-government bodies and employers to assist trade unions and to create conditions conducive to their activities. The state bodies which have such an obligation are the government, ministers, heads of other departments and other state bodies such as regional governors, mayors, and so on. Employers are the employers in the enterprises, companies, firms, organizations, and so forth. State bodies and employers have their own and specific obligations: the government and other state organs should create conditions conducive to the activities of the national and branch trade union organizations at the national or local level within the framework of their competence; employers are obliged to create such conditions on an enterprise level for the basic trade union organizations which exist and function in the respective enterprise.

The essence of this obligation consists in creating conditions for trade union activities to be conducted. It means creating an ambience which facilitates the exercise of trade union activities directed at the promotion and defence of the interests of members and other workers, the establishment of good relationships with the trade unions which permit an introduction and maintenance of a permanent and constructive dialogue, bargaining, etc. This is so because a constructive and fair-play

112. Zh. Stalev et al., *Bulgarsko grajdansko protzessualno pravo*, 170–172.

partnership between trade unions, employers and state bodies is the very basis for the promotion of the interests of any of the parties concerned.

The obligation of the state bodies and employers provided for in Article 46 of the LC is extended in the second sentence. It specifies the general obligation to assist trade unions in the performance of their activities by mentioning the material conditions necessary for the accomplishment of their functions. These conditions are enumerated by way of example: the submission gratuitously for use of real and movable property – buildings, rooms, etc. It is important to underline that all these facilities are to be placed at the disposal of the trade unions gratuitously, i.e., free of charge. Compliance with this obligation attains particular significance under the difficult material conditions the country is facing and in which the trade unions have to realize their activities. Compliance with this obligation is more than ever before absolutely necessary to assure real conditions for all activities of the trade unions.

§3. Employers' Organizations

544. The right of employers to organize is recognized by Article 49, paragraph 2 of the Constitution. It is a fundamental (constitutional) right, further developed in Articles 5, 33, 42 and 49 of the LC. The right of employers to organize has its own legal framework in Bulgarian law for the first time since the end of the Second World War. In the past, during the era of a centrally planned economy based on the domination of the state ownership, this right was practically unknown as employers as such did not exist. The only real employer was the state, and all directors, managers, and so on in state-owned enterprises were state employees. They were members of the same trade unions together with other workers and employees, even though they had their own economic interests different from the interests of the wage earners engaged in the respective state-owned enterprises under their subordination as dependent workers.

545. One part of the legal regulation is common to the right of employers to organize themselves and the workers' and employees' freedom of association and right to organize. This is the legal rule about the independence of the employers' organizations (Article 33 of the LC) and their participation in the discussion of labour and social security issues (Article 42 of the LC). This has already been discussed (*see* above §2). Another part of the legal framework of the employers' right to organize consists of some specific aspects of the employers' organizations. Only these aspects will be discussed further (*see* below, paragraphs 542–651).

546. The fundamental differences between the freedom of association and right to organize workers and employees on the one hand, and of employers on the other hand, consist of three main points:

(1) the subjects of this right;
(2) the purpose of the workers' and employers' associations;
(3) the means by which the employers' organizations act to achieve their respective purpose.

These three points shape, above all, the specific legal and sociological appearance of the workers' and employers' organizations.

547. Subjects of the envisaged freedom are the employers. Para. 1, item 1 of the Supplementary Provisions of the LC contains the legal definition of the concept 'employer'. According to paragraph 1, item 1.

An employer shall denote any natural and juridical person or subdivision thereof, as well as any organizationally and economically autonomous formation (enterprise, establishment, organization, cooperative, economy, shop, household, company and the like), who independently hires workers and employees under relation of employment.

This definition is a broad one. It contains two basic elements:

(1) The employer is a natural or juridical person. If a natural person, he or she must have civil legal capacity. It could also be a juridical person (body corporate) which has acquired this status by the legally established procedure (by law, by an act of permission, or with the founders' approval).[113] If the employer is a corporate body, the quality of employer may be determined by its subsidiary as well as any other formation (enterprise, office, organization, cooperative, etc.), regardless of whether that formation is itself an avowed body corporate or not. But in that case it must be economically and organizationally independent. This means that it must have its own exclusive field of activity or a distinct part of it must be exclusive, its own separate organization and separate finances (its own balance sheet and bank account).
(2) The employer hires another's labour force under a labour *nexus*, to be his/her worker or employee in the performance of the employer's activity. This means that he/she may independently hire and dismiss persons as workers and employees. The number of hired workers or employees makes no difference, nor does the kind of premises on which the employer's activity is performed. It may be public (state or municipal owned), private or a mixture.

The main consequence stemming from this broad definition of the concept of employer is that it widens the possible circle of persons who can be employers. This new solution is a legislator's expression and further development of the proclaimed principle of free economic initiative laid down by the Constitution (Article 19, paragraph 1) and its prescription saying that 'the law creates and guarantees equal conditions for economic activity to all citizens and juridical persons' (Article 19, paragraph 2). These provisions of the Constitution, in fact, lay down some basic requirements of the market economy. The LC, owing to it being the subject of regulation, is one of the key set of laws called upon to give expression to the constitutional requirements for the development and approach to the market economy. So it is from this angle that one ought to evaluate both the juridical and the socioeconomic significance of paragraph 1, item 1 of the Supplementary Provisions of the

113. V. Tadjer, *Civil Law*, 82–84.

LC in defining the concept of employer and further for an understanding of the right to organize according to Article 49, paragraph 2 of the Constitution and Article 5 of the LC.

548. The specific purpose of employers' organizations is defined in Article 4, paragraph 2 of the LC. This provides: 'to represent and protect their economic interest. The economic interest of the employers is that which is connected with the economic activity of the respective enterprise – its efficiency and profitability. These are the employers' issues of general interests which have found specific expression in the field of labour relations, namely organization of the labour process, effective and rational utilization of the labour force of workers and employees, increased production, higher productivity of labour, investments made in safe and healthy working conditions, expenditure in salaries as a part of the cost of production, etc. These are specific issues in the employers' interest vested in and stemming from labour relations.

549. The last point concerns the means by which the employers' organizations act to achieve their purpose. These are enumerated by way of illustration in Article 5, paragraph 2 of the LC as follows: 'collective bargaining, participation in tripartite cooperation and other activities according to the law'. An employers' organization takes part in collective bargaining when this is realized at municipal, branch or national levels. As will be seen further, collective labour contracts are concluded at enterprise, municipal and branch level (*see* below, Chapter 4). The employers' organization takes part in collective bargaining only when the collective bargaining is conducted at municipal and branch level; it is the relevant individual employer who participates in the collective bargaining at enterprise level. The tripartite cooperation normally takes place at municipal, branch and national level (*see* below, general Introduction, Chapter 4, §3). In accordance with the very essence of the tripartite cooperation the employers' organizations take part in this and never an individual employer. As to the 'other activities according to the law' as provided for in Article 5, paragraph 2 of the LC, they embrace for instance: the peaceful settlement of collective labour conflicts, launching a campaign about some questions common to all employers such as costs of production, taxability, relief of tax.

550. As a result of the country's new economic development, the transition to a market economy since the end of 1989 as well as the new legal framework, different employers' organizations (about fourteen) were created. The large number of employers' organizations is an expression of pluralism. At the same time it expresses the organizational and structural weakness of employers' organizations. Most of them have national and only a few branch and local structures and organs, which do not permit a real organization of their membership through the country, to conduct internal organizational life and activities to adopt their programmes to their activity. The lack of national experience organizing themselves freely over the last six decades is also a negative factor in the establishment of employers' organizations. On the other hand, because state ownership continues to be a predominant feature of the national economy, complete independence of the employers' organizations (which unite employers of the public sector) from the state and state organs has not yet been achieved. This is one of the main problems which hinders the strengthening and consolidation of employers' organizations.

551. In the presence of real pluralism, the problem of representativeness of employers' organizations arises as a natural one. This is, however, solved by the law. Article 35 of the LC establishes the legal criteria for recognition of the employers' organization as representative on a national level.

552. The criteria for representativeness of the employers' organizations provided for in Article 35 of the LC underwent an intensive and contradictory development within a short period of time in 2012. Surprisingly, the amendments to the LC of January 2012 (prom. OJ, No. 7 of 2012) introduced in Article 35, paragraph 1, items 1 and 5 of the LC certain criteria that were new and unknown until then. According to them:

> In order for an organization to be recognized as a representative employers' organization at a national level, it should satisfy the following requirements: 1. it should unite branch and sector structures employing 100 thousand persons insured under an employment contract; … 5. it should not perform activities explicitly assigned solely thereto by virtue of a Law or a normative act.

These provisions were challenged before the Constitutional Court as being unconstitutional and inconsistent with the generally accepted norms of international law and the international treaties that Bulgaria is a party to (Article 149, paragraph 1, items 2 and 4 of the Constitution).

Decision No. 7 of 19 June 2012 on constitutional case No. 2 of 2012 proclaimed these provisions unconstitutional and inconsistent with the international treaties that Bulgaria is a party to and, on good grounds, in my opinion, these provisions were exposed in detail in the motives of the said decision of the constitutional jurisdiction. The two criteria which are challenged are new ones. They do not determine the strength and influence of the employers' organization which seeks recognition as a representative one. In its essence, the employers' organization is an alliance of employers – natural persons and legal entities – and not an alliance of 'branch and sector structures' of unclear composition. The inclusion of the number of the employer's workers and employees and the increase in this number up to 100,000 considerably limits the participation of small business employers in the social dialogue; however, it is these very employers that represent the predominant part of employers. On the other hand, the inclusion of the criterion according to which 'the employers' organization should not perform activities explicitly assigned solely thereto by virtue of a Law or a sublegal normative act' does not correspond to the nature of the employers' organization and focuses on the nature of activities it performs and not on the protection of its members' interests, and this contravenes Article 3, paragraph 1 of the ILO Convention No. 87. And lastly, the inclusion of these new criteria for representativeness of employers' organizations increases their number (to five in total) and violates the principle of symmetry in the recognition of representativeness of the trade union and employers' organizations. That creates imbalance in the attitude of the state to the employers' and trade union organizations and gives advantage to the large business employers to the detriment of the representation of the small and medium-sized business.[114]

553. According to the operative provision of Article 35, paragraph 1 of the LC, the criteria for representativeness of the employers' organizations are:

(1) membership of at least 1,500 members and a total of at least 50,000 workers and employees in all members of the employer's organization; or 100,000 workers and employees in all members of the employer's organization;
(2) organizations of the employers in more than one-quarter of the activities designated by a code of up to two digits in the Economic Activities Classification approved by the National Statistical Institute, with a membership of at least 5% of those insured under an employment relationship in each economic activity or at least ten members in each economic activity;
(3) an organization of employers which has local bodies in more than one-fifth of the municipalities within the country and a national body;
(4) the respective organization must have the capacity of a legal person, acquired under the procedure of Article 49, paragraph 1 of the LC at least three years prior to submitting the request for recognition of representativeness.

554. This feature of the representativeness of employers' organizations is designed to characterize the organizational structure of the respective employers' organization. The other problems concerning the recognition of the employers' organizations as representative are solved in the same way as those concerning the trade unions. The employers' organizations are recognized as representative by the Council of Ministers. Any refusal to recognize may give rise to appeal to the Supreme Administrative Court. All subdivisions of employers' organizations recognized as representative at the national level, are also treated as representative at branch and local level (*see* above §2).

555. Five employers' organizations have up to now been recognized as representative by the Council of Ministers for the next four years (OJ, Nos 664, 665, 668, 669 and 670 of 11 August 2016, OJ No. 64 of 2016). They are the following:

(1) Confederation of Employers and Industrialists in Bulgaria.
(2) Bulgarian Chamber of Commerce and Industry.
(3) Bulgarian Industrial Chamber.
(4) Association of the Industrial Capital in Bulgaria.
(5) Union for Private Economic Enterprise.

114. 'Decisions and Rulings of the Constitutional Court – 2012', *supra.*, 107–112.

§4. Legal Personality of Trade Unions and Employers' Organizations

556. Trade unions and employers' organizations are recognized by the legal system as being subjects with rights who may own their own property and can take part in civic activities. Within a certain framework, they can also undertake economic activities which are auxiliary to their basic function. An example of this would be their publishing activities, their efforts to maintain and utilize their real property (buildings, offices), participation in legal proceedings and so on. For this purpose legal personality can be granted to trade unions and employers' organizations as well as to their subdivisions.

557. The amendments to Article 49 of the LC made in July 2018 (prom. OJ, No. 59 of 2018) introduced considerable changes in the procedure for recognition of trade union and employers' organizations as legal entities. It is through these changes that a general procedure was adopted for the acquisition of the capacity of a legal entity by way of entering the trade union and employers' organizations in registers which were created especially for them – separate registers for the trade union organizations and the employers' ones (*see* below paragraphs 558–559). The new legal regulation is derived from the provisions of Chapter 55 of the Civil Procedure Code and Article 49 of the LC.

558. The acquisition of the capacity of a legal entity on the part of trade union and employers' organizations takes place in accordance with the same procedure, namely through an entry of the organization into a separate official court register, which is maintained by the respective district court (Article 595 of the Civil Procedure Code and Article 49 of the LC). The entry is made in the respective register of the district court within the territory of which the specific trade union or employers' organization is located. The entry is carried out in accordance with the procedure laid down in Articles 596–597 of the Civil Procedure Code and is grounded on the decision of the respective competent territorial court. The registers are public ones and each citizen or legal entity has access thereto.

559. The entries made in the court register show certain particulars which identify the respective trade union or employers' organization. They are laid down in Article 596 of the Civil Procedure Code and are complemented with new particulars reflecting the specifics of the trade union or employers' organizations under Article 49, paragraph 4 of the LC and comprise: the type and name of the organization, its seat, address, statutes, governing bodies and names of the persons who represent the organization and the like, as well as any subsequent changes that have occurred in the particulars entered, so that the individualization of the organization is kept updated (Article 49, paragraph 5 of the LC).

In principle, the entry is made at a closed session of the district court, except where the court finds it necessary that it should take place at an open session of the court, or this is explicitly provided for in law. The decision regarding the entry is subject to immediate execution (Articles 602–609 of the Civil Procedure Code). The capacity of a legal entity arises at the time of entry. It is through the same procedure that the capacity of a legal entity is acquired by any subdivision of the respective trade union or employers' organization provided that the respective subdivision is entered in the statutes of the organization (Article 49, paragraph 2 of the LC).

The court entry of trade union and employers' organizations has the nature of an official public announcement of the facts and particulars relating to their identification, and of the fact of their existence, and does not constitute interference in their functions or activity. Primarily, the entry has a certification effect.

The specific thing that special attention should be drawn to is that the entry of trade union and employers' organizations is carried out under the procedure laid down in Chapter 55 of the Civil Procedure Code for the entry of legal entities and not under the Law on the Commercial Register and the Register of Non-Profit-Making Legal Entities, although – by their legal nature – the trade union and employers' organizations are non-profit-making legal entities.[115]

560. The Law on Non-Profit-Making Juridical Persons, adopted in 1999 (*see* above, paragraph 553) introduced the division of non-profit-making juridical persons in two groups: non-profit-making juridical persons that perform activity for public benefit and non-profit-making juridical persons that perform activity for protecting the interests of their members or those of certain persons. The first group of juridical persons comprises state universities, state theatres and the like. Their activity is for the benefit of an unlimited number of citizens and the whole society. These juridical persons are supported financially by the state by way of tax, credit-interest, customs duty and other financial reliefs. It is obligatory for them to be registered in a special central register at the Ministry of Justice and the state exercises direct current and annual control over their activity and functions (Articles 38–44 of the law cited). The non-profit-making juridical persons that perform activity in the interest of their members are: political parties, other non-governmental organizations, etc. They do not receive financial support from the state. However, on account thereof, their activity is not placed under the control of the state.

561. From the viewpoint of this division, the trade unions and employers' organizations that have the capacity of juridical persons belong to the category of non-profit-making juridical persons that perform activity for private benefit within the meaning of Article 37, paragraph 3 of the law cited. They are private law organizations and are established for giving expression and protection to the interests of their members. The trade union organizations are established in order to protect the socioeconomic interests of the workers and employees (Article 49, paragraph 1 of the Constitution and Article 4 of the LC), and the employers' ones to protect the interests of their members, the employers, these interests being connected with the organization and efficient use of the workforce employed by them (Article 49, paragraph 2 of the Constitution and Article 5 of the LC). The appurtenance of the trade unions and employers' organizations to the non-profit-making juridical persons that perform activity for the protection of the interests of their members deprives them of the state's financial support. However, on account thereof, they enjoy greater

115. P. Goleva, Kr. Stoychev, *Yuridicheski Litsa s Nestopanska Tsel* [*Non-Profit-Making Legal Entities*], (Sofia: Bulgarian Centre of Non-Profit-Making Law, 2018), 96–102.

freedom in performing their functions in protection of the interests of their members. This also grants them greater independence from the state and its influence and precludes its interference in the performance of their activities.

Chapter 3. Workers' Participation

§1. General Remarks

562. Workers' and employees' participation in the management of their enterprise has been tangibly and essentially curtailed with the amendments to the LC in November 1992. Here the law swung to the other extreme, trying to react to the 'powers' of the labour collectives under the 1986 version of the LC which were unjustifiably wide ranging but unapplied in practice. Instead of seeking moderate and acceptable solutions to these problems by taking into account the social and democratic role which contemporary international development and experience attach to workers, representatives and participation, the legislator adopted the 'easiest' solution by considerably playing down the role of workers' representatives.

563. The legal regulation of workers' participation is now basically contained in the LC, Article 6–6a regarding the general assembly of workers and employees and Article 7 regarding the legal possibility of workers and employees to participate in the management of the enterprise in cases provided for by the law. They are quite general in their nature. Some legal provisions can also be found in Chapter XIV of the LC under the heading 'Social-Communal and Cultural Services in the Enterprise', namely in Articles 293, 299 and 300, as well as in Article 137 of the Commercial Law. The indicated legal framework will be briefly analysed in the following paragraphs.

§2. Participation in the Enterprise

I. Organs

564. The main bodies of workers' participation are the following:

(1) general assembly (assembly of the representatives) of workers and employees;
(2) representatives of the workers and employees.

These bodies are not expressly enumerated in the law. Nevertheless, their existence can, without doubt, be concluded by way of interpretation of Articles 6 and 7 and 7a of the LC.

565. The general assembly embraces all workers engaged in the enterprise, regardless of how labour relationships were established, by contract of employment, election, competitive examination, etc., for an unspecified length of time, fixed-term labour contract, for full-time, part-time or short-time work, etc. They all form the general assembly of workers and employees and nobody can be excluded by anybody. Instead of a general assembly, an assembly of representatives shall be formed by decision of the general assembly itself in cases where the basic workers' collective is deemed too large or where for example the enterprise consists of distant divisions or works in shifts as this hampers the convocation of a general assembly. The general assembly decides the quota of representation on the assembly of representatives (one representative of every two, five, ten, etc., workers) according to the total number of the workers and employees employed in the enterprise. The representatives are elected by the general assembly in conformity with the procedure established by the latter. The assembly of representatives, if any, shall have the same rights as the general assembly and shall perform identical functions. The general assembly (the assembly of representatives) is a self-governing body. It adopts regulations and determines the procedures of its activity (Article 6, paragraph 2 of the LC).

566. Other bodies of workers' participation are the representatives of the workers. They are of two kinds:

(1) representatives elected by the general assembly. Representation may be by one or more workers in the enterprise. The number is determined by the general assembly (Article 6, paragraph 1 and Article 7, paragraph 1 of the LC);
(2) representatives of the workers and employees for information and consultation on important matters specified in the LC (Article 7, paragraph 2 of the LC);
(3) representatives of the workers and employees for information and consultation on labour organization matters (Article 7a of the LC).

II. Functions

567. The above-mentioned bodies of workers' participation have inherently different functions.

568. The general assembly (assembly of representatives) of workers and employees has two kinds of functions. The first one is to elect representatives who will defend matters of common interest to all wage earners, e.g., matters of labour and social security, and who will take part in the discussions and decisions on questions concerning the management of the enterprise (Articles 6 and 7 of the LC). The second group embraces functions by means of which the general assembly itself participates directly in the decision-making of some social questions in the enterprise. These questions may involve: determining the manner of utilization of funds for social-communal and cultural services in the enterprise (Article 293 of the LC), providing opportunities of utilization of social funds not only to the workers but also to members of their families (Article 299 of the LC), providing the possibility of social funds in the enterprise to be used not only by the workers but also by the pensioners who used to work for the enterprise (Article 300 of the LC).

569. The functions of workers' representatives are very generally indicated by the law. By virtue of Article 7, paragraph 2 of the LC the functions of workers' representatives are to protect the matters of common interest of workers and employees, e.g., matters of labour and social security, before the employer or competent public authorities. 'To protect' means to defend the demands and claims of workers and to insist on them being met. As regards elected workers' representatives and participation in the management of an enterprise (Article 7, paragraph 1 of the LC), their functions are to take part in the discussions and decisions – posing the relevant questions such as expressly indicated by law. But the only case up to now in which participation of a workers' representative is provided for in law is in Article 137, paragraph 5 of the Commercial Law. By virtue of this legal provision the general assembly of a public limited liability company takes decisions on matters of labour and social affairs only after hearing the opinion of the workers' representative. It is evident that participation of the workers' representative in this case consists of expressing a standpoint on the social and labour matter under discussion and not of taking part in the decision-making itself. Only the general assembly is considered competent to partake in the decision-making of the respective public limited liability company.

570. The amendments to the LC of March 2001 introduced important new points in the legal framework regarding the role and functions of the workers' and employees' representatives. They consist in the further development, extension and specification of their rights in the functioning of labour legal relations in the enterprise. Specific cases have been explicitly provided for, these being cases in which the employer is obliged either to make prior consultations with the representatives of the workers and employees in making decisions concerning important issues of labour legal relationships in the enterprise or to give information thereto regarding the important measures he has undertaken, the latter concerning the workers and employees in the enterprise. Here are the most important thereof:

(1) The obligation of the employer to notify and inform in advance the representatives of the workers and employees in those cases where he intends to make large-scale dismissals. In the notification thereof the employer is obliged to specify not only the forthcoming large-scale dismissal, but also the numerous circumstances particularising it, as well as the reasons that cause it, and the number and categories of workers and employees who will be dismissed, the time when the dismissal will take place, the criteria which shall be used for selecting the workers and employees subject to dismissal and the like (Article 130a of the LC).
(2) In the event of extending the working time for economic reasons by two hours per eight hours' working day or by one hour per reduced working day (the length thereof being six or seven hours) for a period of sixty working days within the calendar year, the employer is obliged to make consultations with the representatives of the workers and employees prior to introducing the extended working time in the enterprise or in separate units thereof (Article 136a of the LC).

(3) In the event of introducing reduced working time because of a decrease in the amount of work, the length thereof being not less than one-half of the length of the working day established by law, and the period of this reduced working time lasting for up to three months within a calendar year, the employer is obliged to make prior consultations regarding it with the representatives of the workers and employees (Article 138, paragraphs 2 and 3 of the LC), etc.

(4) Due to the particular nature of their work, the employer is entitled to lay down a working day of non-fixed duration for certain job positions. These are the ones the holders of which are obliged to perform their labour duties even where their working time is over. These job positions are determined after consultations with the workers' and employees' representatives under Article 7, paragraph 2 of the LC (Article 139a, paragraph 1).

(5) According to Article 181, paragraph 1 of the LC, the employer is obliged to issue internal labour regulations for the enterprise. These regulations specify the rights and obligations of the workers, the employees and the employer under the employment relationships, and set out the organization of labour in the enterprise (the start and end of the working time, the organization of the working time and the like) in compliance with the particular features of the activity in the enterprise. The regulations are issued after the employer has held consultations with the workers' and employees' representatives under Article 7, paragraph 2 of the LC (Article 181, paragraph 2 of the LC).

Chapter 4. Tripartite Cooperation

571. Tripartite cooperation is a new phenomenon in Bulgarian social and legal reality. It came into existence at the beginning of the 1990s, along with the deep democratic changes in the country, and forms a part thereof. It results from the severe social problems that the country abounds in, and is one of the mechanisms through which the solution of these problems is sought. During the last twenty-five years it has undergone periods of 'upsurges' and 'downturns' and has gained considerable experience. At the beginning, its actions were 'reactive' and 'campaign-type' ones – for solving specific matters, such as: resolution of acute collective labour disputes and on-going strikes, updating the minimum wage and indexation of labour remuneration. In the most recent decade, in spite of the difficulties that accompany its functioning, it became more stable and the need for applying it gets ever more clearly recognized by the periodically changing governments and by the social partners (employers' and trade union organizations).

§1. Legal Regulation and Scope of Tripartite Cooperation

572. Through the amendments to the LC of November 1992, Article 3 of the LC gave the first explicit regulation – though rather general – of tripartite cooperation. On the grounds of the painful experience gained in the 1990s, this regulation was enriched through the 2001 and 2002 amendments to the LC, which introduced the new Article 3a–3e of the LC.

Tripartite cooperation in employment relationships was also encouraged by the Law on the Economic and Social Council adopted in 2001 (prom. OJ, No. 41 of 2001, as amended), which institutionalized the social dialogue and the consultations on the economic and social policy between the government and the civil society organizations (Article 2 of the Law).

573. A number of special social and labour laws also regulate tripartite cooperation: the SIC (1999, as amended), the Law on Fostering Employment (2001, as amended), the Law on Healthy and Safe Working Conditions (1997, as amended), the Law on Collective Labour Disputes (1990, as amended) and the Law on Health Insurance (1998, as amended). The regulation of tripartite cooperation contained in these laws consists in setting up a tripartite basis – with the participation of the government and the social partners – of the representative employers' and trade union organizations, and the management and consultation bodies acting in various aspects of employment relationships and social security ones.

574. The essence of tripartite cooperation is clearly formulated in Article 3 of the LC, according to which 'The state regulates the employment relationships and those directly related thereto, as well as the social security relationships and the matters regarding the standard of living, in collaboration with and following consultations with the workers' and employees' representatives and the employers' ones.'

Tripartite cooperation is legally binding. Those acts of the government and its members (the Ministers) and other state bodies which are adopted without prior consultations with the social partners are unlawful and are repealed by the Supreme Administrative Court when appealed against.

575. Tripartite cooperation concerns three main groups of important matters:

(1) employment relationships: these are matters relating to the conclusion of employment contracts and the entry into one's official duties, labour remuneration, working time, rest and leave, healthy and safe working conditions, the workers' and employees' professional qualification, the social and community services as well as the cultural ones provided by the enterprise, the social responsibility of the enterprise, etc.;
(2) security relationships: they concern social security and health insurance of the citizens, the categorization of labour, the scope of the insured persons, the number of insurance-covered social risks, the grounds for and the amounts of insurance indemnities in cases of temporary and durable incapacity for work, unemployment benefits, amounts of pensions, quality and accessibility of medical assistance, etc;
(3) matters of living standards: they concern the degree to which the workers and employees meet the basic vital necessities with their labour incomes and the redistribution of the gross domestic product. The scope of these matters was fixed in Decision No. 860 of the Council of Ministers dated 2 November 2004 covering thirteen groups of key matters which – directly or indirectly, yet considerably – determine the way of life and the living standard of the citizens, along with the labour and social security relationships (*see* above items (1) and (2)), such as: social support, taxes, budget policy, labour market policy, health care, education, science and culture, matters regarding the determination of an integrated indicator of assessing poverty and living expenses, creating and maintaining the social infrastructure, environmental issues which concern the interests of the employers, workers and employees.

§2. National System for Tripartite Cooperation

576. Institutionally, tripartite cooperation is an aggregate of bodies which are functionally connected with each other by the common tasks they perform, acting jointly in a specific way for the purpose of regulating the labour and social security relationships and the living standard matters through collaboration and dialogue in solving the problems. However, these bodies do not form a uniform system of hierarchical structure or managerial dependence among them. Each of its bodies acts independently within its subject matter and territorial competence.

577. The tripartite cooperation bodies are set up on the territorial and sectoral principle. They consist of four types of body:

(1) The NCTC is created at the national level. It consists of a Deputy Prime Minister who chairs the NCTC and one more government member – depending on the subject of the matters under discussion which are included in the agenda – who takes part in the meetings of the Council, as well as two representatives of each representative employers' and trade union organization. Commonly, the said government member is the Minister of Labour and Social Policy; however, he/she may as well be the Minister of Health Care, or the Minister of Economy, or the Minister of Finance, etc., if the matters under discussion fall within their fields of activities. The Council discusses Bills and draft acts of the Council of Ministers (decrees, rules, ordinances, etc.) which concern the employment and social security relationships and the living standard matters.

(2) Sectoral and branch councils for tripartite cooperation. They are set up by sectors and branches of activity. They comprise representatives of the respective Ministries, state agencies and representatives of the representative employers' and trade union organizations in the branch. They discuss the specific issues of the employment and social security relationships as well as matters regarding the living standard which concern the working conditions, etc.

(3) District councils for tripartite cooperation. They are set up in the 28 districts of the country and comprise two representatives of the district administration who are designated by the district governor and two representatives of each representative organization of employers or trade unions. These councils discuss and give opinions about the specific matters of employment, labour market and the living standard in the district.

(4) Municipal councils for tripartite cooperation. They are created in the country's 265 municipalities, the latter being the basic administrative and territorial units of the country. These councils consist of two representatives of the municipality who are designated by the mayor of the municipality and two representatives of each of the representative employers' and trade union organizations. They discuss and express opinions about specific matters of employment, labour market and the living standard of the municipality's population, and the workers and employees working in the municipality.

578. According to the supplement to the LC made in July 2015 (prom. OJ, No. 54 of 2015), tripartite cooperation under Article 3, paragraphs 1 and 2 of the LC (*see* above paragraph 571–577) is extended through the creation of the two paragraphs 3 and 4.

According to Article 3, paragraph 3 of the LC, upon request of the representative trade union and employers' organizations and in the judgement of the state, agreements can be concluded between the social partners on the adoption of normative acts regarding certain issues falling within the scope of tripartite cooperation. The 'judgement of the state' is given by its competent bodies, depending both on the nature of issues covered by the agreement and on the type and rank of the normative act they will be regulated in. If the draft of the normative act concerns a Bill regarding which the Council of Ministers will exercise its right to legislative initiative or a normative act of the Council of Ministers under Article 114 of the Constitution and Article 6 of the Law on Normative Acts, the judgement is given by the Council of Ministers. If the draft concerns a normative act issued by a Minister under Article 115 of the Constitution and Article 7 of the Law on Normative Acts, the judgement is given by the respective line Minister, etc. An agreement concluded between the social partners on the content of a normative act is presented to the state body which has made the judgement.

According to the new paragraph 4 of Article 3 of the LC, 'the implementation of the agreement under paragraph 3 is carried out by the state'. This means that the competent state body is obliged to discuss the draft that has been coordinated by the social partners, and give its opinion about it, including proposals and supplements thereto, and, in case of approving it, must take measures for its adoption: if it is a Bill, the state body must exercise its right to legislative initiative and introduce the Bill in the National Assembly, and follow the normal constitutional procedure for its adoption; or, if it is a government's normative act of subordinate legislation, the state body must carry out the final adoption of the act; or, if it is a draft of a line Minister's normative act of subordinate legislation, the state body can make the respective proposals and supplements and sanction it in accordance with the Law on Normative Acts.

579. The decisions of the councils for tripartite cooperation are made by common consent (Article 3e, paragraph 4 of the LC). This is a high requirement for decision-making, which is satisfied after long-continued discussions and negotiations among the three parties represented in the councils.

580. The legal nature of the decisions of the councils for tripartite cooperation is dual. On the one hand, these decisions are final juridical acts from the viewpoint of the internal life and activity of the councils for tripartite cooperation. They do not need the approval or sanction of another body and express the will of the members of the respective council and the interests of the party this council represents. On the other hand, these decisions have a consultative, i.e., a recommendable nature for both the state body and any other public body they are submitted to – the Council of Ministers, the respective Minister, district governor or municipal mayor. They are intended to support the adoption of a final act by the respective state body or local authority which reflects, as largely as possible, the combination and balance of the conflicting interests of the parties represented. Ultimately, the final act is adopted by the competent state body – the Council of Ministers, the respective Minister, district governor, municipal council or mayor.

Chapter 5. Collective Labour Contract

581. After more than four decades during which genuine collective bargaining was neglected and collective labour contracts were used as a means to attain maximum production results and fulfilment of the economic plans, the role of collective labour contracts as a means of improving working and living conditions was restored in 1990. Since that time the collective labour contract has occupied an important place in the system of labour regulation in accordance with the specific legal and social functions assigned to it. These functions are to establish working conditions which are more favourable than those of a minimum legal standard. Accordingly, a completely new legal regulation was devoted to the collective labour contract within the framework of the amendments to the LC in November 1992 and in March 2001. It is contained in Chapter IV, Articles 50–60 of the LC.

§1. Object of the Collective Labour Contract

582. Pursuant to Article 50 of the LC

The collective labour contract regulates matters on labour and social security of workers and employees, which are not regulated by imperative provisions of the law (paragraph 1). The collective labour contract cannot contain clauses which are less favourable to workers and employees than those provided for in the law (paragraph 2).

These legal provisions determine the subject matter of the collective labour contract and the level of collective bargaining.

583. The subject matter of collective bargaining is determined by two criteria. The first is the nature of questions which can be regulated by means of a collective labour contract. These are matters on labour relations and social security of workers and employees engaged in the relevant enterprise or branch. Matters on labour relations are those concerning remuneration, working hours, rest periods, leave, safety and healthy working conditions and the like. Matters on social security concern the scope of insured persons and covered social risks, insurance contributions, kind of social security benefits, etc. The second criterion is that the matter on labour relations and social security which may be the subject of the collective labour contract has not been regulated by an imperative provision of the law. These are questions which are not at all regulated by the law. The reasons for this non-regulation – omission by the legislator or deliberate abstention of the legislator to regulate some problem – are not important. It is important to establish that these are matters on labour relations and social security relations which are not regulated by the law. However, if the relevant questions are regulated by the law, they may not have been regulated by imperative but by suppletive legal provisions. In contemporary Bulgarian labour law these are legal provisions which establish only the minimum standard and give an opportunity by means of collective labour contracts to provide for more favourable working conditions, e.g., higher remuneration, longer leave, shorter working time, and so on. In the new version of the LC, the number of this kind of legal provisions is relatively high, which enlarges the scope of practical use of collective labour contracts.

584. The law does not allow collective labour contracts to include clauses which are less favourable than those of the minimum standards as provided for in the legal provisions. Parties cannot contract below the level of minimum standards. They may improve on them, i.e., agree to more favourable working conditions. This is the basic social meaning and significance of a collective labour contract for the workers and in the interest of trade unions. This also explains the reticent position which employers sometimes have towards collective bargaining, because for them more favourable working conditions means higher production costs and more costs for the allowance of manpower. Nevertheless, if a collective labour contract contains working conditions less favourable than the provided minimum legal standard, the respective stipulations in the collective labour contract shall be null and void because of the conflict with the imperative legal provisions. Such stipulations have no legal effect; consequently, no rights can be derived from them, nor can they give rise to any obligations. Instead of these stipulations, the minimum legal standards established by the relative imperative legal provisions will be applied.

§2. Parties to the Collective Labour Contract

585. According to Article 51, paragraph 1 of the LC the collective labour contract is concluded between an employer or employers' organization, on the one side, and the respective trade union organization at enterprise level, trade union or trade union federation, on the other. Consequently, the parties to the collective labour contract are employer, employers or their organizations and trade unions. This means that not only an employer in an economic branch, i.e., carrying out an economic activity, realizing revenue and profits with a certain degree of autonomy, may be a party to the collective labour contract but also any employer who hires workers and employees in non-economic branches (education, health, science, culture). The understanding under current law that collective labour contracts can be concluded in economic as well as non-economic branches follows from the text of Article 51, paragraph 1 of the LC which mentions only 'an employer', without making a distinction as to the branch in which the employer operates. No subsequent agreement or consent by any other body is required for an employer or trade union organization to exercise their contractual capacity and conclude a collective labour contract.

586. As regards level, collective labour contracts may be concluded for different branches, sectors, municipalities or at enterprise level. In practice, at least for the moment, the most widespread contracts are collective labour contracts concluded at the enterprise level.

587. Collective labour contracts at enterprise level may be concluded between a trade union organization, either a representative or a non-representative one, and the employer. If there is only one trade union organization in the enterprise it has the capacity to conclude collective labour contracts. But when there is more than one trade union organization in the enterprise, which is the most common case in practice, it is advisable for the trade union organizations to reach an understanding in order to be able to conclude a common collective contract with the employer. If they do not reach such an understanding, then the general assembly of all workers and employees will by secret ballot and with a majority of at least two-thirds decide which of the trade union organizations should conclude the collective labour contract. If there is only one trade union organization, the employer signs the collective labour contract with this organization. If there is more than one trade union organization without an understanding to act together and to sign a common collective labour contract, the employer signs the collective agreement with one of them in conformity with the decision taken by secret ballot by the general assembly after the presentation of the proposals of each trade union organization at the general assembly (assembly of representatives). According to Article 51a, paragraph 3 of the LC, only one collective labour contract can be signed with a single employer regardless of the number of existing trade union organizations in the enterprise. This solution was adopted by the amendments to the LC in November 1992 in order to facilitate collective bargaining and to encourage the trade union organizations to join their efforts to reach an understanding which is in their common interest and offers them an opportunity to get more favourable conditions in the collective labour contract.

588. The collective labour contracts by sectors and branches are concluded only between the respective representative employers' and trade unions organizations (Article 51b of the LC). They are based on agreements between the national trade union organizations and the employers' organizations, which determine the general principles regarding the scope and procedural framework of the collective labour contracts by sectors and branches. The sector and branch trade union organizations work out a project for the collective labour contract and submit it to the respective representative sector and branch employers' organizations. It is on the grounds of this project that the collective bargaining is conducted and the final sector and branch collective labour contracts are concluded (*see* below, §3). The sector and branch collective labour contracts regulate the particularities of the working conditions of the workers and employees in the respective sector or branch.

589. An important feature of the collective labour contracts at sector and branch level is the opportunity of extending their field of application, this being provided for through the amendments to the LC of March 2001. Pursuant to Article 51b, paragraph 3 of the LC, in the event that the collective labour agreement at sector or branch level has been concluded among all representative trade union and employers' organizations of the respective sector or branch, at the parties' common will, the effect of the contract may be spread over all enterprises of the respective sector or branch, i.e., even over those employers, workers and employees that are not members of the respective representative trade union and employers' organizations. In this way the effect either of the whole branch or sector collective labour agreement or of separate clauses thereof may be extended.

590. The new legal framework of March 2001 concerning the collective labour contracts explicitly provided for the opportunity of concluding collective labour contracts by municipalities (Article 51c of the LC). Such collective labour contracts may be concluded for activities financed by the municipal budgets or for those people who are employed in the sphere of education (schools), culture (cinemas, theatres, museums, etc.), health (hospitals, pharmacies), etc. These collective labour contracts are concluded between the representative trade union and employers' organizations. The general projects for them are worked out by the local units of the respective trade union organizations and are submitted to the local units of the representative employers' organizations. On the grounds thereof the collective bargaining is conducted and the collective labour contracts are concluded (*see* below, §3).

§3. Collective Negotiations and the Conclusion of the Collective Labour Contract

591. Concluding the collective labour contract is preceded by collective negotiations between the parties. According to the level at which the collective labour contract is concluded (at enterprise, branch, sector, etc.) the negotiating parties are the relevant trade union organizations and the employer (at enterprise level) or the representative trade unions and employers' organizations (when the collective labour contract is concluded at branch, sector, and municipal level). In the course of these negotiations a review is carried out as to compliance of the expired collective labour contract (if any) and, at the same time, the contents of new clauses in the draft of the new collective labour contract are determined by means of discussions.

592. Pursuant to Article 52 of the LC the initiative to start collective negotiations is left to the trade union organization. In general, starting and conducting collective negotiations in order to conclude a collective labour contract is a right of the trade union. There is no obligation on the trade union to negotiate collectively. Of course, the genuine interest of trade unions as representatives of the workers and employees do not allow them to thoughtlessly and arbitrarily relinquish this right and, normally, they exercise it very thoroughly and regularly. But legally speaking, if a trade union organization decides, for one reason or another, not to initiate collective negotiations and not to conduct and conclude a collective agreement it is entitled to do so, and neither the employer nor any other body can compel the trade union organization to negotiate. On the other hand, according to current Bulgarian legislation no organ, body or organization may initiate and negotiate the conclusion of collective labour contracts on behalf of workers and employees. In this sense one can affirm that only trade unions have the capacity to conduct collective bargaining on behalf of workers and employees in order to conclude a collective labour contract.

593. Quite different is the situation with the employers. They are obliged to participate in and conduct collective negotiations. Their common obligation in this respect embraces two groups of concrete obligations. They are provided for in Article 52 of the LC. These obligations are:

(1) to take part in the collective negotiations which are proposed by the relevant trade union organization which is entitled to start and conduct them. This means that the employer who is invited by the respective trade union organization to start and conduct collective bargaining may not refuse to take part in it. He is obliged to reply positively to this initiative and to accept the invitation;
(2) to present information to the trade union organization which has initiated the collective bargaining. This information embraces:
   (a) whether the collective labour contracts binding the parties concerned are based on the principle of economic, territorial or organizational affiliation. It is necessary for the trade union representatives who conduct the collective negotiations to know in which context the present collective negotiations are conducted in order to know how to direct them. It is also necessary in order to compare and conform the present collective bargaining with treaty obligations already reached with the same employer, with concessions which the employer has already made within the framework of other collective agreements binding him, etc.;
   (b) a substantial part of information data on the economic situation which may be meaningful for the conclusion of the respective collective labour contract. It is information on the economic situation of the enterprise for the time being, on its economic programme, on the technical outfit and the degree of productive use, the marketing situation and output realization, the prospects of future development of the enterprise, the employment situation and the prospects of an enlarged or decreased workforce, expected turnover income, profits and losses, organization of work and the like. The required information has to be 'meaningful for the conclusion of the respective labour contract'. These are questions on the basis of which the trade union representatives will formulate their claims and demands and will seek to validate them by elaboration and discussion of the draft of the collective labour contract. This information must be 'timely, reliable and comprehensible'. The information is 'timely' when it is provided at the moment it is needed for being used in the process of conducting collective negotiations on determining the content of the collective labour contract. It is 'reliable' when it is truthful. And it is 'comprehensible' when it is possible for the trade union leaders, workers and employees to understand it. Owing thereto, the employer must express its content in a way which is simple, precise and easy to understand. On the basis of this information, the representative trade union may formulate, define and amend their proposals contained in the draft of the collective labour contract.

594. Where the information required by the representatives of the trade unions constitutes a business or company's secret of the employer and its divulgence could result in damages to the employer, the latter may act in two ways: (1) to refuse to provide it; (2) to provide it with the explicit requirement to and obligation of the trade union representatives not to spread it. These reasonable limitations on the required information (limited to information 'meaningful for the conclusion of the respective collective labour contract') are imposed to comply with the desire to safeguard commercial secrets of the employer and to force the parties to concentrate only on questions which are relevant to labour and social security problems as the subject matter of collective bargaining. The employer may also decide not to give certain information when the requested information is not meaningful for the conclusion of the respective collective labour contract. The employer's denial in this instance would be justified, because the employer is not obliged to supply such information.

595. The above-mentioned obligation on the employer to take part in the collective bargaining and to submit certain information to trade union representatives is of a legal (juridical) nature. That is why, pursuant to Article 52, paragraphs 2 and 3 of the LC, non-accomplishment of these obligations by the employer involves a liability. The liability of the employer may consist of having to pay compensation for consequential damages. The non-fulfilment may be expressed in two ways:

(1) by means of an open and categorical refusal of the employer to fulfil his obligations to negotiate a collective labour contract and/or to submit the requested information concerning the collective agreements binding the parties concerned and the data on the economic situation of the enterprise meaningful for the conclusion of a collective labour contract;
(2) by way of a delay (retard) on the part of the employer in fulfilling his above-mentioned obligations. Employers are considered as causing delay when they do not fulfil their obligation to take part in the negotiations of a collective labour contract within a term of one month of receiving the invitation to start collective bargaining and when they fail to fulfil their obligation to submit the necessary information within fifteen days following receipt of a written statement by the trade union representatives.

Damages caused by the non-fulfilment of these obligations by the employer, including the delay in their fulfilment, are estimated in every concrete case according to the total number of workers covered by the respective collective labour contract, the losses sustained by them regarding their remuneration, expected new leave, improvement of working conditions and the like. Since it is a civil (financial) liability; the non-fulfilment of the relevant obligation has to be the cause. The meaning and destination of this liability are to affirm the significance of collective bargaining, to increase its role, to accustom the employer to observe the rules of collective bargaining and to respect fair play and to instil the spirit of partnership in regulating labour relations.

596. During the course of collective negotiations between the employer and trade union representatives a draft collective labour contract is drawn up, its contents are specified and the rights and obligations of the parties are determined, necessary time limits are set and the amount of sums for carrying out the respective undertakings and the funds from which they will be taken are also determined. The collective negotiations are conducted and the contents of the draft contract are determined by mutual agreement between the parties. In the course of discussing the issues, each party makes certain concessions with a view of reaching an agreement.

The procedure for conducting the discussions of the draft collective labour contract is not expressly regulated by law. This is not an omission of the law but a deliberate approach adopted by the legislator, the meaning being to make the conduct of these discussions more free and flexible. The rules of this procedure, the timing and agenda of the collective bargaining, the setting up of working groups on different chapters and problems concerning the collective labour contract, and so on, are subject to the decisions taken by the contracting parties during deliberations. These questions are part of the contracting autonomy of the parties. In each case they are decided according to the actual circumstances under which the discussions are conducted.

597. If, after the discussions and mutual concessions they reach an agreement, the collective labour contract is concluded (*see infra*). It could also be concluded on the questions on which an agreement was reached. As regards the questions on which no agreement was attained, the procedure on collective labour conflicts is to be followed pursuant to the law on the settlement of Collective Labour Conflicts (*see* below, Chapter 5).

598. The collective labour contract is concluded in writing (Article 53, paragraphs 1 and 2 of the LC). It is a form *ad solemnitatem*, i.e., necessary for its existence and not only as evidence that it has been concluded. This is a common form of concluding a contract without any notarial certification being necessary, either of contents or of the signatures of the contracting parties.

599. The collective labour contract is signed by the parties; on behalf of the employers, by the employer himself or by a person entrusted by the employer. The contract is signed on behalf of the trade union organization by the chairman of the respective trade union committee. Signing the collective labour contract is a confirmation and an extension of the form, in writing, in which it is concluded.

600. The collective labour contract has to be in duplicate; three copies are required, one is sent to each of the respective parties and one to the Labour Inspectorate. 'Possession' of a duplicate of the concluded and signed collective labour contract by each of the parties to the contract is necessary in order to allow each party to exercise its rights and obligations stemming from the contract and to observe the application of the collective labour contract as a whole. As regards the significance of 'possession' of a duplicate of the collective labour contract by the Labour Inspectorate, *see* below. Each of these three copies of the collective labour contract represents the official text which certifies its contents. Copies of the duplicates may be made and officially certified in order to send them to the subdivisions of the employer's enterprises, if any, or to the trade union organizations, if necessary, to submit them to competent state organs such as administrative tribunals.

601. A concluded and signed collective labour contract is not subject to subsequent approval, reaffirmation or verification. In this way the 'sovereign' determination of the contents of the collective labour contract by the will of the parties is definitively reaffirmed. But the amendments to the LC in November 1992 did introduce a procedure of registration of collective labour contracts with the Labour Inspection (Article 53, paragraphs 3–5 of the LC). This procedure poses some important legal questions (*see* below).

602. First of all registration of the collective labour contract is mandatory and not an optional matter. Its significance is to publicize the contents of the respective labour contract. This means that the collective labour contract has the contents indicated in the duplicate which is registered. Registration creates a common confidence in the contents of the registered collective labour contract. But registration as such does not have any constitutive significance for the collective labour contract: the contract is deemed to have been concluded as of the date of signature by the parties (*see* below) and not as of the date of registration. The law does not explicitly state if the registered collective labour contract becomes generally known to all interested people. Despite the fact that the law keeps silence on this problem, a positive conclusion in this sense could be made from the general objective of registration, namely to publicize the concluded collective labour contract. From the declarative (publicizing) significance of registration stems the conclusion that a collective labour contract which, for one reason or another, was not registered is still valid. Non-compliance with the obligation to register the collective labour contract may result in the respective person being administratively liable, but not of the concluded collective labour contract being invalid (null).

603. The registration is operated by a special register. It is an official state register. This register records the parties to the contract, date and place of the concluded collective labour contract, time period during which the respective collective agreement will be operative, etc. The main idea is by means of registering the minimum of data to 'individualize' the concluded collective labour contract.

604. Registration of collective labour contracts is made in a special register of the Labour Inspectorate located in the area of the head office of the employer who is a party to the respective collective agreement. In case the employers have seats in various areas, the registration shall be made with one of the labour inspectorates (Article 53, paragraph 3 of the LC). This rule applies to collective labour contracts concluded at enterprise level or at the level of a group of enterprises. A different rule has been established concerning the registration of the collective labour contracts concluded at the national level and branch level. These contracts are entered in the register of the Chief Labour Inspectorate by the Ministry of Labour and Social Policy in Sofia. This category of collective labour contracts may also refer to those concluded according to different professions. Although they are not expressly mentioned among the collective labour contracts which are registered with the Chief Labour Inspectorate, this conclusion could be drawn by way of interpretation bearing in mind that this kind of collective labour contract is applied to all workers of the same profession at the national level. Any dispute on competency of the relevant Labour Inspectorate to make or not to make a registration of the respective labour contract is considered and settled by the Minister of Labour and Social Affairs.

605. The procedure of registration of the concluded collective labour contract with the Labour Inspectorate is established by Article 53, paragraph 4 of the LC. Pursuant to this legal provision

An entry should be founded on written application of each of the parties within a term of one month of the respective labour inspectorate receiving the collective labour contract. A duplicate of the agreement signed by the parties concerned should be enclosed with each of the applications, as well as an electronic form of the document.

The law does not provide for a term in which registration should be made after the collective agreement has been signed. But, bearing in mind the meaning and function of registration (*see* above), it is normal that the registration ought to be carried out with the shortest possible delay upon the signing of the collective labour contract. The analysed legal disposition imposes the obligation on 'each of the parties' to the collective agreement to submit the written application. This solution is not very satisfactory because it could lead to some uncertainty in cases where either party relies on the other to submit a written application for the registration. In practice, the employer normally makes a written application for registration. There is nothing to prevent both parties making the written application for registration – the employer and the respective trade union organization together. The written application should be directed to the competent Labour Inspectorate. The meaning and objective of this written application is twofold: on the one hand to make known to the Labour Inspectorate that a collective labour contract has been signed and, on the other hand, to ask the competent Labour Inspectorate to take the necessary steps to enter the concluded labour contract in the special registry for this purpose. The competent Labour Inspectorate is obliged to register the forwarded labour contract within one month of its receipt. The law does not stipulate whether the Labour Inspectorate verifies the contents of the collective labour contract or simply registers it. But it is beyond any doubt that the Labour Inspectorate has no authority to either approbate (approve) or reject a collective labour contract on the occasion of its registration and within the framework of the procedure of registration. Also the Labour Inspectorate cannot decline (refuse) registration of the respective collective agreement. Registration is not a means of exercising any control over the contract's conformity with the law but only to enter the respective collective labour contract in the special register of the Labour Inspectorate. Nevertheless, if on the occasion of following the procedure for registration the Labour Inspectorate establishes that certain clauses in the collective labour contract are unlawful (for instance, they provide for less favourable working conditions than those prescribed by law – shorter leave, longer working hours, less compensation, and so on), it is obliged to make these known to the parties to the collective labour contract, focusing their attention to the unlawfulness of the respective clauses. In such cases, the Labour Inspectorate has to notify the parties that those clauses are null and void because they are contrary to the law. It may further ask the parties to eliminate these clauses. But even in these cases, the Labour Inspectorate cannot refuse registration of the collective labour contract.

606. The duplicate of the collective labour contract addressed to the Labour Inspectorate is kept by the Labour Inspectorate. It is at its own disposal as well as at the disposal of all interested persons. It is the genuine significance of the third copy of the collective labour contract.

607. The amendments to the LC made in December 2008 provided that copies of all collective labour agreements entered in the offices of the Labour Inspectorate (the district inspectorates and the General Labour Inspectorate) are submitted to the National Institute for Conciliation and Arbitration (*see* below Chapter 6), which establishes and maintains the information system of collective labour agreements. These copies are sent officially by the respective offices of the Labour Inspectorate in which the collective labour agreement was entered (*see* below). This obligation is aimed at establishing and maintaining a uniform national information system of all collective labour agreements within thc country, regardless of the level at which they are concluded and the office of the Labour Inspectorate with which they are registered.

608. Pursuant to Article 54, paragraph 1 of the LC, the collective labour contract comes into force on the day of its conclusion unless provided otherwise. The date of conclusion of the collective labour contract is as stated. Normally this is the moment from which the collective labour contract takes effect. But this moment may fall after the day of its conclusion and signature or it may be retroactive. It is also possible that some clauses come into effect from the moment of signature, other after the day of signature, and another group of clauses retrospectively from a date specified in the contract. Different solutions or combination in this direction are possible and admissible if the parties so decide. This is the meaning of the legal provision of Article 54, paragraph 1 of the LC 'unless it (i.e., the collective labour contract) provides otherwise'. From the moment the collective labour contract enters in force, it becomes effective, i.e., both rights and obligations can be fulfilled.

609. Collective labour contracts are effective for a period of one year unless provided otherwise (Article 54, paragraph 2 of the LC). The period of one year is the normal duration of collective labour contracts. This has been determined because, presumably, for one year the working conditions in the enterprise will remain stable and secure and consequently, contractual rights and obligations retain their validity and actuality. The parties to the contract may provide for a longer period, but not more than two years, or shorter than one year; such a clause has to be explicit. In the absence of such a clause, the normal rule of one year applies. If the parties decide to establish another (shorter or longer) duration they have to take into account the actual economic situation in the respective enterprise or branch, the dynamic changes in labour and social security relations as well as in the general standard of living. At present, while a difficult economic situation prevails in the country, the normal duration of collective labour contracts is for one year. On the other hand, there is nothing to stop the parties including express clauses on different issues or different periods of duration. In such cases, the specified periods will apply for the indicated items. Upon the expiry of the specified term the parties will start new negotiations and conclude a supplementary (partial) agreement which will constitute part of the collective labour contract.

610. During the period of collective labour contract, it may, as a matter of course, be amended or supplemented with the mutual consent of the parties (Article 56, paragraph 1 of the LC). In practice, various circumstances may make this a necessary step: sharp modification in the economic position of the enterprise, new questions arising in connection with hygiene and the safety for certain categories of workers or at certain workplaces in the enterprise, fresh requests of workers or the trade union organization, rapid growth of the inflation rate, changes in technical and technological equipment in the enterprise and the like. In these cases, the amendments or supplements to the collective labour contract are effected by following the same procedure as for the original drafting, discussion and conclusion (Article 56, paragraph 2 of the LC).

611. One of the most important questions related to the collective labour contract is about its validity and application (to persons). This is regulated by Article 57 of the LC. The Application of the collective labour contract means that its clauses, the rights and obligations stemming therefrom, apply to the individual labour relations between workers and employees, on the one hand, and the employer, on the other hand, and that the rights and obligations become part of their individual labour relationships. The workers to whom the collective labour contract applies can be divided in two groups:

(1) workers who are members of the trade union which is a party to the collective labour contract;
(2) workers who are not members of the trade union which is a party to the respective collective labour contract.

These two groups of workers are submitted to a different regime as regards the effectiveness of the concluded contract.

612. First of all, the collective labour contract affects workers and employees who are members of the trade union which is a party to the said contract (Article 57, paragraph 1 of the LC). Justification for the application of the labour contract in this case is membership of the respective workers of the trade union (party to the contract). Stemming from their membership in the said organization, application is their privilege over other workers and employees. In this case the collective labour contract applies personally to an indefinite circle of workers and employees – all those who are members of the respective trade union at the moment of conclusion and entry into force of the collective labour contract as well as those who will enter into an individual labour relationship with the respective employer and/or are members of the same trade union organization. This is a consequence of the normative character of a collective contract which as every normative act is effective personally to an indefinite circle of persons and not to persons listed by names. All other subsequent supplements or modifications to the collective labour contract made in conformity with Article 56 of the LC (*see* above) also affect this group of workers and employees.

613. Pursuant to Article 57, paragraph 2 of the LC those workers and employees who are not members of the trade union which is a party to the collective labour contract may join a contract concluded by their employer with a written application to the trade union. This category involves all workers in the enterprise, in the enterprises or in the branch, etc., according to the level at which the collective labour contract is concluded and the scope of its effectiveness. These workers may be workers who although not members of the trade union which is a party to the concluded contract, but are a member of another trade union operating in the same enterprise or branch, or workers who are not at all members of any trade union. The collective labour contract may be effective to this so-indicated circle of workers following the special procedure of joining such as is provided for in Article 57, paragraph 2 of the LC.

614. Joining the collective labour contract is a subjective right of every individual worker or employee who is not a member of the trade union which is a party to the collective contract. This means that it depends upon the judgement of the respective worker whether and when to join the collective labour contract concluded by his/her employer. This judgement is made by the worker taking into account his/her interest and the advantages to him/her in joining the contract. If, for instance, he/she has already obtained more favourable conditions of work by means of special clauses in his/her individual labour contract with the employer he/ she will not join the concluded collective labour contract because it will not be advantageous to do so.

615. Joining is done by means of a personal written application. In it, the worker should only express his/her request to join the collective labour contract. No reasons are necessary. The application is directed to the employer and to the trade union organization – parties to the collective labour contract. The meaning of this application is to make known to the parties to the collective labour contract the demand of the interested worker to join the contract exercising his/her subjective right. Neither the employer nor the relevant trade union organization may question the validity of the request or whether it is well founded. Nor can they impose on a worker any conditions as a prerequisite for joining. They may only notify the application for joining and cannot refuse, decline or postpone joining under any circumstances.

616. The collective labour contract becomes applicable to the workers who join it to the same extent as is applicable to the workers who are members of the trade union who is a party to the said contract. The purpose and the sense of the law in this respect is to equalize the effect of the collective labour contract on all workers – those who are members of the trade union which is a party to the contract, and those who are not – in order to offer them equal opportunities to enjoy more favourable conditions of work provided for in the contract and to make them a common good for all workers.

617. The majority of cases joining the concluded collective labour contract do so at the moment of its conclusion and entry into force, but there is nothing to prevent workers from joining the collective labour contract concluded by their employer later – during the period of its applicability. In any case, joining has effect in the future, i.e., upon the receipt of the written application for joining by the employer and the trade union – parties to the respective collective labour contract.

618. The same procedure of joining the concluded collective labour contract is followed in the case of modifications and new supplements to the contract. Any worker who is not a member of the trade union – party to be modified or supplemented collective labour contract – may ask to join by directing a written application to his/her employer and to the respective trade union.

619. Pursuant to the change in Article 58 of the LC of June 2006, the employer is obliged to notify all the workers and employees in the enterprise of both the collective labour agreement and the collective labour agreements by branches, sectors and municipalities that are binding on him/her. The legal provision does not explicitly specify the way in which the employer is to perform this obligation of his/hers; therefore, he/she is free to choose the way himself/herself. He may do it by notifying the workers and employees at the general meeting of the workers and employees, submitting the respective information to the workers' and employees' representatives under Article 7a, who have to transmit this information to all the workers and employees, etc.

620. The employer is also obliged to make available to the workers the text of the collective labour contract (Article 58 of the LC). The text may be put in an accessible place with the management of the enterprise so that every worker can acquaint himself/herself with its contents, can consult it in order to know his/her rights, decide whether to join it or not, etc. A certified copy of the effective collective labour contract may be placed on the notice board in the enterprise. This obligation on the employer concerns not only the initial text of the collective labour contract but also any subsequent modifications and supplements. On the other hand, this obligation on an employer is not only connected with a collective labour contract concluded by him at enterprise level, but also with collective labour contracts at branch, professional or national level whichever is applicable to the employer.

621. The National Institute of Reconciliation and Arbitration (NIRA) processes the data from the copies of the collective labour contracts and the annexes thereto, analyses them by date of signing and date of entry into force, including the changes therein agreed through the annexes. The data regarding the number of effective collective labour contracts at the level of an enterprise under Article 51a of the LC are complemented with those of the employed persons they are binding on with regard to all the indicators about which information is available. As for the collective labour contracts at a municipal level, data are presented about their disposition by regions and districts; as for the collective labour contracts at a branch level, data are presented about their appurtenance to the nomenclature of economic data under A-21 of the 2008 Economic Data Classification of the National Statistical Institute. In the recent eight years there has been a slight drop in contracting, judging by the number of enterprises and the number of persons employed for whom the collective labour contracts are in force as at 31 December of the respective calendar year. The yearly numbers of enterprises in which there are collective labour contracts signed for the period 2011–2018 are: year 2011 – 2080; year 2012 – 2207; year 2013 – 2138; year 2014 – 2020; year 2015 – 1975; year 2016 – 1862; year 2017 – 1824; year 2018 – 1652.

It is in correspondence with the decreasing number of enterprises in which there are collective labour contracts signed that the number of workers and employees is also decreasing, and so is the percentage thereof to whom the collective labour contracts apply. In the data below the first number shows the total number of workers, the second one – the number of workers to whom the collective labour contracts apply, and the third one, which is in brackets, shows the percentage of workers to whom the collective labour contracts apply by years, as follows: year 2011: 2,242,488 – 300,556 (13.4%); year 2012: 2,218,718 – 334,843 (15.18%); year 2013: 2,226,403 – 325,827 (14.6%); year 2014: 2,240,544 – 318,129 (14.2%); year 2015: 2,318,712 – 313,688 (13.5%); year 2016: 2,358,607 – 312,541 (13.3%); year 2017: 2,276,546 – 321,532 (13.6%); year 2018: 2,291,172 – 301,414 (13.2%).[116]

§4. Content of the Collective Labour Contract

622. The content of a collective labour contract is the scope of questions to which it refers. It can be very different and varies largely from one collective labour contract to another. It depends upon the concrete economic situation and working conditions in the respective enterprise, branch, profession and the like.

623. As indicated above (*see* §1 of this chapter), the collective labour contract may cover questions on labour and social security relations which are not regulated by imperative provisions of the law. Proceeding from the basic legal provision, the questions which are most often regulated by collective labour contracts in practice may be grouped in the following six sections: remuneration, employment security and redundancy, compensation, leave, hygiene and safety and social insurance, social and communal services (they will be briefly discussed below). But, of course, depending on the scale of the enterprise, branch, profession, any peculiar features of the working conditions and any specific problems, the number of sections may increase.

116. These are data from the National Institute of Reconciliation and Arbitration, in the collection: *Collective Labour Disputes* (Sofia: NIRA Publishing House, 2019), 3.

I. Labour Remuneration

624. There are two main problems in this section:

(1) the amount of minimum monthly wages. Normally this is higher than the national minimum wage. The amount, as established by the branch collective labour contract, can differ from one branch to another. For instance, the stipulated amount for 2019 in comparison with the national minimum wage was: in the Chemical Industry 129%, in Construction 153%, in Commerce 148%, in Light Industry 134%, in Engineering 128%, etc.;
(2) the amount of the stipulated monthly starting wage for bargaining. In 2019 this was in the different branch collective labour contracts in comparison with the national minimum monthly wage: Chemical industry for auxiliary staff – 126%, for skilled workers 144%, for experts 150%, for experts with managerial functions and for managerial staff – 178%, Metallurgy – for skilled workers – 160%, for managerial staff – 169%, etc.[117]

II. Employment Security; Redundancy

625. In the present situation of unemployment (*see* above, general Introduction), redundancy and employment security is one of the most important topics for discussion within the framework of collective bargaining. The collective labour contracts at branch level and those concluded at enterprise level in 2019 provided for some specific stipulations in order to avoid redundancy, e.g., the introduction of part-time work (energy, metallurgy), consultations with the trade unions or with the tripartite bodies at branch level where redundancy exceeds 7% of the staff (energy, post and telecommunication, food processing industry), the creation of new jobs, etc.[118]

III. Leave

626. In almost all collective labour contracts concluded at branch and enterprise level the contracting parties stipulate longer annual paid leave than that provided for in Articles 155 and 156 of the LC (*see* above, Part I, Chapter 3, §3). The regular annual paid leave is between twenty-two and twenty-five working days (chemical industry, construction, commerce, post and telecommunication, engineering, light industry, metallurgy, energy, etc.), instead of the minimum legal duration of twenty working days as provided for in Article 155 of the LC. The supplementary annual paid leave for unhealthy working conditions is also longer: from six to sixteen

117. These data are from *Kollectivno troudovo dogovariane 2019, Spravochnik* [*Collective Bargaining 2019, Reference Book*] (Sofia: KNSB, 2019), 3–24. The national minimum monthly wage in 2019 is BGN 560 (about USD 320) from 1 Jan. 2019; in 2020 it is BGN 650 (about USD 372).
118. These data are from *Kollectivno troudovo dogovariane 2019*, 26–29.

working days (Mines, Energy, Chemical Industry, etc.), instead of the minimum legal standard of five working days as provided for in Article 156 of the LC[119] (*see* above Part I, Chapter 4, §3).

IV. Compensation

627. The collective labour contracts stipulate provisions for special compensation in the cases of dismissal as a result of total or partial closing of the enterprise, reduction in staff or fall in output. Such compensation may vary from two to six months' wages depending on the length of service (chemical industry, light industry, agriculture, energy, food processing industry, etc.).[120]

V. Hygiene and Safety and Social Insurance

628. The obligations on the employer in this field consist in the implementation of concrete measures rendering safe machinery and equipment, the restoration of the natural environment, the supply of personal safety devices and special working clothes and the like. In the field of social insurance such obligations refer to the proper organization of work in canteens with special dietary feeding requirements, at health centres and sanatoria (if available in the enterprise or in the branch) for rendering assistance to workers who have fallen ill, etc. Moreover, the main task is not so much to secure fulfilment of the legal requirements in this sphere because this is obligatory anyway, but rather to include measures of application which coincide with the specific conditions prevailing in the individual enterprise or the respective branch, as well as envisaging new measures which take into account the peculiarities in working conditions at a given enterprise or branch.

629. The peculiar thing about this section is that it includes questions which are not directly connected with the labour process, but go beyond this and affect the daily life of workers, the interest, concerns and problems with which they are faced outside and apart from their work at the enterprise. As a matter of fact, the question deals with their living conditions and establishes an employer's duty to help improve such conditions satisfying the needs of the workers. This is achieved through the implementation of undertakings such as: the construction, providing of equipment and maintenance of children's crèches, kindergartens and summer camps for the children of workers, workers' canteens, shops for foodstuffs, barbers' and hairdressing saloons, multiple service establishments in the region of the enterprise, the construction of departmental housing and its distribution, the maintenance and management by the enterprise of workers' accommodation, the construction of workers' holiday homes and the distribution of cards entitling them to spend their holiday there, securing the workers' transport to and from their homes and their place of work with vehicles belonging to the enterprise, and so on. Unfortunately,

119. These data are from *Kollectivno troudovo dogovariane 2019*, 44–49.
120. These data are from *Kollectivno troudovo dogovariane 2019*, 32–34.

because of the great economic difficulties most enterprises have had to face in the past few years, there has been a tendency to substantially decrease the relative significance of this section within the framework of the collective labour contracts.

§5. Claims in Case of Non-fulfilment of the Collective Labour Contract

630. Pursuant to Article 59 of the LC, when an employer fails to fulfil the contractual obligations, the trade union as a party to the respective collective labour contract, as well as any worker or employee to whom this contact applies, may lodge a claim against the employer.

631. This legal provision establishes a claim for non-performance of the employer's obligation as stipulated in the collective labour contract as well as for damages caused by non-performance or partial discharge only. In other words, depending on the specific obligation which has not been discharged, the interested person may have a claim for, e.g., the supply of personal safety devices, special working clothes, payment of the stipulated labour remuneration, annual paid leave to be enjoyed.

632. The following have the right to claim: the trade union organization – party to the respective collective labour contract – and each individual worker and employee to whom the said contract applies (*see* above, §3 of this chapter). The trade union organization lodges a claim where non-fulfilment concerns all workers or a great number of them, i.e., where it concerns a common interest. The individual worker or employee may put in a claim where the non-fulfilment concerns himself/ herself, or when, for one reason or another, the trade union organization remains inactive (does not undertake anything) about lodging a claim.

633. These claims are against the employer as a party to the respective collective labour contract, which he has failed to discharge. The employer is the respondent in the judicial dispute. The procedural nature makes these claims civil actions. They are addressed in the ordinary courts. Examination of any claim by the courts is carried out in conformity with the procedure provided for in the Code of Civil Procedure and, more precisely, by following its rules about claims procedure (Articles 103–309).

634. The fact that Article 59 of the LC establishes a claims procedure in cases of non-fulfilment of the collective labour contract by an employer does not mean that a dispute concerning a common interest of the workers cannot be settled as a collective labour dispute in conformity with the procedure established by the Law on Collective Labour Conflicts (*see* Chapter 5, below). This way is still open to the parties at issue if the dispute is a collective one. As a matter of fact, in the case of non-fulfilment of a collective labour contract, it is highly desirable that the parties make an effort to settle the dispute by negotiation. But if they do not succeed in reaching an agreement to settle the collective labour dispute, the legal suit procedure may be adopted. This is the objective of Article 59 of the LC.

§6. Invalidity of the Collective Labour Contract

635. It was through the amendments to the LC of March 2001 that the explicit legal framework of invalidity of the collective labour contract was established. Until that time there was no such legal framework and this used to be a serious gap in the legislation. Now this legal framework is contained in the new Article 60 of the LC.

Each collective labour contract may be claimed to be declared invalid, regardless of the level it was concluded at: enterprise, municipality, branch or sector level. Depending on the nature of the fault and the parts of the collective labour contract affected thereby, the invalidity of either the whole collective labour agreement or certain clauses thereof may be claimed.

636. The claim for declaring the invalidity of the collective labour contract may be made by two groups of legal subjects:

(1) By the parties to the collective labour contract. They are determined according to the level that the collective labour contract has been concluded at. As for a collective labour contract that has been concluded at enterprise level, these are: the employer and the trade union organization which has concluded the contract, as for the sector and branch collective labour contracts and also for the collective labour contracts concluded at municipal level, these are the representative employers' and trade union organizations of the respective sector, branch or municipality.
(2) The claim for declaring the invalidity of the collective labour contract may also be made by each worker or employee that the respective collective labour contract is applied to. This can be either each worker or employee who is a member of the trade union organization which is a party to the collective labour contract, or each worker or employee who, in spite of not being a member of such a trade union organization, or of any other trade union organization, which is not a party to the collective labour contract, has joined the collective labour contract in accordance with the procedure set forth in Article 57, paragraph 2 of the LC (*see supra*, §3).

637. The claim for declaring the invalidity of the collective labour contract may be made on two grounds:

(1) 'Contravention of the law': this ground means contravention of the imperative provisions of a law within the precise legal meaning of this term – a normative act adopted by the National Assembly, and it also means contravention of the imperative provisions of a sublegal normative act issued by a state body. Such acts are: Decrees of the Council of Ministers, Rules, Regulations and Instructions issued by the Council of Ministers or a Minister authorized thereof by law. The 'contravention of the law' means that the collective labour

contract provides for something which is different from and inconsistent with what the law has established within the meaning explained above.

(2) 'Circumvention of the law': it is present where an unlawful result is achieved through the collective labour contract indirectly, in a roundabout way. For instance, such cases where the collective labour contract specifies a job of a permanent nature as a temporary, seasonal or short-term one for the purpose of circumvention of the prohibition on concluding fixed-term labour contracts of a permanent nature under Article 68, paragraph 2 of the LC.

638. The claim for declaring the invalidity of the collective labour contract may be made by way of filing a claim with the court. The statement of claim specifies the grounds for invalidity, i.e., what the contravention of the law or circumvention thereof consists in, which law or sublegal normative act, and which article thereof, the collective labour contract contravenes or circumvents, etc. The statement of claim is filed with the regional court by place of concluding the collective labour contract. The claim filed is considered in accordance with the rules of the three-instance proceedings: regional court, district court and Supreme Court of Cassation pursuant to the provisions of Articles 103–309 of the Civil Procedure Code.

639. The consequences of the court's declaring the invalidity of the collective labour contract – or of certain clauses thereof – is that the latter are not applied any more to the relations between the parties to the collective labour contract and do not give rise to rights and obligations between the employer and the workers and employees. However, these consequences occur after the court's decision on declaring the invalidity of the collective labour contract has taken effect and has been delivered to the parties. It is from that moment on that the court's decision obliges the parties to the collective labour contract to align their conduct with the new situation resulting from declaring the invalidity of either the whole collective labour contract or separate clauses thereof.

Chapter 6. Collective Labour Disputes

§1. General Remarks

640. Collective labour conflicts and their legal regulation is a new problem in Bulgarian labour law and industrial relations. Regulation of collective labour conflicts is contained in the Law on the Settlement of Collective Labour Disputes, adopted on 6 March 1990 (OJ, No. 21 of 1990, as amended) at the very beginning of the country's process of political upheaval and democratization after the overthrow of the totalitarian regime on 10 November 1989.

641. The most important topics of the new regulation are the following: recognition of collective labour disputes, establishment of a procedure for their peaceful settlement, legal recognition of the right to strike as a fundamental right of the workers and employees and the prohibition to lockout. These topics will be discussed further below (*see* §§2–5).

642. Among all matters regulated by the Law on the Settlement of Collective Labour Disputes, the right to strike is the most important topic and achievement and with historical significance. In recognizing the right to strike, the socialist ideological tenet on this matter which dominated legislation and official theory after the Second World War was ended. According to this tenet and given the existing political and economic structure of society in which the state was deemed to express the radical interest of the working class, striking was not a necessary means of defending economic and social interests. The realities and the historical experiment carried out by the socialist countries in Eastern Europe after the Second World War – including Bulgaria following the Soviet model of socialist society – have categorically refuted this tenet. Now in the process of democratization Bulgaria's national legislation on industrial disputes is taking its first steps in mastering the new approaches to the settlement of such disputes.

§2. Notion of Collective Labour Disputes

643. Collective labour disputes are characterized by their subjects, object, nature and procedure of settlement. These matters will be analysed below.

644. The subject of collective labour disputes are the workers and employees, on one side and the employer, or employers, on the other. On the side of the workers it is not necessary that they are organized in a trade union. This is usually but not always the case. From a legal point of view a group (collective) of workers not organized in a trade union may be the subject of a collective labour dispute. However, it is necessary to have, on the side of the workers, a collective in order for the labour dispute to qualify as a collective one. The employer is a person (natural or legal) who hires the manpower (labour force) of workers and employees. As the subject of a collective labour dispute, this may be either an individual employer, a group of employers or an employers' organization. The collective character of the labour dispute springs from the presence of collective workers and their common interest in the dispute. Consequently, a collective character on the side of the employer is not necessary. It does not matter whether the employer or the workers are engaged in the private or public sector. In both cases collective labour disputes may arise.

645. The object of a collective labour dispute is 'about what' the collective labour dispute arises. It is defined by Article 1, paragraph 1 of the Law[121] and embraces three groups of disputes according to the level at which the dispute may arise:

(1) disputes arising from the labour relationship such as remuneration, additional payments, leave, working time, health and safety, collective redundancies, and all other questions connected with the arising, contents or termination of the labour relationship;
(2) questions stemming from social security. These are questions about social security, risks, different kinds of benefits, social security contributions, occupational diseases and accidents at work, family allowances. The employer is obliged to pay the required contribution for his employees. The cost of social security has mounted considerably over the last four years and additional social security benefits are provided by means of collective agreements;
(3) questions (disputes) about standard of living. Despite the general meaning of this notion ('standard of living') included here, there are questions such as different kinds of compensation because of the rapid growth of the rate of inflation, supply of free medication, payment of part of rent, gratuitous meals in canteens.

It is obvious that the scope of collective labour disputes is quite broad and the concept is a loose one.

646. The legal nature of collective labour disputes is determined by two features:

(1) The dispute normally involves several workers.
(2) The dispute flows from a common (collective) interest of the workers, acting in combination (collectively) to defend that common interest which affects all (or several) workers. It is precisely this 'community' of interest of several workers which represents the 'texture' of the collective labour dispute and makes a genuine collective labour dispute that of a labour dispute in which various individuals take part.

647. In the legislation of Bulgaria, as of most countries, a distinction is made between disputes of rights and disputes of interest. Despite the fact that there is no

121. When in this chapter 'the law' is cited without any other indication as to title, it refers to the Law on the Settlement of Collective Labour Disputes, 1990 (OJ, No. 21 of 1990, as amended).

clear definition of these different kinds of disputes, it could be said that disputes of rights are those arising from recognized and established subjective rights. It does not matter 'where' in law the right is recognized: in the Constitution, in the Law, in a sublegal normative act, in a collective agreement, etc. What does matter is that the respective right is recognized, and the parties' dispute is about exercising the right, the extent of the right, whether the right applies to the subject who alleges to be entitled to it, etc. The solving of these disputes consists in pronouncing 'what the law says about' (*jurisdictio*). Disputes of rights involve the interpretation and application of already established norms, and therefore also of the rights of the parties. Disputes of interest are those which consist in the establishment of subjective rights, their creation, and introduction into the relations between the parties. Both parties in this case defend their interest in establishing or changing on non-establishing or retention of the respective subjective rights. Normally, as a result of these kinds of disputes, the respective rights are inserted in a collective labour contract or in another type of agreement between the controversial parties. Most cases of collective labour disputes are about disputes of interest. But this does not mean that collective labour disputes of rights are altogether excluded. The legal provision of Article 59 of the LC which entitles the trade union to lodge a claim against an employer who fails to fulfil the contractual obligation stemming from the concluded collective agreement is a categorical example of a collective labour dispute of rights (*see supra*, Chapter 4, §5).

648. Another distinction is drawn up between individual and collective labour disputes. Generally, individual labour disputes essentially concern individual labour relations. One of the parties is always a worker or employee, i.e., the individual acting in defence of his/her rights and interest stemming from the individual employment relationship. The other party is the employer and, normally, the individual employer. An individual dispute may become collective if it forms a threat to a common interest, for instance where a trades union militant was unlawfully dismissed or if the employer blankly refuses, without any justification, to satisfy a legitimate right of workers. Individual labour disputes are mostly disputes of rights. They are resolved by the courts according to the rules provided for in Articles 357–362 of the LC and in the Code on Civil Procedure (*see supra*, Part I, Chapter 10).

649. Pursuant to the law, collective labour disputes may be peacefully settled by means of negotiation, voluntary arbitration or by pressure and force, i.e., by means of strikes. A completely different procedure is applied in either *modus operandi*. The normal and most frequently used procedure is the peaceful settlement of the collective labour dispute. From the legal viewpoint, this is the most desirable outcome of the collective labour dispute that has arisen. It is the goal that the efforts of the Law on the Settlement of Collective Labour Disputes, 1990, are primarily aimed at. According to the philosophy of this Law, strikes are the last and extreme means – *ultimum remedium* for the settlement of collective labour disputes.

§3. Peaceful Settlement of Collective Labour Disputes

650. Pursuant to the legal framework established by the Law on the Settlement of Collective Labour Disputes, the voluntary settlement of the collective labour disputes is achieved through the application of four methods: (I) direct negotiations; (II) mediation; (III) conciliation; (IV) voluntary labour arbitration. They are the subject of the exposition coming next.

I. Settlement by Means of Negotiation

651. This is the first stage of settling collective labour disputes, which is an obligatory one to be followed by the parties as soon as the dispute arises (Article 3 of the law). Negotiations are direct, i.e., they have to take place between the opposing parties: workers and employees on the one side and the employer on the other. During these negotiations both the workers and the employer may be represented by their representatives. On the part of the workers such representation may be (and most frequently is) their trade union organization. But it is also likely (and, in practice, especially in the existing situation of trade union pluralism and dispersal of trade union organizations) that for the negotiations, the workers elect their representatives ad hoc. They may belong to the trade union's militants or not, as the workers themselves decide. As regards the employer, he may personally participate and be in direct contact and negotiation or nominate a representative from among his deputies, leading personnel, specialists, etc., as he decides.

652. At the very beginning of direct negotiations and before they start, the workers who normally are the instigators of the collective labour dispute have two obligations:

(1) to submit to the employer, in writing, their requests. It is not necessary to explain these in detail, or to give a motivation. It suffices to merely indicate the questions about which the dispute has arisen and, if necessary, to add some short notes or explanations on the requests;
(2) to inform the employer of the names of any representatives who will take part in the direct negotiations (Article 3, paragraph 2 of the law).

It is evident that these preliminary obligations are intended to facilitate and to allow better organization of the forthcoming direct negotiations.

653. The procedure on how direct negotiations are conducted is 'freely decided' by the opposing parties (Article 1, paragraph 1 of the law). This is a very important though peculiar feature of the procedure of direct negotiations. It means that there are no legal rules laid down on any particular course of action, but there are rules decided upon between the parties as an eloquent expression of the autonomy of the social partners and as one of the basic principles in this matter.

654. The direct negotiations themselves consist of full explanations and the suggestion of articulate arguments by the workers in order to substantiate (to give proof) the validity of their requirements, in order to convince or make the employer accept and satisfy them. Normally the employer is not, at once, prepared to accede completely to the workers' demands. The employer, in turn, may suggest arguments refuting or denying the grounds on which the worker's requirements are based. And so negotiations and genuine bargaining may sometimes continue for days. During these negotiations both parties try to prove their professional capabilities, knowledge and ability to conduct the negotiations, to argue their position, to make necessary and unavoidable concessions and compromises in order to reach a final agreement. In this regard the parties at issue, both the workers' representatives and the employer and his nominated representatives, go through a form of apprenticeship in the difficult art of negotiations and in order to attain an agreement by means of negotiation. They are not yet used to doing this. If the parties reach an agreement, the collective labour dispute is settled. This is the most desirable outcome of a collective labour dispute. At the end of procedure for the settlement of a labour dispute, the parties elaborate on the agreement in writing and sign it.

655. If during direct negotiations the parties do not succeed in reaching an agreement, pursuant to Article 4 of the law, the next possible stages in the negotiations are open to them.

656. The next three stages and methods of voluntary settlement of collective labour disputes are regulated under Article 4–4a of the law cited. They have two main points in common: (a) they are applied after the application of the direct negotiations under Article 3 of the law cited has failed, as one of the parties or both of them have not wanted it, or, in spite of being applied, the direct negotiations have not brought about reaching an agreement between the parties for the voluntary settlement of the collective labour dispute; (b) these methods are organized and realized by and in cooperation with a new state body which was established through the amendments of 2001 to the Law on the Settlement of Collective Labour Disputes – the National Institute for Conciliation and Arbitration at the Minister of Labour and Social Policy (Article 4a of the law cited).

II. Settlement by Means of Mediation

657. Mediation is an activity that aims at inducing the parties to the dispute to negotiate with each other and to make mutual concessions in order to reach an agreement and settle the dispute voluntarily. This activity is performed by persons-mediators, who have been especially charged with this function and have been approved by the Supervisory Board of the National Institute for Conciliation and Arbitration (*see* above, paragraph 651). It is in cooperation with the mediator and with the help of his/her efforts, that each of the parties to the dispute 'covers its own part of the distance', which divides them, so they can 'meet' and reach an agreement for voluntary settlement of the dispute. The mediation for voluntary settlement of collective labour disputes may also be carried out by the trade union and employers' organizations through the parity participation of their representatives for voluntary settlement of the collective labour dispute between the parties.

III. Settlement by Means of Conciliation

658. Conciliation is realized in cooperation with conciliators, who are persons that have been especially charged with the realization thereof. Their mission, although close to the role and mission of the mediators, is somewhat different. The conciliatory function of the conciliator consists of suggesting ideas, making proposals, developing versions for achieving voluntary settlement of the collective labour dispute. He/she makes efforts so that each party to the dispute be induced, severally or jointly, to accept these proposals. For this purpose the conciliator hears out the parties, either severally or jointly. All in all, he/she conducts the whole procedure for finding a way out for the voluntary settlement of the collective labour dispute to be achieved. And wherever necessary, he/she also exercises discreet pressure upon the parties, in order to 'bring' them to reaching an agreement for voluntary settlement of the dispute. The conciliation is organized by the National Institute for Conciliation and Arbitration. It may also be realized by representatives of the employers' and trade union organizations.

659. If the parties attain an agreement in the course of direct negotiations, mediation or conciliation, they conclude an understanding (a covenant) which has the force of a collective agreement (§l of the Supplementary and Final Provisions of the law), sign it and, in this way, the dispute is settled. Where there is a failure in the negotiations, the last chance to reach an agreement by peaceful means is by way of arbitration (*see* below).

IV. Settlement by Means of Arbitration

660. The arbitration procedure is provided for in Articles 5–8 of the Law. The arbitration established by the law is a voluntary one. The dispute may be brought to arbitration only by mutual consent in writing of the parties at issue (Article 5, paragraph 1 of the law). Arbitration may be applied apart from the procedure of direct negotiations (*see supra*, section I). Normally this procedure is applied wherever there is a failure in the process of the direct negotiations including those with assistance of representatives of superior employers' and trade union organizations.

661. Arbitration may be carried out by an arbitrator sitting on his own or a college of three arbitrators. The arbitrators may be chosen by the parties from among those included in the list of arbitrators compiled upon the proposal of all trade unions and employers' organizations and approbated by the Supervisory Board of the National Institute for Conciliation and Arbitration. Some of the arbitrators are lawyers. However, to be approbated as arbitrator the law does not stipulate any formal requirements as to professional qualifications. When the parties consent to refer the dispute to an arbitrator sitting on his own, they nominate one. If they decide to bring the dispute to an arbitration panel both parties nominate an arbitrator and the so-nominated arbitrators elect a president from among the arbitrators on the approbated list.

662. The arbitration hearing is held in public in the presence of the summoned parties at issue. During the sitting the parties' representatives are heard, explanations are given and documents and other trial records may be cited as evidence. If necessary, other persons may be summoned and experts' opinions may be called upon (Article 6 of the law).

663. The arbitration award is decided upon by a majority of the arbitrators in cases of a hearing by an arbitration panel. This is based on the evidence produced during the hearing of the case. If the collective labour dispute is one of rights, the arbitration award ought to be based on the legislation in force. The arbitration award is pronounced in writing and should be motivated. It is a final decision and there is no appeal. The arbitration award is mandatory on the parties involved and is immediately enforceable (§1 of the Supplementary and Final Provisions of the law).

664. In confirmation of the fundamental principle of amicable settlement of collective labour disputes, on which the legal regulation thereof is set up (*see* above paragraphs 650–663), in recent years special attention has been given to encouraging and strengthening the parties' activity for settling the disputes through direct negotiations between the disputing parties 'on the spot' on which the disputes have occurred. The latter are settled through 'a freely regulated procedure' between the parties. This procedure is increasingly being agreed on in the collective labour contracts, which also provide for the terms in which direct discussions shall take place, the frequency of the meetings between the parties to the dispute and the like. In the settlement of collective labour disputes through direct negotiations between the parties, serious assistance is rendered by the National Institute of Reconciliation and Arbitration. In 2017 and 2018, it is 20% of all the collective labour disputes occurring in the enterprises that have been settled in this way.[122]

§4. Strikes

I. Notion

665. As has already been pointed out, a strike is the ultimate, yet normal means for the settlement of a labour dispute. 'Ultimate means' here does not indicate that it is an extraordinary or exclusive means, but only that it is used after having tried to settle the collective labour dispute in a peaceful and voluntary way through direct negotiations including those with the assistance of representatives of superior

122. *See* collection: *Deistvashti Kolektivni Trudovi Dogovori i Kolektivni Trudovi Sporove* [*Operative Collective Labour Contracts and Collective Labour Disputes*] (Sofia: Publishing House of the National Institute of Reconciliation and Arbitration, 2019), 57–59.

employers' and trade union organizations.[123] The strike is a means of unilateral pressure by workers on an employer in order to compel him to satisfy their requests which have been put forward within the framework of the initiated collective labour dispute. According to Article 11, paragraph 1 of the law, a strike is a temporary cessation of work. During such cessation of work, the worker (the striker) is temporarily not fulfilling his/her obligation to furnish his/her labour and fulfil his/her labour duties; but he/she has no intention to terminate his/her individual labour contract. The *animus* of the worker on strike is neither to put an end to the employment contract, nor to breach it, but only to temporarily cease work to protest against, e.g., the unsatisfactory wages and working conditions in the enterprise, branch, etc. This protest is directed at the employer or employers. Through the strikes workers exert pressure on the employer in order that the latter may yield to the force and meet the workers' demands. This pressure is legally regulated, admitted and permitted. What is more, the striker wants to return to his/her job after the strike is over. On the other hand, the strike is a 'concerted action'. This means that several workers are involved. It is a collectively decided action in which various workers participate. Under Bulgarian law a strike by one person is theoretically possible if the decision to strike is made following the procedure as provided for in the Law (*see* below, section III).

666. During the strike the individual labour relationships of the strikers continue to exist. They are merely suspended. More precisely, fulfilment of the workers' obligations arising from such relationships is stopped (suspended). After the strike, the strikers resume the jobs and their employment contracts continue to be normally, adequately and completely performed.

667. A striker has no right to remuneration during the period he/she is on strike: a worker who does not report for work has no right to remuneration. If a worker reports for work at a plant which is on strike, the employer has to provide him/her with work and pay him/her. In practice, strikers – union members as well as non-unionists – are paid strike benefits from strike funds, created by the trade unions, during the strike.

II. Types of Strikes

668. Pursuant to Article 50 of the Constitution and according to their purpose, the law regulates and allows only economic strikes of workers and employees. These are strikes about demands stemming from labour and social security relations and the standard of living (*see* above, §2 of this chapter). Hence, strikes of persons who are not workers and employees (pupils, students, soldiers and the like) are not allowed. Not allowed either are the so-called political strikes, i.e., strikes against the government, Parliament or other authorities, established in conformity with the Constitution, in their capacity of organ of public power. However, in practice, it is

123. J.-M. Verdier, Al. Coeret & M.-A. Souriac, *Droit du travail, Volume V, Rapports collectifs, 14-ème éd.* (Paris: Dalloz, 2007), 249–253.

very difficult to distinguish between political and economic strikes. It is even more difficult in the present situation where protest by way of strikes against low wages and bad working conditions is very often mixed with and transformed into a protest against the general economic and social politics as exercised by the government and the Parliament.

669. Another classification of strikes is made after the form they take. According to this criterion, the differentiates between three types of strikes:

(1) regular (normal) strikes – where workers strike in order to defend their own economic and social interests (Article 11, paragraphs 1–3 of the law). This is the typical kind of strike;
(2) warning strikes (Article 11, paragraph 5 of the law). These may be declared without notice being given to the employer. The maximum duration of such strikes is one hour. This short stoppage of work is intended to underline the threat of possible further serious strike action if the employer does not satisfy the requests put forward by the workers;
(3) strikes of solidarity (Article 11, paragraph 4 of the law). The aim is to exert pressure on another employer. These strikes express the solidarity and support for other workers of another employer. They are of moral significance for the workers who are on 'regular' strike.

670. In the last few years there has been a growing importance of 'sit-ins' or 'occupations'. The last one (January–February 1994) consisted of the occupation by students and lecturers of the University 'Saint Kl. Ohridski' in Sofia. It was declared as a last resort to defend the interest of higher education and against the low percentage of financial resources provided by the state budget. Despite the declared purpose (and the high-minded, noble and justifiable requirements in the case of the recent occupation of the University of Sofia), sit-ins are illegal. It is a violation of property and constitutes an infringement of the freedom of labour of other workers who want to work, as well as of the freedom of an employer and his managerial staff.

671. The number of strikes in the country since 1990 has been considerable. In 1990 there were 1,300 strikes with 1.4 million strikers, in 1991 there were 850 involving 1 million strikers, in 1992 the country faced 1,100 strikes whilst in the first half of 1993 there were 350 strikes.[124] The boom of strikes in 1990 was due to the multitude of severe social problems inherited from the totalitarian regime after it had been ousted and the boom in 1992 was due to anti-trade union politics as proclaimed by the government of the day. During the recent years – since 1993 – there has been a clear tendency towards a decrease in the number of strikes.

124. These data are cited from *Otcheten doklad na Koordinazionnia Savet na KNSB*, 89–99.

III. Prerequisites and Procedure

672. Article 11, paragraph 1 of the Law establishes two main material prerequisites for going on strike. They are the following:

(1) The parties involved in the collective labour conflict have not succeeded in reaching an agreement within the framework of direct negotiations (*see* above, §3 of this chapter). It underlines the obligatory character of direct negotiations, on the one hand, and the fact that such negotiations have been duly followed by the parties but have not produced the required outcome.
(2) The employer has not fulfilled his obligations to the workers. These obligations may be contained in a collective agreement or in any other understanding concluded during a previous collective labour conflict, etc.

It goes without saying that these obligations should be related to the matters stemming from labour and social security relations and the standard of living. These prerequisites are alternatives, i.e., the presence of either condition is sufficient. Certainly, both conditions may exist at the same time.

673. The law also establishes some procedural rules to be followed by workers when they go on strike. They are the following:

(1) The necessity for a decision to go on strike taken by the workers of the enterprise, branch etc. (Article 11, paragraph 2 of the law). This decision is made by simple majority of the workers employed in the enterprise. The law does not determine how this decision is to be taken – in secret or by public vote. Written proceedings are normally drawn up for the decision to be made on this matter. Such written proceedings will be further necessary in a lawsuit about the lawfulness of the strike (*see* below section VI – Lawful and Unlawful Strikes).
(2) Serious efforts should have been made for voluntary settlement of the collective labour dispute that has arisen. This requirement is a confirmation of the principal view upheld by the legislator, according to which the strike is an ultimate means of settling the collective labour disputes and it should be applied only after efforts have been made for the voluntary settlement thereof and the means of voluntary settlement of the dispute have been exhausted (*see* above, paragraphs 645–658) without bringing about voluntary settlement of the dispute by way of an agreement between the parties. More specifically, this requirement means: (a) direct negotiations between the parties have been conducted pursuant to Article 3 of the law cited; however, in the course thereof no agreement between the parties has been reached; (b) following the parties' failure to reach an agreement for voluntary settlement of the dispute, and according to their own will, they have proceeded to mediation and conciliation pursuant to Article 4 of the law cited; however, no agreement has been reached between the parties for voluntary settlement of the dispute in the course of application of these procedures.

(3) The employer has failed to fulfil his obligations to the workers and employees. These obligations of the employer may arise out of various sources: the law, the collective labour contract between the parties, agreements between the parties reached in the course of direct negotiations between them or resulting from the application of procedures for conciliation, mediation or awards of the labour arbitration under Articles 3, 4, 5–8 of the law cited.
(4) Workers who go on strike are obliged to inform the employer about the impending strike by means of a written statement. This written statement must be directed to the employer at least seven days before the strike is to start (Article 1, paragraph 3). It also has to contain: the date and hour on which the strike will start, its duration and organizer and the leaders of the strike. This is important to the employer in order for him to take the necessary measures to organize his activities during the stoppage of work.

674. According to the legislation, strikes may be organized by the trade unions as well as the workers themselves. In the latter case the workers who go on strike elect from among them a strike committee and adopt other rules concerning the course of action and so on. For this reason the national legislation does not recognize so-called wildcat strikes (*grèves sauvages*). Certainly over the last three years strikes have normally been organized by the trade unions.

IV. Protection of Essential Supplies and Services

675. For obvious reasons the right to strike cannot be unlimited. Legal solutions should be provided for in order to prevent harm and losses to society as a whole. In this context, one of the limitations is the protection of essential supplies and services during a strike.

676. Pursuant to Article 14 of the law the workers and the employer are obliged to assure, by means of an agreement in writing, the continuing provision of essential supplies and services during the strikes, suspension or stoppage of which may otherwise generate serious danger to people. Such essential supplies and services have to be provided in the following activities, the non-fulfilment or stopping of which may create danger for:

(1) the life and health of citizens in need of urgent or emergency medical care, or of those whose hospital treatment has started;
(2) the production, distribution, transfer and supply of gas, electrical energy and heat power; the satisfactory communal and everyday life and transport services for the population; interruption of television broadcasting, radio broadcasting and the fixed-network voice telephone services;
(3) inflicting irreparable damages to public or personal property or the natural environment;
(4) the public order.

This agreement should be concluded at least three days before the strike is to start (Article 14, paragraph 2). Nevertheless, if the parties involved do not achieve an agreement, the problem will be decided by way of arbitration – by a single arbitrator or an arbitration board nominated by the government or an authority empowered by it (Article 14, paragraph 3 of the law). By the way, this is the only case in which the national legislation provides for obligatory arbitration aiming to prevent harm and losses, especially those inflicted upon society as a whole and being out of proportion or intolerable.

677. Although the strike marks the most acute stage in the development of a collective labour dispute, it does not put an end to the relationships between the parties to the dispute. Even at this phase of strained relationships between the parties, the law stays true to its fundamental idea of voluntary settlement of disputes. This is evidenced by Article 15 of the Law on Settlement of Collective Labour Disputes, which says: 'During a strike the parties put efforts into settling the dispute through direct negotiations, mediation or in some other appropriate way.' The initiative of continuing the direct negotiations or resorting to any of the other methods of voluntary settlement of the dispute can be taken by any of the parties at any time. While the strike is going on, it is important that the parties continue communicating with each other, trying to find a way out of it in a mutually acceptable manner. In practice, it is during this time that mutual consent is reached to termination of the strike on the grounds of Article 15 of the Law on Settlement of Collective Labour Disputes with mutual concessions and compromises between the parties.

V. Limitations on the Freedom to Strike

678. Another manner in which legislation has introduced some limitations on the freedom to strike is provided for in Article 16 of the law. Pursuant to this legal provision, strikes are formally prohibited in certain cases; the list of cases is exhaustive. They may be summarized in four groups.

679. The first group embraces the cases in which the purpose of the strike goes beyond its objective as a means of defence of collective economic interests of workers stemming from labour relations and social security relations and the standard of living. To this group belong strikes in which workers put forward requirements which are contrary to the Constitution, have a political character, or are utilized for resolving individual labour disputes (Article 16, items 1, 5 and 7 of the law).

680. The second group includes the cases in which strikes are banned in certain branches or spheres of activity because these are considered very important for the society as a whole. For this reason the lawmaker prohibits strikes in these branches and spheres, in order to protect the general (public) interest as well as to prevent harm and losses to society as a whole. Consequently, strikes are forbidden in spheres of activity such as: Ministry of Defence, Ministry of Internal Affairs, Judiciary – courts, public prosecutor's offices and bodies of preliminary inquest (Article 16, items 4 and 6 of the law cited).

681. It is worth noting explicitly that the restrictions which used to exist as regards the prohibition on strikes of the workers and employees in certain sectors and spheres of activity, such as the generation, distribution and supply of electricity and gas, communications and health care under the 1990 Law on the Settlement of Collective Labour Disputes, were lifted by the 2006 Law on the amendments thereto. Their lift was a result of long-continued negotiations between the social partners – the representative trade union and employers' organizations – which were conducted from the spring until the autumn of 2006 within the framework of the discussions on the Bill on amendments to the Law on the Settlement of Collective Labour Disputes held under the auspices of the Commission on Labour and Social Policy at the 40th National Assembly. These negotiations ended successfully – the social partners agreed upon the lift of the restrictions. As a mechanism compensating for the lift of these restrictions and for the extension of the workers' and employees' freedom to exercise their right to strike, minimum activities were determined that have to be performed during the period of a strike by the workers and employees involved in a strike in the above-mentioned sectors and spheres (prom. OJ, No. 87 of 2006, *see* above paragraph 674).

682. The third group embraces the cases of violation of the established rules concerning the settlement of collective labour disputes, such as the rules on direct negotiations in settling collective labour disputes, rules of procedure (e.g., decision taken by simple majority of the workers in an enterprise to go on strike, the obligation of the organizer of the strike to inform the employer on the forthcoming strike) and rules on the protection of essential supplies and services. To this group also belong the cases in which a strike is carried on despite the fact that there exists an agreement between the parties involved or an arbitration award for the settlement of the collective dispute (Article 16, item 3 of the law). An interdiction of strikes in these cases is imposed in order to ensure the observance of the legal regulation established for the settlement of collective labour disputes.

683. The fourth group includes the cases in which strikes are carried on during a natural disaster and urgent restoration works whilst life-saving services are necessary to combat the consequences flowing from such incidents (Article 16, item 2 of the law). The justification of an interdiction here is to be found in the exclusiveness of the circumstances engendered by Acts of God (force majeure) occurring in the whole country or in the locality where the relevant enterprise is situated.

VI. Lawful and Unlawful Strikes

684. The main principle in this area consists of the presumption introduced by the Law according to which all strikes are deemed to be lawful unless the contrary is established by the court. Nobody may qualify the strike as wrongful (unlawful) before the competent court has so decided. Nevertheless, the presumption is a refutable one (*juris tantum*) and may be refuted in the court's judgment following the judicial procedure prescribed by the Law (Article 17 of the law).

685. The claim for the establishment of unlawfulness of a strike may be lodged by the employer and the workers not participating or having participated in the strike. Only these two groups of persons are entitled to ask for the court's judgment on the (un)lawfulness of the given strike. This is a civil action against the workers who have participated in the strike. The claim is lodged before the district court which is the only court competent to hear such a case. Geographically seen, the case falls within the jurisdiction of the district court if the seat of the employer is within the district. The case is heard in open court with the participation of the public prosecutor. The judicial procedure to be followed in the hearing of a case is the ordinary procedure established by the Code of Civil Procedure. The district court's decision may be appealed to the appellate court. The decision of the latter may be appealed against to the Supreme Court of Cassation within thirty days in accordance with the procedure and on the grounds laid down in Article 280 of the Civil Procedure Code. The decision of the Supreme Court of Cassation is final. Thus, unlike the previous legislation, the disputes over the lawfulness of a strike are subject to consideration under the normal three-instance adversary judicial proceedings, which corresponds to their importance and juridical complexity.

686. Certainly, the main problem in the hearing of these cases is about the notion of unlawfulness of the strike. This notion is not legally defined. In this situation, the jurisprudence deduces the basic legal criteria for appreciation of the lawfulness or the unlawfulness of a strike from the prohibition established in Article 16 of the law. This approach is correct and well-founded. When the law enumerates exhaustively the cases in which strikes are banned in such a way, it establishes the criteria for appraisal of the conformity of the strikes with the legal requirements. Infringement of these so-enumerated legal interdictions makes a strike unlawful.

§5. Lockout

687. A special regulation is devoted to lockouts by means of Articles 20 and 21 of the law. In order to give more protection to the workers, especially during the present difficult transitional period to a market-oriented economy, the period of a general slump in production and rising unemployment, the Law prohibits lockouts.

688. According to the law, the interdiction of a lockout embraces three kinds of action on the part of the employer which are forbidden. This gives the lockout in the context of national legislation a certain specific and broader meaning in comparison with the usual meaning of this notion as the closure of a plant by an employer in order to exert pressure on the workers during a collective conflict, rather than merely for economic or technical reasons.

689. The kinds of operations prohibited by the Law are the following:

(1) The law forbids the employer to suspend the activity of the enterprise or its subdivisions with the purpose to prevent or to suspend a strike, or to frustrate the requests put forward by the workers from being satisfied. Consequently,

the lockout is characterized not only by the operation being a prohibited one but also by the 'anti-strike' purpose (*animus*) with which it is undertaken. These actions by an employer are forbidden during the whole period after the declaration of a strike, whilst it is going on, and until it finishes (Article 20 of the Law).

(2) During the period under (1) the employer is prohibited from dismissing a worker for the above-mentioned 'anti-strike' purposes, i.e., to prevent or to suspend a strike, or to frustrate the demands submitted by the workers within the framework of the collective labour conflicts from being satisfied, whose ultimate and sharpest stage is the strike (Article 20 of the Law).

(3) During the strike the employer is prohibited from recruiting new workers and probable strike-breakers from outside the enterprise in order to ensure the normal continuity of his activity, from undermining the courage, perseverance and willingness of the strikers to attain satisfaction of their demands. The only exception to this interdiction allowed by the law is for the provision of essential supplies and services according to Article 14 of the law (*see* above, section IV). This exception is only temporary and applicable only for the duration of the strike (Article 21 of the Law).

690. In the case of a violation by the employer of any of the above-indicated prohibitions within the framework of the interdiction of lockouts, his acts are annulled by the courts at the request of the persons concerned. The most important problem in this regard is proof that the disputed actions of the employer are undertaken after the declaration, during the strike and before it is finished and, with the anti-strike purpose as just indicated, i.e., with 'lockout or anti-strike *animus*'. In this situation the employer will bear the burden of proof that he did not undertake these operations at all, or that he did undertake them but with another purpose in mind and not with the purpose to prevent or suspend the strike, or to frustrate the satisfaction of the workers' requests put forward by them within the framework of the pending collective labour conflict.

691. Violation of the so-established legal prohibitions also constitutes an administrative infringement and is punished as such with fines imposed by the Labour Inspectorate (Article 22 of the law). Establishment of infringements committed, the issue of penal orders for punishment, appeal and enforcement are regulated by the Law on Administrative Breaches and Punishments.

Selected Bibliography

Legislation

Mrachkov, V., *Sbornik Troudovi zakoni* [*Collection Labour Laws*], 2nd ed., Sofia: Publishing House Sibi, 2001.

Judicial Decisions

'Sbornik Postanovlenia i Talkouvatelni Reshenia na Varhovnia, Sad po grajdanski dela, 1953–2014' [Collection of Resolutions and Decisions of the Supreme Court], in *Civil Law Cases*, Sofia: 'Fenea' Publishing House for periodicals, 2016.

Buletin na Varhovnia Sad na Republika Balgaria [*Bulletin of the Supreme Court of Cassation – Republic of Bulgaria*], 1993–2018, Sofia: Supreme Court of Cassation.

Sadebna practica – Kodeks na trouda [*Judicial Practice – Labour Code*], 3rd edn., Sofia: Publishing House Soloton, 2000.

Specialized Monographs

Filipova, Th., *Disciplinarno uvolnenie* [*Disciplinary Dismissal*], Sofia: University Printing House 'Paissiy Hilendarski', 2015.

Guenova, Y., *Predpriatieto polzvatel v individualnoto trudovo pravootnoshenie* [*The User Enterprise in Individual Employment Relationship*], Sofia: University Printing House 'Paissiy Hilendarski', 2015.

Guevrenova, N., *Specialna zakrila na rabotnitzite i sloujitelite s namalena rabotosposobnost* [*Special Protection of the Employees with Reduced Capacity for Work*], Sofia: Publishing House Sibi, 2013.

Ianoulov, I., *Troudovo provo* [*Labour Law*] 2nd edn., Sofia: Izdatelstvo Sv. Kl. Ohridski, 1948.

Milovanov, K., *Troudov dogovor: skljuchvane, izmenenie, prekratiavane* [*Labour Contract: Conclusion, Modification and Termination*], 3rd edn., Sofia: Publishing Complex Trud i Pravo, 2016.

Mingov, E., *Prekratiavane na troudovia dogovor poradi obshti osnovania* [*Termination of the Labour Contract on General Grounds*], Sofia: Publishing House Sibi, 2004.

Mrachkov, V., *Pravna zachtita srechtou nepravilno ouvolnenie* [*Legal Protection Against Unlawful Dismissal*], Sofia: Izdatelstvo na Balgarskata Akademia na Naoukite, 1971.

Selected Bibliography

Mrachkov, V., *Balgarskoto troudovo zakonodatelstvo i mejdunarodnite troudovi konvencii i preporaki* [*Bulgarian Labour Legislation and International Labour Conventions and Recommendations*], Sofia: Izdatelstvo Naouka i Izkoustvo, 1978.

Mrachkov, V., *Kolektivni troudovi sporove i pravo na stachka* [*Collective Labour Disputes and the Right to strike*], Sofia: Universitetsko Izdatelstvo 'Sv.Kl. Ohridski', 1992.

Mrachkov, V., *Troudovo pravo* [*Labour Law*], 10th edn., Sofia: Publishing House Sibi, 2018.

Mrachkov, V., *Dogovorat v troudovoto pravo* [*The Contract in Labour Law*], Sofia: Publishing House Sibi, 2010.

Mrachkov, V., *Imoushtestvena otgovornost na rabotodatelia* [*Financial Liability of the Employer*], Sofia: Publishing House Sibi, 2013.

Mrachkov, V., *Subektivno pravo i subektivni trudovi prava* [*Subjective Law and Subjective Labour Rights*], Sofia: Publishing House Sibi, 2017.

Mrachkov, V., Sredkova, K. & Vassilev, A., *Komentar na Kodeksa na trouda* [*Commentary on the Labour Code*], 12th edn., Sofia: Publishing House Sibi, 2016.

Radoilski, L., *Troudovo pravo na Narodna Republica Balgaria* [*Labour Law of the PR of Bulgaria*], Sofia: Izdatelstvo Naouka i Izkoustvo, 1957.

Sredkova, K., *Troudovo pravo, obshta chast* [*Labour Law, General Part*], Sofia: Universitetsko Izdatelstvo 'Sv. KI. Ohridski', 2010.

Sredkova, K., *Troudovo pravo. Specialna chast, Dial I* [*Labour Law, Special Part, Section I*], Sofia: Universitetsko Izdatelstvo 'Sv. KI. Ohridski', 2011.

Vassilev, A., *Obezchtetenia po troudovoto pravootnoshenie* [*Indemnities on the Labour Relations*], Sofia: Publishing House Sibi, 1997.

Vassilev, A., *Troudovo pravo*, Bourgas: Publishing House Bourgaski Svoboden Universitet, 1997.

Index

The numbers given here refer to paragraph numbers.

Index

Index

www.ingramcontent.com/pod-product-compliance
Ingram Content Group UK Ltd.
Pitfield, Milton Keynes, MK11 3LW, UK
UKHW020135290926
15471UKWH00003B/494

9 789403 527208